THE PACIFIC WAR
AND JAPAN'S DIPLOMACY
IN ASIA

THE
PACIFIC WAR
AND
JAPAN'S
DIPLOMACY
IN
ASIA

HATANO Sumio

Japan Publishing Industry Foundation for Culture

PUBLISHER'S NOTE
This book follows the Hepburn system of romanization of Japanese words. Except in familiar place names, long vowels are indicated by macrons. The tradition of placing the family name first has been followed for Japanese, Chinese, and Korean names.

The Pacific War and Japan's Diplomacy in Asia
Hatano Sumio. Translated by the Japan Institute of International Affairs (JIIA).

Published by
Japan Publishing Industry Foundation for Culture (JPIC)
2-2-30 Kanda-Jinbocho, Chiyoda-ku, Tokyo 101-0051, Japan

First English edition: March 2021

© 1996 Hatano Sumio
English translation © 2021 The Japan Institute of International Affairs (JIIA)
All rights reserved

Originally published in the Japanese language under the title *Taiheiyō sensō to Ajia gaikō* by University of Tokyo Press in 1996.
English publishing rights arranged with University of Tokyo Press.

This book is the result of a collaborative effort between the Japan Institute of International Affairs (JIIA) and Japan Publishing Industry Foundation for Culture (JPIC).

Jacket and cover design: Miki Kazuhiko, Ampersand Works

Printed in Japan
ISBN 978-4-86658-128-6
https://www.jpic.or.jp/

Table of Contents

Introduction

"Bitter experience has taught us that it is often easier to win a war than to achieve a war aim . . ."

— Louis Francis Albert Victor Nicholas Mountbatten[1]

One of the rare English-language books that the Japanese were eager to read during World War II was *Conditions of Peace* by Edward Carr. The editorial of the daily *Asahi Shimbun* on November 27, 1943, for instance, reads as follows:

> According to *Conditions of Peace*, the significance of the current world lies in its nature as a revolution against three major principles of democracy—liberal democracy in terms of politics, the principle of self-determination in terms of international politics, and liberal economy in terms of economy—that were predominant in the nineteenth century. The Allies' purpose for war—to defend democracy—became deadlocked and, in particular, the principle of self-determination, which was the "first principle of the Atlantic Charter," has already hit a stumbling block . . .

Around the same time, a British intellectual published *Charters of the Peace*, aiming to call attention once again to the significance of the Atlantic Charter. The author argues as follows:

> . . . the essence of this war is not a battle with Rommel's tactics or competition over the Spitfire's technology. It is a "battle of philosophy" over a new international order. As long as the war in Asia is fought mainly in the region where there is no consensus on the future of colonialism, it

---

1 V. P. Menon, *The Transfer of Power in India* (Princeton University Press, 1957), p. 415.

is essential to convince peoples in Asian colonies that a victory by the Allies will promise them much freer and better living conditions than what can be expected from the independence that Japan gave them out of charity in order to fight this war effectively.[2]

While these two commentaries present completely contrasting prospects for the historical significance of the Atlantic Charter, they share the common political background that actualized those prospects both on the Allied side and the Axis side. And it was a series of "Asian peoples' liberation" policies carried out by Japan that appeared to be steadily achieving results, including the permission for independence granted to Burma and the Philippines in 1943. This shows that, behind the intensification of the war, the issue of how to treat colonies had emerged as an international controversy.

This book explores how the issue of the treatment of colonies was handled mainly during the Pacific War, perceiving the issue as part of wartime diplomacy in the wider sense of the term. Generally, wartime diplomacy is required to fulfill two missions: (1) to contribute to the waging of the ongoing war, and (2) to lead to termination of the war to the advantage of one's own side. In the case of Japan during the Pacific War, the central target of diplomacy that could meet these two ends was the Soviet Union, with which Japan had maintained neutral relations. Nevertheless, the target of Japan's wartime diplomacy was not limited to the Soviet Union, or to Germany and Italy, or neutral countries in Europe. Japan's main theater of war had been the Asia Pacific region including the four-year-long war with China. In the Asia Pacific region, Japan could pursue autonomous diplomacy toward an early peace settlement, whereas in Europe, Japan's diplomacy had to rely on others. When the transfer of authority for diplomacy in the Greater East Asia region to the newly established Ministry of Greater East

---

2 W. Arnold-Forster, *Charters of the Peace: A Commentary on the Atlantic Charter and the Declaration of Moscow, Cairo and Teheran* (London: The Camelot Press, 1944).

Asia was discussed at the Privy Council in 1942, former Foreign Minister Ishii Kikujirō argued that if the Japanese government expected the Ministry of Foreign Affairs to prepare peace, management and accomplishment of a Greater East Asian diplomacy centered around China would be the most important aspect. It was Asia that had been perceived as the central stage of this kind of diplomacy.

The authority of the Ministry of Foreign Affairs, particularly concerning China diplomacy, had been reduced since the Manchurian Incident, and after the commencement of hostilities with Britain and the United States, the establishment of the Ministry of Greater East Asia further deprived the Foreign Ministry of much of its jurisdiction over foreign policy toward Asia.[3] Still, the reduction of its authority concerning diplomacy in Asia and the downsizing of its organization did not necessarily lead to a decline in the ministry's influence. One reason was that, after the eruption of the war, there still remained in Asia independent entities such as Manchukuo, the National Government of the Republic of China in Nanjing, and Thailand, as well as unoccupied regions that were targets of Japan's diplomacy. More than that, the issue of independence–or autonomy of colonies in the region—continued to be pursued, making the Foreign Ministry's presence a necessity.

Needless to say, administration of occupied territories is outside the jurisdiction of the Foreign Ministry. In the case of the occupation of Japan,

---

3   With the establishment of the Ministry of Greater East Asia in November 1942, the East Asia Affairs Bureau, the South Sea Affairs Bureau, and the Research Department of the Ministry of Foreign Affairs were abolished. The ministry was thus composed of the four bureaus of political affairs, treaty, trade, and research. The number of full-time officials at the head office was reduced from fifty-six (regular staff) to thirty-seven. Furthermore, later the trade bureau was also abolished (to be replaced by the newly established wartime economic bureau), and some divisions of the political affairs bureau and the research bureau were merged to reduce the number of officials as part of an administrative reorganization in November 1943. The result was a reduction of the work force quota at the ministry by 20 percent. The majority of the intelligence gathering and research activities were transferred to the Political Affairs Bureau, making the Political Affairs Bureau–centrism in the wartime diplomacy all the more pronounced. (Nippon Gaikō Nenkansha, ed., *Nippon gaikō nenkan: Shōwa 18-nen* [Japanese Yearbook of Foreign Relations: 1943 Edition] and Ministry of Foreign Affairs record A5-0-0-9 *Kakugi kettei jikō no jisshi jōkyō chōsa kankei ikken* [Survey Related Documents on the Implementation Status of Cabinet Decided Policies].)

administration of the occupied territory—Japan—was designated as falling within the jurisdiction of the occupation forces as a part of their operations. As American historian Peter Duus points out, however, the principle of self-determination had already been embedded in international relations as an "unavoidable code of conduct" since the end of World War I. Therefore, for imperial powers to put occupied territories under military administration and entrust their government to colonial offices during the inter-war period would make them liable to be denounced as colonialists. And this was one factor behind the tolerance toward "independence" and "autonomy" that Japan cited at the time of the Manchurian Incident and the Second Sino-Japanese War.[4] During the Pacific War, Japan adopted a system of allowing independence for occupied territories in Asia after a certain period of military administration. This policy left space for the diplomatic authorities to become engaged. And the Ministry of Foreign Affairs became a devout supporter of these measures.

The main objective of the present volume is to analyze Japan's treatment of occupied territories in Asia after the commencement of the war as well as the process of the formation of major policies toward unoccupied territories from the viewpoint of struggles, compromises, and coordination among major actors, including the Ministry of Foreign Affairs, the Ministry of Greater East Asia, and the Imperial Japanese Army and Navy. For the sake of analysis, the rivalry between the Foreign Ministry, on the one hand, and the Imperial Army and Navy, on the other, is used as an axis.[5] The Imperial

---

4 Peter Duus, "Introduction: Japan's Wartime Empire; Problems and Issues," in Peter Duus et al., eds., *The Japanese Wartime Empire, 1931–1945* (Princeton University Press, 1966). For the Japanese considerations on the principle of self-determination and possible international repercussions, see Y. Tak Matsusaka, "Managing Occupied Manchuria, 1931–1934," in this volume.

5 One of the tasks entrusted to the General Affairs Division, General Affairs Bureau of the Ministry of Greater East Asia was "matters related to research and policy planning related to administration of occupied territories" (Article 8 Section 4 of *Daitōashō bunka kitei* [Task Demarcation Regulation of The Ministry of Greater East Asia]). As this fact indicates, works related to the administration of occupied territories were transferred to the Ministry of Greater East Asia upon its establishment. Nevertheless, by retaining substantial influence through the appointment of Sugihara Arata, director of Research Department 1, to the post of director of General

Army and Navy were in charge of the military administration of the occupied territories after completion of military exercises, and their decisions carried significant weight in the Japanese government's decision on whether or not to abolish military administration in an occupied area. Contention within the Japanese government over the treatment of the occupied territories centered on whether the policy of respect for sovereignty and early independence was appropriate or not in light of the war requirement to minimize the cost of occupation by obtaining the cooperation of local peoples in the war effort, while accomplishing the priority goal of procuring natural resources. In this book, I attempt to shed light on this contention, not on the local level in Asia but on the central government level.

The Foreign Ministry's tolerance toward the independence of Asian colonies as well as its argument for unified diplomatic route derived from its intention to respond, albeit in a limited fashion, to Asian nationalism even during the war. And it was Shigemitsu Mamoru, the person most responsible for the wartime diplomacy, who was determined to stress these lines more clearly. The present volume values the significance of a series of new policies for Greater East Asia implemented under Foreign Minister Shigemitsu, such as the new China policy geared toward the Nanjing government, sanctioning the independence of Burma and the Philippines, the Joint Declaration of the Greater East Asia Conference, the liberation of French Indochina, and so on. The process of formation of these measures is the focus of the analysis of this volume.

Affairs of the Ministry of Greater East Asia, by far the most important post in the new ministry, and by deliberately avoiding the definition of the range of "authentic diplomacy" (Article 1 of *Daitōashō kansei* [Organization and Functions of the Ministry of Greater East Asia]), the Ministry of Foreign Affairs was able to retain the substance of centralization of diplomacy. Although the objective of this book requires reference to official records of the Ministry of Greater East Asia, no substantive records or documents on operations of the ministry exist at either the Foreign Ministry or other government organizations including the National Archives of Japan. Currently, therefore, only records of activities of the Ministry of Greater East Asia that had been distributed and circulated to the Foreign Ministry or other government organizations are available. Therefore, at this point, it is impossible to systematically trace the policies of the Ministry of Greater East Asia's Asian diplomacy, which admittedly poses a limit to the analysis herein.

Investigation of the above themes is also an attempt at exploring the meaning of "Asian peoples' liberation," one of Japan's proclaimed war aims, in terms of policy. Even if Japan's occupation of Asian colonies might have reduced the power of the colonial masters and helped promote the decolonizing of Asia, it should be noted that Japan's Asian peoples' liberation policy was not necessarily consistent with that tendency. As a matter of fact, Japan's policy was characterized more by confusion and inconsistency. Because Japan did not enter a war with the United States, Britain, and the Netherlands with decolonization as its main war goal, the objectives entrusted to Japan's occupation policy were not monolithic. In fact, they were highly ambiguous, making intra-government relations all the more contentious.

The series of new policies implemented under Shigemitsu were not perceived as simple instruments to mobilize Asian peoples into the war and, thus, obtaining their cooperation. Advocates of those policies were indeed aware of the issue of decolonization as an international debate. That awareness must have intensified the domestic struggle over decisions and the implementation of these policies. This is the hypothesis behind the analysis in this book. As Christopher Thorne's study[6] and others have pointed out, the major point of contention in Asia at the time of World War II was the pros and cons of colonialism. For the United States, which aimed at the permeation of anti-colonialism through the means of world war, Japan's Asian peoples' liberation policy was a target of suspicion and apprehension. But, more than that, the position taken by the United States put it in constant conflict with European countries, which did not hide their desire to return to Asia as colonial masters. The question is whether the various controversies in postwar Japan over these new policies really had little to do with the international context. This book is but a first step in clarifying this question.

---

6 Christopher Thorne, *The Issue of War: States, Societies, and the Far Eastern Conflict of 1941–1945* (New York: Oxford University Press, 1985); ibid., *Allies of a Kind: The United States, Britain, and the War against Japan, 1941–1945* (New York: Oxford University Press, 1978).

Chapter 1

Opening of War against the United States, Britain, and the Netherlands and a Plan to End the War

1. A Plan to End the War against the United States, Britain, and the Netherlands, and Chiang Kai-shek's China

On the day the Pacific War broke out, the diary of the War Guidance Office, Imperial Headquarters Army Department, recorded the success of the attack on Pearl Harbor and the Malayan Campaign as "an ideal start of a war." But the official log also noted, "How should we pursue termination of this war? This will be the most difficult task in the current war,"[1] thus betraying the Imperial Headquarters' apprehension about prospects for the war's conclusion. Let us first look into what vision the war guidance authorities of the Imperial Japanese Army and Navy had regarding the end of the war.

Immediately after the September 6, 1941, decision at the Gozen Kaigi (Imperial Council) on the *Teikoku kokusaku suikō yoryō* (Guidelines for the Execution of Imperial Policy), officials of the Bureau of Military/Naval Affairs of the Imperial Army and Navy proposed the *Tai-Bei-Ei-Ran sensō shidō yōkō* (Outline for the Guidance of War against the United States, Great Britain, and the Netherlands). The proposal was drafted with an eye to its adoption by the Liaison Conference between the government and the Imperial General Headquarters or the Imperial Council as a comprehensive war plan encompassing measures to be taken toward the termination of the war, measures toward occupied territories, the pretext for opening the war, and various external measures.[2] While the full picture of the proposal was unknown until today, it was not adopted as national policy automatically. In the midst of the political turmoil that culminated in the dissolution of the third Konoe Fumimaro cabinet in October 1941, the proposal was tentatively treated as an understanding between the army and the navy.

---

1 Dai hon-ei rikugunbu [Imperial Headquarters Army Section] same as *Sano honbu* [Army General Staff Office], *Kimitsu sensō nisshi* [Confidential War Diary] (December 8, 1941).

2 Kōseishō Hikiage Engokyoku, ed., *Ishii Akiho Taisa kaisōroku* (The Memoir of Colonel Ishii Akiho), 1946, pp. 170–184. (*Ishii Memoir* henceforth)

This was because it was feared that formalizing the proposal could foster an atmosphere that suggested reconciliation with the United States might be possible, thus making people suspect an ulterior motive behind the military's claim to the contrary. Nevertheless, when the commencement of the war became inevitable at the November 2 Imperial Council, each item contained in the proposal was separately scrutinized once again in order to prepare for specific necessary measures accompanying the start of a war. After this process, the items thus deliberated eventually became decisions by the Liaison Conference or the Imperial Japanese Army and Navy. For example, the measures to be taken toward ending the war became the *Tai-Bei-Ei-Ran-Shō sensō shūmatsu sokushin ni kansuru fukuan* (Tentative Plan to Hasten the End of the War with the United States, Britain, the Netherlands, and China; *Fukuan* henceforth) and were adopted as a Liaison Conference Decision on November 15, 1941. The proposal's measures toward occupied territories were adopted as the *Nanpō senryōchi gyōsei jisshi yōryō* (Principles for the Implementation of Military Administration in the Occupied Southern Area) as a Liaison Conference Decision on November 20. Both of these items were taken from the original proposal for the *Outline for the Guidance of War against the United States, Great Britain, and the Netherlands* and retouched. It was from this second stage that the Ministry of Foreign Affairs began participating in war planning.[3]

This suggests that controversy over the *Outline for the Guidance of War against the United States, Great Britain, and the Netherlands* centered on the following three points.

---

3 Ibid., and verbal comments of Takayama Shinobu (former staff officer, Imperial Headquarters Army Section) on August 20, 1978. The author has relied on *Sugiyama Memo, jō* [Sugiyama Memorandum, vol. 1] edited by the Army General Staff Office (Hara Shobō, 1989), pp. 523–525, for the description of *Fukuan*.

(1) Controversy over War Objectives

The first issue concerned setting out war objectives. The army staff, including Satō Kenryō, director-general of the Bureau of Military Affairs, argued for including construction of a Greater East Asia Co-Prosperity Sphere and a Greater East Asia New Order as war objectives, along with self-reliance and self-defense. The navy staff, centered around Lieutenant Colonel Fujii Shigeru of the Bureau of Naval Affairs, argued for limiting the objective to self-reliance and self-defense alone.[4]

A glance at the series of decisions regarding measures for southern territories adopted by the Imperial Council since the beginning of 1941 reveals that, while the purpose of measures related to southern territories was limited almost exclusively to self-reliance and self-defense until the September 6 Imperial Council, there was a tendency for establishment of a Greater East Asia New Order to be included in the purpose after Japan decided to wage war against the United States, Britain, and the Netherlands.[5] It should be understood, however, that this tendency was not a reflection of a shift in the points of contention in the negotiations with the United States or debates within Japan. Instead, it merely reflected an aspect of certain arguments consistently found in documents on national policies produced around the same time: Japan's national policy is to "establish a Greater East Asia Co-Prosperity Sphere and, thereby, contribute to consolidation of world peace" and, to accomplish this firm goal, it was necessary not only to settle the war with China but also to "consolidate the foundation for self-reliance

---

4 *Ishii Memoir*, pp. 172–173.
5 Hatano Sumio, "Nippon no 'shinchitsujo' rinen to sensō mokuteki," *Shin bōei ronshū*, vol. 8, no. 3, 1981, pp. 32–40.

and self-defense" by advancing into southern territories.[6]

In other words, consolidation of a foundation for self-reliance and self-defense was perceived to be a precondition for construction of the Greater East Asia Co-Prosperity Sphere, Japan's steadfast national policy, and an indispensable process toward attaining that goal. Therefore, the slogans of self-reliance and self-defense and construction of a Greater East Asia Co-Prosperity Sphere were not contradictory as objectives of the war against the United States, Britain, and the Netherlands. In his affidavit, Tōjō Hideki, former prime minister and a Class A war criminal suspect explained the objective of the war, stating, "Needless to say, the motivation behind the use of force was Japan's quest for self-reliance and self-defense. Once the war erupted, Japan tried to carry out its Greater East Asia policy, i.e., establishment of a new order of co-prosperity in East Asia, that it had long pursued."[7] This affidavit reveals that Tōjō had understood the relation between self-reliance and self-defense and establishment of the Greater East Asia Co-Prosperity Sphere.

The cabinet meeting convened on December 12, 1941, four days after the opening of the war, decided to name the war against the United States, Britain, and the Netherlands, and including the Second Sino-Japanese War, the Greater East Asia War. Accordingly, the Cabinet Intelligence Bureau announced, "the name 'Greater East Asia War' signifies that it is a war with the objective of constructing a Greater East Asia new order; it does not mean that the war zone will be confined to the Greater

---

6　Draft explanation to the prime minister on *Jōsei no suii ni tomonau teikoku kokusaku suikō yōkō* [Outline of Implementation of the Imperial Policy accompanying Changes of Situations] on July 2 in *Sugiyama Memorandum*, vol. 1, p. 261. The briefing material for the September 6 Imperial Council on the outline of implementation of the imperial policy states the purpose of a war against Britain and the United States is "to expel American, British, and Dutch influences from East Asia in order to consolidate the sphere for the Empire's self-reliance and self-defense and, at the same time, to construct a new order in the Greater East Asia" (ibid., p. 322). This also shares the same argument.
7　Tokyo Saiban Kenkyūkai, ed., *Tōjō Hideki sensei kyōjutsusho* [Affidavit of Tōjō Hideki], Yōyōsha, 1948, pp. 141–150.

East Asian region."[8] When the "no separate peace" agreement was signed on December 10, 1941, between Japan, Germany, and Italy, each of the signees promised the others to work toward the establishment of a new postwar order. It appears that behind this decision on the war name was Japan's intention to stress to its Axis partners its determination to uphold the tripartite war agreement. However, there was no discussion of what establishment of a new order meant either among the Axis partners or even within the Japanese government. Foreign Minister Tōgō Shigenori's reply at a December 10 meeting of the Privy Council of Japan's review committee makes this clear. The committee met to discuss the tripartite agreement. When queried by council member Obata Yūkichi, Tōgō replied that there had been no concrete discussion on the new order with Germany and Italy.[9]

Thus, at the government level the understanding of the war aim drifted between self-reliance and self-defense and establishment of the Greater East Asia Co-Prosperity Sphere (or construction of the Greater East Asia new order). Neither the Imperial Army nor Navy could idly stand by regarding this issue because it could affect the awareness of officers and soldiers who planned operations and engaged in battle. That was why the discussion on the *Outline for the Guidance of War against the United States, Great Britain, and the Netherlands* became a heated debate. Nevertheless, no unity on the objectives of the war was achieved before the start of the war; this undoubtedly had repercussions on missions under subsequent operations.

---

8 Furthermore, the cabinet's standard for explanation on amendments of various laws accompanying the decision on the war name clearly states, "the objective of the war against Britain and the United States is construction of a Greater East Asia new order." (*Daitōa sensō no koshō o sadametaru ni tomonau kaku hōritsu chū kaisei hōritsuan setsumei kijun* [Cabinet's Standard for Explanation on Proposed Amendment of Various Laws Accompanying the Adoption of Greater East Asia War as the War Name]), Cabinet.

9 Obata Yūkichi also questioned how the government perceived the proposed new order, to which Foreign Minister Tōgō replied without details, i.e., "we intend to construct a new order by forming a political and economic bloc around the core of Japan, Manchukuo, and China, in which each East Asian people attain a proper place." (Ministry of Foreign Affairs Record A7-0-0-9-14 "Matters Related to the Greater East Asia War/Japan-Germany-Italy Joint Waging of War against Britain/'No Separate Peace' Agreement/Cooperation toward Construction of a New Order")

For instance, the *Dairikumei dai 564-gō* (Emperor's Order on the Army no. 564), which instructed Imperial Japanese Army troops to prepare for the capture of southern territories based on the November 5 decision of the Imperial Council, cited both self-reliance and self-defense as well as construction of the Greater East Asia new order as the reason for the preparations. In contrast, the order to naval troops (*Taikairei dai 1-gō*) issued at around the same time cited only self-reliance and self-defense.

This discrepancy between the army and the navy could have been caused by their differing expectations regarding the duration of the war. The Imperial Army thought it would be a long, drawn-out war, while the Imperial Navy imagined it would be a short, decisive battle. If a long-term war was envisioned when Japanese troops occupied the southern territories, the government would undoubtedly be held accountable for the accomplishment, or lack thereof, in the construction of the Greater East Asia new order and the Greater East Asia Co-Prosperity Sphere, which had been a slogan since 1940. Lieutenant Colonel Ishii Akiho (promoted to colonel in November 1941) of the Army Department's Military Affairs Bureau, who had participated in the drafting of the *Outline for the Guidance of War against the United States, Great Britain, and the Netherlands*, was one of a few army staff officers who persisted in setting self-reliance and self-defense as the sole war aims. Understanding that self-reliance and self-defense was the minimum condition for Japan's economic survival, Ishii argued that, for the peace settlement, Japan had to stick to a narrow war objective. Nevertheless, such was the political environment that even Ishii had to admit, "Once a war is started, it will be impossible to end it unless the construction of the Greater East Asia Co-Prosperity or the Greater East Asia new order is achieved."[10]

---

10 *Ishii Memoir*, pp. 172–173.

(2) A Scenario for Termination of the War

The second point of contention was measures for termination of the war, including management of diplomacy during the war. According to Colonel Ishii, the essence of the *Outline for the Guidance of War against the United States, Great Britain, and the Netherlands* was "to cripple the Chiang Kai-shek government, drive Britain into submission, in collaboration with Germany and Italy, and deprive the United States of the will to continue fighting." In short, defeating Chiang Kai-shek's Republic of China government in Chongqing and Britain were deemed as the direct path to ending the war.[11] Nevertheless, as we will see later, the Imperial Army did not envision any specific measures for crippling the Chongqing government aside from the seizure of foreign concessions and the capture of Hong Kong.

Measures against China after the war began had been a consistent subject of discussion among the Imperial Army and Navy and the Ministry of Foreign Affairs since early November 1941. The army and navy were requested to "keep in mind when carrying out subsequent measures against China that operations against China were merely a part of the Empire's world war." In terms of operations, the army and navy were required to "minimize exhaustion of the troops in China as much as possible." In other words, they were instructed to "avoid aggressive operations in China as much as possible."[12] There was no hint of a perception that settlement of the Second Sino-Japanese War—that is, subjugation of the Kuomintang government in Chongqing—should be prioritized over termination of war against the United States, Britain, and the Netherlands. Instead, ending the Second Sino-Japanese War was treated as subordinate to the war against the

---

11 Ibid., pp. 182–183.
12 "Tai Bei-Ei-Ran kaisen no baai ni okeru teikoku no tai-Shi hōsaku" [The Empire's China Policy in the Event of War against the United States, Britain, and the Netherlands] (November 10, 1941), "Juichi-gatsu itsuka Gozen Kaigi kettei: Teikoku kokusaku suikō yōryō ni kansuru taigai sochi" [Decision at November 5 Imperial Council: External Measures Related to the *Guidelines for the Execution of Imperial Policy*] (Liaison Conference decision, November 13) (Ministry of Foreign Affairs Record A1-1-1-0-30 33, *Matters Related to the Second Sino-Japanese War*, vol. 33).

United States, Britain, and the Netherlands.

Therefore, in reality, the only opportunity to end the war would be provided when Japan defeated Britain in collaboration with Germany and Italy. The *Fukuan* essentially followed this line of argument. The scenario for termination of the war presented by *Fukuan* was for Japan to bring southern territories under its influence, thus consolidating the foundation for a long-term war, and subjugate Britain—the greatest ally of the United States in Europe as well as East Asia—and the Chiang Kai-shek government. Accomplishing this would leave the United States with no other option than to abandon its intention to continue the war. But the *Fukuan* did not offer any concrete measures for subjugating Chiang's government, aside from the vague "aggressive pursuit of political maneuvering measures." Instead, it devoted more space to describing a strategic scheme of war collaboration among the Axis countries.

In essence, the *Fukuan* proposed that Japan should attempt to sever Australian and Indian connections with Britain through political maneuvering and measures disruptive to trade in order to engineer their alienation from Britain. The *Fukuan* requested Germany and Italy to "carry out military operations in the Near East, North Africa, and the Suez and, at the same time, take measures against India." As a method for tripartite cooperation, the *Fukuan* proposed the "strengthening of liaison and cooperation via the Indian Ocean." Strategic cooperation with Germany and Italy was indispensable in order to defeat Britain and, therefore, Japan's war in Asia and the Pacific had to be positioned as an integral part of the Axis' tripartite war effort.

In other words, Japan's war plan at the outset was constructed on the premise of victory or, at least, the invincibility of Germany on the European front. It was not structured in a way that Japan could take its own initiative to end the war.

If the defeat of Britain and subjugation of the Chongqing government were to be direct opportunities for Japan to end the war, then the scheme to mediate a peace settlement between Germany and the Soviet Union, on the assumption that Japan's relations with the latter could be stabilized, was a secondary opportunity that Japan counted on. Supposing that Japan's initiative could accomplish peace between Germany and the Soviet Union, Germany would be liberated from its war with the latter, enabling it to concentrate its war effort against Britain. It was also envisioned that the Axis countries could bring the Soviet Union into their camp, which would make it possible for them to threaten the British Empire's lifeline by pushing the Soviet troops southward to the Middle East/India region. However, since the war between Germany and the Soviet Union was at a delicate stage around the time Japan commenced hostilities with the Allies, sounding out the intentions of those two countries alone was found to be a "highly sensitive and difficult" task. Therefore, this scheme did not become a high priority among various measures proposed by the *Fukuan*.[13]

The *Fukuan* contains the following lines:

Measures should be considered to promote a peace settlement between Germany and the Soviet Union in order to bring the latter into the Axis camp and, at the same time, to coordinate our relations with the Soviet Union. When the situation allows, Soviet troops should be encouraged to advance into areas of India and Iran.

As "should be considered" indicates, the *Fukuan* did not say that Japan would or should engage in these measures.

Still, the expression "mediation of a peace settlement between Germany and the Soviet Union" was heard in the Imperial Japanese Army General Staff Office even immediately after the outbreak of the war between the two countries.[14] It was a diplomatic theme that was persistently pursued

---

13 *Ishii Memoir*, p. 171.
14 *Kimitsu sensō nisshi* [Confidential War Diary] (June 25, 1941).

throughout the duration of the war. Externally, such a settlement was almost the only measure by which Japan could obtain a favorable peace settlement on its own initiative; domestically, it was one of the few measures that the Army, Navy, and the Ministry of Foreign Affairs could jointly promote.[15]

(3) Policies on Occupied Territories and Envisioning Termination of the War

The third point of contention was measures regarding the occupied territories. The unique characteristic of Japan's war plan at the outbreak of the war was the vision that linked termination of the war to measures related to the occupied territories. The Imperial Japanese Army General Staff Office had set up in February 1941 a study section within its G1 Bureau (operations) to study administration in the occupied territories. In April of the same year, the study section compiled a *Nanpō sakusen ni okeru senryōchi tōchi yōkō an* (Agenda Proposal for the Governance of Occupied Territories in the Southern Sphere of Operations) and the *Gunsei jisshi yōkō* (Principles for Military Administration) for each region. The centerpiece of these studies, the *Senryōchi tōchi yōkō an* (Agenda Proposal for the Governance of the Occupied Territories), found indirect rule—that is, restoring and managing indigenous government organizations in accordance with the traditional organizational practices in that region—to be fundamental to the governance of the occupied territories. The proposal set out procurement of

---

15 See Hosoya Chihiro, "Taiheiyō Sensō to Nippon no taiso gaikō" [The Pacific War and Japan's Soviet Policy], Hosoya Chihiro. *Ryō taisen kan no Nippon gaikō* [Japan's Diplomacy in the Inter-War Period] (Iwanami Shoten, 1988); Kudō Michihiro. *Nisso Chūritsu Jōyaku no kenkyū* [Study on the Soviet-Japanese Neutrality Pact], Nansōsha, 1985; Moriya Jun. "Dai 2-ji Taisen chū no Nichidoku kōshō ni kansuru ichikōsatsu" [An Observation on the German-Japanese Negotiations during World War II], *Kokusai seiji*, vol. 89, 1988. Recent studies mainly based on German primary sources include: Ōki Tsuyoshi, "Dokuso wahei kōsaku o meguru gunzō−1942 nen no keii o chūshin ni" [People Engaged in the German-Soviet Peace Settlement−Centered around Developments in 1942], Kindai Nippon Kenkyūkai, ed., *Nenpō kindai Nippon kenkyū 17* [Selected Essays on Modern Japanese Studies 17] (Yamakawa Shuppansha, 1995), and "Dokuso wahei mondai to Nippon" [German-Soviet Peace Settlement Issue and Japan] presented at Taiheiyō Sensō shūketsu 50-shūnen kokusai gakujutsu kaigi [International Academic Conference Commemorating the 50th Anniversary of the End of the Pacific War], August 1995, Shimoda, Japan.

natural resources and restoration of public order as the goals of the military administration. It also proposed the following two principles: (1) to avoid "hasty announcements on the future restoration of sovereignty and reforms of government organizations, except in the British colonies"; and (2) to "respect their sovereignty, treat them as independent countries, and refrain from interfering in their governments in the case of friendly countries whose incumbent governments approve our military activities."[16]

In short, the agenda proposal revealed the Imperial Japanese Army General Staff Office's intention to, in principle, tolerate the sovereignty and independence of Indonesia (Dutch East Indies), depending on the degree of its cooperation with Japan, while retaining military administration for the time being in the British colonies including Burma, British Malaya, and British Borneo. Noteworthy here was the special treatment of the Philippines. Instead of applying regional principles for military administration, for the Philippines, the army compiled the *Taibei sensō ni tomonau hitō shori hōsaku-an* (Agenda of Policies toward the Philippines during the War against the United States). This set of policies stated, "The main purpose of operations in the Philippines should be destruction of the American bases of operations there. The capture of materials and resources need not be given serious consideration." In other words, Japan would not impose military administration in the Philippines but would respect the sovereignty of the incumbent government in the Philippines, hoping to secure the latter's cooperation with Japan. In this sense, the Philippines was to be treated on a par with Thailand and French Indochina.

These studies by the Imperial Japanese Army General Staff Office had been revisited since August 1941 in conjunction with planning for the

---

16 *Nanpō sakusen ni okeru senryōchi tōchi yōkō an* [Agenda Proposal for the Governance of Occupied Territories in the Southern Theater of Operations] compiled by Study Section, G1 Bureau, Imperial Japanese Army General Staff Office, March 1941, (*Nanpō gunsei/nansei gunsei 62* [Southern Region Military Administration/Southeastern Region Military Administration 62], a collection at the National Institute of Defense Studies, Japan).

Southern Operations, and it appears that they provided a basis for discussions leading up to the *Outline for the Guidance of War against the United States, Great Britain, and the Netherlands*. Compared with the conclusions of the G1 Bureau's study section, it is noteworthy that the proposal spelled out the clear intention of accepting the independence of Burma and the Philippines. The independence of Burma was clearly positioned as a part of the political strategies aimed at crippling Britain. As we will see in more detail later, the Minami Kikan (a secret intelligence organization) was established under the jurisdiction of the Imperial Japanese Army General Staff Office in the spring of 1941 to engage in engineering Burma's independence, which was expected to prompt the independence of India.

In the case of the Philippines, the proposal followed the conclusion of the study section—that is, the sovereignty of the Philippines would be respected. It proposed that Japan should let the incumbent Quezon administration stay in power and, depending on the intentions of the United States, hand over the Philippines to the United States, because this would contribute to an early end to the war. This indicates that tolerance of independence for the Philippines and Burma was not out of consideration due to nationalism or the zeal for independence in the two regions but was a measure that Japan hoped would lead to an early end of warfare. It was the war against the United States in the case of the Philippines, while it was the war against Britain in the case of Burma.

It has been pointed out, however, that specifically what was meant by the "autonomy" of Indonesia was extremely obscure.[17] It was impossible to link tolerance toward Indonesian autonomy to the end of any war, and it was only natural for the meaning of this treatment of Indonesia to become highly ambiguous unless it was understood in the context of respect for nationalism of the Indonesian people.

Thus, the independence of both the Philippines and Burma could be

---

17 *Ishii Memoir*, pp. 177–178.

connected to Japan's war plan as measures to prompt the termination of the war. This stance was reflected in *Fukuan* which stipulated that Japan could take advantage of Burma's independence to stimulate the independence of India. As for the Philippines, *Fukuan* stated that "the incumbent administration should be upheld for the time being and deliberation should be conducted to utilize this measure to prompt the end of the war." Near the end of *Fukuan*, it was written that "consideration should be given to treatment of the Philippines" as "a measure to promote a peace settlement with the United States." It is a well-known fact that the Imperial Japanese Army had stressed the "separability of Britain and the United States" during the process leading up to the start of the Pacific War. The desire of the army to confine the war to Britain (and the Netherlands) was reflected in the deliberation process for the drafting of the *Outline for the Guidance of War against the United States, Great Britain, and the Netherlands*. According to Colonel Ishii, the Imperial Army would not cease to pursue ways to avoid going to war against the United States.[18] It may be said that the treatment of the Philippines proposed in *Fukuan* was a reflection of this kind of awareness.

It should be pointed out here that the *Principles for the Implementation of Military Administration in the Occupied Southern Area*, which was adopted by the Liaison Conference on November 20, five days after the decision on the *Fukuan*, did not touch on the independence of Burma and the Philippines. Instead, the *Principles* set forth a policy that seemed to directly contradict the goal stated in the *Fukuan*. While the *Principles* set forth the policy of indirect military rule as well as three goals of the military administration, the document particularly stressed the policy of "rapid procurement of important national defense resources" and stipulated principles including incorporation of developed and procured resources into the resources mobilization plan and means of transporting those resources

---

18 *Kōtani Etsuo Taisa kaisōroku* [The Memoir of Colonel Kōtani Etsuo] coordinated by Kōseishō Hikiage Engokyoku, 1956.

to Japan. To accomplish these purposes, the *Principles* stated that the "local population must be made to endure heavy burdens that would unavoidably affect the public welfare of these people." This was a clear indication of the *Outline*'s expectation that these regions would function as logistic bases for the war against Britain or the four-year-long war against China.

According to Colonel Ishii, behind these stipulations was a lesson Japan had learned from its failure in the occupied territories in China. As represented by the establishment of the Wang Jingwei regime and the North China Political Affairs Committee, the Japanese occupation forces entrusted administration to prominent local politicians. At the same time, however, they interfered greatly with those local politicians on the pretext of "supervision and cooperation," thus turning local people against Japan. In other words, it was the intention of the *Principles* to maintain the explicit military administration policy and to entrust the government of the occupied regions to the expeditionary forces instead of establishing a puppet government. Having been the adviser on political affairs in Hebei (north China) as a staff officer of the Japanese North China Area Army, Ishii admitted that, "everything we tried ended up being inconclusive due to the official position that the Second Sino-Japanese War was a mere incident and not a war." Regarding southern China, Ishii disclosed that Japan could fully enforce military administration without any pretention because in that case, it was clearly a war.[19] As a matter of fact, during the Second Sino-Japanese War, the official stance of "not imposing military administration and, instead, relying on the autonomy of the Chinese side as much as possible" was persistently upheld. It was structured so that the special operations section set up within the headquarters of the expeditionary force supervised and advised the governing body of the Chinese side.[20]

---

19 Ishii Akiho, "Nanpō gunsei nikki" [Diary of Military Government in the Southern Territories] in Bōeichō Bōei Kenkyūsho Senshibu ed. *Shiryōshū/Nanpō no gunsei* [Documents on Military Administration in the Southern Territories], Asagumo Shimbunsha, 1985, p. 443, pp. 453–454.

20 Bōei Kenshūsho Senshishitsu, *Shina Jihen rikugun sakusen 2* [Imperial Japanese Army Operations in China during the Second Sino-Japanese War], Asagumo Shimbunsha, 1973, p. 250.

Incidentally, *Principles for the Implementation of Military Administration in the Occupied Southern Area* stated that the treatment of the occupied territories "should be addressed separately" and did not touch on the issue of independence for the Philippines and Burma. According to Ishii, the independence of these two regions had already been "agreed on among all as a matter of common sense" and the absence of the issue in the *Principles* would not obstruct further study of the issue of independence of these regions. The *Principles*, however, made it clear that the main objective of the occupation policy was to procure resources for national defense and other necessities to wage war, not to encourage the independence of the occupied territories. Thus, it should be said that the independence of these two regions was an extremely exceptional measure that was approved only in connection with the plan to end the wars.

2. Opening of War and the Ministry of Foreign Affairs

(1) German-Soviet Peace Settlement and the China Problem

Two weeks into the war, Amō Eiji, recently retired as deputy foreign minister, wrote in his diary, "War is going on but the presence of the Foreign Ministry is ever so small, and I have nothing to do. While it is regrettable that I cannot contribute to the war effort at this time of national crisis, there is really nothing I can do about it." In subsequent diary entries, Amō often deplored the "increasingly diminishing importance of the Foreign Ministry."[21] The decline of the Foreign Ministry's position could also be assumed from the fact that it was often left out in the cold during the process of deciding a series of external measures after the opening of the war.[22]

---

21 Amō Eiji Nikki/Shiryōshū Kankō Iinkai, ed., *Amō Eiji nikki/shiryōshū, dai 4-kan* [Amō Eiji Diary/Reference Materials, vol. 4], 1979, entries on December 23, 1941 and January 29, 1942.
22 Ministry of Foreign Affairs was not informed of the January 10 Liaison Conference decision until immediately before the conference, about which the ministry openly expressed displeasure as "an abrupt proposal" (*Kimitsu sensō nisshi*, January 7).

Facing waning morale within the ministry staff, Foreign Minister Tōgō tried to inspire officials, saying, "We must end this war at the most advantageous opportunity for Japan. I expect every Foreign Ministry official to contribute to the study and exploration of such an opportunity even at the sacrifice of other tasks."[23] Taking into consideration the delicate international position of Japan at the time of the start of the war, however, it was nearly impossible to seek a general peace agreement. The only possible path to an early peace settlement was "to create opportunities for individual peace settlements first, upon which the opportunity for a general peace could be attained." For this to be realized, it was considered that the priority, for the time being, would be to approach the Soviet Union and settle the "China problem."[24]

At the start of the war, the "maintenance of tranquil relations" with the Soviet Union was a priority for Japan, even superseding the alliance with Germany. When war broke out between Japan and the United States, the Soviet Union did not change its strategy of concentrating its military might on its war against Germany; therefore, it did not harden its attitude toward Japan, either.[25]

Believing that the first step toward a peace settlement advantageous to Japan and an early end to the war should be to force the Soviet Union to withdraw from the war against Germany, Tōgō became a strong advocate of mediation of the German-Soviet peace settlement rather than simply pursuing the maintenance of tranquil relations as the sole goal of Japan's Soviet diplomacy. When the Soviet ambassador to Japan Konstantin Alexandrovich Smetanin returned home in January 1942, Tōgō promised that Japan would

---

23 "Kurihara Ken memo" [Kurihara Ken Memorandum], Kurihara Ken and Hatano Sumio, eds., *Shūsen kōsaku no kiroku, jō* [Record of Maneuvering to End the War, vol. 1], Kōdansha, 1986, pp. 36–37.

24 Tōgō Shigenori, *Jidai no ichimen* [An Aspect of the Time], Hara Shobō, 1985, pp. 298–302.

25 Alexei Filitov, "Nippon no Taiheiyō Sensō totsunyū to So-Nichi kankei" [Japan's Entry to the Pacific War and Soviet-Japan Relations], Nakai Akio et al., eds., *Dokuso Nichibei kankei to 50-nen go* [German-Soviet and US-Japan Relations and 50 Years Later], Nansōsha, 1993, pp. 79–80.

do its best to mediate any negotiation between the Soviet Union and Germany for a peace settlement.[26] Tōgō also insisted at prewar discussions on the *Fukuan* and at the March 1942 deliberation on the *Sensō shidō taikō* (General Principles for Waging War) that these documents should clearly stipulate that Japan would mediate peace negotiations between Germany and the Soviet Union. Tōgō even sounded out, albeit casually, the German reaction when he met German ambassador to Japan Eugen Ott toward the end of March 1942. The Imperial Japanese Navy also had been enthusiastic about a bilateral peace settlement, and it sounded out the German reaction via Paul Wenneker, German naval attaché to Japan, as early as late October 1941. The navy continued to approach Germany through Wenneker into the spring of 1942.[27] The navy became active regarding the issue of a German-Soviet peace settlement because it aimed at establishing security in the north in preparation for the Japan-Germany joint operations in the Indian Ocean. Hitler, however, consistently refused peace negotiations with the Soviet Union.[28]

While the Imperial Japanese Army General Staff Office and the Army Ministry acknowledged the importance of the German-Soviet peace settlement, they nonetheless remained passive toward it. They took the stance that, "Under the current circumstances, to respond positively to a request [for mediation in peace negotiations] from either Germany or the Soviet Union would increase the pressure on Japan in its northern periphery and lead to further harm." Behind this prediction was an apprehension that the Soviet Union might strengthen its pressure on Japan once it was liberated from its war against Germany via a peace settlement. When Foreign Minister Tōgō notified the Imperial Japanese Army General Staff Office of his contact with Ambassador Ott and requested a feasibility study, the General Staff

---

26 *Noguchi Yoshio kōkyōsho* [Affidavit of Noguchi Yoshio] (Kyokutō Kokusai Gunji Saiban sokkiroku 335-gō [Proceedings of the International Military Tribunal for the Far East no. 335]).
27 Ōki, op cit., pp. 249–282.
28 Milan Hauner, *India in Axis Strategy: Germany, Japan, and Indian Nationalists in the Second World War* (Stuttgart: Klett-Cotta, 1981), pp. 402–403.

Office reconfirmed its stance that Japan should not take the initiative in the German-Soviet peace settlement and gave notice to that effect to ministers of the army and foreign affairs.[29] However, if either Germany or the Soviet Union proposed a peace settlement, it was understood that "since it would not be possible for the Empire of Japan to remain indifferent, the country should make due preparations and conduct necessary studies." Subsequently, the Imperial Japanese Army General Staff Office and the German embassy jointly attempted a variety of maneuvers via official and nonofficial channels, but they all failed to change the mind of German Foreign Minister Ulrich Friedrich Wilhelm Joachim von Ribbentrop, who had remained reluctant about a peace settlement with the Soviet Union. This led to the de facto abandonment of the attempt in September 1942.[30]

As we will see later, Germany had consistently requested Japan's participation in the war against the Soviet Union. It appeared that one of the reasons that the Imperial Army rejected the German request in 1942 was its judgment that it was desirable to retain the leeway for Japan to take initiative in a peace settlement between the two countries. Participation in the war against the Soviet Union would not only exhaust Japan's national power but also make it difficult for Japan to handle its Northern Territories dispute if and when the two countries reached a unilateral peace agreement while Germany maintained overwhelming superiority.[31] It was deemed more desirable for Japan to retain its own initiative for a German-Soviet peace settlement than to join the war against the Soviet Union, which would waste its national strength and constrain its freedom of action vis-à-vis a German-Soviet peace settlement.

The "China problem" referred to the settlement of the four-year-long Second Sino-Japanese War. Most militarily and politically effective solutions

---

29 *Kimitsu sensō nisshi*, April 13, 1942.
30 Ōki, op cit.
31 Telegraphs #872-829 of deputy chief of staff on August 5, 1942 addressed to the military attaché of the German embassy (included in Zaidoku Bukanshitsu Chūdoku Bukan Denpō Tsuzuri, a collection of telegrams at the National Institute for Defense Studies, Japan).

had been exhausted. Large-scale military operations ceased to be carried out after the Canton Operation/Battle of Wuhan in the autumn of 1938. These were gradually replaced by political strategy, which became increasingly important. Political strategy consisted of either maneuvering to break down the Chongqing government or negotiating toward a ceasefire and a peace settlement. Such maneuvering was to be done through one of the following routes: via the Nationalist government in Nanjing (Wang Jingwei regime) or via a direct approach to the Chongqing government. Both channels, however, had been clogged up since the Japanese government had recognized the Nanjing regime in November 1940.

The previous quotation from the *Fukuan* of November 15 attached equal importance to "crippling the Chongqing government" and "defeating Britain," deeming both as important opportunities to end the war. Accordingly, the Liaison Conference convened immediately after the opening of the war decided that, in relation to the "matter concerning the maneuvering to cripple the Chongqing government according to changes in circumstances," Japan should aim at overthrowing the said government by "applying strong pressure upon its fatal weakness" as well as through maneuvering based on intelligence activities.[32] In the discussion on measures to address the China problem convened around the same time among representatives of the Imperial Army and Navy and the Foreign Ministry, however, it was decided that, until important resources in the southern regions were secured and a system for long-term self-sufficiency in resources was firmly established, Japan should "refrain from direct negotiations with the Chongqing government or measures that could give the impression that Japan was anxious to overthrow that government." Thus, the decision by the Liaison Conference cannot be interpreted as a measure toward the Chongqing government to be actively pursued.[33] And that was

---

32 *Sugiyama Memorandum*, vol. 1, p. 570.
33 "Tai Bei-Ei-Ran kaisen no baai ni okeru teikoku no tai-Shi hōsaku" [The Empire's China Policy in the Event of War against the United States, Britain, and the Netherlands] (November 10, 1941).

why no concrete instruction was given to the China Expeditionary Army.[34]

During the planning of the *Sensō shidō taikō* (General Principles for Waging War) in March 1942, Foreign Minister Tōgō questioned the Imperial Army's negative posture toward measures vis-à-vis the Chongqing government, saying, "Is it not inappropriate for the army to sit back and feel contented with the so-called maneuvering based on intelligence activities vis-à-vis the Chongqing government? Isn't there something the army should be doing militarily?"[35] This was Tōgō's way of tacitly suggesting more proactive operations toward the said government. The General Staff Office nonetheless remained passive, and Tanabe Moritake, deputy chief of the General Staff, merely explained that to carry out an attack on Chongqing would be practically impossible.

Colonel Horiba Kazuo, staff officer of the China Expeditionary Army, once wrote that the opening of war against the United States, Britain, and the Netherlands had deprived the Second Sino-Japanese War of its original status and degraded the provision of instruction on that war to a secondary position, making the war's future dependent on developments in the south.[36] From the viewpoint of the China Expeditionary Army, which had exerted itself to settle the war against China, the *Outline for Leadership of War against the United States, Great Britain, and the Netherlands* was as good as abandoning the effort to conclude the war. It wasn't until mid-1942 that the Imperial Japanese Army General Staff Office launched full-fledged preparations for 5-Gō Sakusen (Operation No. 5)—an aggressive attack on Chongqing—in response to the request of the China Expeditionary Army.

---

34 Itō Takashi et al., eds., *Zoku gendaishi shiryō 4: Rikugun Hata Shunroku nisshi* [Documents on Contemporary History 4: Diary of the Imperial Japanese Army's Hata Shunroku], entry of December 25, 1941, Misuzu Shobō, 1984.

35 *Sugiyama Memorandum*, vol. 2, p. 52.

36 Horiba Kazuo, *Shina Jihen sensō shidōshi* [History of War Guidance during the Second Sino-Japanese War]. Jiji Tsūshinsha, 1962, p. 40, pp. 747–749.

(2) Ministry of Foreign Affairs and Rule of the Occupied Territories

The drafting of policies on the rule of the occupied territories immediately before and after the opening of the war was done solely at the initiative of the General Staffs of the Imperial Japanese Army and Navy. One reason for this was the *Senji kōtō shireibu kimmu rei* (Instructions on Tasks of Wartime Higher Headquarters) (Gunrei Riku Otsu 1-Gō, February 1929), which stipulated that the "commander of the army of a territory should supervise administration of the areas of its military operations." This wording indicates that the planning of various measures for the occupied territories was considered to be within the jurisdiction of military command in the broad sense of the term. The stipulation's more important political background was, as mentioned earlier, the army's reflection on the ruling of the occupied territories in China through establishment of a puppet government as well as its awareness of the difference in the form of war between the Second Sino-Japanese War, which had been started without declaration, and the war against the United States, Britain, and the Netherlands, for which it was possible for Japan to make its position clear.

Although at first the Ministry of Foreign Affairs was permitted to engage principally in the continuation or abolishment of the military administration in occupied territories and post-military administration measures—not the military administration itself—over time the Foreign Ministry became actively involved in the issue of governance in the occupied territories. And this was due to the fact that measures for the occupied territories had been closely connected with the termination of the war schemes in the earlier war plans. Secondly, the ministry had a great interest in the issue of the independence of those territories after the end of military administration. The Foreign Ministry's first step toward this active involvement was Foreign Minister Tōgō's strong argument at the November 20, 1941, Liaison Conference for the insertion of "remarks" in the main text of the *Principles for the Implementation of Military Administration in the Occupied Southern*

Area. The wording that Tōgō advocated was "military administration organizations should be coordinated with or relegated to the new apparatus as the Japanese government establishes it."[37] Underlying Tōgō's assertion, which was rejected, was a competition over the reform of government organizations in the occupied territories, including China. This competition could be regarded as a preliminary skirmish toward the establishment of the Ministry of Greater East Asia.

From the late 1940s, a scheme for establishment of a new government organization in the occupied territories, with an eye on the proposed construction of the Greater East Asia Co-Prosperity Sphere, had gradually materialized around the Kōain (East Asia Development Board). In essence, it was an organizational plan that prioritized military considerations. One proposal was to put measures for territories within the Co-Prosperity Sphere under a new organization separate from the Foreign Ministry. This would expand and reinforce the Kōain. The other proposal was to expand the authority of the Imperial Japanese Army and Navy General Staff Offices (Imperial Headquarters), which was a scheme to put priority on military considerations. The Ministry of Foreign Affairs, in contrast, was contemplating a scheme to integrate the Kōain and the Tai-Man Jimukyoku (Bureau of Manchurian Affairs) into an organization under the auspices of the Foreign Minister for the sake of unification of the diplomatic route.[38]

Thus, it can be said that behind Tōgō's suggested wording to the effect that government organs of military administration should be promptly relegated to a civilian government organization was intended to restrict establishment of a new organization around the nucleus of the Kōain, because that was substantially no different from continuation of the military administration. In other words, Tōgō's wording was an argument for prompt abolishment of military administration, which attracted little support at the Liaison Conference.

---

37 *Sugiyama Memorandum*, vol 1.
38 Baba Akira, *Nitchū kankei to gaisei kikō no kenkyū* [Study of Sino-Japanese Relations and Foreign Policy Organization]. Hara Shobō, 1983, pp. 384–391.

However, the policy to "decide important matters related to the military government at the Imperial Headquarters–Government Liaison Conference," which was also advocated by Tōgō at the same November 20 Liaison Conference, was adopted—despite strong opposition. This decision signified that the Foreign Ministry had succeeded in obtaining a bridgehead in securing its influence in the decision-making on the organization issue and the independence issue. Colonel Ishii observed that these assertions by Foreign Minister Tōgō were manifestations of the Foreign Ministry's jurisdiction.[39] Behind the Foreign Ministry's argument for an early abolishment of military administration was its own agenda to tolerate prompt autonomy or independence for the occupied territories.

The issue of independence of the occupied territories once again became a subject of deliberation among the Imperial Japanese Army, the Imperial Japanese Navy, and the Ministry of Foreign Affairs immediately after the start of the war. The independence of Indonesia (Dutch East Indies) was the point of contention. While the Imperial Navy (particularly its General Staff Office) took a negative stance, claiming it was desirable to occupy the entire territory of Indonesia, the Foreign Ministry insisted on forming an Indonesian federation among the Celebes, Java, and Sumatra islands on the premise of their autonomy.[40] It is held that the Foreign Ministry's argument was based on the *Nanpō chiiki shori yōkōan* (Proposal on Principles for Handling the Southern Occupied Areas),[41] which had been drafted immediately after the beginning of the war.

The ministry's proposal was comprised of the following four components: (1) to allow the Philippines to become independent; (2) to let the Dutch East Indies become independent as a Federation of Indonesia composed of the provinces capable of self-government (Java, Sumatra,

---

39 *Ishii Memoir*, p. 241.
40 *Kimitsu sensō nisshi*, December 23, 1941.
41 *Kyokutō Kokusai Gunji Saiban sokkiroku, dai 3-kan* [Proceedings of the International Military Tribunal for the Far East, vol. 3], Yūshōdō Shoten, 1968, p. 377.

and Celebes), while mandating to Japan the provinces without that capability (Dutch Borneo, New Guinea, and Timor); (3) to incorporate the colonies along the Strait of Malacca, including Singapore and British Borneo, into the territory of the Empire of Japan to be supervised by the Empire's governor-general stationed in Singapore; and (4) to make Malaya a protectorate of the Empire.

In the later-day explanation of his final compromise proposal on the Ministry of Greater East Asia, Foreign Minister Tōgō asserted that, by putting regions necessary for the war and defense of Greater East Asia under Japan's direct control while upholding the principle of respect of sovereignty in other regions, Japan could avoid falling into British- and America-style colonialism.[42] This must have reflected the thinking behind the Foreign Ministry's compromise proposal almost in its entirety.

It should be noted that the Foreign Ministry's initial attitude toward the issue of independence of the occupied territories could be found in the *Tai Doku-I-So kōshō-an yōkō* (Outline of Negotiating with Germany, Italy and the Soviet Union) from the time of Matsuoka Yōsuke's tenure as foreign minister (1940–1941). The third section of this document stated that residents of regions within the Greater East Asia Co-Prosperity Sphere should in principle be allowed to remain or become independent. The exceptions were peoples who were not capable of independence; for these peoples, Japan should grant the maximum degree of autonomy within their capability and assume responsibility for offering guidance in self-government. As Matsuoka himself admitted, this policy regarding the occupied territories' independence was taken into consideration in proposing a long-range plan for the nation. It was drafted as a long-term plan centered around economic advancement overseas,[43] and, as such, it did not seem to have a strong, direct impact on *Proposal on Principles for Handling the Southern*

---

42 Baba, op cit., pp. 421–423.
43 *Sugiyama Memorandum*, vol 1, pp. 173–176.

Territories.[44] Nevertheless, these two documents shared a policy of allowing local residents to maintain independence or autonomy according to their respective capabilities.

After discussions on independence issues immediately before and after the beginning of the war, the Foreign Ministry's proposal on a Federation of Indonesia was turned down. It was decided instead that Japan should refrain from approving Indonesia's independence or autonomy. This proposal of the Foreign Ministry met particularly adamant opposition from the Imperial Japanese Army and Navy General Staff Offices.

Subsequently, the Foreign Ministry submitted a proposal on the independence of Java, with the consent of the Imperial Japanese Army, to the March 1942 Liaison Conference, which discussed the post–Southern Operations handling of the occupied territories. Details of this proposal are not known, but the explanation by Yamamoto Kumaichi, director-general of the Foreign Ministry's East Asian Affairs Bureau, gives us some clue. Yamamoto comments, "While it is conceivable to grant the occupied territory a high degree of autonomy before letting it become independent, it should be permissible to decide on its independence beforehand if it is to become independent anyway in the near future." Judging from Yamamoto's words, it appears that the Foreign Ministry singled out Java, which had been under the jurisdiction of the Imperial Japanese Army, from the Federation of Indonesia scheme and proposed its independence. In any event, the independence of Java was shelved on the grounds that it would be premature.[45]

(3) Controversy over Independence of the Philippines

Meanwhile, Prime Minister Tōjō remained cautious regarding the independence issue, as seen in his remark at an intra-ministerial conference of the Army Ministry on January 10, 1942. The prime minister said, "I have not yet

---

44 Among works that see strong relations between the two is William G. Beasley, *Japanese Imperialism, 1894–1945* (Oxford: Clarendon Press, 1987), pp. 256–257.
45 *Sugiyama Memorandum*, vol. 2, pp. 100–103.

declared to anyone whether [the occupied territories] should be annexed to Japan or become independent, and I do not intend to comment on this issue for the time being."[46] However, after seeking the Imperial Japanese Army's internal scrutiny of the content, Tōjō abruptly submitted to the January 15 Liaison Conference a proposal on the handling of overseas territories, including the independence issue. The proposal was submitted as a draft of a speech to be delivered in the National Diet.[47] Tōjō's intention here was not altogether clear. But the draft contained important content related to the handling of the occupied territories. In this draft, a commitment that "the Empire of Japan would gladly grant the honor of independence [to the Philippines] if it appreciates the true intention of the Empire and plays a part in construction of the Greater East Asia New Order" was followed by a statement that "the Empire's intention is no different for the Dutch East Indies and Burma."

While the portion on the Philippines and Burma was an announcement of a previously established policy, the speech draft's reference to Indonesia stirred a controversy. Finding it "a fairly bold statement," the Imperial Japanese Army General Staff Office demanded that the Army Ministry delete this reference to Indonesia, with which it could hardly concur.[48] In the end, the revision of the speech draft by the Imperial Japanese Army and Navy General Staff Offices was adopted. Accordingly, it was decided that Prime Minister Tōjō's speech at the seventy-ninth session of the National Diet on January 21 would not touch on the independence of Indonesia.[49]

46 "Kinbara Setsuzō gyōmu nisshi tekiroku" [Excerpts from Kinbara Setsuzō's Diary], January 10, 1942 (a collection at the National Institute of Defense Studies, NIDS).
47 *Kimitsu sensō nisshi*, January 15, 1942.
48 Ibid.
49 In the January 21, 1942 conference among directors-generals, Muto Akira, director-general of Bureau of Military Affairs, Army Ministry announced, "We should refrain from a premature announcement on territorial jurisdiction of the occupied territories. That of Hong Kong and Malay should belong to Japan. Independence should be granted to the Philippines and Burma. If the Dutch East Indies and Australia collaborate with the Empire, it shall try to improve their convenience, but it should not announce their independence." "Kinbara Setsuzō gyōmu nisshi tekiroku" [Excerpts from Kinbara Setsuzō's Diary], January 21, 1942 (a collection at NIDS).

Foreign Minister Tōgō, however, actively supported Prime Minister Tōjō's speech draft, and particularly its policy pledge on the independence of the Philippines. Tōgō's support was partly based on an ulterior motive. Because Tōgō saw the pledge as "something handed down from the US promise of independence to the Philippines," Tōgō thought "this policy could hopefully diminish obstacles to a subsequent peace settlement with the United States by letting that nation know that Japan had no territorial ambitions in the southern occupied territories and, at the same time, that Japan's Philippines policy was identical to that of the United States."[50]

As is well known, independence for the Philippines had been promised by the Tydings-McDuffie Act of 1934, and the archipelago was preparing itself for its imminent independence under the leadership of the Commonwealth of the Philippines. The above remarks by Tōgō revealed that his support of independence for the Philippines was motivated by his wish to eliminate obstacles to a peace settlement with the United States as much as possible, by minimizing the capture of the Philippine Islands and persevering respect for the sovereignty of the Commonwealth of the Philippines. I have already shown that the argument for independence for the Philippines had been widely discussed within the Japanese government at that time as well as within the Imperial Japanese Army. One week into the war, the War Guidance Section of the Imperial Japanese Army General Staff Office drafted a proposal concerning the handling of the Philippine Islands in "an attempt to promptly end the battle on the Philippine Islands." The same section subsequently presented a "draft declaration of independence for the Philippines" to the Imperial Japanese Navy on January 7, 1942.[51] While the exact content of this draft declaration is unknown, it is said that the Army General Staff Office maintained the policy of supporting the incumbent Manuel Quezon administration in organizing a central government

---

50 Tōgō, 1985, p. 303.
51 *Kimitsu sensō nisshi*, December 15, 1941 and January 7, 1942.

and allow the Philippines to become an independent republic after a certain period of military administration.[52]

Because Quezon fled Manila shortly afterward, Jorge Bartolome Vargas, the mayor of Manila, became the next to be backed up by the Imperial Japanese Army. It is believed that the Japanese Fourteenth Army stationed in the Philippines was envisioning the establishment of a Wang Jingwei regime-like government in the archipelago. However, Colonel Ishii Akiho, who had been assigned to the Southern Expeditionary Army as a senior staff officer, insisted, "It should be a proper order to first have them establish a mere administrative organization—something akin to an executive branch of government—instead of a full regime, and to put it under the military commander's supervision." Ishii flew to Manila in mid-January 1942 to convince the leaders of the Japanese Fourteenth Army of this objective. It was Ishii's view that a military commander should instruct and issue orders to the chief of the administrative organization rather than collaborate with him.[53] Consequently, when the first instruction from the commander-in-chief of the Japanese Fourteenth Army was issued on January 23, it instructed Vargas to "assume the post of the chief of the central administrative organization to promptly integrate and unify residual administrative organs in the archipelago and carry out administrative tasks under the instruction and command of the commander-in-chief of the Japanese Fourteenth Army."[54] A similar system in which the chief of the administration organization carried out administrative tasks under the instruction and command of the commander-in-chief of the occupation

---

52 Ōta Hiroki, "Firipin ni okeru saishoki no Nippon gunsei" [Early Japanese Military Administration in the Philippines], *Seiji keizai shigaku*, no. 122 (July 1976), pp. 47–48, and Maruyama Shizuo. *Ushinawaretaru kiroku: Taika/nanpō seiryaku hishi* [Lost Records: Secret History of Political Tactics against China and the Southern Region]. Kōraku Shobō, 1950, pp. 245–246.
53 Ishii Akiho, "Nanpō gunsei nikki" [Diary of Military Government in the Southern Occupied Territories], p. 445.
54 Ōta Hiroki, "Firipin ni okeru Nippon gunsei kikan to Hitō gyōseifu (II)" [Japanese Military Administration Organization in the Philippines and the Local Administrative Organization (II)], *Seiji keizai shigaku*, no. 129 (February 1977), p. 20.

force was also adopted in Burma.[55]

As we have seen, while the policy of utilizing the existing government organization (indirect military administration) was narrowly upheld, the idea that respect for the Philippines' sovereignty or its early independence would be beneficial at the time of a peace settlement with the United States suffered setbacks soon after the outbreak of the war. And this happened not only in the Philippines but also in Burma around the time when the Southern Operations completed its initial stage. One reason behind these setbacks was the thinning of connections between independence of the occupied territories and the plan to terminate the war, which will be discussed in detail in the next chapter.

3. Conclusion: In the Context of the Peoples' Liberation Movement

During his speech at the seventy-ninth session of the National Diet on January 21, 1942, Prime Minister Tōjō declared that establishment of the Greater East Asia Co-Prosperity Sphere was the final aim of the war. He said that the basic policy of the Greater East Asia Co-Prosperity Sphere was to "allow each country and each people in East Asia to have its own place and consolidate an order of co-existence and co-prosperity based on morals centered around the Empire of Japan." On that basis, Tōjō revealed the existing policies of securing the Malay Peninsula and Hong Kong as the stronghold of the Greater East Asia defense, while allowing the Philippines and Burma to become independent. The daily *Asahi Shimbun* commented on this speech on three consecutive days and praised the speech as a "major revolution in ideology of war" that "surpassed the Atlantic Charter, a manifestation of the British and American intention to imperialistically

---

55 Ōta Tsunezō, *Biruma ni okeru Nippon gunseishi no kenkyū* [Study of History of Japanese Military Administration in Burma], Yoshikawa Kōbunkan, 1976, p. 524. (Chūō gyōsei chōkan ni atafuru shirei [Instruction on the Chief of Central Administrative Organization], July 22, 1942.)

rule the world" and "truly explicated the method for peoples' liberation."[56] As a matter of fact, the prime minister had implied in his earlier answers in the National Diet that liberation of Asian peoples was an integral part of construction of the Greater East Asia Co-Prosperity Sphere.[57] Thus, the argument for peoples' liberation was raised to the status of Japan's war aim, and it became a goal of its own.

To be sure, Japan did not enter the war having raised the issue of peoples' liberation and colonial rule as its aim for war. But Japan had to camouflage its true purpose of procurement of national defense resources and economic exploitation of the occupied territories.[58] Furthermore, because Japan thought the direct path toward ending the war lay in the war against Britain, Japan had to uphold a noble cause for its military aggression in the Malay Peninsula, Burma, and even India, above and beyond the self-sufficiency and self-defense argument. These factors made it imperative for Japan to cite the liberation of people's suffering under British imperial rule.

While Foreign Minister Tōgō's foreign policy speech shared with Tōjō's Imperial Diet speech the argument that the liberation of East Asia and construction of the Greater East Asia Co-Prosperity Sphere were the purposes of the war, Tōgō's speech contained more committed arguments on the following two points. First, in order to make the point that the Pacific War was not a so-called war of aggression, Tōgō stressed that while Japan

---

56 "Daitōa sengen no sekaishiteki igi" [Global Historical Significance of the Greater East Asia Declaration], *Asahi Shimbun*, January 23–26, 1942.

57 Prime Minister Tōjō touched on respect of cultures, customs, and freedom of religion of each local people in the House of Representatives' plenary session on the budget on January 23 and remarked that, "Since the Empire of Japan is in the process of liberating Asian peoples, we need to encourage local peoples [in the occupied territories] to participate in the construction of the Greater East Asia Co-Prosperity Sphere." In other words, in Tōjō's mind the process of peoples' liberation and the process of establishing the Co-Prosperity Sphere were perceived as an integral unit.

58 An attempt to perceive the Japanese argument for peoples' liberation in the context of how to camouflage intended economic exploitation is found in the deliberation on economic construction at the Council for the Co-Prosperity Sphere of Greater East Asia (4th Division). See Kawahara Hiroshi, *Shōwa seiji shisō kenkyū* [Study of Political Thought in the Shōwa Era]. Waseda Daigaku Shuppanbu, 1979, pp. 285–303.

had to hold on to the regions that were necessary for the defense of East Asia, an "appropriate status" should be recognized in accordance with each people's traditions, cultures, and other elements in the regions occupied by Britain and the United States. It is conjectured that this "appropriate status" perhaps meant autonomy or independence. As mentioned earlier, what Tōgō had in mind was a method of placing territories that were essential for Japan's war efforts and Greater East Asia defense under Japan's direct control while upholding the principle of respect for sovereignty in other territories as a means for Japan to avoid lapsing into British-American style colonialism. While Tōgō expressed himself less explicitly in his Diet speech, he conveyed the same message.

The second point that Tōgō stressed in his speech was that the philosophy of the Greater East Asia Co-Prosperity Sphere was not of a closed and exclusive nature. He emphasized that it was obvious that economic exchanges between the Co-Prosperity Sphere and friendly nations outside the Sphere would gradually become prevalent as establishment of the Sphere progressed. Tōgō characterized his speech as an expression of the ideology that respect for sovereignty would be upheld for countries inside the Co-Prosperity Sphere and such notions as block economy and *lebensraum* (living space) should be ruled out. In this way, he clearly differentiated his perception of the Co-Prosperity Sphere from that of Prime Minister Tōjō. While the process of Asian people's liberation was simultaneously that of creation of the Greater East Asia Co-Prosperity Sphere in Tōjō's perception, respect for the sovereignty of territories within the Sphere was not a premise for development of the Co-Prosperity Sphere for Tōjō.

In short, the issue of contention was how to incorporate peoples of the occupied territories into the Greater East Asian Co-Prosperity Sphere after their liberation. While Tōgō envisioned, politically, an early termination of military administration and approval of autonomy and independence and, economically, an open, non-exclusive regime based on exchanges with external countries, Tōjō held the completely opposite image.[59] These totally different visions of the Co-Prosperity Sphere came to be directly reflected in the issue of the Ministry of Greater East Asia (see chapter 3).

---

59 See Tōgō (1985), p. 304.

Chapter 2

Political Battle over Advance into West Asia

1. *Sensō Shidō Taikō* and the Plan to Defeat Britain

In the Army Ministry's meeting for division chiefs issued near the end of January 1942, Nagai Yatsuji, director of military affairs, reported on future war instructions. Nagai referred to the studies conducted by the Imperial Japanese Army and the Imperial Japanese Navy on whether or not to escalate military operations so as to take advantage of the remarkable accomplishments seen in the early stages of the war. Nagai wrote the following:

> If Japan can overcome Britain, then it would be possible to draw the United States into peace negotiations, but there is no reason to amend the overall policy if Japan cannot bring Britain to heel, and fight the United States until that country loses the will to fight. Even if Britain does not capitulate, because Australia and India are substantially separated from Britain and cannot be expected to cause the immediate fall and subjugation of Britain, its influence over Australia and India is predicted to be reduced significantly. Therefore, it is imperative to execute military operations against Australia and India with urgency.[1]

Pointing out that the only way to prompt the end of war was to persist with the plan to cripple Britain, Nagai urged the Imperial Army's support for the Imperial Navy–led operations to sever Australia and India from Britain. The Imperial Navy agreed with the strategy of Operation FS (Fiji and Samoa) to cut the supply and communication chains between Australia and the United States. Accordingly, it conducted a small-scale Indian Ocean raid around Ceylon Island on March 14 through early April as the fourth-stage of the first step in the operation to sever India from Britain. The major goal of the Combined Fleet led by Admiral Yamamoto Isoroku, however, remained,

---

1 *Kinbara Setsuzō gyōmu nisshi tekiroku* [Excerpts from Kinbara Setsuzō's Diary], entry on January 29, 1942, (a collection at the National Defense Medical College).

from beginning to the end, to conduct a decisive battle with the US fleet in the Pacific. While the cutting of communications between Britain and India through the invasion of Ceylon and establishment of a liaison with Germany and Italy were part of the operational goals in the Imperial Navy Second-Stage Operation Plan ratified on April 15, 1942, they did not take precedence over Operation MI (Midway) to devastate US fleets or Operation AI (attack on Hawaii).[2]

The aggressive posture of the Imperial Navy was also reflected in the *Sensō shidō taikō* (General Principles for Waging War) of March 1942, which set out the basic strategies that would follow the Southern Operations. As is well known, the *General Principles for Waging War* ended up adopting, at least on paper, both the navy's aggressive operational schemes and the army's assertion about securing the southern occupied territories and consolidating a long-term self-sufficient regime.[3] But from the viewpoint of accelerating a conclusion to the war, the *War Instruction Outline* confirmed that Japan's central strategy was to subdue Britain, explicitly designating the purpose of war as "crippling Britain and depriving the United States of its will to fight." In that sense, the *General Principles for Waging War* did not contain any new decisions. Therefore, it was stated that "seeing as this content is not greatly different from the existing plan, it would not be necessary to submit it to imperial decision or convene an Imperial Council."[4] Thus, the *General Principles for Waging War* was positioned as a Liaison Conference decision.

In any event, in order to effect the strategy of cutting off communications between Britain and India, a joint operation in which the Imperial Navy captured Ceylon Island and German troops advanced into the Middle

---

2 Nomura Minoru. "Taiheiyō Sensō no Nippon no sensō shidō" [Japan's War Instructions during the Pacific War], Kindai Nippon Kenkyūkai, ed., *Nenpō Kindai Nippon Kenkyū 4: Taiheiyō Sensō* [Annual Report on Modern Japan Studies 4: Pacific War], Yamakawa Shuppansha, 1982, pp. 36–38.
3 For instance, see Nishiura Susumu, *Shōwa sensōshi no shōgen* [Testimonies on the History of Wars during Shōwa] Hara Shobō, 1980, p. 167.
4 Imperial Japanese Army General Staff Office, ed., *Sugiyama memo, ge* [Sugiyama Memorandum, vol. 2]. Hara Shobō, 1989, p. 54.

East (Suez) was considered essential. The Imperial Army and Navy urged the German navy to advance into the Middle East and the Indian Ocean via the military attaché (Lieutenant General Nomura Naokuni) and the naval attaché (Vice-Admiral Banzai Ichirō) stationed in Germany. They also explored the possibility for the German navy to invade the British mainland. Around the time of the fall of Singapore, the leadership of the German navy was seriously studying the operation plan to advance into the two regions that the Japanese military had requested.[5] The Japanese military attaché who had met the German directors of naval and army operations in mid-February reported, however, that while the German military recognized the importance of the operations in the Middle East, those goals fell second to Germany's primary concern for operations vis-à-vis the Soviet Union. According to these German army and naval officers, although Germany had not yet abandoned the plan to invade the British mainland, it had decided that the plan should be carried out after the war against the Soviet Union had achieved a major aim.[6]

Judging from the German attitude, which made it quite clear that it would be hopeless to expect German and Italian troops to advance into the Middle East promptly, the Imperial Army nevertheless continued to view German-Japanese cooperation in the Middle East as the key to the progress of the war. Consequently, the Imperial Army began to envision a long-term scenario to advance into the Caucasus in the period between spring and summer, to be followed by advances into West Asia.[7] The strategic aim of the German-Japanese joint penetration into West Asia to isolate India did not seem feasible unless it was acted on in concert with the German and Italian

---

5 Milan Hauner, *India in Axis Strategy: Germany, Japan, and Indian Nationalists in the Second World War* (Stuttgart: Klett-Cotta, 1981), pp. 398–402.

6 February 16 telegram of the military attaché stationed in Germany addressed to the Chief of Staff (included in the compilation of army and naval attachés stationed in Germany), a collection at the National Institute for Defense Studies, Japan.

7 "Kinbara Setsuzō gyōmu nisshi tekiroku" [Excerpts from Kinbara Setsuzō's Diary], entry of March 18, 1942, (a collection at the National Defense Medical College) and *Sugiyama memo, ge*, p. 68.

Middle East operations and supported by the Imperial Japanese Navy.[8]

When the German troops started their advance into the Caucasus toward the end of June 1942, the Imperial Japanese Army General Staff Office predicted that this summer offensive would play out with the overwhelming superior German troops capturing the Caucasus by the end of 1942 at the latest. The Army General Staff Office also believed that the German troops would advance further into Suez and launch their West Asia operations by the spring of 1943.[9] Accordingly, G-1 (operations) of the Army General Staff Office started a study of the possibility of dispatching a government mission to Germany in line with the "West Asia offensive" strategy to isolate India via penetration into West Asia and the disruption of navigation routes in the Indian Ocean. Because this government mission was envisioned to include "a prominent figure" who would bring with him a proposal on the German-Soviet peace settlement, the German side was reluctant to receive the mission. In the end, a liaison mission devoid of the original duties was accepted by Germany in January 1943.[10]

The Imperial Navy, which had been devastated at the Battle of Midway, decided to abolish Operation FS, which had aimed at isolating Australia from the United States and launching an Indian Ocean raid, to which the main forces of the Combined Fleet were to be mobilized, in response to the German and Italian invasion of North Africa (toward the end of May 1942) and the Italian prime minister's request by telegram for the Imperial Navy to advance into the Red Sea region. The Imperial Navy decided to do this, although it had not altogether abandoned the plan of a decisive battle

---

8 "Kinbara Setsuzō gyōmu nisshi tekiroku" [Excerpts from Kinbara Setsuzō's Diary] (entry on section chiefs' conference of the Army Ministry on March 18), and Imoto Kumao, *Sakusen nisshi de tsuzuru Daitōa Sensō* [The Greater East Asia War as Depicted by Military Operation Diary], Fuyō Shobō, 1979, pp. 117–118.
9 *Tanaka Shin-ichi Chūjō kaisōroku* [Memoir of Lieutenant General Tanaka Shin-ichi] (dictated in 1956), a collection at the National Institute for Defense Studies, Japan.
10 *Kōtani Etsuo Taisa kaisōroku* [Memoir of Colonel Kōtani Etsuo] (Kōseishō Hikiage Engokyoku, ed., 1956).

with the US fleet in the Central Pacific.[11] When Nagano Osami, chief of the Imperial Japanese Naval General Staff, reported to the emperor on July 11, 1942, he explained the Imperial Navy's decision as its response to the "increased possibility of consolidating the invincibility of the Axis powers" thanks to the northern African operations by the German and Italian troops. It showed that, for the first time, the Imperial Japanese Navy sought to focus its main operations in the Indian Ocean.

While the interests of the Imperial Army and Navy converged in the Middle East and West Asia, measures vis-à-vis Burma and India were the centerpieces of corresponding political measures. And these measures were pursued both within and outside the region. Internally, measures consisted solely of maneuvers directed at India and Burma to be carried out by the Imperial Headquarters Army Section (Imperial Japanese Army General Staff Office), including the expeditionary army troops in the field. (The Imperial Japanese Navy General Staff Office was in charge of operations directed at Australia). External measures took the form of propaganda on the Japanese government's policy, to be carried out mainly by the Ministry of Foreign Affairs. The division of duties among actors in these measures was extremely clear-cut,[12] as shown in the following activities toward Burma.

2. Political Battle over Burmese Independence

(1) Minami Kikan and Maneuvers Regarding Burma

Maneuvering regarding the independence of Burma had already been conducted by the Minami Kikan, a secret intelligence organization that was

---

11 Bōei Kenshūsho Senshishitsu, ed., *Daihon-ei Kaigunbu: Rengō Kantai, dai 3-kan* [Imperial Headquarters Navy Section: Combined Fleet, vol. 3], Asagumo Shimbunsha, 1970, pp. 55–60.

12 January 10 Liaison Conference decision on "Jōsei no shinten ni tomonau tōmen no shisaku ni kansuru ken" [On Matters Related to Immediate Measures in Response to Changes in the Situation] and "Tai-Indo-Gōshu shisaku ni kansuru riku/kaigun mōshiawase" [Understanding between the Imperial Army and Navy on Measures toward India and Australia], *Sugiyama Memo, ge* [Sugiyama Memorandum, vol. 2], pp. 4–7.

founded in Bangkok in February 1941 with Colonel Suzuki Keiji as its chief. The Minami Kikan reported directly to the Imperial General Headquarters. The major emphasis of the measures for Burma was the prompt inducement of Burmese volunteers (members of the Thakin Party) inside Burma to carry out active independence movements everywhere in the country.[13] Military action by the Imperial Army was limited to deploying a small number of troops to capture the region around Moulmein in south Burma for use as a base to support the Burmese independence movement. It was hoped that by seeing Burma being granted independence, the Indian people would intensify their quest for secession from Britain and for independence. In this way, Burmese independence was viewed as potentially giving indirect support to the already existing movement of the Indian people for the independence of India.[14]

As soon as war was declared against Britain and the United States in December 1941, the Southern Expeditionary Army ordered the 15th Army to advance into Thailand and capture southern Burma; the 5th Division of the 15th Army assembled in Bangkok in late December. The mission of the Minami Kikan immediately after the opening of the war was to lead members of the Thakin Party to riot inside Burma and destroy government organizations. At the same time, the Minami Kikan was mandated to organize a volunteer army of insurgents, which was to become the core of the independent regime, and consolidate the foundation of an independent Burma. Having advanced into Bangkok together with the 15th Army, the Minami Kikan succeeded in establishing the Burma Independence Army (BIA) and began maneuvering activities aimed at Burma.

Yet as the Burma campaign advanced, the policy of the Imperial

---

13 Saitō Teruko, "Kaisenki ni okeru tai-Biruma kōsaku kikan: Minami Kikan saikō" [Organization for Maneuvering toward Burma at the Opening of the Pacific War: Minami Kikan Revisited] in Tanaka Hiroshi, ed., *Nippon gunsei to Ajia no minzoku undō* [Japanese Military Administration and Nationalist Movements in Asia], Ajia Keizai Kenkyūsho, 1983, pp. 99–104.
14 March 7 entry on "Sekai jōsei handan (sankō)" [Assessment of the World Situation (for reference)], *Sugiyama memo, ge,* p. 68.

Japanese Army General Staff Office rapidly changed. Now it envisioned the occupation of the entire territory of Burma. Early on December 21, 1941, when Colonel Hattori Takushirō, director of the G1 (operations) of the Imperial Japanese Army General Staff Office, arrived in Saigon, he ordered the capture of the important regions in Burma, including Mandalay and Akyab in central and western Burma, respectively. The aim of this was to sever the Chiang Kai-shek support route and eliminate British influence in Burma. At the same time, Hattori also requested that the Minami Kikan's maneuvers be coordinated with the military campaign.[15] Although initially somewhat baffled, the Southern Expeditionary Army accepted Hattori's proposals on the condition that the attack would be limited to Rangoon and its vicinities. On January 22, 1942, the Imperial General Headquarters Army Section issued an order to capture key regions in Burma (*Tairiku Mei* #590), whereby the 15th Army was instructed to capture Mandalay and other regions. Thus, the mission of the Southern Expeditionary Army became one that eyed the capture of the entirety of Burma.

When ordered to capture key regions in Burma, Lieutenant General Iida Shōjirō, commander-in-chief of the 15th Army, announced on January 22 that the purpose of the advance into Burma was to drive out British influence so as to liberate the Burmese people and assist their attaining independence. And the Minami Kikan, also, was to advance into Burmese territory with the volunteer army to work toward the reorganization of the local administrative apparatus and reform traditional local leadership in preparation for an independent Burma.[16] These instructions were based on the policy of respecting "traditional local autonomy organizations" as long as their presence would not disturb the "execution of the military's operations and establishment

---

15 Bōei Kenshūsho Senshishitsu, ed., *Biruma kōryaku sakusen* [Operation to Capture Burma], Asagumo Shimbunsha, 1967, p. 72.
16 "Shōwa 16-nendo rikuamitsu dai-nikki, dai 42-gō" [FY1941 Rikuamitsu Diary no. 42], *Biruma kōryaku sakusen*, pp. 118–119.

of an independent government."[17] That is, Minami Kikan's activities were endorsed on the premise that expanding the range of the invasion in Burma would not affect the policy to grant early independence for Burma.

The rapid turnabout in policy for the Burma invasion operation induced an upswell of arguments in both the Southern Expeditionary Army and the Army General Staff Office calling for suppression of an early independence. While the Minami Kikan held on to the original vision of early independence for Burma with the volunteer army as the nucleus of the independent regime, the Southern Expeditionary Army and the Army General Staff Office opposed that scenario. Instead, they set out a policy to maintain military administration under the Imperial Army for the time being. The Southern Expeditionary Army was particularly critical of approving an early independence, claiming that, while establishment of a "powerful new regime" remained the basic policy, the approval of this new regime should be granted after the end of the war.[18] The Imperial Japanese Army General Staff Office, for its part, had been bitter about the Minami Kikan's aggressive actions since the outbreak of the war, as detected from its critical stance toward Prime Minister Tōjō's reference to Burmese independence in the draft of his January 21 speech.[19] In particular, it is said that the most ardent critic of the argument for early independence for Burma, Colonel Ishii Akiho (senior staff officer of the 3rd section of the Southern Expeditionary Army and formerly with the Military Affairs Bureau of the Army Ministry), tried hard to dissuade army leaders from approving early independence, quoting his bitter experiences with the founding of the Wang Jingwei regime during

---

17 Dorothy Guyot, "The Burma Independence Army: A Political Movement in Military Garb," in Josef Silverstein, ed., *Southeast Asia in World War II: Four Essays*, (Yale University Southeast Asia Studies Monograph Series No. 7, 1966), pp. 51–65.

18 *Biruma kōryaku sakusen*, pp. 123–124, Ishii Akiho, *Nanpō gunsei nikki* [Diary of Military Administration in Southern Territories], Bōei Kenkyūsho Senshibu, ed., *Shiryōshū nanpō no gunsei* [Documents on Military Administration in the Southern Territories], Asagumo Shimbunsha, 1985, pp. 443–445.

19 *Kimitsu sensō nisshi* [Confidential War Diary], entries of January 15, 21, and 22, 1942.

his extended assignment in North China.[20]

The fall of Rangoon on March 8, 1942, forced Japan to face a choice between continuing a Japanese military administration in Burma or granting immediate independence. Colonel Suzuki of the Minami Kikan requested full-scale support for prompt recognition of independence on the basis of the general message contained in Prime Minister Tōjō's speech at the National Diet in the wake of the fall of Rangoon (although Tōjō did not explicitly refer to Burma's independence). The Southern Expeditionary Army, however, rejected the request from the Minami Kikan on the basis of the Principles Governing the Administration of the Occupied Southern Regions and set out a policy of forgoing early independence and continuing the military administration for the time being, during which time preparations for eventual independence would be made. Then on March 22, 1942, Colonel Suzuki *arbitrarily* announced the formation of the Burma Baho Government. Suzuki made the announcement under his name in Burmese, Bo Mogyo. Whether Suzuki's action had been endorsed by the 15th Army or not remains open to debate. In any event, it was a manifestation of the Minami Kikan's alacrity for early recognition of independence for Burma.[21] But the Imperial Japanese Army General Staff Office and the Southern Expeditionary Army leaned heavily toward implementation of military administration, as represented by their adoption of the 15th Army's *Senryōchi tōchi yōkō* (Principles Governing the Administration of the Occupied Southern Regions), which stipulated that "while it is considered that an independent regime should be

---

20 Ishii, op cit., p. 454.

21 Ōta Tsunezō, *Biruma ni okeru Nippon gunseishi no kenkyū* [A Study on History of the Japanese Military Administration in Burma], Yoshikawa Kōbunkan, 1967, p. 46; Intelligence Bureau, Government of Burma, *Burma during the Japanese Occupation*, 1st Oct. 1943, (Confidential), pp. 1–2. According to a report compiled by Intelligence Bureau of Government of Burma, Burma Baho Government was formed around Thakin Tan Ok as its chief by way of integrating local committees. This government issued its first directive prior to April 7, 1942. The same report states that it is not known whether the establishment of this government had been endorsed by the relevant authorities or whether the said government believed in the volunteer army's slogans of "Asia for Asians" and "Fight for Free Burma." (Ibid., pp. 2–3.)

established in Burma, it is predicted that its actual establishment will be, at least for the time being, after the end of the Greater East Asia War."[22]

Upon announcement of the military administration on June 3, 1942, the Minami Kikan and the BIA were dissolved. Colonel Suzuki was transferred to the headquarters of the Imperial Guard (as of June 15), while the BIA was reorganized as the Burma National Army. The *Hayashi Shūdan senryōchi tōchi yōkō* (General Plan for the Rule of the Occupied Areas under the Hayashi Army Group) issued on the same day by Iida Shōjirō, the commander of the Hayashi Army Group, reconfirmed the policy at the beginning of the war on control of occupied areas, stipulating that as much as possible the Southern Expeditionary Army's self-support needs and procurement of resources for Japan's national defense (article 7) should be obtained solely at the local level without anticipating support from the outside, regardless of the burden placed on local populations.[23] The document also contained articles that restricted the argument for early independence for Burma, particularly as it came from the Minami Kikan, arguing that the establishment of an independent regime should be envisioned after the end of the war (article 2) and that Japan should remain noncommittal on the timing and the form of independence (article 40).

Burma shares borders with India and China, and it was anticipated that the Allies would launch a counteroffensive from these two neighboring countries. The strategic position of Burma was defined as a "western wall" or an "outer shell" to help consolidate Greater East Asia's preparedness for a long-term war. From the viewpoint of orchestrating an end to the war with China, Burma occupied a strategic position in terms of severance of Chiang Kai-shek's support route. These notions of Burma's strategic position were also reflected in the Imperial Army's post–Southern Operations troops deployment plan. Of

---

22 *Shiryōshū Nanpō no gunsei* [Documents on Military Administration in the Southern Territories], p. 275 and Bōei Kenshūsho Senshishitsu, ed., *Biruma kōryaku sakusen* [Operation to Conquer Burma], pp. 445–451, and Ishii, op cit., p. 454.
23 Ōta, op cit., pp. 487–490.

the six divisions of troops to remain in the southern territories, in accordance with the plan to withdraw troops from the southern territories (troop management proposal), three were allotted to Burma, which was an exceptionally large number compared with one division in Java, one division in Sumatra, one division in Indochina, and three independent garrisons in the Philippines. It was toward the end of May 1942 that this troop management proposal was reported to the emperor by Sugiyama Hajime, chief of the General Staff.[24] Sugiyama's report coincided with the timing of the Imperial Army's decision to establish a military administration in Burma.

(2) Setback of the Argument for Burma's Independence

On June 29, 1942, the Army General Staff Office put the 15th Army under the direct jurisdiction of the Southern Expeditionary Army. It also again issued an instruction pertaining to the Southern Expeditionary Army's basic mission. The instruction defined Burma—along with British Malaya, Sumatra, Java, and British Borneo—as an area where attempts should be made to familiarize the local population with the Japanese military administration. This instruction finally settled the issue of independence for Burma.[25] Thus, construction of a "Burma for the Burmese people" that Prime Minister Tōjō had stressed no longer necessarily meant Burma's independence. In other words, Burma's role as a key to Greater East Asia defense became more important than its role as a "base of measures to influence India."[26] When in early July the Southern Expeditionary Army was reminded of the

---

24 Section 2 of the Imperial Japanese Army General Staff Office, "Nanpō senryō chiiki no genjō to heiryoku unyō ni tsuite" [On the Status of Southern Occupied Territories and Troop Deployment] compiled in *Shōwa 17-nen jōsō kankei tsuzuri kan-1* [File of Documents Reported to the Emperor in 1942, vol. 1] a collection at the National Institute for Defense Studies, Japan. For the troop management proposal, see Bōei Kenshūsho Senshishitsu, ed., *Daihon'ei Rikugunbu, dai 4-kan* [Imperial General Headquarters Army Section, vol. 4], Asagumo Shimbunsha, 1972, pp. 157–160.
25 *Shiryōshū Nanpō no gunsei* [Documents on Military Administration in the Southern Territories], p. 23.
26 "Biruma ni kansuru bōryaku jisshitō ni kansuru ken" [Matters Related to Implementation of Strategies for Burma], February 6 included in Bōei Kenshūsho Senshishitsu, ed., *Biruma kōryaku sakusen* [Operation to Capture Burma], p. 122.

importance of an early independence for Burma from the viewpoint of its impact on India, it rejected the idea, insisting that "it is inconceivable that the acceleration of Burma's independence by six months to one year would have a spillover effect on India."[27] This shows that, while only a half year earlier Burma had been a territory that had to be made independent to facilitate measures against India, now what happened in Burma had become a totally separate issue from the Indian issue.

On July 22, 1942, the commander-in-chief of the 16th Army issued a "directive addressed to the chief of the central administrative organization" in which it was stated that the chief of administration in Burma would act as instructed by command orders from the commander-in-chief of the Southern Expeditionary Army.[28] This was the same arrangement as had been proposed for the Philippines. This directive was based on the suggestion from Colonel Ishii of Section 3 of the Southern Expeditionary Army that the military commander should not simply "cooperate with" the local chief of administration but should "command and issue orders" to him. This suggestion had been derived from Ishii's bitter experience of establishing a puppet government in China (the Wang Jingwei regime), which allowed endless interferences from the Japanese side, resulting in failure to win the support of local people.[29]

Around the same time, the military administration headquarters of the Southern Expedition Army issued instructions on measures for local peoples in which it was stressed that extra care should be taken to avoid any commitment to the local residents regarding the handling of the occupied territories because "the final decision had been put on hold as national policy." While it had been a "secret intention of the central government" to "approve independence [for the Philippines and Burma] at an appropriate timing in the future," it should be kept in mind that the independence of these countries

---

27 *Biruma kōryaku sakusen*, pp. 492–493.
28 Ōta, op cit., p. 524.
29 Ishii, op cit., p. 445.

would fall under the strong military, diplomatic, and economic controls of the Empire of Japan.[30] This instruction clearly shows that, even in those occupied territories that had been scheduled for the granting of independence, the mode of independence that the Minami Kikan had envisioned was already out of the question.

Detecting these changes, Ba Maw, head of the provisional civilian administration in Burma and, later, head of state under the Japanese military administration, observed that, as the influence of the Southern Expeditionary Army increased, its headquarters became dominated by a "Korean clique," the members of which had the "sense of superiority of the conqueror . . . who, I came to realize, was not sure itself whether it was fighting to retrieve Burma from Britain or to bring it under its own purview. The majority of this clique was hoping to somehow keep Burma as a Japanese possession, like Korea and Manchuria."[31]

The intra-government battle over independence for Burma in the early days of the war can also be characterized as a conflict over the need to procure national defense resources and military operation requirements overriding the argument for an early independence as represented by the Minami Kikan. And this process was clearly reflected in external announcements of the Japanese government. It was Prime Minister Tōjō's speech at the National Diet on January 21, 1942, that made the first reference to Burma's independence. After stating that the Philippines would be given the honor of independence, Tōjō added that "What the Empire of Japan intends to do with Burma is no different from the Philippines."[32] The draft of the prime minister's speech at the time of the fall of Singapore (adopted by the Liaison Conference on February 9) stated that "We intend to promptly grant the honor of independence and active cooperation to the Burmese people's

---

30 Ibid., p. 294.
31 Ba Maw, *Breakthrough in Burma: Memoirs of a Revolution, 1939–1946* (New Haven, Yale University Press, 1968), p. 181.
32 *Kanpō gōgai* [Official Gazette, extra issue], January 22, 1942, House of Representatives Stenographic Record no. 2.

construction of Burma." But the actual speech delivered on February 16 declared, "We intend to promptly render active cooperation to the Burmese people's construction of Burma," omitting "the honor of independence." Mid-February coincided with the beginning of the confrontation between the Minami Kikan and the Southern Expeditionary Army over Burma's independence and military administration. And the intricacies of the situation were reflected in the prime minister's speech.[33]

Furthermore, in the prime minister's speech after the fall of Rangoon, there was no mention of independence, either in the draft submitted to the Liaison Conference or the speech actually delivered on March 12. After merely stating that "Burma for the Burmese people is about to be completed," the prime minister devoted the entire speech to the military significance of the capture of Rangoon.[34] This indicates that the early independence of Burma was now out of the question, in both Burma and Tokyo.

In contrast to rhetoric on the issue of Burma's independence, which was gradually toned down in the series of speeches by the prime minister, the significance of the liberation of India and construction of an "India for Indians" became increasingly emphasized.

3. Political Battle over Independence for India

(1) The "India Crisis" and Maneuvering Aimed at India

In response to Britain's declaration of war in September 1939, the governor-general of India immediately declared war against Germany. This decision completely ignored the contention of Indian nationalists that India's participation in the war must be decided by the Indian people themselves. The Indian National Congress—the government party in particular—had

---

33 *Sugiyama memo, ge* [Sugiyama Memorandum, vol. 2], pp. 18–20; *Kanpō gōgai*, February 17, 1942, House of Representatives Stenographic Record no. 16.

34 *Sugiyama memo, ge*, pp. 61–63; *Kanpō gōgai*, March 13, 1942, House of Representatives Stenographic Record no. 17.

resolved that, if Britain approved India's right to self-determination and its right to establish its own constitution, India would be prepared to fight alongside Britain. This was tantamount to a de facto rejection by India of collaboration with Britain. Nevertheless, while the Government of British India and the British government were willing to make concessions needed to secure wartime preparations, they had no intention of making compromises that could affect the future of British rule of India. While provincial governments, which were non–Indian National Congress and predominantly Islamic, were inclined to collaborate with Britain's war efforts, the Indian National Congress rejected the resignation of provincial cabinet members and all cooperation with the war effort. It instead confirmed its policy of non-compliance and demanded that a constitutional convention be convened immediately. The Government of British India, in response, did not alter its policy of suppressing elements that were obstructive to the war effort but maintained the standard tactic of divide and rule by securing the support of the Muslim population while, at the same time, suppressing aspirations of the predominantly Hindu nationalists.[35]

The Japanese military advances into Southeast Asia in the first half of 1942 strongly impacted the obstinate British attitude toward the rule of India. Japanese troops first occupied Singapore on February 15, followed by capturing Rangoon on March 8 and Java on March 9. The Government of British India appealed to the British government that the crisis threatened India. In response, Prime Minister Winston Churchill reshuffled the cabinet to form a Labor Party–led cabinet on February 19, to which he appointed Clement Richard Attlee, who had had extensive experience with India, and British Ambassador to the Soviet Union Richard Stafford Cripps, to deputy prime minister cum secretary of state for dominion affairs and minister of aircraft production, respectively.

---

35 Takenaka Chiharu, "Kenryoku ijō eno seiji katei" [Political Process toward Transition of Power], *Tōyō bunka kenkyūsho kiyō*, no. 101, November 1986, pp. 133–136.

At the same time, international pressure on Britain to reconsider the Indian issue grew increasingly strong. When Chiang Kai-shek traveled to India, he sent a letter to the US government in which he observed that Indian people had no intention of shouldering the burden of war unless autonomy was granted to India. In the US Congress, arguments were heard that the United States should pressure Britain to grant autonomy to India, using American material assistance to Britain as leverage, and induce India to participate in the war against Japan.[36] On March 10, President Roosevelt wrote to Prime Minister Churchill to convey his own proposal on the India issue and request Britain's reconsideration of the issue.[37]

Under such international pressure, even Prime Minister Churchill was forced to revisit the India issue. He announced in mid-March the dispatch of the Cripps mission to India to discuss the future autonomy of the country and political measures during the wartime. The mission arrived in India on March 22, bringing with it a proposal known as the Cripps proposal. This proposal consisted of three points: (1) an organ to create a constitution should be set up among representatives of British India immediately after the end of the war (and provinces not wishing to take part in this organ should be allowed to adopt their own constitutions); (2) the Indian Union should be established as a completely autonomous political entity; and (3) participation by representatives of various political parties in India in the wartime regime should be expanded. Still, leaders of the Indian National Congress including Jawaharlal Nehru and Mohandas (Mahatma) Gandhi would not compromise their demand for the de facto transfer of power during wartime and, particularly, they would not give in even an inch in their demands for India's right to self-determination in military decisions. Other factions, including the All India Muslim League and Hindu Mahasabha, also expressed their rejection of the Cripps proposal. Although the Cripps mission extended its stay in

---

36 Ibid., p. 144.
37 US Department of State, *Papers relating to the Foreign Relations of the United States, 1942*, vol. 1 (US Government Printing Office, 1955), pp. 615–616, Takenaka, op cit., pp. 144–145.

India to work out a compromise proposal, negotiations broke down, and the mission returned home in mid-April.[38]

The failed Cripps mission negotiations, however, did not result in a major schism among the Allied countries. Chiang Kai-shek, in particular, requested that the United States intervene to solve the problem, out of his sympathy with the Indian National Congress. The US government, for its part, was apprehensive about the possibility of this adversely affecting unity among the Allies, the Indian National Congress side monopolizing India's military decision-making, and Britain's total wartime mobilization system being weakened. US Secretary of State Cordell Hull was critical of the idea of the US increasing pressure on Britain on this issue out of concern about cooperative relations between the two countries. For the sake of maintaining cooperative relations among the Allies, Hull believed it was unwise to pour criticism on the issue of colonies on the European colonial masters. US President Roosevelt also valued US-UK bilateral cooperation, although he had felt that British responses were not prudent.[39] Churchill stressed to Roosevelt that, from the military viewpoint, Britain's argument was quite legitimate because the Indian National Congress represented only a small number of Indian elites. Churchill also warned Chiang Kai-shek that, should the Indian National Congress side monopolize the military decision-making, the leadership of Gandhi, based on nonviolence and civil disobedience, and conduct by pro-Japan factions in India would create a situation that was unfavorable to China.[40] Through these exchanges, Roosevelt became increasingly negative toward hasty settlement of the issue of autonomy for India and was inclined to shelve the issue by the summer of 1942 as the military threat of Japan crept up on east of India.

---

38 William R. Louis, *Imperialism at Bay: The United States and the Decolonization of the British Empire, 1941–1945* (Oxford: The Clarendon Press, 1977), pp. 160–188.

39 Christopher Thorne, *Allies of a Kind: The United States, Britain, and the War against Japan, 1941–1945* (New York: Oxford University Press, 1978), pp. 144–145. Gary R. Hess, *American Encounters India, 1941–1947* (Baltimore: The Johns Hopkins University Press, 1971), pp. 60–76.

40 Takenaka, op cit., pp. 145–148.

(2) Fujiwara Kikan and Decisions at the Tokyo Conference

The fall of Singapore had the effect of stimulating anti-British independence movements among Indians residing in such Asian territories as Hong Kong, Malay, Java, Shanghai, and the Philippines. Among Indian prisoners-of-war who had fought Japan as members of the British Indian Army, some became sympathetic with the cause of Indian independence. And it was the Fujiwara Kikan (also known as F Kikan) under the leadership of Major Fujiwara Iwaichi that played the role of organizing these Indians in Southeast Asia. Maneuvering for anti-Britain collaboration with Japan was already under way by Section 8 (in charge of strategy) of the Imperial Japanese Army General Staff Office as of the summer of 1941 in collaboration with the Indian Independence League, a secret society organizing the anti-British independence movement among Indians living in Southeast Asia. Fujiwara entered Thailand in September 1941 under instructions from Chief of General Staff Sugiyama Hajime with a mandate to organize the anti-British movement among Indian residents in various locations in Asia, using Bangkok as an operational base. In Thailand, Fujiwara organized the Fujiwara Kikan with the help of Military Attaché Tamura Hiroshi. Fujiwara Kikan's role in the early days was to propitiate Indian residents and induce their collaboration with Japan's military operations against Britain as the Malayan Campaign advanced.[41]

As Fujiwara came to collaborate closely with Captain Mohan Singh, a leader of the anti-British movement among surrendered Indian soldiers and who had voluntarily offered cooperation, Fujiwara recognized support of India's independence as his main objective. According to Fujiwara, Britain's dropping out of the fighting was key to ending the war, and India's attitude toward Britain would play an important role toward that end. It was necessary, according to Fujiwara, for Japan to engineer India's defection from the

---

41 Nagasaki Nobuko, "Indo kokumingun no keisei: Bankoku ketsugi made" [Formation of the Indian National Army: Up to the Bangkok Resolutions], Nagasaki Nobuko, ed., *Minami Ajia no minzoku undō to Nippon* [Nationalism Movement in South Asia and Japan], Institute of Developing Economies, pp. 13–19.

Allied camp through nonmilitary means. To that end, Fujiwara considered it necessary to support India's complete independence. By refraining from directly interfering in the anti-British movement, Japan could earn Indian people's determination to cooperate with construction of the Greater East Asia New Order.[42] Mohan Singh put together a First Indian National Army, which participated in the Battle of Singapore as a lightly armed special task force. After the fall of Singapore, the number of soldiers joining the First Indian National Army soared, reaching, it is said, 42,000 by the end of August 1942.[43] As the operations aimed at India advanced, Fujiwara's activities were recognized by the central command of the Imperial Army in February 1942 as part of the measures to give rise to anti-British riots inside India and prompt the crippling of Britain.

Section 8 of the Imperial Japanese Army General Staff Office, for its part, convened the Tokyo Conference under the chairmanship of Rash Behari Bose with the purpose of unifying various anti-British independence movements. Bose was the Japan representative of the secret society known as the Indian Independence League and, as such, he had mediated communications between the League and the Fujiwara Kikan. Bose had earned the trust of leaders of the Japanese military, including Chief of General Staff Sugiyama. The three-day Tokyo Conference was convened March 20–22, 1942. The participants, including Giani Pritam Singh Dhillon of the Indian Independence League (who was later killed in a plane accident) and Captain Mohan Singh, leader of the First Indian National Army, discussed the organization of independence movements and recognized the Indian Independence League as an organization for Indian independence among Indians residing in various Asian locations.[44] Participants of the Tokyo Conference also made

---

42 Fujiwara Iwaichi, *Fujiwara Kikan* [Fujiwara Kikan], Hara Shobō, 1966, pp. 183–184.
43 Nagasaki, op cit., pp. 20–28.
44 "Tai Indo shisaku no keika" [Progress of Measures toward India] (November 8, 1945) and "Sensōchū ni okeru waga tai Indo shisaku keika gaiyō" [Summary of Progress of Japan's Measures toward India during the War] (Ministry of Foreign Affairs Record A7-0-0-9-29 "Daitōa sensō kankei 1-ken/Indo mondai" [Matters Related to the Greater East Asia War/Indian Issue]).

the following requests of the Japanese government: (1) military operations toward India should be carried out solely by the First Indian National Army under Indian commanders; (2) India's complete sovereignty and independence should be guaranteed; (3) the future creation of a constitution should be entrusted solely to representatives of Indian people; and (4) the position of the Indian army within Japanese-occupied territories should be recognized. In short, the Indian activists made it clear that the Japanese government's respect for India's sovereignty and guarantee of India's future independence were prerequisites for Indians' collaboration with Japan's war efforts. The Japanese side avoided making a clear response due to its policy to refrain from any guarantee or commitment that could constrain its future options.[45]

On the occasion of this Tokyo Conference, the Army General Staff Office decided to reorganize the Fujiwara Kikan to establish anew an Iwakuro Kikan (headed by Colonel Iwakuro Hideo) to carry out larger-scale measures toward India. The Iwakuro Kikan was organized in Saigon toward the end of April 1942, and it grew into a large-scale organization of some 250 members. It was engaged in such measures as propaganda activities aimed at Indians residing in other Asian locations, infiltration of "revolutionaries" into India, and reinforcement of the First Indian National Army.

(3) Crippling of a Scheme for a Joint Statement by the Axis Countries

On February 16, 1942, in the wake of the fall of Singapore, Prime Minister Tōjō delivered a speech at the 79th session of the National Diet in which he stressed that the true intention behind military advances into Burma was destruction of Britain's military strongpoints and defeating the Chongqing government. Tōjō declared that it was by no means Japan's intention to antagonize the Burmese people. He reiterated Japan's position toward India,

---

45 Nagasaki, op cit., pp. 38–43. According to the above "Tai Indo shisaku no keika," Prime Minister Tōjō found the requests insolent and refused to give a reply.

stating, "The Empire of Japan expects that India will restore its original position as a country of Indian people and the Empire will not hesitate to extend whatever assistance it can to Indians' patriotic efforts."[46]

On March 12, at the occasion of the conquest of Rangoon, Prime Minister Tōjō once again appealed to India, saying:

The Empire of Japan has no intention to antagonize Indian people at all . . . In Burma, India's eastern neighbor, "Burma for the Burmese people" is about to be realized. I am convinced that it is this day that "India for the Indian people," a long-standing aspiration of 400 million Indian people, shall be realized . . . [47]

When failure of the Cripps mission was reported, Tōjō issued a statement on April 12, announcing that this was an ideal opportunity for people in India to construct a government for the Indian people and restore what India should have been from the beginning. He continued, "At this heaven-given opportunity, I expect that the Indian people will cast off years of the yoke of Britain and push forward toward realization of India for the Indian people."[48]

Meanwhile, the Ministry of Foreign Affairs compiled a proposal for a Japan-Germany-Italy trilateral joint statement on India and Arabia and requested the Army General Staff Office to study it. Colonel Iwakuro Hideo's trip to Tokyo provided the General Staff Office with the opportunity to study the proposal. It was hoped that, with the establishment of the Iwakuro Kikan to launch the engineering of Indian independence on a full scale, this proposed joint statement would have a "tremendously encouraging impact on independence movements in India" in line with advancement of

---

46 *Kanpō gōgai* [Official Bulletin, extra issue], February 17, 1942, House of Representatives Stenographic Record no. 16.
47 *Sugiyama memo, ge*, pp. 61–63.
48 Ibid., pp. 108–109.

the maneuvering for independence.[49] At the same time, there was a hidden intention to induce Germany into a proposed German-Japanese joint operation to cross through West Asia.

The proposed statement reiterated Japan's previous arguments about India. Observing that India and Arabia were "at a crossroads between remaining a running dog of the British Empire and serving the decaying British imperialism to the end, on the one hand, or rising up to expel British imperialism, the long-standing enemy, from India and West Asia . . . and establishing India for the Indian people and Arabia for the Arabian people, on the other," the proposed joint statement declared that Japan, Germany, and Italy would not hesitate to render any possible cooperation if Indians and Arabians decided to move forward toward achieving independence.[50] Particularly noteworthy was the statement that "Japan, Germany, and Italy do not have an ambition to replace Britain in India and Arabia, and the three countries hope that India for the Indian people . . . is promptly realized." This was a declaration that the Axis countries had no ambition for ruling India in place of Britain and that they would guarantee India's independence.[51] This proposal was adopted by the Liaison Conference on April 11 and given to the German government for its own deliberation.

On the German side, a scheme for the Axis countries to jointly assist India's independence had been proposed several times to the German government before the beginning of the Japan-US war by Chandra Bose, who was in Germany. More concretely, Bose proposed such actions as the organizing of an Axis force to advance into India, carrying out operations for the formation of an interim government, and a joint declaration to guarantee the "freedom and independence" of Arabia and India in the face of the announcement of the Atlantic Charter.[52] The German response to these

---

49 *Kimitsu sensō nisshi* [Confidential War Diary] (April 7, 1942 entry) and *Sugiyama memo, ge,* p. 110.
50 Ibid.
51 Nagasaki, op cit., p. 35.
52 Hauner, op cit., chapters 3–4.

proposals was, however, by no means enthusiastic. Hitler, in particular, who had been exploring the possibility of a compromise vis-à-vis Britain, was highly critical of this kind of joint activity that might provoke Britain.[53]

Receiving the proposal on a joint statement from Japan, Chandra Bose in Germany welcomed it, while the Italian leaders also called for German acceptance of the Japanese proposal. In anticipation of Hitler's disapproval, the German government compiled a revised version, with which Reich Minister of Foreign Affairs Joachim von Ribbentrop tried to persuade Hitler. Although it is not clear which portions of the Japanese proposal were revised, revisions were made because the Japanese original proposal was too abstract and lacking in detail, and its definition of the Arabic people was also obscure. Hitler was apprehensive that the joint statement might disappoint those in Britain who hoped for a peace settlement with Germany. In response, Ribbentrop tried to persuade Hitler that those in Britain who supported a peace settlement with Germany would not mistake the proposed joint declaration as an attempt by the Axis powers to replace Britain in India. On the contrary, Ribbentrop stressed, it would give those elements further incentive to pursue peace with Germany. But Hitler would have none of it and only permitted Bose to advance into East Asia.[54]

In early May, Foreign Minister Ribbentrop gave notice to the Japanese government that Germany would defer the adoption of the joint declaration. As reasons for the rejection, he argued that a joint declaration on the Middle East, if not India, might reveal the military operational plans of the Axis side and that the military power of Germany and Italy had not yet advanced into these regions. Chandra Bose, for his part, warned German and Italian leaders that, if they let this golden opportunity for a joint action concerning

---

53 For a perspective that it was more important to Hitler to bring Britain to the peace negotiations table by establishing the Axis' overwhelming superiority in the Far East than to destroy Britain's rule of India, given his dogma on human races, see Morise Kōkichi, "Chandora Bōsu no Indo dokuritsu shien to Nichi-Doku-I sangoku dōmei" [Chandra Bose's Assistance to India's Independence and the Japan-Germany-Italy Tripartite Alliance], *Gunji shigaku*, no. 99 & 100, 1990, pp. 196–197.
54 Hauner, op cit., p. 361, pp. 476–480.

the liberation of India slip away, following the failure of negotiations by the Cripps mission, it would allow Japan to act on behalf of its own national interests alone, paying no heed to the interests of other Axis members. Conveying this warning to Hitler, Ribbentrop once again tried to persuade him to reconsider. But barring the Axis side obtaining an overwhelming superiority in the Middle East and the Indian Ocean, thus triggering anti-Britain riots in India, Hitler basically had no intention of taking joint action to topple Britain's rule of India.[55]

According to German historian Milan Hauner, the launch of the Caucasus campaign by German troops toward the end of June 1942 was a period in which the possibility for joint military operations in the Middle East that the Axis countries had longed to realize was at its peak. What the German side requested of Japan for the time being, however, remained the same: an attack on the Soviet Union instead of partnership in a German-Japanese joint military operation in the Indian Ocean. Under instructions from Hitler, Ribbentrop met Japanese Ambassador to Germany Ōshima Hiroshi on July 9 and demanded that Japanese troops attack Vladivostok and advance into the Lake Baikal area, claiming that successful campaigns of the German troops in the Caucasus and North Africa through the Near East would lead to the victory of the Axis side.[56] But the Liaison Conference on July 25 decided to reject this German request. Ambassador Ōshima conveyed the decision to Ribbentrop when the two met toward the end of July. Ōshima communicated to Ribbentrop that it would not be until after the successful launchings of the China campaign and the military operations against the United States in the South Pacific—in other words, the following year—that Japan would start war against the Soviet Union.[57]

55 Ibid., pp. 480–483.
56 Ibid., pp. 503–504.
57 *Sugiyama memo, ge*, pp. 137–138, Hauner, op cit., p. 504.

4. Failure of Maneuvering in India

(1) The Bangkok Resolutions

In mid-June 1942, a conference to discuss India's independence was convened in Bangkok. One hundred and several dozen representatives of Indian residents in Southeast Asia as well as representatives from the First Indian National Army attended the conference. It was at this conference that the Indian Independence League was formally recognized. The First Indian National Army was recognized as the military arm of the India Independence League with Bihari Bose as its commander-in-chief. While it was the understanding of the War Guidance Section of the Imperial Japanese Army General Staff Office that the Iwakuro Kikan supported this conference, the involvement of the Iwakuro Kikan remains unknown.[58]

The resolutions adopted at the Bangkok Conference contained demands almost identical to those of the Tokyo Conference: treatment of the First Indian National Army as an equal to the Axis alliance troops; inviolability of Indian territory and sovereignty; exercise of influence on other countries to recognize India's independence and sovereignty; and elimination of foreign interference in the future creation of the Indian constitution. Admitting that the continued presence of Britain in India would cause tremendous damage to India, the Bangkok resolutions praised nationalistic movement leaders in India for having stayed away from the war on the British-Allied side and, instead, having explicitly and dauntlessly demanded Britain's withdrawal from India. This was an open admission of loyalty to the movements of the Indian National Congress. Thus, the Bangkok resolutions recognized the Indian National Congress as "the only political organization that is generally accepted as representative of the Indian people" and "action plans [of the independence movement] must be guided and directed so as to coincide with the objectives and intentions of the Indian National Congress."

---

58 *Kimitsu sensō nisshi* [Confidential War Diary], entries of June 16, 1942.

It was a demand that meant Japan in effect recognized the movements of the Indian National Congress. At the same time, though, the resolutions also expressed the conference participants' hope that an invitation could be extended to Chandra Bose in Germany to return to India and requested Japan to arrange it.[59]

Frustrated by Hitler's lack of interest in assisting India's independence, Chandra Bose hoped to move promptly into Asia, believing it to be his duty as a leader of the "Indian people's revolution" to fight British and American imperialism.[60] The original point of contention between Chandra Bose and Nehru over independence for India can be summarized as follows. While Nehru perceived the independent issue in the context of fascism vs. anti-fascism or imperialism vs. anti-imperialism, highly valuing cooperation with China, Chandra Bose had no views on the issues involving imperialism and anti-imperialism. As such, Bose would not hesitate to collaborate with any force, including fascist nations, that was interested in the anti-British struggle. Bose's position caused an insurmountable schism with Nehru.[61] Thus, the contradiction found in the Bangkok resolutions—that is, on the one hand, advocating unity with the Indian National Congress movement, while, simultaneously hoping for Bose's return to Asia, on the other—is considered to be one of the reasons behind the Indian National Congress's refusal to cooperate with the Indian Independence League and the activities of the First Indian National Army.

In any event, the Bangkok resolutions were much more adamant in demanding Japan's clarification of its intention and its approval of the included demands than the Tokyo Conference. The Japanese government once again shied away from formal announcement of its intention and remained negative toward extending an invitation to Bose. The attitude

---

59 Nagasaki, op cit., pp. 45–49, Hauner, op cit., pp. 490–493.
60 Hauner, op cit., p. 483, pp. 486–487.
61 Oshikawa Fumiko, "Dainiji sekai taisenki no Indo dokuritsu undō: Gandi, Nerū, Bōzu o chūshin ni" [Independence Movements in India during World War II: Focusing on Gandhi, Nehru, and Bose] in Nagasaki, ed., op cit., pp. 102–103.

of the Japanese government can be attributed to the uncertain prospects of independence movements inside India and the trends within the Indian National Congress, topics we will revisit in subsequent chapters.

Japan's abstention from clarifying its position became one of the causes deepening mistrust of Japan within the Indian Independence League. Around the time of the Bangkok resolutions the schism between the Indian Independence League and the First Indian National Army became conspicuous. Also, the conflict between the more civilian element in the League, which had been critical of Mohan Singh's "military dictatorship tendency," and the First Indian National Army as well as criticism of Bihari Bose's attitude toward Japan among League members surfaced around this time.

(2) "Operation No. 21" and Setback of India Maneuvering

After Richard Cripps returned home, the Indian National Congress faced the crisis of a breakup caused by the confrontation between Gandhi, who argued for Britain's immediate, full-scale withdrawal from India and resistance to Japan's advance into India with "nonviolence and noncooperation," and Nehru, who predicted that these measures would only benefit the fascist side by creating a vacuum of power in India. In the end, the two sides made concessions to one another in the July 14, 1942, resolution (known as the "Quit India" resolution) of the executive committee of the Indian National Congress. The resolution included a decision on noncooperation with Britain's war efforts and the demand for Britain's withdrawal from India. The resolution declared that a "nonviolence and civil disobedience" movement would be launched if the demand for British withdrawal were rejected. The national committee of the Congress adopted the resolution on August 7. Out of fear of anti-British riots, the Government of British India immediately arrested key members of the Indian National Congress and started to crack down on the Congress-led movements.

As is well known, the anti-British riots at that time were not systematically organized. They remained sporadic and uncoordinated anti-government movements all over India and were suppressed within roughly two weeks. This lack of systematic organization was said to be attributed mainly to the weakening of the leftwing faction of the Congress, which, of all the factions among the elitist gathering, had valued connection with ordinary people.[62]

Although the anti-British riots in India in the summer of 1942 were the first impulses for American anti-colonialism, the US was already strongly inclined toward tolerance of continued British rule of India until the end of World War II. Therefore, the possibility for India to attain autonomy or the promise of independence through US mediation was already eliminated. The subsequent US stance toward India remained passive: it did not support British India policy but it refrained from interfering. According to American historian Gary R. Hess, American failure to support India's independence became one of the causes of President Roosevelt's deepened interest in the Indochina problem.[63]

Incidentally, anti-British riots in India also became one of the causes that further inspired the Japanese military to attempt to advance into India. On August 5, 1942, the Southern Expeditionary Army submitted to the Imperial Army General Staff Office a "view on expansion of the defense area vis-à-vis northeast India" with the goal of capturing eastern Assam. The Southern Expeditionary Army was encouraged by the unexpectedly successful Burma campaign and the internal unrest in India following the departure of the Cripps mission. The major aim of the proposal was to promote the advance of Japan's maneuvers directed at India. The Army General Staff Office responded by instructing the Southern Expeditionary Army on August 22 to prepare for the campaign to advance into eastern India. The supreme command staff of the Imperial Army and Navy took the initiative in deliberations on a post–Southern Operations basic strategy. The

---

62 Takenaka, op cit., pp. 149–150.
63 Gary R. Hess, "The Emergence of U.S. Influence in Southeast Asia," in Iriye Akira and Warren Cohen, eds., *American, Chinese, and Japanese Perspectives on Wartime Asia, 1931–1949* (Wilmington: Scholarly Resources Inc., 1990), pp. 197–198.

strategy set the Asian continent (Burma and China) as well as the Indian region as the chief targets of the offensive and the northern region (the Soviet Union) and eastern region (Pacific Ocean) as the areas to endure protracted wars. These policies had come to be recognized as the backbone of the new *War Instruction Outline* along with the 51–Gō Sakusen (Operation No. 51, which later became 5-Gō Sakusen (Operation No. 5) to threaten the home ground of the Chongqing government, which had been proposed at around the same time.[64] The proposed campaign to advance into eastern India was named 21-Gō Sakusen (Operation No. 21) and was scheduled to launch in mid-October.

It was the now fully-organized Iwakuro Kikan that was expected to be engaged in operations regarding India, which were to be coordinated with Operation No. 21. In September 1942, after Operation No. 21 was issued, Colonel Iwakuro compiled a "view on military operations toward India," which stressed the necessity for maneuverings within India (e.g., fostering the anti-British independence spirit and the pro-Japan spirit, etc.) to be coordinated with military operations against India. The assumption was that, unless accompanied by the military campaign, "it would probably be impossible to completely expel Britain's influence from India by maneuvering alone." In this view, while administration of the occupied territory was to be entrusted to Indian people, maneuvering for India's independence was positioned as a measure subservient to the military campaign toward India. It was a departure from the days of the Fujiwara Kikan when exercises by Japan's forces were to be avoided and the military advance into India was entrusted to the First Indian National Army.[65]

In stark contrast to Iwakuro's aggressive scheme for an advance into

---

64 "Riku-kaigun kyoku buchō kaigi no gōi" [Agreements at army/navy directors-general conference] *Kōtani Etsuo Taisa kaisōroku* [Memoir of Colonel Kōtani Etsuo], July 9, 1942.

65 "Tai-In shisaku ni kansuru iken" [A View on Military Operations toward India] (September 15, 1942) compiled in *Nanpō gun sakusen kankei shiryō tsuzuri* [Compilation of Documents Related to the Operations of the Southern Expeditionary Army] as *Ishii shiryō* no. 11, a collection at Bōei Kenshūsho Senshishitsu.

India was the judgment of the G-2 Bureau (intelligence) of the Imperial Japanese Army General Staff Office. G-2 compiled its view on the campaign against eastern India around the same time. Particularly noteworthy was the attention that G-2 paid to the influence of the military campaign against India upon the nationalist movement in India. G-2 proposed restraint regarding massive military advances on the basis of the following three considerations. (1) If the Japanese military advanced into India, Britain might use the action as an excuse to break down and propitiate the nationalist movement in India to convert it from an anti-British to an anti-Japanese movement. (2) There was a high probability that Japan's military action would make the Indian National Congress suspicious of Prime Minister Tōjō's promise on the construction of India for the Indian people and make India "temporarily terminate the anti-British struggle to resist our military actions against India." (3) There was a possibility that the US would take advantage of Japan's advance into India to mediate a British-Indian compromise by, for instance, guaranteeing India's independence.[66]

The direct reason for the cancellation of Operation No. 21 was the lack of physical resources. Japan's military power was exhausted due to the fierce battles in the southeast Pacific (Guadalcanal Island) which started in early August 1942. This means that G-2's view was not necessarily the main reason why Operation No. 21 was not implemented. Still, it is conceivable that G-2's position calling for constraining the military operation against India to a limited defensive one exercised a certain influence. And the analysis by G-2 that a Japanese military advance into India might make the Indian National Congress suspicious of Prime Minister Tōjō's promise of India's independence and force India into a resistance struggle against Japan appears to be one of the reasons why the Imperial Army hesitated to launch

---

66 Sanbō Honbu Dai 2-Bu, "Gun no tōbu Indo shinkō ga Indo minzoku undō ni atafuru eikyō" [Influence of the Military's Advance to the Eastern India on the Nationalist Movement in India] September 5 (Bōei Kenshūsho Senshishitsu, ed., *Daihon'ei Rikugunbu 5* [Imperial Headquarters Army Section 5], Asagumo Shimbunsha, 1973, pp. 69–72).

a large-scale military advance into India.

In other words, the cancellation of Operation No. 21 showed that there remained an element within the Imperial Army which still expected the nationalism movement centered around the Indian National Congress to convert to a "pro-Japan, anti-Britain" movement. And this explained, at least partially, the cold shoulder given to the Iwakuro Kikan and the First Indian National Army by the Imperial Japanese Army mainstream as well as the army's lack of a response to the Tokyo and Bangkok resolutions. This was also a reason why the Army General Staff Office remained passive toward inviting Chandra Bose to return to India.

Expectations on its role notwithstanding, the Iwakuro Kikan steepened its realistic inclinations, perceiving maneuvering for independence as part of its cooperation with the military operation on the assumption that there would be a massive military campaign by the Japanese military. Because of this thinking, the Iwakuro Kikan became increasingly distanced from the idealism and the policy of noninterference in the movements in India upheld by the Fujiwara Kikan.

Toward the end of November 1942, representatives of the Indian Independence League, including Mohan Singh, submitted a letter to the Iwakuro Kikan requesting once again the Japanese government's responses to the unanswered articles of the Bangkok resolutions. The letter was a request that the Japanese government show its clear support for and guarantee of India's complete independence and sovereignty, which were the core of the Bangkok resolutions. Iwakuro, however, refused to deliver the letter to the Japanese government and announced that (1) the Japanese government was not obliged to recognize the Bangkok resolutions; (2) the Japanese government had no intention of making a separate announcement or resolution on the independence of India; (3) all captured Indian soldiers, except those who had participated in the founding of the First National Indian Army, would be treated as prisoners of war; and (4) the future of the First Indian National

Army was in the hands of the Japanese government.[67] Mohan Singh, who was about to be removed from duty, felt that the First Indian National Army had been deprived of its raison d'être. On December 21, 1942, he made the following announcement:

> The First Indian National Army will be dissolved shortly. It is regrettable as well as lamentable that we had to come to this decision. However, the current situation has made it impossible for the First Indian National Army to take the leadership in attaining its goal—that is, elimination of the enemy's interference, control, and exploitation and achievement of complete independence.[68]

The crisis of the First Indian National Army spilled over to the Indian Independence League, resulting in the reduction of its membership to only two, including Bihari Bose, by February 1943. At that point, there was no other measure that could salvage the Indian independence movement from the crisis than the return of Chandra Bose from Germany.

5. Conclusion: Outcome of the Argument for the Liberalization of India

It is obvious from British Prime Minister Winston Churchill's memoir that the Japanese troops' West Asia campaign was perceived as a crisis that could shake up the overall war plan of the Allies (that is, primacy of the defeat of Germany). In fact, in the spring of 1942, Churchill appealed to US President Franklin D. Roosevelt over the "grave situation in the Indian Ocean." Churchill was referring to what would happen if the Imperial Japanese Navy dispatched its fleets and main force aircraft carriers to the Indian Ocean. It

---

67 Hauner, op cit., p. 597.
68 Ibid., pp. 681–689 (Document No. 9).

would be impossible for Britain to counter this offensive, resulting in loss of command of the seas.[69] Loss of command of the seas in the Indian Ocean and the Bay of Bengal would allow Japanese troops to advance into eastern India, which was tantamount to severance of the liaison route with China via Burma, gravely affecting the war plans of the United States and Britain.[70] Although the Imperial Navy "suddenly disappeared," never to reappear in the Indian Ocean, Churchill could not escape a sense of crisis.[71]

According to Hauner, had a German-Japan joint military operation targeting India been launched in the first half of 1942, when the Axis side held overwhelming superiority, in accordance with the bilateral military agreement of January 1942, Britain would have been forced to withdraw from India, causing tremendous damage to the Allies.[72] Despite the golden opportunity called the "crisis in India" in the first half of 1942, the Axis powers failed to exercise any influence on the issue of India's independence whatsoever. As witnessed during the negotiations for the Germany-Japan military agreement at the time of the opening of World War II, the position given to the Soviet Union in the basic strategies of both countries differed greatly. The German side had consistently put much more emphasis on attacking the Soviet Union—and requested Japan to do so—than on launching an Axis joint military operation in the Middle East and the Indian Ocean. Also, it had proven impossible to induce Hitler, who had been obsessed with compromise vis-à-vis Britain, to sanction aggressive measures against India.

On the Japanese side, the expectation that the nationalist movement centered around the Indian National Congress would convert to an anti-Britain, pro-Japan movement led Japan to take a cool attitude toward the

---

69 Winston S. Churchill, *The Second World War: The Hinge of Fate* (Boston: Houghton Mifflin Company, 1950), pp. 183–184.
70 F. H. Hinsley, *British Intelligence in the Second World War: Its Influence on the Strategy and Operations*, vol. 2 (London: HMSO, 1981), pp. 356–357.
71 Churchill, op cit., pp. 186–187.
72 Hauner, op cit., p. 19.

Indian Independence League and the First Indian National Army. This expectation also became one of the causes behind Japan's hesitation to launch a massive-scale military advance into India. In the end, though, Japan failed to take any positive measures to prompt the independence movement of the Indian National Congress or any action that could influence the movement. In short, Japan's "measures for independence" of peoples in occupied territories in Asia remained, from beginning to end, extremely expedient ones that were subservient to the military strategy. No in-depth soul-searching on the issue of independence was conducted in Japan.

The scheme of early independence and/or respect for the sovereignty of Burma and the Philippines at the earlier stage of the war had been derived from the viewpoint of bringing an early end to the war against Britain and the United States. It was by no means a measure taken in consideration of those peoples' aspirations for independence. Therefore, the moment it became clear that independence for Burma would not influence the independence movement in India at all, the argument for Burma's early independence was put on the backburner. The argument for Philippine independence, too, was destined to perish soon after the opening of the Pacific War. Because of military needs, the activities of the Iwakuro Kikan were also reversed from those intended to assist India's independence movement to efforts to suppress that movement.

Thus, as we have seen, the Axis countries failed to coordinate their actions in order to launch a joint war operation, nullifying the dream of "penetration into West Asia."

Toward the end of February 1942, when the crisis of India became imminent, President Roosevelt, who throughout the war had been constantly concerned about settlement of the colony issue, drafted a letter addressed to Prime Minister Churchill in which Roosevelt strongly condemned European countries' indifference to reviewing old, "rule and obedience" or "master and slave" relations with their colonies and constructing a new relationship. He further pointed out

. . . this rather recent surge under the generic name of "Asia for the Asiatics" has in a sense come rather suddenly upon the Dutch and the British, for the very good reason that you . . . have not had time to work out a different plan for the future. . . . I feel that there is real danger in India now that there is too much suspicion and dissatisfaction in too many places, and that resistance to Japan would therefore not be nearly as sincere and wholehearted as it should be . . . [73]

While Roosevelt decided to refrain from sending the portion of his letter in which he criticized Britain, the draft of the letter reveals how such slogans as "establishment of Burma for the Burmese people" and "establishment of India for the Indian people" that Japan had proudly proclaimed at the time of the crisis of India were perceived by Allied leaders who found the issue of colonies very important.

In the spring of 1942, American Sinologist Owen Lattimore wrote, "Burma has fallen. Japan now holds a land wedge that threatens to split India and China apart entirely. . . . Up till now, . . . the United Nations, in the Pacific theater, has been . . . fighting a makeshift war." Now, they have had to shift their weight more to Asia. Lattimore also wrote:

The Japanese have proclaimed the liberation of Asia . . . an Asia for the Asiatics. Their propaganda, in spite of their spectacular victories, has had as yet no great effect. Indeed, this propaganda . . . was probably intended more for us [the Western powers] than for the colonial peoples. . . . If those of the United Nations that are colonial Powers attempt to set foot again in their lost colonies as conquerors or reconquerors, . . . the danger is that the propaganda of Asia for the Asiatics . . . may suddenly become very powerful if Japan can present herself as the defender of

---

73 Thorne, op cit., pp. 242–243.

colonial Asia against white reconquest.[74]

Just as the European colonial powers were nonchalant about their colonies in Asia, so was Japan nonchalant about the creation of a concrete program that was appropriate for such grand slogans as "independence of Greater East Asian peoples" and "construction of India for the Indian people." As Japan's draft proposal for a joint statement on India and Arabia was criticized even by Germany, its own ally, as being "short of concreteness and its definition of the Arabic people was also obscure,"[75] many of Japan's statements were mere political propaganda devoid of any substance and, therefore, they failed to arouse Asian peoples' sympathy. The scheme to advance into West Asia was conceived because the defeat of Britain was considered to be the key to ending the war promptly. If Japan were to justify its military operations in the area from the Malay Peninsula to Singapore, to Burma, and all the way to India, self-sufficiency and self-defense would not be adequate. In the end, Japan had to resort to the "liberation" of peoples who were supposed to be suffering under British rule, and this became one of the reasons for "liberation of East Asia" to be employed as Japan's war purpose without any in-depth examination of its meanings or implications.

---

74 Owen Lattimore, "The Fights for Democracy in Asia," in *Foreign Affairs*, vol. 20, no. 4 (July 1942), pp. 694–699.
75 Hauner, op cit., p. 480.

Chapter 3

Construction of the Greater East Asia and the Ministry of Greater East Asia

1. The Greater East Asia Co-Prosperity Sphere and the Surmounting of Colonialism

In his speech at the National Diet in the wake of the fall of Singapore, Prime Minister Tōjō Hideki announced that it was the intention of his cabinet to work out measures for the construction of Greater East Asia "extensively mobilizing governmental and nongovernmental wisdom and capabilities alike." On February 21, 1942, a week after that speech, the Daitōa Kensetsu Shingikai (Greater East Asia Establishment Council) was founded as an advisory commission to the prime minister. Some thirty members were appointed to the council, with Hoshino Naoki, chief cabinet secretary, as its secretary-general. As we saw in chapter one, Prime Minister Tōjō and Foreign Minister Tōgō Shigenori differed greatly in their perceptions of the Greater East Asia Co-Prosperity Sphere. Nonetheless, as long as liberation of Asian peoples was the pretext of the war, at least continuation of Western colonial rule in the region had to be eliminated at any cost. The Daitōa Mondai Chōsakai (Research Group on the Greater East Asia Issue) of the Kokusaku Kenkyūkai (Research Institute of National Policy), which had long tackled this issue, for instance, stressed the following point in its interim report, *Daitōa Kyōeiken kensetsu hōsaku an* (Proposal on Measures to Construct the Greater East Asia Co-Prosperity Sphere):

> While [the Greater East Asia Co-Prosperity Sphere scheme] by nature does not allow for the existence of colonies such as those traditionally ruled by western colonial masters, it is only in East Asia that Japan can prove that it can do without a colony in its co-prosperity sphere and present such a model to the world.[1]

---

1   Kokusaku Kenkyūkai, ed., *Kokusaku Kenkyūkai shūhō* [Weekly Newsletter of Kokusaku Kenkyūkai], vol. 18, no. 3, pp. 6-7.

How, then, could Japan present a model of management of a co-prosperity sphere without colonization? It was the Greater East Asia Construction Council that was entrusted with the task of tackling this issue at the state level.

The Greater East Asia Construction Council vigorously discussed the matter and, on May 4, 1942, submitted its basic recommendation. The *Daitōa kensetsu ni kansuru kiso yōken* (Fundamentals for the Founding of a Greater East Asia], set out the council's basic philosophy that "the essential mission is to establish a new order based on moral principles of its own in which, under the guidance or rule of the Empire of Japan, each country and each nation within the sphere can attain its own proper place."[2]

American anthropologist Ruth Benedict once pointed out that the expression "let each nation attain its own proper place," a customary epithet that appeared in almost all related Japanese government documents during the war, represented a peculiar sense of order which had been the basis of class perception prevalent in the Japanese people's family relations and their relations with the community and the state.[3] And reference to this expression in the context of the Greater East Asia Co-Prosperity Sphere signified that it was applied as the principle of a desirable international order in the sphere. Hidden in "let each nation attain its own proper place" was the Japanese notion of "one's lot" or "one's proper status," which derives from the perception of work ethics and social class consciousness.[4] Thus "let each nation attain its own proper place" meant that the independence of nation and state would be guaranteed only when each one faithfully played its role in accordance with its own lot and, thereby, served the guiding

---

2   The basic recommendation of the Greater East Asia Construction Council is quoted from Ishikawa Junkichi, *Kokka sōdōinshi shiryōhen dai-4* [History of National Mobilization: Reference Materials no. 4], Kokka Sōdōinshi Kankōkai, 1976, pp. 1,257–1,351.

3   Ruth Benedict, *The Chrysanthemum and the Sword: Patterns of Japanese Culture* (Boston: Houghton, 1946), pp. 20–74.

4   Kawahara Hiroshi, *Shōwa seiji shisō kenkyū* [Study of Shōwa Political Thought], Waseda University Press, 1979, pp. 117–120.

nation (i.e., the Empire of Japan).

This type of belief in hierarchical order would never allow penetration of the western-style principle of the self-determination of nations. For instance, the *Daitōa Kyōeiken ron* (On the Greater East Asia Co-Prosperity Sphere), a report compiled by the Ministry of Navy's research department in July 1942 with the help of various intellectuals, stated, "Such democratic ideas of international order as the principles of self-determination of nations or national individualism have to be thoroughly demolished." The report continued on to declare that liberalization of peoples "must be based on self-realization that only through active voluntary contribution in the construction of the Greater East Asia Co-Prosperity Sphere can peoples in East Asia attain genuine self-liberalization." In other words, *On the Greater East Asia Co-Prosperity Sphere* concluded that "liberalization of East Asian peoples must be a centripetal integration; it should not be a centrifugal fission."[5]

In short, according to the Japanese perception, "independence" and "autonomy" were to be granted by the guiding country, i.e., Japan, at its own initiative. They were by no means responses to independence movements or local people's demands. Edward H. Carr, English historian, diplomat, journalist and international relations theorist, pointed out that World War I had given momentum to various "racial and linguistic groups" to claim "political independence and statehood by virtue of their quality as nations, when the claim of all independent states to effective membership of the international

---

5 Doi Akira, ed., *Shōwa shakai keizaishi shiryō shūsei* [Collection of Documents on Shōwa Social and Economic History] vol. 17 (Daitō Bunka Daigaku Tōyō Kenkyūsho, Gen'nandō Shoten, 1992), pp. 8–25. On this issue, an opinion leader declared that "one's proper place" introduced by the Greater East Asia Construction Council was "a clear-cut answer to the so-called Wilsonian principle of self-determination of nations" in his speech in autumn 1943. He explained that, while the Wilsonian principle of self-determination of nations was monolithic, a series of measures taken by Japan, including independence of Burma and the Philippines as well as political participation of the locals in Java, were all measures suitable to their respective positions. It appears that this was a general understanding of the issue among the Japanese in those days. See Ōkawa Shūmei et al., *Fukkō Ajia ronsō (3)* [Collection of Essays on Asia's Reconstruction vol. 3], Nippon Kokusai Kyōkai, 1944, pp. 151–152.

community. Membership in the international community thus became ostensibly a matter not of might but of right."[6] In contrast, the issue of various peoples' political independence was never perceived to be a matter of right in prewar Japan.

The image of the Greater East Asia Co-Prosperity Sphere, the ideal set out by the Greater East Asia Establishment Council, in economic terms, was that of Japan being in charge of "planned trade" and "industrial regulation" as the guiding state and of political, diplomatic, and trade relations with extra-sphere regions being under the guiding state's supervision. According to this ideal, freedom of diplomatic conduct or complete independence of peoples inside the sphere was totally impermissible. The proposal on the Ministry of Greater East Asia was submitted as an organization that presupposed the above image of the Co-Prosperity Sphere.

2. Contention over Administrative Organization in the Occupied Territories

(1) Proposal on Kōain and Argument for Unification of Diplomatic Routes

The fall of Singapore gave momentum to intra-government discussions on the body to manage the Greater East Asia region including southern territories. Secret studies were conducted jointly among the Kōain (East Asia Development Board), Army Ministry, Cabinet Planning Board, and Ministry of Navy. Participation by the Ministry of Foreign Affairs was thus blocked. A proposal on the desirable body was completed on March 10, 1942. This March 10 proposal almost completely followed in the footsteps of the proposal on the expansion of the structure and functions of the East Asia Development Board. The latter referred to the prewar scheme proposed by the Development Board on reorganization of the Ministry of Foreign Affairs that called for

---

6 E. H. Carr, *Nationalism and After* (London: Macmillan, 1945), pp. 41–42.

setting up a Gaiseishō (Ministry of Foreign Policy) or a Kōashō (Ministry of East Asia Development) in order to unify external state affairs (political and economic) with the ultimate goal of separating foreign policy vis-à-vis the Greater East Asian Co-Prosperity Sphere region from policy for regions outside of that sphere. The proposal included such schemes as integration of a part of (or all of) the functions of the Ministry of Foreign Policy into the Imperial General Headquarters as well as unification and integration of local government organizations in the sphere under the Imperial Japanese Army and Navy troops. It was an attempt to permeate the region with the principle of the primacy of military operations.

In contrast, the prewar proposal from the Ministry of Foreign Affairs was permeated with the ideal of unification of diplomatic routes even in the Greater East Asia region, even though it did not oppose integration of functions of the Bureau of Manchurian Affairs and the East Asia Development Board into the proposed Ministry of Foreign Policy. The Foreign Ministry's proposal aimed at accomplishing this ideal by strengthening the power of the minister for Foreign Policy, allowing him to monopolize command authority over local government organizations and restricting, in principle, incumbent military personnel from joining the rank and file of the Ministry of Foreign Policy. The argument was that political and foreign affairs of the Greater East Asia region should be handled by the same chain of responsibility as other regions. In contrast to the East Asia Development Board proposal, which had presupposed continuation of the military administration in the occupied areas, the Foreign Ministry's proposal premised an early termination of military administration (e.g., the granting of independence) and restoration of diplomatic functions in the occupied areas. Neither side gave in before Japan entered the Pacific War.[7]

---

7 Baba Akira, *Nicchū kankei to gaisei kikō no kenkyū* [Study on Sino-Japan Relations and Organization for Foreign Policy], Hara Shobō, 1985, pp. 384–391. Unless otherwise specified, the author relies on Ministry of Foreign Affairs document M1.1.0.7/3 (Matters Related to Establishment of the Ministry of Greater East Asia) vol. 3 for the ministry's historical document on the establishment of the Ministry of Greater East Asia, including exchanges of telegrams.

The March 10 proposal argued that diplomatic and consular clerical work and colonization work concerning Manchuria, China, Siam, and French Indochina should be transferred, for the time being, from the Ministry of Foreign Affairs and the Ministry of Colonial Affairs to the East Asia Development Board and that ambassadors and ministers stationed in these regions should be guided and supervised by the president of the Development Board. Ultimately, the proposal aspired for the establishment of the Ministry of East Asian Development as a unitary organ of policy affairs and guidance for the Greater East Asia Co-Prosperity Sphere region. In other words, it was proposed that the Ministry of East Asian Development be established when Japan's occupied territories were transferred from the military administration stage to the establishment stage. Before that period, the East Asia Development Board was to attend to administration (including diplomatic clerical work) as an interim organ. As such, the Development Board's chief mission was to cooperate with military operations and the military administration in these regions.[8]

The Greater East Asia Co-Prosperity Sphere as envisioned by the March 10 proposal was divided into permanent territories (Hong Kong, the Federation of Malaya, Borneo, New Guinea, and parts of the Philippines, Dutch East Indies, Burma, Australia, and India) and areas to be independent under the protection of Empire of Japan (the Philippine archipelago, French Indochina, Burma, Indonesia, Australia, and India). The Greater East Asia Co-Prosperity Sphere envisioned in the March 10 proposal was identical with the vision presented in the basic recommendation of the Greater East Asia Construction Council, in the sense that it was a "Japan as the guiding country" scheme where "both permanent territories and areas to be independent under the protection of the Empire of Japan would systematically attend to economic development, trade, monetary and currency affairs, and traffic and communications, not to mention politics and diplomacy, under

---

8   Baba, op cit., pp. 393–399.

the strong control and guidance of Japan."[9] It was the "reformist" military personnel and bureaucrats centered around the Cabinet Planning Board who had substantially drafted the March 10 proposal. They were also the central actors in the management of the Greater East Asia Construction Council, and they drafted its report as well. In that sense, it was only natural that the March 10 proposal shared the same vision of the Greater East Asia Co-Prosperity Sphere with the council.[10] It was not only the "reformist" bureaucrats that shared these visions of the Co-Prosperity Sphere. Still, the viewpoint to prioritize acquisition of national defense resources, perceiving occupied territories as the logistic base to support reinforcement of Japan's warring capability (capacity to mobilize physical resources), was more strongly reflected in these visions.

For instance, toward the end of February 1942, Sakomizu Hisatsune (director of Section 1, Department 1 of the Cabinet Planning Board), who, as assistant to the chairman of the Greater East Asia Construction Council, was in charge of coordinating the views of the council and various government ministries, enumerated three requirements for construction of the Greater East Asian economy. In his speech at the Research Institute of National Policy, Sakomizu said that the economy (1) had to complete the national defense system with the primary aim of improving military preparedness; (2) should be based on the principle of self-sufficiency under the guidance of Japan; and (3) should be contributed to by each people commensurate with their respective capacity (i.e., to let each people have its own position). These requirements accurately represented the thinking of reformist bureaucrats who prioritized the need for acquisition of national defense resources in the economic structure and its operation

---

9 Ibid., p. 395.
10 Furukawa Takahisa, *Shōwa senchūki no sōgō kokusaku kikan* [Wartime Shōwa's Comprehensive National Policy Organs], Yoshikawa Kōbunkan, 1992, pp. 269–275, 282–283.

of the Greater East Asia region.[11]

And it was the East Asian Affairs Bureau of the Ministry of Foreign Affairs that was developing a scheme which clearly conflicted with the above proposal on Kōain.

(2) East Asian Affairs Bureau's Proposal vs. Proposal of Jūninkai

The East Asian Affairs Bureau of the Ministry of Foreign Affairs had been working on a separate scheme that collided head on with the other visions. The independent study by the East Asian Affairs Bureau culminated in a proposal on enlargement of its own bureau by absorbing and integrating the East Asia Development Board as an external bureau of the Foreign Ministry. On the basis of this scheme, the East Asian Affairs Bureau compiled a proposal on the Ministry of Foreign Policy in mid-August. The proposal included the following organizational features: (1) the posts of directors-general of the East Asian Affairs Bureau and the European and American Affairs Bureau would be instituted under the minister for foreign policy, and all local organizations within the Greater East Asia Co-Prosperity Sphere would be put under the minister's direct command and supervision; (2) no incumbent military personnel can become heads of local organizations, be it an embassy or a consulate; and (3) local organizations of the East Asia Development Board should be integrated into the organizations of the Ministry of Foreign Policy, and the chain of command and areas of administrative responsibility among local organizations should be clearly delineated. Overall, the proposal was permeated with the principle of unification of diplomatic routes.

As if to give a push to studies conducted by the Foreign Ministry, another

---

11 On the notion of "to let each people [of the Greater East Asia] have its own position" in economic construction of the sphere, Sakomizu introduced the pet argument of his colleague at the Cabinet Planning Board, Mōri Hideoto, who stressed that Japan should be in the leading position of samurai (quoting the pre-Meiji Restoration class system of the samurai, the farmer, the artisan and the tradesman) in the Greater East Asia Co-Prosperity Sphere. See Sakomizu Hisatsune, "Kon gikai ni arawaretaru shoshisaku" [Various Measures Introduced in the Current National Diet], *Kokusaku Kenkyūkai Shūhō*, vol. 4, no. 10, 1942, pp. 2–12.

group called the Jūninkai (Group of Ten) was even more zealously trying to put together a scheme for the governing organization for the Greater East Asia. The Group of Ten, which was composed of retired diplomats and ambassadors or ministers in-between assignments had been functioning as an advisory committee to the foreign minister. Upon the opening of the Pacific War, its membership expanded rapidly as the Japanese overseas legations were closed one after another. On December 22, in the wake of the attack on Pearl Harbor, chief members of the Group of Ten (Arita Hachirō, Hotta Masaaki, Horinouchi Kensuke, Matsudaira Tsuneo, Debuchi Katsuji, Hayashi Kyūjirō, Yamakawa Tadao, Tanaka Tokichi, Matsuda Michikazu, Amō Eiji, and others) reconfirmed their commitment to stay in close collaboration through frequent meetings centered around Arita.[12]

It was the issue of diplomacy toward the Soviet Union and the governing organization for the Greater East Asia that this group took up first after the outbreak of the war. Horinouchi, Hotta, and Amō took the leadership.

In mid-March 1942, Amō completed a draft proposal on the government organization in the Greater East Asia Co-Prosperity Sphere. The draft proposal was adopted unmodified by the Group of Ten on March 17. While the details of its content remain unknown, judging from Amō's characterization of the proposal as "mostly an argument to maintain the Ministry

---

12 Amō Eiji Nikki Shiryōshū Kankōkai, ed., *Amō Eiji nikki/shiryōshū* [Amō Eiji Diary and Reference Materials] vol. 4, 1982 (entry of December 22, 1941). It is said that the Group of Ten gathering among ex-diplomats and ambassadors and ministers in-between assignments was organized in the mid-1930s as an amity group of free discussion on current affairs. The group was characterized by its persistence with the pro-Britain-US stance as represented by its advice to US Ambassador Joseph Grew and the Japanese Ambassador to the US Nomura Kichisaburō in order to break the deadlock of the bilateral negotiation before the attack on Pearl Harbor (see *Debuchi Katsuji nikki* [Debuchi Katsuji Diary], October 30, 1939). Therefore, people like Matsuoka Yōsuke and Shiratori Toshio were not invited to the group. The group remained highly active during the war and members frequently met, sometimes with the foreign minister joining them, to discuss important issues of the times. The group offered its opinions on important measures to the government. Nevertheless, only a few documents or studies exist on its activities. As far as my limited knowledge can tell, Takahashi Katsuhiro's study report based on *Debuchi Katsuji nikki* (on strengthening of the Anti-Comintern Pact and activities of ex-diplomats to break the deadlock of the US-Japan negotiations) is the only one available (delivered at Yoshida Shigeru Kenkyūkai on July 2, 1993). It was through Mr. Takahashi's introduction that I became aware of *Debuchi Katsuji nikki*.

of Colonial Affairs," it is conjectured that it did not propose establishment of new organizations or expansion of the East Asia Development Board. Instead, it perhaps proposed that independent nations in the Greater East Asia region should be under the jurisdiction of the Ministry of Foreign Affairs, while administration of occupied territories should be under the jurisdiction of the Ministry of Colonial Affairs. Subsequently, the Group of Ten continued to meet to discuss the Amō proposal and, on May 26, the group discussed the "necessity of putting independent nations [in the Greater East Asia Co-Prosperity Sphere] under the jurisdiction of the Ministry of Foreign Affairs."[13] It is conjectured that this view of the group was passed on to Foreign Minister Tōgō via Arita and other members.

Exposed to these studies and also having heard of the East Asia Development Board proposal, Tōgō told Prime Minister Tōjō on July 12 that establishment of a new ministry to singlehandedly attend to foreign affairs, political affairs, and cultural affairs within the Greater East Asia Co-Prosperity Sphere would not be wise. He expressed his opposition to the proposal to make the problematic East Asia Development Board a permanent organization. Tōgō stressed that Manchuria, China, French Indochina, and Thailand, as well as southern occupied territories that were expected to become independent, should be placed under the jurisdiction of the Ministry of Foreign Affairs, arguing that the "unification of diplomatic routes would be absolutely necessary regardless of the government organization to be established."[14]

Nevertheless, by mid-July, the Tōjō cabinet drew up a proposal to establish the Tōashō (Ministry of East Asia) as a unitary comprehensive organization to attend to all policy matters (excepting "pure" diplomacy) concerning all the countries and new territories within the Greater East Asia Co-Prosperity Sphere. It was a proposal on organizational reform to

---

13 Ibid., May 26, 1942.
14 Baba, op cit., pp. 403-404.

concentrate and mobilize the total strength of the Greater East Asia in the expansion of Japan's various capabilities. Slightly differentiated from the March 10 Ministry of East Asia Development proposal by the insertion of the phrase "excepting 'pure' diplomacy," this cabinet proposal appeared to pay some consideration to the Ministry of Foreign Affairs, which ardently argued for unification of diplomatic routes. Nevertheless, the cabinet proposal's main thrust was cooperation with the supreme command staff (the chief of the Army General Staff Office and the president of the Naval General Staff Office) for administration of the occupied territories.

On August 29, a cabinet proposal on establishment of the Ministry of Greater East Asia was presented to Foreign Minister Tōgō via Chief Cabinet Secretary Hoshino Naoki. The August proposal was similar to the mid-July proposal on establishment of the Ministry of East Asia.

Tōgō opposed the August proposal, not only because of the Foreign Ministry's stake in the unification of diplomatic routes, but also because he believed that only when Japan respected other peoples' independence and refrained from unnecessary interference would the people in the region genuinely collaborate with establishing the Greater East Asia Co-Prosperity Sphere. Particularly in the case of China, Tōgō said, "Bluntly speaking, due to the fact that the Empire of Japan's interference in domestic affairs was so excessive, the Republic of China has become less enthusiastic toward [collaboration with] Japan." This was why he could not agree with the proposal to establish the Ministry of Greater East Asia, which was tantamount to an expansion of the East Asia Development Board.[15]

On August 31, Tōgō requested that the cabinet meeting to decide on the proposal presented in mid-July be postponed. Nonetheless on September 1, Tōjō submitted the July proposal to the cabinet meeting for deliberation. Tōjō rushed to settle the matter so that establishment of the Ministry of

---

15 Itō Takashi et al., eds., *Tōjō naikaku sōridaijin kimitsu kiroku* [Confidential Records of Prime Minister Tōjō], University of Tokyo Press, 1990, pp. 83–84.

Greater East Asia could be handled as a part of the issue of rationalization of administrative organizations. Afraid of the cabinet's dissolution, the emperor instructed Navy Minister Shimada Shigetarō to mediate the confrontation between Tōgō and Tōjō. When Shimada conveyed this emperor's wish to Tōgō in the evening of September 1, Tōgō presented a compromise proposal to Shimada.

Tōgō's compromise proposal recommended that all the non-military clerical work of independent nations (including those that were scheduled to be independent in the future) in the Greater East Asia Co-Prosperity Sphere be handled by the Ministry of Foreign Affairs, which was to singlehandedly tend to all the policy affairs concerning foreign countries, while clerical work pertaining to economic measures as well as the military administration in the Co-Prosperity Sphere should be under the jurisdiction of a organization to be established. In his explanation of the compromise proposal, Tōgō argued that Japan should respect the sovereignty and territories of independent countries within the Greater East Asia region (including those scheduled to be independent in the future), with the exception of occasions when some other approach was required for establishment of the Co-Prosperity Sphere and waging of the war, and ruling other regions as directly controlled territories. According to Tōgō, setting things up this way would prevent Japan from falling into the pitfalls of "British-American-style colonial policy."[16]

As introduced in chapter one, at the opening of the war, Tōgō was already convinced of the desirability of an early end to military administration. Accordingly, he had argued whenever he could that rule of the occupied territories should be based on the principle of respect for the sovereignty of that territory or approval of early independence, so that Japan would not be accused of aggression. The only exception should be the areas that Japan needed to hold on to for the war effort and the defense of the Greater East Asia Co-Prosperity Sphere. A similar argument was repeated in

---

16 Baba, op cit., pp. 421–423.

Tōgō's compromise proposal, but much more clearly. In a nutshell, overall recognition of "independent states" in the Greater East Asia Co-Prosperity Sphere whose sovereignty and territories were guaranteed, albeit under certain constraints due to war requirements, was the premise for the argument for unification of diplomatic routes. But this compromise proposal was unacceptable to Prime Minister Tōjō. At this rejection, Tōgō singlehandedly tendered his resignation.

Meanwhile, Horinouchi of the Group of Ten convened an emergency meeting of the group in the morning of September 1, attended by Yamakawa, Debuchi, Arita, Hotta, Horinouchi, and Amō. They reached the unanimous conclusion that, because the plan for a new government organization for the Greater East Asia they had been studying as a group was totally incompatible with the Tōjō cabinet's proposal on the Ministry of Greater East Asia, the resignation of Foreign Minister Tōgō was understandable.[17] It is conjectured that this view of the Group of Ten might have had a significant influence on Tōgō's decision to resign alone.

(3) Foreign Ministry's Reaction and Proposal on the Greater East Asia Conference

The debate over the establishment of the Ministry of Greater East Asia would have serious bearing upon the unification of diplomatic routes. In that sense it was a critical issue comparable to the proposed creation of the Bōekishō (Trade Ministry) in 1939. At that time, almost every Foreign Ministry bureaucrat above the *kōtōkan* (senior official) level threatened to resign en masse. But the debate this time did not loom large enough to result in a united action across the ministry.[18] This was partly because the Foreign Ministry bureaucrats took into consideration the critical wartime situation, in which political unrest should be avoided. But, more importantly, the

---

17 *Amō Eiji nikki*, September 1, 1942.
18 Nishi Haruhiko, *Kaisō no Nippon gaikō* [Japan's Diplomacy Remembered], Iwanami Shoten, 1970, p. 127.

argument that a separate organization other than the Foreign Ministry was called for administrating the occupied territories must have been seriously taken into account.

Participants in the meeting among senior officials of the Foreign Ministry on September 2 agreed that they should set forth the general principle of integrating the entire organization of the Foreign Ministry into the proposed Ministry of Greater East Asia from the viewpoint of unification of diplomatic routes. Realistically, however, they were more inclined toward a view that it would be wiser to leave all the trivial business of the occupied territories to the new ministry, while retaining the Foreign Ministry's substantial influence by sending in its competent officials to the new ministry, allowing it to "concentrate more on the study and implementation of higher-level world policy than previously."[19]

Thus, the Foreign Ministry gradually shifted the emphasis toward securing its substantive influence through loaning diplomats to the Ministry of Greater East Asia. The Foreign Ministry was also determined to maintain close contact and connections with personnel of the new ministry for the same purpose. Consequently, it was decided at the cabinet meeting on September 29 that the appointment and dismissal of heads of legations (or senior staff of embassies) who were concurrently diplomats of the Foreign Ministry stationed in the Greater East Asia region should be subject to closed-door consultations between the ministers of foreign affairs and Greater East Asia. The cabinet meeting also decided that smooth exchange of human resources should be pursued between the two ministries.[20]

Among key posts in the Ministry of Greater East Asia, the Foreign Ministry secured such posts as deputy minister (filled by Yamamoto Kumaichi); directors of the general affairs division, the education and training division, and the examination division of the General Affairs Bureau;

19 Baba, op cit., pp. 427–429.
20 Foreign Minister Tani Masayuki's October 2 telegraph addressed to the Japanese embassy in Beijing.

director of political affairs of the China secretariat; and secretary-general and directors of political affairs and cultural affairs of the southern territory secretariat. It was of particular significance that the Foreign Ministry succeeded in securing the post of the director of the general affairs division of the General Affairs Bureau, and to that post appointed Sugihara Arata (director of Section 1 of the Research Department), who had extensive experience in China. This division was (according to the regulations pertaining to the division of labor in the Ministry of Greater East Asia) in charge of research, surveys, and planning concerning administration of the occupied territories. Although Sugihara had been one of the most vocal opponents to the establishment of the Ministry of Greater East Asia, he was transferred to the newly established ministry to devote himself to the planning of new policies toward China.

As is well known, the proposal to establish the Ministry of Greater East Asia was opposed by the majority of the members of the Privy Council's Review Board (Suzuki Kantarō, chairman). Only Isawa Takio supported it. At the board's plenary conference on October 28, Chairman Suzuki, by way of summarizing the anti-establishment arguments, recited the report of the Review Board and pointed out that the establishment of the Ministry of Greater East Asia would not only split diplomacy into two different routes but also hurt the pride of independent nations in the region and cripple the expectations of those hoping for independence, adversely affecting the willingness of peoples in the region to collaborate with the Greater East Asia Co-Prosperity Sphere. In response, Tōjō declared, "Typically, diplomacy exists between two confronting states. That kind of situation is not found in the Greater East Asia Co-Prosperity Sphere. What exists instead are foreign affairs with the Empire of Japan as the leader."[21] When, toward the end of December 1942 in the wake of establishment of the Ministry of

---

21 Fukai Eigo, *Sūmitsuin jūyō giji oboegaki* [Memorandum of Important Agenda at Privy Council], Iwanami Shoten, 1953, pp. 251–268.

Greater East Asia, Wang Jingwei, president of the Republic of China (the Nanjing Nationalist regime), visited Japan to request Japan's assistance in his government's participation in the war, Tōjō told Wang, "There should be no fence between brothers. . . .When a child comes home, he is not requested to present his business card and make a formal entry from the front door."[22] From that time onward, Tōjō repeated the same allegorical story to various VIP guests from countries in the Greater East Asia region who came to Japan prior to the Greater East Asia Conference.

It is noteworthy that an important discussion took place during the same plenary conference of the Privy Council's Review Board that eventually resulted in the Greater East Asia Conference. During the conference, Privy Councilor Ishii Kikujirō, disagreeing with the proposal to establish the Ministry of Greater East Asia out of fear of splitting diplomacy into two different routes, suggested several alternatives could be imagined for dealing with the issue of collaboration in the war by the peoples in the Greater East Asia region. One alternative was to hold a Greater East Asia Conference. In order to encourage collaboration in the successful completion of the Greater East Asia War by countries in the Greater East Asia region, Ishii argued, convening an international conference to promote solidarity in the region should be more effective than establishing a Ministry of Greater East Asia because the creation of such a ministry could arouse antipathy among the peoples in the region. While the details of Ishii's proposal are unknown, it is known that Prime Minister Tōjō stated, "As an adviser to the emperor, I have the responsibility to hold fast to [the proposal on the Ministry of Greater East Asia]" and "it [the proposed Greater East Asia Conference] can never be an alternative to the establishment of the said ministry." Nevertheless, he promised that the idea for a conference would be studied further.[23] And this became one of the origins of the Greater East Asia Conference.

---

22 *Tōjō naikaku sōridaijin kimitsu kiroku* [Confidential Records of Prime Minister Tōjō], p. 139.
23 Fukai, op cit., p. 265.

3. The Issue of Local Government Organizations and Ambassador Shigemitsu

(1) Local Government Organization Issue: Emergence of "Two Roles in One Person" Argument

The proposal on the Ministry of Greater East Asia submitted to the September 1, 1942, cabinet meeting stipulated that all the local government organizations, including Japanese ambassadors and ministers, in Manchuria, China, Thailand, and French Indochina would be placed under the jurisdiction of the Ministry of Greater East Asia. It further stipulated that the status of employees of these local government organizations should be such that their operations would be carried out under the instruction and supervision of the minister for Greater East Asia. The proposal on the organization and function of the Ministry of Greater East Asia that was adopted by the September 15 cabinet meeting also stipulated that the minister for Greater East Asia should administer various government affairs concerning the Greater East Asia region (excepting "pure" diplomacy) and instruct and supervise all the diplomats and consular officials stationed in the region. The question was how to proceed with the reform of local government organizations along the lines of these reform principles, particularly in China.

The main concern of the proposal on Kōain was to prevent a situation with two sources of political power, which could emerge when the Japanese government started directly taking measures in China in order to reinforce the capability of the Republic of China government in Nanjing. On the premise that local government organizations would employ the Japanese officials, the proposal stipulated that (1) it should be completely understood that the nature of the local government organization was to be that of an organization in a battlefield in wartime; (2) the ambassador and the commander-in-chief should be unified in one person (two roles in one person); and (3) just as a military commander-in-chief needs staff of his own within the supreme command staff to assist him, a general affairs department and a research department should be established to assist the ambassador as organizations to provide the planning, guidance, and supervision necessary for the internal guidance of the Nationalist government personnel. In short, local government organizations as recommended by the proposal on the Ministry of Greater East Asia tended toward institutions to execute military administration by the Japanese military.[24] This proposal strongly reflected the conviction of the Imperial Japanese Army.

As far as the administration of the southern occupied territories was concerned, the Imperial Japanese Army General Staff Office had been greatly concerned about (1) the division of labor with the Army Ministry, on the basis of the official position that military administration was a matter of supreme command; (2) the future direction of occupied territories (whether they would be independent or continue to be ruled by military administration); and (3) measures aimed at nationalist movements. With regard to the issue of the Ministry of Greater East Asia, the Imperial Japanese Army General Staff Office had maintained "an expectant attitude from beginning to end" as the issue had been out of the range of "matters of supreme command" ever since the issue had surfaced in the central government.[25] Concerning the issue of local government organization in China, in particular, the Imperial Japanese Army General Staff Office argued vigorously for the roles of "military commander and ambassador [to be filled by] one person."[26] The China Expeditionary Army shared this view.[27]

While some in the Imperial Japanese Army, like Lieutenant Colonel

24 *Daitōashō setchi ni tomonau genchi kikō (an)* [Proposal on Local Government Organizations Accompanying Establishment of the Ministry of Greater East Asia] (no date given) and *Daitōashō setchi ni tomonau genchi kikō no setsumei* [Explanation of Proposal on Local Government Organizations Accompanying Establishment of the Ministry of Greater East Asia] (September 12).

25 *Kōtani Etsuo Taisa kaisōroku* [Colonel Kōtani Etsuo Memoir], Kōseishō Hikiage Engokyoku Chōsei, 1956.

26 *Kimitsu sensō nisshi* [Secret War Diary] (September 5, 1942).

27 Itō Takashi et al., eds., *Zoku gendaishi shiryō 4: Rikugun Hata Shunroku nisshi* [Documents on Contemporary History vol. 4: Daybook of Hata Shunroku of the Imperial Japanese Army], Misuzu Shobō, 1984, entry of September 18, 1942 (*Hata Shunroku nisshi*, henceforth).

Tsuji Masanobu of the General Staff Office, opposed the idea of "one person in two roles" because "it is appropriate that a commander of military operations is positioned higher than an ambassador to whom he gives guidance," the general inclination in the army was to approve the "one person playing two roles" argument. In contrast and based on advice from the fleet command of the China Area Fleet, the Imperial Japanese Navy opposed this argument so that China would not be a "duplicate of Manchuria"; it also adamantly disagreed with the appointment of an acting military officer to an ambassadorship.[28] Thus emerged a situation that was described as the "unmanageably uncompromising attitude of the Navy."

A direct negotiation between ministers for the Imperial Army and Navy was convened to break the impasse. At the negotiation, the navy minister demanded that, if "one person in two roles" was to be adopted, then the minister to Shanghai and the minister assisting the Japanese ambassador as his chief of staff should be navy officials.[29] In the end, the two sides reached an agreement on September 17, 1942, that the posts of ambassador to China and minister to China would be filled by civilian officials. The War Guidance Office of the Imperial General Headquarters Army Section summarized the negotiation outcome as the "miscarriage of the 'one person with two roles,' system, the main feature of the Ministry of Greater East Asia, in the face of formidable resistance from the Imperial Navy."[30] Thus, toward the end of September, it was decided between the army and the navy that (1) civilian officials would be appointed as Japanese ambassador to China and as minister to Shanghai; (2) the posts of ministers to Beijing and Zhangjiakou would be filled by the current directors of local liaison departments; (3) the status quo should be maintained in Hainan (to be administered by the Special Service Unit of the Imperial Navy and the consul-general);

---

28 *Kimitsu sensō nisshi*, entry of September 8, 1942.
29 Ibid., entry of September 14.
30 Ibid., entry of September 17.

and (4) all the consul-general posts would be filled by civilian officials.[31]

This inter-ministerial agreement notwithstanding, the China Expeditionary Army argued vigorously for "assigning necessary military personnel to the ambassador or minister's side to assist them" with the aim of implementing "one person with two roles" by intensifying organizational relations between the ambassador and the army. In consultation with the China Expeditionary Army, the Army Ministry compiled its final proposal on October 15, 1942. The proposal, while reconfirming that ambassadors would be a civilian officials, suggested that (1) for security and law enforcement which only the military could provide, the commander-in-chief of the China Expeditionary Army should attend the ambassador; (2) the bare minimum number of army personnel should be assigned to the embassy, using the military attaché system; and (3) ministers to Beijing and Zhangjiakou should be concurrent positions for general officers attached to headquarters of the Japanese North China Area Army and the Mongolia Garrison Army, respectively. With this final proposal, the Army Ministry commenced coordination with the Imperial Navy.[32] At the army-navy joint research session on October 20, it was decided that, while civilian officials should be appointed as the ambassador to China, minister to Shanghai, and consul-general, senior officials of the East Asia Development Board's Liaison Department should be appointed as ministers plenipotentiary to Beijing and Zhangjiakou. This move essentially allowed army generals to wield the real power.[33] Accordingly, Major General Shiozawa Kiyonobu, deputy director (acting director) of the North China Liaison Department, and Major General Iwasaki Tamio, director of the East Asia Development

---

31 Baba, op cit., pp. 448–449.
32 "Daitōa genchi kikō seibi ni kanshi Shina hakengun sōsanbōfukuchō tono kondan yōshi" [Summary of Consultation with the Deputy Chief of Staff of the China Expeditionary Army Concerning Consolidation of Local Government Organizations in Greater East Asia], (October 15, 1942 at Army Ministry), *Shōwa shakai keizaishi shiryō shūsei* [Collection of Documents on Shōwa Social and Economic History], vol. 17, pp. 216–218.
33 *Kimitsu sensō nisshi*, entry of October 29, 1942.

Board's Mengjiang Liaison Department, were appointed as the ministers to Beijing and Zhangjiakou, respectively.

Meanwhile, the Ministry of Foreign Affairs was demanding unified control of "pure diplomacy" by ambassadors, particularly in relation to political organizations in China. More concretely, it requested confirmation of the ambassador's prerogative to instruct and supervise ministers to Beijing, Zhangjiakou, and Shanghai as well as consuls-general, except matters regarding the military. It also demanded specification of relations between the Special Service Unit and local organizations of the Ministry of the Greater East Asia.[34] In the end, while the adoption of the proposal for "one person with two roles" was avoided thanks to the help of the Imperial Navy, the "special circumstances" of North China which the Imperial Army had stressed were substantially recognized because it was agreed that (1) the posts of minister to Beijing and Zhangjiakou were to be filled by army officers and that (2) these ministers should be under the direct instruction of the minister of Greater East Asia for "specific matters" (as per the October 15 proposal).

Whether to maintain or abolish the Special Service Unit was another point of contention between the Imperial Army and Navy and the Ministry of Foreign Affairs. The latter stressed the necessity of coordinating relations between the Special Service Unit, which actually gave guidance to local organizations in China, and consulates. As far as the future of the Special Service Unit was concerned, there were three options: (1) to abolish it, (2) to integrate it with consuls-general; and (3) to leave it to the discretion of the local office of the Ministry of Greater East Asia (the consul-general) on the assumption of its eventual abolishment. Each of these options had potential problems. The first option would possibly nullify unification of the source of policy measures. The second option would require the integrated consul-general and Special Service Unit to be directed, as a consul-general,

---

34 Baba, op cit., pp. 447–448.

by the minister, while, as a member of the Special Service Unit, be directed by the military. The third option would necessitate Japanese civilian officials giving inside guidance to Chinese organizations until the Special Service Unit was abolished, hurting the pride of the Chinese people.

G-2 of the Imperial Japanese Army General Staff Office (intelligence) argued for retaining the unit; G-1 (military operations) rejected that.[35] While details of the subsequent coordination process remain unknown, it is known that the directors-general of the Bureau of Military Affairs and the Bureau of Naval Affairs reached an understanding toward the end of September 1942 that, while the Special Service Unit would be retained for the time being, its authority would be transferred to the consul-general or the Chinese local organization, excepting on matters related to public order.[36] In the Army Ministry's October 15 proposal, the transfer of authority was to be of limited range, consequently allowing for the effective co-existence of civilian organizations and the Special Service Unit. But, as we shall see in chapter 4, the "new China policy" would completely wipe out the above co-existence.

(2) Ministry of Greater East Asia Issue and Ambassador Shigemitsu

Because Japanese Ambassador to China Shigemitsu Mamoru had received hardly any information from Tokyo, news of the establishment of the Ministry of Greater East Asia came as a shock. Perceiving the proposed new ministry as "a kind of colonialist device," Shigemitsu immediately considered resigning from his post. There was another reason behind Shigemitsu's decision to resign, which was quite different from Foreign Minister Tōgō's reason for resigning. It was because the establishment of the new ministry would "completely antagonize the spirit of the new China policy" that Shigemitsu had been assiduously preparing since he had been stationed in

35 *Kimitsu sensō nisshi*, entry of September 8 and 9, 1942.
36 Baba, op cit., pp. 448–449.

China in early 1942.[37] In early October, however, Shigemitsu was dissuaded from resigning by Prime Minister Tōjō, newly appointed Foreign Minister Tani Masayuki, and Minister for Greater East Asia Aoki Kazuo.[38] Shigemitsu changed his mind because it was explained to him that the new ministry had been established so that the new China policy could be implemented and that for this reason Aoki and Tani had been appointed to their new posts. Aoki was top economic adviser to the Nanjing government who had been sympathetic toward the new China policy, and Tani was head of the Cabinet Intelligence Bureau and had shown understanding toward the new China policy.[39] Those who succeeded in dissuading Shigemitsu argued that the Ministry of Greater East Asia had been established in order to prompt the shift of Japan's China policy toward non-interference in the Nanjing government and realization of China's independence and autonomy—the very aim of the new China policy.

In the discussion of local government organizations in China accompanying establishment of the Ministry of Greater East Asia, Shigemitsu was most apprehensive about the continued recognition of "special circumstances" in Mengchiang and North China as a premise. This was because one of the major thrusts of the new China policy that Shigemitsu had envisioned was the gradual reduction of the proclaimed "special circumstances" of North China which had made the Chinese people in general suspicious of Japan's hidden intentions.[40]

In the process of determining details of the local government organizations in China, the Ministry of Foreign Affairs drafted the minister for Greater East Asia's instructions addressed to the Japanese ambassador to

---

37 Shigemitsu Mamoru, *Shōwa no dōran, ge* [Shōwa in Turmoil, vol. 2], Chūō Kōronsha, 1952, p. 165 and *Hata Shunroku nisshi*, entry of September 27.
38 *Hata Shunroku nisshi*, entry of October 8, 1942.
39 Shigemitsu, op cit., p. 166.
40 "Tai-Shi shinhōshin no suishin ni tsuite" [On Promotion of the New China Policy] (April 5, 1943), Ministry of Foreign Affairs document A7.0.0.9-41-2.

China and heads of the Japanese legations in China on October 22.[41] In the draft, there were two stipulations that the Imperial Army found problematic: (1) while the minister to Zhangjiakou (Mengchiang) was put in charge of affairs in the region controlled by the Mongol United Autonomous Government that were under the jurisdiction of the Ministry of Greater East Asia under the instruction of the Japanese ambassador, the said ambassador would not prevent the minister from attending to affairs related to Japanese residents and cooperative works with the Mongol United Autonomous Government (excepting affairs related to the Nationalist government and relations with third party countries) at his own discretion, and (2) similarly, the minister to Beijing would not be blocked from doing cooperating with the North China Political Affairs Committee (excepting affairs related to the Nationalist government and relations with third party countries) at his own discretion. The Imperial Army, apprehensive about the possibility of ministers to Mengchiang and Beijing acting literally at their own discretion, demanded that the Foreign Ministry modify these stipulations. The revised stipulation said, "The ministers to Mengchiang and Beijing should be under direct instruction of the minister for Greater East Asia for cooperative actions with the Mongol United Autonomous Government and the North China Political Affairs Committee."[42]

Ambassador Shigemitsu criticized the modification, which now put the ministers to Mengchiang and Beijing under the direct command and supervision of the minister for Greater East Asia, stating that it essentially endorsed "special circumstances in Mengchiang and North China" or their "exceptional positions," leaving these regions at the discretion of the North China Expeditionary Army, which would aggravate the Nanjing government.[43] Shigemitsu told Tani that, after all the hard work that went into establishing

41 "Daitōashō setchi ni tomonai zai-shi kikan ni taishi sashiatari torubeki sochi" [Measures to Be Taken at Once toward the Japanese Government Organizations in China Accompanying Establishment of Ministry of Greater East Asia] (October 22, Ministry of Foreign Affairs).

42 Foreign Minister Tani's telegram addressed to Ambassador Shigemitsu on October 30 (#780).

43 Ambassador Shigemitsu's telegram addressed to Foreign Minister Tani on October 28 (#1,514).

the Ministry of Greater East Asia, he found it highly disagreeable that government organizations in China seemed to have increased their tendency to make south and north China more divisive. In response to Shigemitsu's question, the deputy minister for Greater East Asia Yamamoto Kumaichi reminded Shigemitsu that the ministers to Mengchiang and Beijing were directed and supervised not only by the Japanese ambassador to China but also by the minister for Greater East Asia and explained that the inclusion of "excepting affairs related to the Nationalist government and relations with third party countries" was a product of the Foreign Ministry's painstaking efforts.[44] Insertion of this phrase implied that matters related to the Nanjing government and the third party countries were within the jurisdiction of the Japanese ambassador and ministers. In other words, the Foreign Ministry succeeded in specifying that, even in Mengchiang and North China, relations with the Nationalist government in Nanjing were under the jurisdiction of the Japanese ambassador to China.

While it is not clear how Shigemitsu received Deputy Minister Yamamoto's explanation, it was, in any event, necessary for the ambassador to China to hold centralized authority to direct and supervise local government organizations for the new China policy to be carried out effectively. What the Foreign Ministry had done can be seen as an attempt to specify the authority of the Japanese ambassador and consolidate chains of command among government organizations in China, taking advantage of the establishment of the Ministry of Greater East Asia as an opportunity to reform local government organizations for the realization of the new China policy.

Aoki, who was anticipated to become minister for Greater East Asia, shared the same perspective. From his experience as the top fiscal adviser to the Nanjing government, he had been aware that the most important measure for strengthening the Nanjing government was a gradual move toward recognizing its autonomy, particularly concerning its economic measures.

---

44 Foreign Minister Tani's telegram addressed to Ambassador Shigemitsu on October 30 (#780).

Aoki explained to Zhou Fohai, second in command of the Executive Yuan in Wang Jingwei's collaborationist Reorganized National Government of the Republic of China, that the establishment of the Ministry of Greater East Asia would "unify and simplify the negotiation partner for the Nationalist government, which in itself would be an improvement." But he also warned that, when its leadership "was not too familiar with the true aim of the strengthening of the Nationalist government, control over China would be much tighter than before."[45]

These exchanges seem to indicate the new China policy which was uppermost in the minds of both Shigemitsu and Aoki. They concluded that, if the establishment of the Ministry of Greater East Asia brought with it unification and simplification of local government organizations in China, it would not be wise to stand in opposition. To them, the big question, was rather who would be in the key positions and how would all the proposed regulations be carried out. Particularly as long as ministers to Mengchiang and North China were Imperial Army officers, Shigemitsu and Aoki feared that substantive recognition of these regions as "exceptions" could come about. This put them constantly on alert regarding who would be appointed to these two posts. As a matter of fact, during Shigemitsu's tenure as foreign minister, he replaced Lieutenant General Shiozawa Kiyonobu as minister to Beijing because Shigemitsu found Shiozawa obstructive to the new China policy.

Privy Councilor Ishii Kikujirō reminisced that Shigemitsu, when he was the foreign minister, appeared to overwhelm the Ministry of Greater East Asia when it came to measures toward China. Ishii attributed the successful avoidance of the pitfall of duel diplomacy, at least partially, to deliberate abstention from limiting the range of "pure diplomacy" in the Greater East Asia region allowed to the Foreign Ministry.[46] Seeing a limit to what he

---

45 Sai Tokukin (Cai Dejin), ed. *Shū Futsukai nikki* [Zhou Fohai Diary], entry of September 9, 1942, Misuzu Shobō, 1992.
46 Fukai, op cit., p. 256.

could do, nevertheless, Shigemitsu as the foreign minister decided to carry out unification of Japanese diplomatic routes by concurrently assuming the post of minister for Greater East Asia himself.

4. Conclusion: Nationalism vs. Government Structure in the Occupied Areas

At a meeting of section directors of the Army Ministry on March 18, 1942, Nagai Yatsuji, director of the Military Affairs Section, stated the following concerning the administrative organizations in the occupied territories:

> It appears that there have been so many arguments that the issue has been deadlocked . . . For instance, while the Supreme General Command Staff straightforwardly wishes to simply colonize the occupied territories, the Foreign Ministry has strongly opposed it, in part, in consideration of its own personnel problems.

The Foreign Ministry's own personnel problems referred to the drastic decrease in the number of posts and the resultant stagnation of opportunities for promotion within the ministry. Nagai observed that "this is why the Foreign Ministry hoped the occupied territories would have administrative organizations to which it could dispatch its officials."[47]

The Foreign Ministry's argument for an early termination of military administration and unification of diplomatic routes was not only a manifestation of the sectionalism within the ministry. As Tajiri Akiyoshi, who later became deputy minister for Greater East Asia, pointed out, if the establishment of the Ministry of Greater East Asia meant "for the occupied territories to be treated as an extension of Japan's domestic politics and to be exploited

---

47 "Kinbara Setsuzō gyōmu nisshi tekiroku" [Summary of Kinbara Setsuzō's Diary], entry of March 18, 1942 (a collection at the National Defense Medical College).

as a means for Japan to wage war," from beginning to end, it would make Asian peoples turn against Japan, nullifying the preconditions for termination of the war.[48] In other words, to perpetuate the Co-Prosperity Sphere and conceive "the occupied territories to be permanently unchanging" would be dangerous not only from the viewpoint of an early end of the war but also from the anticipated rise of independence movements in Asia in the future.[49]

In particular, when pursuing the termination of war with China, it was "necessary to put mutual respect of nationalism into concrete action," which called for measures to guarantee to China that diplomatic relations would be between two independent nations, respecting China's independent and autonomous position.[50] In this sense, the Ministry of Greater East Asia issue and the new China policy immediately after the emergence of the former were, from the viewpoint of the Ministry of Foreign Affairs, two parallel issues. Basically, there was heated disagreement between the view that to respond to nationalistic demands of the occupied territories and grant them independence and respect for their autonomy would be effective in securing Asian peoples' cooperation in the war effort and the view which did not believe this. What made Shigemitsu different from others, who were only concerned about securing Asian peoples' cooperation in the war effort, was his willingness to respond to nationalism in Asia, albeit in a limited manner, taking advantage of the war to do so. And his new China policy should be regarded as the first step toward this goal.

Privy Councilor Fukai Eigo once observed that the scheme to establish the Ministry of Greater East Asia "might have been prompted as a counter to Ambassador Shigemitsu's argument."[51] While the relationship between the plan for establishment of the Ministry of Greater East Asia and the new

---

48 Tajiri Akiyoshi, *Tajiri Akiyoshi kaisōroku* [Tajiri Akiyoshi Memoir], Hara Shobō, 1978, pp. 100–102.
49 Yamada Hisanari, *Beranmei gaikōkan* [Rough-Tongued Diplomat], Kongō Shuppansha, 1966, pp. 68–69.
50 Tajiri, op cit., pp. 101–102.
51 Fukai, op cit., p. 269.

China policy that Ambassador Shigemitsu had been promoting around the same time was a tricky one, without doubt these two were contradictory. Particularly obvious was the conflict between the Imperial Army and East Asia Development Board, which demanded "two roles performed by one person" appointments in the government organizations in China, and the Ministry of Foreign Affairs, which argued that it was the ambassador that should play the central role. Even though the two sides both aimed at strengthening the Nationalist government in Nanjing, the Imperial Army and East Asia Development Board side had presupposed the strengthening of the Nanjing government's war preparedness and participation of Japanese officials in local government organizations from the viewpoint of the primacy of military operations. And this was entirely incompatible with Shigemitsu's argument for self-reliance and self-autonomy. Thus, the new China policy was to be launched, harboring the above ambivalence.

Chapter 4

Evolution of the New China Policy

1. Introduction: The New China Policy and Its Background

On December 21, 1942, when the battle over Guadalcanal in the southeast Pacific was about to enter the critical stage, the Imperial Council decided on a new China policy known as *Daitōa Sensō kansui no tameno tai-Shi shori konpon hōshin* (Basic Policy toward China in Order to Accomplish the Goal of the Greater East Asia War; Basic China Policy henceforth). Convinced that the Nanjing government's participation in the war was a major opportunity to break the deadlock in Sino-Japanese relations, the Basic China Policy aimed at "strengthening the political power of the Nanjing Nationalist government [Wang Jingwei regime] and completely destroy all pretexts for the Chongqing government to repeat another anti-Japan movement." More concretely, the policy proposed promotion of the Nanjing Republic of China government's "voluntary activities," revision of the policy to make Mengchiang and North China a special zone, abolition of exterritoriality and foreign concessions, revision of the Japan-China Basic Relations Treaty of November 1940, and restrictions on the Japanese monopoly of economic measures.[1]

While the policy goal of strengthening the political power of the Nationalist government had already been set in *Shina Jihen shori yōkō* (Outline for Dealing with the Sino-Japanese Incident) of November 1940, the Imperial Council's decision this time differed in its concrete measures. Compared to the older outline, the Basic China Policy shifted its attitude toward tolerance of self-initiative and freedom, leaving the implementation of measures to the voluntary activities of the Nationalist government. The new policy even shifted toward a willingness to take measures to restore the Republic of China's sovereignty. And hidden in the objective of "completely destroying

---

1 Imperial Japanese Army General Staff Office, ed., *Sugiyama Memo, ge* [Sugiyama Memorandum, vol. 2], Hara Shobō, 1985, pp. 321–322.

pretexts for the Chongqing government to repeat another anti-Japan movement" was the Japanese government's expectation that these measures would strengthen the Nationalist government, which would hopefully lead to a full Sino-Japanese peace encompassing the Chongqing government.

The background of the emergence of this new policy was primarily the worsening of the overall war situation in the latter half of 1942. When the new policy was introduced at the liaison conference between the Cabinet and Imperial General Headquarters (Liaison Conference henceforth) on December 18, Sugiyama Hajime, chief of the Army General Staff, quite candidly stated, "Although I had been confident enough to believe the Chongqing problem could be solved when we forced our way with military power, [the current situation is less than desirable both in the southwest Pacific and the north Pacific.]" In Europe, the Axis partners were in a disadvantageous state, while, domestically, Japan had exhausted its human resources and expansion of production had not been realized as planned. "Under these circumstances, it is essential to find an area where we could attain some leeway so that we could maintain our ability to hold out over the long term." And this area where they could obtain some leeway was nowhere other than China under the rule of the Nanjing government. The new policy was, in short, a proposal to strengthen Japan's ability to recover from pressure was by reducing the military pressure in China and diverting military resources to other regions.

Another backdrop was the British-American announcement on the abolition of extraterritoriality vis-à-vis the Chongqing government made on October 10 ("Double Ten Day," which was the National Day of the Republic of China). While Britain and the United States had earlier expressed their intention to abolish extraterritoriality, a Britain-China negotiation and a US-China negotiation toward this goal had been started separately in October. The rise of public opinion in the Allied countries for complete equal treatment of China, improvements in the military situation in Asia-Pacific, and the Chongqing government's strong wish for abolition of extraterritoriality all contributed to the change of attitudes by the British and American governments. The US decision to accept the Chinese demand in its entirety in its negotiation with the Chinese side put pressure on Britain, which had many vested interests in China. Although the British government did not agree to retrocession of the Kowloon Leased Territory, adjoining Hong Kong, it maintained a positive attitude toward the abolition of extraterritoriality, enabling concerted responses between Britain and the US.[2]

This concerted action by Britain and the US had a significant impact on Japan's measures toward the Nanjing government. For instance, Tsuchida Yutaka, Japanese councilor to Beijing, sent the following message via wire to Foreign Minister Tani Masayuki.

> The British-American abolishment of extraterritoriality appears to have affected the psychology of not only the people around the Chongqing government but also the Chinese people in general. Given this development . . . although we have long stressed the liberation of East Asia, the Chinese people in general may have become suspicious of our sincerity, leading to a highly unpleasant situation in terms of winning people's hearts unless we take some concrete measures—not just propaganda—to prompt Chinese cooperation to counter the British-American political offensive.[3]

Both the Allies and Japan alike regarded the abolition of unequal treaties, including those concerning extraterritoriality, as an effective means of winning the Chinese people's hearts. Accordingly, the two sides competed with one another in hurriedly materializing the return of concessions and the abolition of extraterritoriality.

---

2 Christopher Thorne, *Allies of a Kind: The United States, Britain, and the War against Japan, 1941–1945* (New York: Oxford University Press, 1978), pp. 178–179, pp. 195–197.

3 October 15 telegram of Councilor Tsuchida in Beijing addressed to Foreign Minister Tani (#981), Ministry of Foreign Affairs Document A7.0.0.9.41-1 on Matters related to Greater East Asia War, to Republic of China government's war participation, and to return of foreign concessions and abolition of extraterritoriality.

Nevertheless, against these two backdrops, one internal and the other external, these measures remained mere incentives to draw out the new China policy. They were not the direct engines of the policy. Another, more powerful internal impetus was called on in deciding to implement a new China policy, through which Japan would have to give up considerable vested interests in China.

2. Deciding the New China Policy

(1) "5-Gō Sakusen" (Operation No. 5) and Participation of the Nationalist Government in the War

As discussed in chapter 1, the Imperial Japanese Army did not intensify its military operations in China after the outbreak of the war. This was because it had been stipulated that, in China, "offensive military operations that could consume the Empire's total warring capability should be avoided as much as possible." In terms of political strategy, also, it was considered a matter of course to hold back maneuvering toward Chongqing until "resources [in the southern territories] are secured and preparation for long-term self-sufficiency is completed."

In mid-April 1942, after a stage of the Southern Operations had been completed, the Imperial Japanese Army General Staff Office set out to study large-scale military operations in China in response to a request from the China Expeditionary Army. In early July, the Army General Staff Office started full-scale preparations for the main force of the Expeditionary Army to conquer key areas of Sichuan and threaten Chongqing in the spring of 1943. The military goal of this operation was to reduce war preparations on the Chinese continent and allot the personnel and equipment thus saved to frontal attacks on the US and Britain (the western offensive as well as deployment of forces to the Pacific front) in preparation for the British and American counteroffensives in the Pacific that were predicted to come in the latter half of 1943. In other words, because scaling back on war preparations in Manchuria was not possible in light of the defense needs against the Soviet Union, China became the target of reductions. "Annihilation of the source of the Chongjin government's resistance" was a necessary prerequisite.[4]

Yet strategically, it was expected that military pressure on Sichuan, the headquarters of the Chongjin government, would force the government to accept a peace settlement.[5]

Just as this military operation, code named 5-Gō Sakusen (Operation 5), was about to be launched, the issue of the Nanjing government's participation in the war surfaced. As John H. Boyle, American historian and political scientist, points out, while the Nanjing government's participation in the war had been an issue since the beginning of the war, this did not necessarily mean that the Japanese side had enthusiastically requested the Wang Jingwei regime [the Nanjing government] to participate in the war against Britain and the US.[6] The Japanese side actually hesitated to strongly push through the request because, most of all, it could not count on the Nanjing government to serve as a reliable ally during war. And the Nanjing government itself was fully aware of this. Under these circumstances, both sides entertained a variety of speculations concerning the Nanjing government's participation. For instance, whenever the Nanjing government expressed its willingness to participate in the war, Hata Shunroku, commander-in-chief of the China Expeditionary Army, could not shed the impression that "their ulterior motive is to take over the British and American concessions themselves, and their announcement harbors an extremely utilitarian wish to secure a seat at the postwar peace conference."[7] Also, there appeared to be a conflict of views within the Nanjing government. Those who were positive

---

4   *Kōtani Etsuo Taisa kaisōroku* [Colonel Kōtani Etsuo's Memoir], Kōseishō Hikiage Engokyoku Chōsei, 1954. (*Kōtani Memoir*, henceforth)

5   See, for instance, Itō Takashi et al., eds., *Zoku gendaishi shiryō 4: Rikugun Hata Shunroku nisshi* [Documents on contemporary history vol. 4: Diary of Hata Shunroku of the Imperial Japanese Army], Misuzu Shobō, 1984, entry of September 6 and November 15, 1942 (*Hata Shunroku nisshi*).

6   John H. Boyle, *China and Japan at War, 1937–1945: The Politics of Collaboration* (Stanford: Stanford University Press, 1972), p. 308.

7   *Hata Shunroku nisshi*, entry of December 27, 1941.

about participating in the war took the view that doing so would help the Nationalist government gain popularity and strengthen it. Those who were hesitant about participating based their viewpoint on the uncertainty of Japan's final victory.[8] As estrangement of the people became a serious issue for the Nanjing government due to worsening economic conditions, however, the voices of those supporting participation in the war became dominant.

On the occasion of Zhou Fohai's visit to Japan in July 1942 the Japanese government was formally notified of the Nanjing government's will to join the war. Zhou was second in command of government administration and was head of the financial bureau in Wang Jingwei's regime. While the purpose of Zhou's visit was mainly to discuss currency and fiscal issues with the Japanese government, Zhou had a pre-visit consultation on July 8 with Chen Gongbo, who was to become the second president of the Wang Jingwei regime, and Mei Siping, minister of business of the regime, to discuss the agenda for the trip. During that meeting, Chen proposed that Zhou should sound out the Japanese government on the issue of China's participating in the war. Wang Jingwei promptly approved the proposal.[9] Thus, this proposal was submitted to the Japanese government without prior notice to the China Expeditionary Army or the Japanese embassy. Receiving an ex post facto report on this proposal from Zhou, Commander-in-Chief Hata reprimanded the former, saying, "You should inform your president that the Nanjing government should refrain from going over our heads to submit proposals to Tokyo; such action is highly inconvenient for us."[10]

During his visit to Japan, Zhou met Prime Minister Tōjō Hideki and

---

8 Kajima Heiwa Kenkyūsho, ed., *Nippon gaikōshi 24: Daitōa Sensō/senji gaikō* [Diplomatic History of Japan 24: Greater East Asia War and Wartime Diplomacy], Kajima Kenkyūsho Shuppankai, 1971, p. 249.
9 *Hata Shunroku nisshi*, entry of August 5, 1942. Sai Tokukin (Cai Dejin), ed. *Shū Futsukai nikki* [Zhou Fohai Diary] (translated by Murata Tadayoshi et al.), Misuzu Shobō, 1992, entry of July 8, 1942. (*Shū Futsukai nikki*, henceforth)
10 *Hata Shunroku nisshi*, entry of August 5, 1942.

Foreign Minister Tōgō Shigenori and sounded them out regarding the Nanjing government's participation in the war from the viewpoint of the need to unify public opinion in China and as a measure to reinforce the Nanjing government. The China Expeditionary Army and the Army General Staff Office had held the view that, given the military power of Wang's regime, not much military contribution could be expected from its participation. Besides, it was deemed conceivable that the Wang government might demand compensation for its participation in the war at the peace negotiations. Based on these views, Tōjō did not give Zhou an encouraging response. Tōgō also remained passive, citing possible obstruction in obtaining an overall peace.[11]

If the Japanese government opted to wait for the military effect of Operation 5 then the Nanjing government's participation in the war, which could make full peace unattainable, had to be avoided until the launch of the operation. It was thought that the Nanjing government's participation in the war would deepen the conflict between the Wang and the Chiang regimes, reducing the options of achieving peace through the Wang government. In response to that scenario, Zhou stressed that the Nanjing government's participation would have nothing to do with the complete peace. He argued that China's participation would be effective in strengthening the Nationalist government and that it would not get in the way of complete peace. Zhou also declared that the Nanjing regime would not demand possession of the British and American vested interests or return of the concessions—as if to restrict any future demands for compensation by the regime after the war.[12]

Immediately before Zhou's departure, the Japanese side convened another Liaison Conference, in which it was reconfirmed that the issue of the Nanjing government's participation in the war should be "cautiously studied further in relation to the overall progress of the war."[13] This was conveyed

---

11　*Shū Futsukai nikki*, entry of July 17, 1942.
12　Ibid., entry of August 5, 1942.
13　Ibid., entry of July 30, 1942.

to Zhou. "Overall progress of the war" meant not only the situation on the European front but also the progress of the large-scale military advances into Chongqing (Operation 5), which until the end of August had been code named Operation 51. It was, thus, the decision of the Liaison Conference to wait and see the outcome of this military operation.

The Nanjing government once again expressed its wish to participate in the war when the Hiranuma Kiichirō mission (including Arita Hachirō and Nagai Ryūtarō) visited Nanjing in late September. While the mission's response was nothing above and beyond the decision of the Liaison Conference, the War Guidance Office of the Imperial Army General Staff Office nevertheless started a full-scale study on the issue after the mission returned home as part of measures to strengthen the Nationalist government.[14] The most important element in this study was the timing of Operation 5.

(2) Support of the Emperor

Zhou and his party left for home in early August 1942. The US counter-offensive in the southeast Pacific theater, which took place immediately after Zhou's departure and was a fierce war of attrition over the control of Guadalcanal Island, deprived Operation 5 of its material foundation. Anticipating that Operation 5 would require 50,000 tons of steel and vessels weighing a total 100,000 tons for concentrated transportation, the Imperial Army initiated negotiations with the Imperial Navy. The navy refused to budge even an inch and insisted on devoting everything it possessed to securing command of the air over the Solomon Islands. Meanwhile, the production of steel declined after August, while the wear and tear on vessels progressed much faster than expected.[15] On October 5, 1942, a liaison officer of the Army General Staff Office informed the China Expeditionary Army of Operation 5's postponement; subsequently, the operation's de facto

---

14 *Kōtani Memoir*, pp. 38–39. For the Hiranuma mission, see *Shū Futsukai nikki*, entry of September 14, 17, and 28, 1942.
15 *Kōtani Memoir*, p. 39.

cancellation (at least in 1943) was unofficially announced. The reason given for the decision was mainly "a shortage of vessels that could be mobilized for transportation."[16]

The depletion of national strength (particularly that of vessels) in the Battle of Guadalcanal and the resultant setback of the Operation 5 scheme prompted a fundamental review of measures toward termination of the Second Sino-Japanese War. As a result, policy was shifted toward more reliance on political maneuvers; large-scale military operations were put on hold for the time being.[17] For instance, Tanaka Shin'ichi, director of the G-1 Bureau (operations) of the Imperial Japanese Army General Staff Office, instructed Colonel Tanemura Suketaka of the War Guidance Office to study concessional measures vis-à-vis the Nationalist government, including the abandonment of vested interests. It was an attempt at shifting the major thrust of measures for settling the war with China from military actions to political maneuvers so as to enable the transfer of troops stationed in China to other areas.[18] In light of the failure of measures to strengthen the Nanjing government's political power to bear any tangible results, it was hoped that approval of the Nanjing government's wish to participate in the war would improve the political position of Wang Jingwei, who had been losing popular support due to worsening economic conditions, and promote his government's cooperation with Japan.

---

16 *Hata Shunroku nisshi*, entry of October 5 and November 9, 1942.

17 According to Colonel Kōtani Etsuo, chief of the War Guidance Office of the Imperial Army General Staff Office, "Around this time, prospects for aggressive strategic measures became bleak due to the status of the national warring capability. Instead, expectations of bringing about a major turn of the war situation by aggressively taking political measures have come to surface among the government and the Supreme General Command." (See *Kōtani Memoir*, p. 27.)

18 *Kimitsu sensō nisshi* (entry of December 16, 1942) and *Hata Shunroku nisshi* (entry of January 9, 1943). It is believed that Tanaka Shin'ichi was so skeptical about the likely effect of Operation 5 on the termination of the war with China that he was interested in a change of policy toward China. For instance, he was contemplating "future creation of new principles on establishment of long-lasting Sino-Japanese relations" around an "East Asia League" scheme to be promoted by the appointment of Ishiwara Kanji to deputy chief of staff. *Tanaka Shin'ichi chūjō kaisōroku* [Memoir of Lieutenant General Tanaka Shin'ichi] dictated in 1956 (a collection of the National Institute for Defense Studies, Japan).

And in order to make cooperation with Japan more attractive to China, the Japanese side worked out "compensations" for the Nanjing government's participation in the war, including the following: (1) vested interests of the Allied countries in China would be, in principle, transferred to the Nationalist government, excepting those that were necessary for the management of Greater East Asia; (2) Japanese concessions in China would be returned to the Nationalist government; and (3) the Shanghai and Xiamen International Settlements would be returned to the Nationalist government after the Japanese military established firm control in the two regions. On October 29, 1942, the Liaison Conference adopted these measures and decided to "prompt [China's] earliest possible participation in the war against Britain and the United States in order to promote Chinese cooperation with Japan."

While the Liaison Conference's decision of October 29 showed a strong inclination toward measures to prompt Chinese cooperation with Japan's war effort, it did not include measures befitting the name of a new China policy such as the revisions to the Japan-China Basic Relations Treaty envisioned in the earlier mentioned Basic China Policy. The Liaison Conference's decision this time concluded that, as far as such measures as the transfer of the enemy's assets and the return of Japanese concessions to the Chinese side were concerned, "it would be essential both to make the Chinese side aware that these are fair and proper measures that the Empire of Japan would take to strengthen the friendly nation and to guide the Chinese side away from an insatiable desire for more." It was the emperor's remarks the following day that swept away those perceptions that countered the new China policy. The efforts of Shigemitsu Mamoru, Japanese ambassador to China, in November further persuaded influential figures in Japan.

On October 30, when Prime Minister Tōjō reported to the emperor on the organization and functions of the Ministry of Greater East Asia, the emperor raised three points. First, he said that he was aware that some in the military wrongly believed that *Hakkō Ichiu* ("all eight corners of the world under one roof," universal brotherhood) could be realized by force, and that they must be watched carefully. Second, he said that some views on the establishment of the Ministry of Greater East Asia expressed at the Privy Council were worth listening to and that avoiding regrettable management of the ministry was imperative. Third, the emperor remarked,

> Zhang Qun, a prominent member of the Nationalist government, once said, 'While Western diplomacy cleans out the contents and leaves the box intact, Japanese diplomacy, in contrast, cleans out the box and leaves the contents intact. The true psychology of the Chinese people wishes for the box to be left untouched even if the content is cleaned out.' I think those engaged in Japan's diplomacy should appreciate his remark.[19]

These three points seemed to include a message suggesting that policy toward Greater East Asia—including China—should be revisited on the occasion of establishment of the Ministry of Greater East Asia. Tōjō was particularly impressed by the third point and commented, "Those words of wisdom bring home how critically important it is to consider the Chinese people's pride. This was the first time I have heard this from the emperor. From now on, I shall make every effort to avoid regrettable results on this account."[20] Colonel Kōtani Etsuo, chief of the War Guidance Office of the Imperial Army General Staff Office analyzed the main purport of the emperor's remark to be that "it is utterly impossible to apply the same policy across the board to Greater East Asian countries. To begin with, the spirit of the Imperial Way is not something that can be imposed with force." Kōtani further pointed out that this remark of the emperor exerted influence on "the major shift of Japan's China policy."[21]

---

19 Itō Takashi et al., eds., *Tōjō naikaku sōridaijin kimitsu kiroku* [Confidential Records of Prime Minister Tōjō], University of Tokyo Press, 1990, p. 110.
20 Ibid.
21 *Kōtani Memoir,* p. 30.

(3) Shigemitsu's New China Policy and Persuasion of Influential Persons

When reviewing the decision-making process toward the new China policy, the role played by Shigemitsu Mamoru, Japanese ambassador to China at that time, should not be overlooked.

When Shigemitsu returned to Tokyo in April 1942, he emphasized the significance of the new China policy to Kido Kōichi, Lord Keeper of the Privy Seal. Shigemitsu told Kido that the core of this policy was to "recognize China's independence and autonomy and return China in its entirety to the Chinese people." For Shigemitsu, who had learned at first hand how the conflict with China had led directly to the Pacific War, the war was "totally meaningless for Japan unless it established a relationship between equals based on respect of sovereignty with China and other East Asian peoples."[22]

There were two reasons that Shigemitsu perceived the opening of the Pacific War as an opportunity to realize this new China policy. First, the "outlook of the Japanese people was broadened for the first time after Japan entered the great war." According to Shigemitsu, it was only after Japan entered the war that the Japanese people awakened to Japan's mission to liberate East Asia, and accompanying this awakening there occurred a decline in short-sighted concerns with matters of self-interest alone. Second, due to worsening economic conditions under the Nanjing regime, procurement of materials by the Japanese expeditionary troops became deadlocked, which made voluntary cooperation by the Chinese essential to securing raw materials to be sent to Japan.[23]

Foreign Minister Tōgō was one of the sympathizers with Shigemitsu's new China policy and was convinced that it would be effective as a measure to strengthen the political power of the Nationalist government.

---

22 Kido Nikki Kenkyūkai, ed., *Kido Kōichi nikki* [Kido Kōichi Diary], vol. 2 (University of Tokyo Press, 1967), entry of April 11, 1942.
23 Shigemitsu Mamoru, *Shōwa no dōran, ge* [Shōwa in Turmoil, vol. 2], Chūō Kōronsha, 1952, pp. 162–163.

Unlike Shigemitsu, however, Tōgō was not convinced that the new China policy would lead to mutual compromise between Chiang Kai-shek and Wang Jingwei, because such a policy would make it unnecessary for the Chongqing government to fight against Japan, potentially leading to peace talks between Chiang Kai-shek and Japan.[24] It should not be overlooked that, behind Shigemitsu's above future prospect, which was not shared by Tōgō, were talks he had had with Zhou Fohai and other key persons of the Nanjing government. For instance, when Zhou met Shigemitsu on July 6, he pointed out that, in order to pursue peace through the Nationalist government, "it would be necessary to convince the Chongqing government that Japan has no intention of invading China. But, before convincing Chongqing, Japan must convince us first."[25]

Early in November 1942, after the controversy over the establishment of the Ministry of Greater East Asia was settled, Shigemitsu temporarily returned to Tokyo to persuade Japanese government leaders on the new China policy scheme. Staying for nearly a month in Tokyo, Shigemitsu actively met such prominent figures as Prime Minister Tōjō, the emperor, Lord Keeper of the Privy Seal Kido, senior officials of the Foreign Ministry, military leaders, and members of the Jūninkai (Group of Ten). Shigemitsu met Tōjō twice. While the details of each of these meetings are unknown, the gist of these talks is found in the "memorandum note" that Shigemitsu had prepared for the report to the emperor that Privy Councilor Fukai Eigo was able to read through the cooperation of Sawada Renzō (former vice minister for foreign affairs). It read as follows:

Japan should narrow its range of military administration as much as possible; expand the range of economic and administrative activities to be entrusted to the autonomy and self-initiative of the Chinese people;

---

24 Ibid., p. 167.
25 *Shū Futsukai nikki*, entry of July 6 and 7, 1942.

and let the Chinese people enjoy significant levels of prosperity in their businesses and livelihoods. And along with measures to promote these goals, Japan should also increase support of the Wang regime and thereby accomplish the expected results.[26]

A meeting between Shigemitsu, newly appointed Foreign Minister Tani Masayuki, and Minister for Greater East Asia Aoki Kazuo on November 13, 1942, produced a document that opened with a statement of awareness that "Japan has no other recourse than to attempt a radical shift of conditions through various measures that could make us hopeful about the future of Sino-Japanese relations along with preparing a foundation that facilitates China's cooperation with Japan [in the Greater East Asia War]." On this basis, the document enumerated measures to be taken as follows: (1) cooperation in stabilizing people's livelihood and industrial recovery; (2) return of enemy assets in Chongqing to the Nanjing government and accommodative consideration regarding enemy assets possessed by Britain and the United States; (3) return of foreign concessions; and (4) revision of unequal treaties including abolition of extraterritoriality.[27] From this document, it can be deduced that the trio was not simply requesting the Nanjing government's cooperation with Japan's war efforts. Rather, they were exploring a new policy toward China that could lead to full peace in the future.

Based on the agreement among the three, Aoki, as the minister for Greater East Asia, prepared an explanatory document which he presented to the November 27 Liaison Conference. There was, however, an important perception gap between Shigemitsu and Aoki. Concerning the revision of unequal treaties, including abolition of extraterritoriality, while Aoki believed that concrete measures to realize these reforms could be made

---

26 Fukai Eigo, *Sūmitsuin jūyō giji oboegaki* [Memorandum of Important Agenda at Privy Council], Iwanami Shoten, 1953, p. 269.
27 "Kokumin Seifu sansen mondai" [Issue of the Nationalist Government's War Participation] (November 13, 1942), Ministry of Foreign Affairs document A7.0.0.9-41-1.

within the framework of such existing treaties as the Japan-China Basic Relations Treaty,[28] Shigemitsu had in mind a fundamental revision of that treaty. The difference between the two was reflected intact in the controversy over the revision of the treaty.

(4) Adoption of the New China Policy

Energetic persuasion by Shigemitsu and Aoki significantly influenced government and military leaders. During the November 27 Liaison Conference, Suzuki Teiichi, chief of the Cabinet Planning Board, pointed out that "the China problem must be dealt with from a broader perspective" and stressed that Japan's policy should facilitate the movement for national independence that had followed the Xinhai Revolution of 1911. Finance Minister Kaya Okinori also made a similar remark at the conference. According to *Kimitsu sensō nisshi* (Secret War Journal), those remarks by Suzuki and Kaya were "abruptly proposed without any prior ground work."[29] Satō Kenryō, director-general of the Bureau of Military Affairs of the Army Ministry who participated in the conference *ex officio*, warned participants, "While it is really noble of them to speak of such lofty ideals . . . the military, in actuality, cannot always act on such fine words, given its duty to provide public order and security as well as its own need for subsistence. I beg participants' understanding of this reality." Nonetheless, the War Guidance Office of the Imperial Japanese Army General Staff Office began drafting a new *Tai-Shi shori yōkō* (Outline for dealing with China) toward the end of November to replace the *Outline for Dealing with the Sino-Japanese Incident*.[30]

Chiefly because Tanaka Shin'ichi was an avid promoter of the new China policy, the Imperial Japanese Army General Staff Office took the initiative in drafting the policy. However, on December 6, 1942, in an attempt to push through the supreme general command office's position, Tanaka confronted

---

28 Sugiyama Memorandum, vol. 2, pp. 180–181.
29 *Kimitsu sensō nisshi* [Secret War Journal], entry of November 27, 1942.
30 Ibid.

Prime Minister Tōjō over the issue of impressment of privately-owned vessels. As a result, he was transferred to the Southern Expeditionary Army on December 8. His last instruction to subordinates at the G-1 Bureau was that the army should thoroughly manage relations with China so that surplus forces in China could be mobilized to prepare for situations in the north, thus betraying Tanaka's true concern.[31]

The central person in the drafting of the *Outline for Dealing with China* at the War Guidance Office was Lieutenant Colonel Tanemura Suketaka. He was joined by directors of pertinent sections of the Foreign Ministry, the Greater East Asia Ministry, and the ministries of army and navy, who had assisted the secretary-general of the Liaison Conference. Of particular importance was the contribution by Sugihara Arata, director of the general affairs section of the Ministry of Greater East Asia. As director of the first section of the Foreign Ministry's research department, Sugihara had been the major hardline opponent of the establishment of the Ministry of Greater East Asia. In fact, he once decided to resign from the Foreign Ministry in protest but, through persuasion and pleading from Greater East Asia Minister Aoki, he agreed to join the newly established ministry under Aoki. Owing to this background, Aoki was highly regarded even at the Army General Staff Office as "the central figure in the Ministry of Greater East Asia." Sugihara became a valuable adviser to Tanemura.[32]

The major points to be pursued in drafting the policy were threefold:

---

31 *Kimitsu sensō nisshi* [Secret War Journal], entry of December 16, 1942. When Tominaga Kyōji, director-general of the Personnel Affairs Bureau of the Army Ministry visited Hata Shunroku, commander-in-chief of the China Expeditionary Army, in early January 1943 to brief Hata on the new China policy, he emphasized, "Although it has often been rumored that this decision was first proposed by civilian officials, that is not true. It was proposed by the supreme general command office with the aim of gradual withdrawal from the muddy mess of China." Hearing the explanation, Hata understood that, in a nutshell, the proposal had derived from "former director of G-1 Tanaka Shin'ichi's wish to transfer as many anti-Soviet troops as possible to provide them with training." (*Hata Shunroku nisshi*, an entry on January 9, 1943).

32 Tanemura Suketaka, *Daihonei kimitsu nisshi* [Secret Diary of the Imperial General Headquarters], Fuyō Shobō, 1979, p. 184, and an article on this book on pp. 327–328 in Sugihara Arata, *Meiyū Tanemura Suketaka Taisa o shinobu* [In Memory of My Sworn Friend Late Colonel Tanemura Suketaka].

(1) to avoid interference in the Nationalist government, (2) to coordinate the "uniquely local peculiarities" [or "special regions"], and (3) to abolish and coordinate foreign concessions and extraterritoriality based on the philosophy of respect for sovereignty. The Japanese military stationed in China— the China Expeditionary Army and the China Area Fleet—was apparently passive toward the new policy, citing the need for public order and security as well as military operations. Moreover, attaining a proper balance between the above policy and the need for development and procurement of national defense resources, which had become all the more urgent due to depletion of national strength, was an extremely challenging task. For instance, Finance Minister Kaya—actually a sympathizer of the new China policy— pointed out a problem in the proposal to leave the regulation of goods up to the Chinese side. If coal production from North China was turned into a Sino-Japanese joint venture and entrusted entirely to the Chinese side, in name and in substance, procurement of materials for Japan might slacken and Japan might fail to obtain what it absolutely needed.[33] Because the chief organization to draft the policy was the Army General Staff Office and, fortunately, not the Cabinet Planning Board which was a stronghold of "reformist" bureaucrats, and also because Suzuki Teiichi, chief of the Cabinet Planning Board, was one of the promoters of the new policy along with Finance Minister Kaya, these concerns did not cause the drafting of economic measures to stumble. Nevertheless, apprehensions such as those expressed by Kaya were strongly rooted, even in the Army Ministry.

When the new China policy entered the implementation stage, it was reported at a bureau chief and section chief conference at the Army Ministry that an estimated 400,000 Japanese citizens would lose their jobs due to the policy.[34] As suggested by this prediction, the Army Ministry was not necessarily enthusiastic about the new China policy because it would deprive Japan

---

33 Sugiyama Memorandum, vol. 2, p. 303.
34 *Kinbara Setsuzō gyōmu nisshi tekiroku* [Excerpts from Kinbara Setsuzō's Diary], entry of January 20, 1943 (a collection at the National Defense Medical College).

of much of its vested interests in China. The Imperial Navy was similarly highly passive about the return of the concessions in Kowloon, including Hong Kong—so much so that the Navy General Staff Office protested the Army General Staff Office's argument for the return of Japan's concessions. In the end, an agreement was reached between the two to leave the issue untouched for the time being.[35] Due to opposition and passive attitudes, the Tanemura-Sugihara proposal ultimately included only general principles devoid of any concrete measures to be taken.

Also, whether or not to abolish and revise the unequal treaty and privileges even during wartime became an important point of contention. Although the Tanemura proposal stipulated that "such situations as unequal treaties and violations of sovereignty and independence should be promptly abolished or coordinated," it also stipulated that revision of the Japan-China Basic Relations Treaty should be carried out "after completion of the Greater East Asia War." The latter stipulation was obviously different from the positions of Shigemitsu and the Foreign Ministry.[36] Moreover, the argument for the continuation of "inside guidance" on key functions such as diplomacy and the military as well as minimization of revision of "special region" treatment remained persistent from the viewpoint of respect of the spirit of the Japan-China Basic Relations Treaty.[37]

The central issue of contention at the final stage of the policy drafting was the relation between the new China policy and the Chongqing government. Japan had two options: to terminate moves in establishing peace with the Chongqing government for the time being, focusing instead on development and strengthening of the Nanjing government, or to resume peace efforts toward Chongqing (in substance, maneuvering to induce Chongqing

---

35 *Kimitsu sensō nisshi*, entry of December 18, 1942.

36 *Tai-Shi shori yōkō* [Outline for Dealing with China], entry of December 3, "Tanemura proposal" (Ministry of Foreign Affairs document A7.0.0.9-41-1).

37 *Tai-Shi shori yōkō ni motozuku gutaiteki hōsaku (dai 3-an)* [Concrete Measures Based on the Outline for Dealing with China, third proposal], December 1942 (Ministry of Foreign Affairs document A7.0.0.9-41-1).

to yield), which had been temporarily halted due to the consideration of achieving a full peace between Japan and China. In the end, it was decided that Japan would not approach Chongqing. This was because Japan's inadequate war capability was revealed by the setback of Operation 5 just as military pressure was considered to be essential activities toward an effective peace. Although a strongly worded proposal was submitted by the War Guidance Office during the drafting process, the Army Ministry found it excessive. The proposal insisting that Japan should abandon the Nanjing government's peacetime nature, terminate all operations in seeking peace, and cut off links with Chongqing was going too far. The Army Ministry instead submitted a revised proposal in a softer tone stating, "Until further notice, the Empire of Japan would undertake no peace-seeking operations toward Chongqing."[38]

Originally, Prime Minister Tōjō had not been particularly positive toward the new China policy because it would entail the loss of Japan's vested interests in China. It was partly because the Imperial Japanese Army General Staff Office was an avid supporter of the new policy that Tōjō, too, was converted, becoming an active promoter of the policy. But a more important reason for his conversion was believed to be the emperor's endorsement of said policy. The emperor's support provided the energy to overcome arguments for caution during the drafting process under the general principle of, "while there are a few problems in this policy in terms of requirements for military operations, it is necessary to adopt a policy of dauntlessly letting the Nationalist government attend to all other issues."[39]

On December 21, 1942, the Imperial Council adopted the *Tai-Shi shori*

---

38 Ibid., and *Tai-Shi shori yōkō an* [Proposed Outline for Dealing with China], entry of December 10, 1942.

39 Sugiyama Memorandum, vol. 2, p. 304. For the details of the emperor's enthusiastic support of the new China policy and the dispatch of Takahito, Prince Mikasa, to the China Expeditionary Army as a de facto supervisor, see Shibata Shin'ichi, "Tai-Shi shinseisaku no kettei to Wakasugi sanbō (Mikasanomiya) no Chūgoku haken" [Decision on the New China Policy and Dispatch of Staff Officer Wakasugi (Takahito, Prince Mikasa) to China], *Meiji Seitoku Kinen Gakkai Kiyō*, no. 3, 1989, pp. 32–59.

konpon yōkō (Basic Guideline for Dealing with China)—the new China policy. A few days later, an entry in *Kimitsu sensō nisshi* recorded that, "The *Basic Guideline for Dealing with China* has passed a historical turning point and has taken the first step toward implementation."[40] Nevertheless, as was made clear during the drafting process, perceptions and understandings of the new China policy, which was narrated only in terms of general principles, diverged widely. "Same bed, but different dreams" would be a good way to describe the situation. The adverse effect of this divergence was reflected in the implementation process of the policy.

3. Implementation Process of the New China Policy

(1) Revision of the Unequal Treaty—Chongqing and Nanjing

On January 9, 1943, the Nanjing government declared war against Britain and the US. That same day, it issued a joint declaration of cooperation with Japan against Britain and the US. The governments of Japan and Nanjing agreed to enter negotiations on such issues as return of single-country concessions, retrieval of international concessions, and abolition of extraterritoriality based on the "spirit of respect for the sovereignty of the Republic of China." Although originally the plan was to carry out all of these measures no sooner than mid-January, they were abruptly moved forward. This was due to the fact that the Japanese government had received intelligence in early January that Britain, the US, and the Chongqing regime had already anticipated that a declaration of war by the Nanjing government was forthcoming and had launched sabotage activities. This intelligence prompted the Japanese government to push the Nanjing government to move up the declaration of war.[41]

On January 11, two days after the Nanjing government's declaration of

---

40 *Kimitsu sensō nisshi*, December 24, 1942.
41 *Shū Futsukai nikki* [Zhou Fohai Diary], entry of January 8, 1943.

war, the Chongqing government concluded a new treaty with Britain and the US. The new treaty represented the manifestation of the abolishment of extraterritoriality and reform of the unequal treaty that Britain and the US had announced on "Double Ten Day" (October 10, the National Day of the Republic of China), as introduced earlier in this chapter. In his diary, Chiang Kai-shek wrote of this new treaty that it had been the greatest goal of Sun Yat-sen, who had waged a lifelong battle pursuing it. The accomplishment of this goal was, wrote Chiang, a sublime once-in-a-lifetime delight.[42] Thus, the unequal treaty, which had bound China for one full century since the signing of the Nanjing Treaty in 1842 in the wake of the Opium Wars, was abolished and China's sovereignty was restored. Given that this all took place during wartime, it did not gather too much attention. Nevertheless, an old system was completely terminated.[43] Both the Kuomintang and the Communist Party of China alike welcomed this development. The February 5 and 11 issues of the *Xin Hua Daily* applauded the signing of this new treaty as raising China's international position.[44] From the viewpoint of the Chongqing government, this meant that China had become a member of the Allies both in name and substance.

Interestingly, it was the US and, on the Japanese side, the Imperial Army that were particularly enthusiastic about the return of Hong Kong and other Kowloon concessions. The Imperial Army insisted that "Hong Kong (including the Kowloon concessions) should be promptly returned to China."[45] But due to the Imperial Navy's reluctance, the case was put on hold, "to be settled separately." As we shall later see, the Imperial Navy

---

42 Sankei Shimbunsha, ed., *Shō Kaiseki hiroku* [Confidential Records of Chiang Kai-shek], Sankei Shuppan, 1985 (entry of October 10, 1942).

43 Marius Jansen, "20 seiki ni okeru Taiheiyō Sensō no imi" [Meaning of the Pacific War in the 20th Century] (translated by Takenaka Yoshihiko), Hosoya Chihiro et al., eds., *Taiheiyō Sensō* [The Pacific War], University of Tokyo Press, 1994, p. 609.

44 Chin Kō (Chen Jiang), "Taiheiyō Sensō to Chūgoku" [The Pacific War and China], Hosoya et al., op cit., pp.458–459.

45 *Tai-Shi shori yōkō an* [Proposed Outline for Dealing with China], entry of December 10, 1942, (Ministry of Foreign Affairs document A7.0.0.9-.41-1).

also resisted the return of the Shanghai concessions, resulting in criticism from the Army about its obsession with vested interests. In any event, this situation demonstrated the differing degrees of interest in vested interests in China between the Army and the Navy.

(2) Resistance to the Principle of Separation of Government Business and Military Affairs

With the Nanjing government's participation in the war, the new China policy entered the implementation stage. Hata Shunroku, commander-in-chief of the China Expeditionary Army, wrote in his daily journal in early December 1942 that, seeing as the new China policy was "the last resort when all domestic measures as well as measures toward the Chongqing government are deadlocked, it should not be easy to carry it out."[46] And this prediction turned out to be more than just an imaginary concern. Toward the end of December, the chiefs of staff of armies stationed in China were summoned to Tokyo for thorough briefings on the new China policy. The remarks the emperor made when the proposed organization and functions of the Ministry of Greater East Asia were reported to him were communicated to the summoned officers by the army minister and the chief of general staff. However, these invited representatives of the armies in China argued in one voice how difficult it would be to transfer various authorities to the Nanjing government and the newly established Ministry of Greater East Asia. Their reaction hinted at the challenging prospects for policy implementation.[47]

With the establishment of the Ministry of Greater East Asia, local government organizations in China were now divided into those affiliated with the Greater East Asia Ministry, those affiliated with the Foreign Ministry, and those affiliated with the China Expeditionary Army. Because one of the primary objects of the new China policy was to realize the principle of

---

46 *Hata Shunroku nisshi* [Hata Shunroku Diary], entry of December 3, 1942.
47 *Kōtani Etsuo Taisa gyōmu nisshi* [Colonel Kōtani Etsuo's Diary], entry of December 24, 1942, (a collection of the National Institute for Defense Studies, Japan).

separation of government administration and military strategy, it became necessary to transfer all government business–related matters that the China Expeditionary Army had been handling to the jurisdiction of the Ministry of Greater East Asia. The Army General Staff Office cooperated, and it launched a revision of the China Expeditionary Army's basic tasks, which had been untouched since the beginning of the Second Sino-Japanese War. The Tai-Riku-Mei 757-Gō (Imperial General Headquarters Army Section Instruction #757) issued on February 27, 1943, stressed stabilizing occupied territories and included a newly added article stating, "When securing and guarding the occupied territories to stabilize them, spontaneous activities of the locals, particularly in China, should be encouraged."[48] On the same day, the wartime high command headquarters duty regulations of the Imperial Armies stationed in China were also revised, and the commander-in-chief of the China Expeditionary Army as well as commanders of regional armies and individual armies were no longer instructed to supervise administrative affairs. Also, the reference to "maintenance of public order" was deleted from these regulations. Deputy Chief of General Staff Tanabe Moritake explained to the China Expeditionary Army that the revision was meant to instruct the army to concentrate on its primary duty of engaging in military operations and defense. The reference to public order was eliminated, because it might have led to a misunderstanding that locally stationed armies were in charge of administration of the occupied territories.[49]

From the viewpoint of the China Expeditionary Army, which had been engaged in the maintenance of public order, however, it was highly difficult to distinguish between administrative affairs and military operations and defense in some areas, because the public order situations varied greatly from one occupied territory to another. At the chiefs of staff conference on March 3, 1943, Kawabe Torashirō, chief of staff of the China Expeditionary Army,

---

48 Bōei Kenshūsho Senshishitsu, ed., *Hokushi no chian-sen, 2* [Battle for Chinese Communists in North China, vol. 2], Asagumo Shimbunsha, 1971, pp. 305–307.
49 Ibid., pp. 307–309.

raised this issue. In response, the Army General Staff Office explained that, at times when the administrative functions of the Nationalist government were operating ineffectively, "certain administrative tasks required from the viewpoint of military operations and defenses should be conducted by the China Expeditionary Army and the entire responsibility for the stability shall be entrusted to it."[50] This left a lot ambiguous.

Meanwhile, Prime Minister Tōjō insisted on retaining the army minister's authority to deal with government affairs. He cited the possibility that the army minister's stated authority would be needed on matters within the jurisdiction of either the Ministry of Greater East Asia or the Ministry of Foreign Affairs which directly required the military's cooperation and assistance.[51] Tōjō's argument was turned down by the Army General Staff Office, which found the issue to be within the jurisdiction of the supreme general command.

To begin with, the Army General Staff Office's understanding attitude toward the new China policy was attributable not to its acceptance of the shift toward tolerance regarding the Nanjing government's autonomy, but to the coincidence between the policy and its own plan to create conditions that would allow reallocation of military resources stationed in China to the war against the Soviet Union and to fighting against Britain and the US. For the General Staff Office, the most important aspect of the new China policy was its effect on the promotion of the active involvement of the Chinese side and the strengthening of Japan's military resilience through the reduction of burdens on its troops and a gradual concentration of the military force.[52]

(3) Resistance from Troops Stationed in China

The principle of separation of government operations and military affairs was applied even to the organizational reform of peripheral units of troops

---

50 Ibid., p. 310.
51 *Kimitsu sensō nisshi*, entry of February 25, 1942.
52 *Hokushi no chian-sen, 2*, pp. 308–309.

stationed in China. Thus, Section 4 (government affairs) of the General Staff Office of the China Expeditionary Army and the same section of the Northern China Area Army were abolished. In March 1943, the majority of the work these sections had done was transferred either to the Chinese side or to the Ministry of Greater East Asia. In the case of North China, for instance, work pertaining to government administration on the Japanese side came to be shared by the Ministry of Greater East Asia's office at the Japanese embassy; consulates; administrative advisers to the Chinese government above the prefectural level (adviser to Shinminkai [New People's Society], an activist organization among local people of northern China); and liaison sections below the prefectural level.

The liaison section was a successor to the special service agency under the China Expeditionary Army. Relations between the special service agency, which had actually engaged in guidance activities in China, and consulates were found to be problematic, but in the end, it was decided that both would be retained. In order to unify measures at the rank-and-file level and completely renew the nature of the special service agency, the former was renamed "liaison section" and the internal guidance to the Chinese side was totally abolished.

Sōgun danwa (Informal Announcement from the China Expeditionary Army) on February 26 explained that the task of the liaison section was to handle "matters related to strategic defense and research activities." One by one all the special service agencies in North China were converted to liaison sections by the end of March 1943. Nonetheless, it should be pointed out that the composition of personnel and the content of actual business hardly changed. The only conspicuous change was abolition of the prefectural liaison officers, who were previously assigned to each special service agency as non-regular staff of area armies. They were now counselors of the Shinminkai to provide the Chinese side with indirect assistance. Concurrently, by way of valuing autonomous activities on the Chinese side, a large number of Japanese staff members who had played central roles in the Shinminkai were transferred to other posts.[53]

There was no small amount of opposition to these reforms. According to Commander-in-Chief Hata, who inspected North China in late February, rationalization of personnel had been progressing but, on the prefectural level, abolition of the prefectural liaison officer position had met strong resistance. Hata concluded that, because the great majority of prefectural government affairs were matters related to military operations and defense, of which the military should be in charge, "it is feared that immediate abolishment of the prefectural liaison officers might actually worsen public order."[54]

Among government organizations stationed in China, it was the Imperial Japanese Navy that was most reluctant to carry out the new China policy. This was manifested in the handling of the international concessions in Shanghai. The War Guidance Office of the Imperial Army General Staff Office found that the Navy's proposal on the concessions was "for Japan to take over what the Shanghai Municipal Council (Britain, the US, Portugal, etc.) and the Municipal Administrative Council (French, "conseil d'administration municipal") used to enjoy, an argument of those who are obsessed with vested interests." The gap between the Navy's proposal and proposals from the Imperial Army and the Ministry of Greater East Asia was so immense that deliberations had to be adjourned. While the Imperial Navy regarded the international concession as essentially a "special district" and insisted that "the Empire of Japan should get hold of it," the Imperial Army emphasized "getting the city government of Shanghai under control and wiping out the vested interest–oriented form of control and engagement that Britain and the US had pursued."[55]

In order to avoid a clash between these fundamental philosophies, a very broad compromise proposal was worked out. The compromise proposal

---

53 Ibid., pp. 314–315.
54 *Hata Shunroku nisshi*, entry of February 25, 1943.
55 *Kimitsu sensō nisshi*, entry of February 14 and February 17, 1942.

was approved by the February 24 Liaison Conference as the *Shanhai sokai kaishū sochi yōryō* (Essentials of Measures for Retrieval of the Shanghai Concessions). Japanese residents in Shanghai were temporarily shaken by this decision, and some in the Imperial Navy continued to hamper the return of the Shanghai concessions.[56] These movements inside the Imperial Navy subsided when the Nationalist government adopted regulatory measures to retrieve administrative authority over the Shanghai International Settlement on June 30 (implemented beginning on August 1). Still, the Imperial Navy's negative attitude toward the new China policy lingered unchanged, posing an obstacle to the launch of the new Greater East Asia policy that Shigemitsu was about to promote as an extended version of the new China policy.

(4) Economic Measures Deadlocked

The Basic China Policy pointed in the following two directions as far as economic policy was concerned: (1) to restrict monopoly by the Japanese side as much as possible and, concurrently, utilize the responsibilities and ingenuities of Chinese officials and citizens and (2) to expand procurement of materials necessary to attain the goals of war and to meet the need for the development and acquisition of vital materials.

Of the two directions, the second requirement was particularly urgent due to heavy losses of and damages to vessels in battles in the Southeast Pacific. A decline in maritime transport capabilities resulted, which directly led to rapid depletion of national power. Thus, a policy to concentrate the nation's materials mobilization plan on coal, steel, and aluminum was adopted. To obtain a stable supply of these raw materials, Japan had to rely on North and Central China as well as Manchuria, because of their geographical proximity. In the mutual trade plan within the Greater East Asia region, which had provided the basis for the physical mobilization plan for fiscal year 1943, Japan's import of goods from these three regions

---

56 *Hata Shunroku nisshi*, entry of May 12, 1943.

exceeded 74 percent of the total. In particular, the relative weight of North China had increased rapidly.[57] Colonel Horiba Kazuo, who had long been assigned to the China Expeditionary Army, pointed out, "The major difference between this Basic China Policy and other conventional measures is that it requests China's cooperation, particularly in the form of high-level provision of materials as a part of its participation in the Greater East Asia War."[58] As this observation revealed, the role of North China as a logistical base for Japan was growing rapidly.

North and Central China under the Nanjing government in those days, however, suffered from confusion over currency, hyperinflation, and severe commodity shortages. The situation was caused by, among other factors, the new currency issued by the Nanjing government (fabi), which had failed to overcome its weakness vis-à-vis the older currency and the excessive issuance of military currencies by the Japanese army. Therefore, the Nanjing government was in no condition to accommodate Japanese requests. When Zhou Fohai visited Japanese Ambassador Shigemitsu Mamoru together with Wang Jingwei in late February 1943, he requested emergency solution strategies for the economic crisis. During the interview, Zhou told Shigemitsu that, while he himself was grateful for Japan's return of foreign concessions and abolishment of extraterritoriality,

> Our people do not appear to be overjoyed at these measures. This is because other urgent issues that directly affect them have not been resolved, including the problem of inflation. Foreign concessions were returned and extraterritoriality has been abolished. But these things have nothing to do with their daily lives.[59]

---

57 Nakamura Takafusa, *Senji Nippon no Kahoku keizai shihai* [Wartime Japan's Economic Control of North China's Economy], Yamakawa Shuppansha, 1989, pp. 287-301.
58 Horiba Kazuo, *Shina Jihen sensō shidōshi* [History of War Guidance in the Second Sino-Japanese War], Jiji Tsūshinsha, 1962, p. 678.
59 *Shū Futsukai nikki*, entry of February 23, 1943.

For ordinary people under the Nanjing government, a solution to the economic crisis caused by hyperinflation was a more compelling issue. As such, they were in no mood to welcome a new policy initiative from Japan.

To overcome the economic crisis, the Japanese side took such measures as terminating the new issuance of military currency, shifting to the use of fabi, and abolishing military oversight of the physical distribution control system. Authority over the distribution system was transferred to the National Commercial Control Association that had been newly established in March as the Nanjing government's unified goods and materials distribution control authority. These measures were in line with the first direction proposed by the Basic China Policy—that is, to restrict monopoly by the Japanese side as much as possible and, concurrently, utilize the responsibilities and ingenuities of Chinese officials and citizens. As such, they were a part of the attempt to promote the self-reliance of the Nanjing government. More realistically, however, they were aimed at securing a supply of important materials to be exported to Japan.[60]

Some in the Nanjing government optimistically predicted that inflation would be suppressed because the establishment of the National Commercial Control Association allowed the Chinese side to reclaim its authority to maintain control and paved the way for a relaxation of regulations. The association's functions, however, turned out to be limited. Concealment of important commodities became rampant, particularly in Shanghai, and by the summer of 1943 inflation had reached a catastrophic level. This was attributable not only to the weak regulatory power of the association, but also, and more importantly, to a decline in people's confidence in the Nanjing government and Japan due to Japan's defeat by the increasingly fierce counter-offensive of the Allies in the Southeast Pacific. Chinese citizens became suspicious of the value of the new currency. Although

---

60 Furumaya Tadao, "Nitchū Sensō to senryōchi keizai" [The Second Sino-Japanese War and Economies of the Occupied Territories], Chūō Daigaku Jinbun Kagaku Kenkyūsho, ed., *Nitchū Sensō* [The Second Sino-Japanese War], Chūō Daigaku Shuppankai, 1993, pp. 344–359.

the Nanjing government tried to cope with the situation by promulgating the Nationalist government's ordinance for enforcement of regulations on concealment (April), it turned out to be ineffectual.[61]

Toward the end of May 1943, the China Expeditionary Army reported that economic conditions in Central China were such that prices had doubled in a single year. This meant that there was a limit to what materials Japan could obtain at a reasonable price. It would be difficult to secure the supply of necessary goods and materials even if the Japanese government increased the budget for purchases, because there was not enough of certain materials to be sent to Japan. Unable to overlook such a critical situation, the Japanese government discussed measures to save the Chinese economy at the Liaison Conference in July 1943. The conference decided on an emergency measure of sending 250,000 tons of gold ingot to Central and North China to be sold at local markets to obtain the necessary cash to forcibly buy up cotton yarn—the commodity that had been the most extensively concealed. While this measure succeeded in temporarily ameliorating the concealment of materials—and thus suppressed the price hike—its effect did not last long.[62]

4. Conclusion: Shigemitsu and the New China Policy

Ambassador to the United States Kurusu Saburō, who returned home in the autumn of 1942, highly praised the new China policy and Shigemitsu's contribution to it in various talks, as well as in his report submitted to the Foreign Ministry. Kurusu wrote, "Maneuvers toward China are the primary goal of our wartime diplomacy. . . . A breakthrough in relations with China can be accomplished almost singlehandedly by Japan's determination alone," and "with highly appropriate advice from Japanese Ambassador to

---

61 *Shū Futsukai nikki*, entry of March 11, 1943 and Okada Yūji, *Nicchū Sensō urakataki* [Clerical Staff's Record of the Second Sino-Japanese War], Tōyō Keizai Shinpōsha, 1974, pp. 261–268.
62 *Hata Shunroku nisshi*, entries of May 25 and July 11, 1943.

China Shigemitsu, things are gradually moving in that direction."[63] It may be said that the new China policy was an outcome of the issue of how to settle the Second Sino-Japanese War. Having been given low priority, the issue of settling the Second Sino-Japanese War was reevaluated as an opportunity to autonomously terminate the Pacific War. In other words, the new China policy was significant because it could replace the collapsed political strategy to force Britain to surrender to terminate the Pacific War, which by nature made Japan dependent on Britain's decision.

But Kurusu's perception did not necessarily penetrate all parts of the Japanese government and the military. In fact, the new China policy was not so highly evaluated, even setting aside the setback of its economic measures. Nishimura Susumu, director of the military affairs section of the Army Ministry, for instance, observed that the issue was, after all, whether the spirit and philosophy of the new China policy had spread among officials and citizens in China. From this viewpoint, the new China policy was "merely a reexamination of a wiser alternative for pursuing the same goal."[64] Moreover, while there were some in Japan who supported the policy, saying, "it is necessary to make people understand Japan's true intention and induce the Chongqing government to work toward a peace settlement even at the sacrifice of economic benefits," in the field in China, there were many more in opposition who insisted that "as a war is no fantastic theory, we find no reason to give up the material benefits we have laboriously obtained." In particular, naval officers stationed in China held this view en masse.[65]

Okada Yūji, supreme economic adviser to the Nanjing government, reminisced as follows:

---

63 Kurusu Saburō, *Hōmatsu no 35-nen* [Ephemeral 35 years], Chūō Kōronsha, 1986, pp. 171–172.

64 Nishiura Susumu, *Shōwa sensōshi no shōgen* [Testimony on Shōwa War History], Hara Shobō, 1980, pp. 188–189.

65 "Yamazaki Seijun-shi, 'Tai-Shi shinseisaku ni tsuite'" [Mr. Yamazaki Seijun on the New China Policy] (October 12, 1943), Doi Akira, ed., *Shōwa shakai keizai shiryō shūsei* [Collection of Reference Materials on Shōwa Society and Economy], vol. 11, Daitō Bunka Daigaku Tōyō Kenkyūsho, Gennandō Shoten, 1995, pp. 445–446.

Participation in the war by the Wang Jingwei government drastically changed character. His regime's character as a medium for a peace settlement with the Chongqing government is now lost. Instead, the Wang Jingwei government has metamorphosed into Japan's partner in fighting the great war. And one of its roles as the partner is to supply materials that Japan is critically short of from Central China. Another role is to devote its troops to the maintenance of public order so that Japanese troops in the Chinese continent can be redeployed elsewhere.[66]

It is indeed true that, before its participation in the war, the Nanjing government had been a medium for Japan's peace settlement with the Chongqing government. By participating in the war, the Nanjing government became Japan's war ally. Economically, it was expected to become a base to supply materials to Japan. Militarily, it was expected to contribute to the strengthening of the national defense capability of the Imperial Army as a whole by reducing the burden on Japanese troops in the Chinese continent. In short, particularly for the Imperial Japanese Army, the political measures to respect the Nanjing government's autonomy and tolerance of its self-initiative were, from beginning to end, a means to help Japan wage war against Britain and the US. Achieving a full peace was by no means the primary goal.

Thus, with the failure of economic measures and differing understandings and criticisms from many corners, the new China policy continued to weave about. Shigemitsu alone would not treat the policy as a mere tool to help Japan fight the war against the United States and Britain. Even under these circumstances, Shigemitsu continued to attempt to mobilize the policy as the groundwork for inducing a full peace between Japan and China. As soon as Shigemitsu assumed the post of foreign minister in April 1943, he wrote the following assessment of the new China policy, albeit with the caveat that the policy was still in the process of being implemented:

---

66 Okada, op cit., p. 271.

. . . Its impact, both within and outside China, has already been much greater than expected, and it has left a particularly deep impression on the Chinese people in general. I have reason to infer that the new China policy has remarkably reduced the Chongqing government's so-called will to resist. When the spirit of this new policy is further pursued and various economic and political measures are carried out, I daresay the settlement of the China Incident [the Second Sino-Japanese War] would not be impossible.[67]

As the former ambassador to Nanjing, Shigemitsu was one of the few who were keenly aware of the reality of the new China policy. Still, he held to his assessment, which appeared to turn a blind eye to economic realities. By the end of May 1943, soon after Shigemitsu became the foreign minister, he had already been criticized by the military who felt that "In the end, Shigemitsu ended up twisting his idealism."[68] Such criticism notwithstanding, Shigemitsu continued to devote himself to pushing through the new China policy. He hoped that the universal policy ideal of the new China policy would "leave a particularly deep impression [on the Chinese people] and remarkably reduce the Chongqing government's so-called will to resist," eventually leading to a full peace settlement.

At the same time, the new China policy had another role: to "clearly present the fair spirit of the Japanese people to the Chinese people" through "fundamental correction" of Japan's China policy or "liquidation of ill-directed policy."[69] Therefore, the crux of the new China policy had to be the fundamental revision of the Japan-China Basic Relations Treaty, "an

---

67 *Tai-Shi shinhōshin no suishin ni tsuite* [On Promotion of the New Policy toward China] (April 5, 1943), produced by Ministry of Foreign Affairs with Shigemitsu Mamoru's signature (Ministry of Foreign Affairs Record A7.0.0.9-41-2, "Daitōa Sensō kankei ikken Chūka Minkoku Kokumin Seifu sansen kankei, Nikka Dōmei Jōyaku kankei" [Matters Related to Greater East Asia War, Nationalist Government of the Republic of China's Participation in the War, Japan-China Basic Relations Treaty]).

68 *Kimitsu sensō nisshi*, entry of May 29, 1943.

69 Shigemitsu, op cit., p. 167 and p. 172.

unequal treaty that treated China almost as Japan's colony"[70]—which would lead to eventual restoration of China's sovereignty. Shigemitsu devoted himself determinedly to the realization of the revision.

To put it another way, it was held that with the new China policy, which laid out the goal of abolition of the unequal treaties as its final objective, the "liberation of Greater East Asia," which had come to be featured as the philosophy of the war after the outbreak of the war, on the one hand, and the direction of Japan's China policy, on the other, coincided for the first time.[71] And this must have been the reason why Shigemitsu posited the new China policy as "diplomatic policy to prepare a broad premise or background" for the Sino-Japanese peace settlement targeted ultimately at the Chinese people in general. To him, that was much more than a policy targeted at the Nanjing government alone to be used in bargaining with the Chongqing government. In terms of the actual policy, Shigemitsu's position was to pursue a full peace settlement with China on the assumption that the Japanese government would fully respect the position of the Nanjing government. Shidehara's persistence in this position despite an increasingly weakened Nanjing government was a contradiction and it led him, eventually, to a sticky situation in which he was trapped.

Incidentally, among the Allies it was Britain that was most interested in Japan's new China policy. It is interesting that Britain believed Shidehara was the driving force behind this policy. In the spring of 1943, a section of the British foreign office made the analysis that Japan's adoption of "a compromise policy" toward the occupied territories was largely attributable to Shigemitsu and that its purpose was to lure the Chongqing government toward the Wang Jingwei camp. Arguing that, if Japan granted "genuine independence" to the Wang regime along with financial assistance, a

---

70 *Kihon jōyaku ni kansuru mondai* [Problems Related to the Japan-China Basic Relations Treaty] (April 14, 1943), Ministry of Foreign Affairs Document A7.0.0.9-41-2.
71 A virtually identical view is found in Tobe Ryōichi, "Daitōa Sensō to Shina Jihen" [Greater East Asia War and the Second Sino-Japanese War], *Gaikō Jihō*, no. 1320, July 1995, pp. 48–50.

Japan–Wang regime alliance would be a much greater threat to the Allies in China than Japan's military advances, this analysis stressed the need for the Chongqing government to conduct counter propaganda. At the same time, it also argued that this compromise policy was merely a "thin disguise" for Japan's ulterior motive to reduce military pressure that was mounting elsewhere in China. Even if Japan won the war, the analysis predicted, Wang's China would only be incorporated, along with Korea, into a co-prosperity sphere in which only the interests of Japan, the hegemon of the sphere, would be prioritized. It would be only the British and American camp, which had completely abolished extraterritoriality, that could guarantee an alliance on equal footing with China. Therefore, it was proposed that the Allies should stress this point as a part of counter propaganda.[72] This argument implies that the British-American abolition of the unequal treaty had significance as a countermeasure to Japan's new China policy. At the same time, the new China policy had the effect of highlighting the battle to win over the Chongqing regime, another aspect of the war in China.[73]

---

72 Foreign Research and Press Service, "Japan Policy toward China" (27 March 1943), F1649/351/23/F0371/35948.

73 G.F. Hudson of the Royal Institute of International Affairs, London, also concluded that the objective of Japan's new China policy was to make the Chongqing government break off from the Allied camp, paying a dear price. See G.F. Hudson, "What peace terms could Japan now offer China," 26 June 1943, F3275/351/23/F0371/35948.

Chapter

5

"Independence" of Burma and the Philippines

1. Introduction: Manchukuo Model

It has already been pointed out in the first chapter that the handling of the occupied territories had been linked to Japan's war plan solely from the viewpoint of promoting an early end to the war. Thus, the policies to grant independence to the Philippines (or respect its sovereignty) and to approve the independence of Burma were not the result of Japan's consideration for those peoples' nationalism and/or their demands for independence but rather the results of the primacy of terminating the war in a manner that was advantageous to Japan. But this viewpoint on an early and advantageous end to the war was lost by the time the Southern Operations had completed its initial stage, and the argument for independence of the peoples of the Philippines and Burma itself experienced a setback due to strong opposition from the expeditionary armies and the supreme general command of the Japanese Imperial Army and Navy. As a result, military administration was carried out in these regions. The issue of independence for Burma was separated from the Indian issue, while the independence of the Philippines ceased to be connected with the peace settlement with the United States. This development indicates that, as an early end to the war became hopeless, the connection between independence for the occupied territories and the scheme for ending the war became more remote. Also, the importance of these territories as logistical bases for Japan in its war against China as well as Britain and the US increased further.

In August 1942, the Military Administration Headquarters issued a directive on measures for local peoples in which it was stressed that extra care should be paid to avoid making any commitment to local residents regarding the handling of the occupied territories because "the final decision had been put on hold as a national policy." At the same time, the directive also stipulated as follows:

As repeatedly stated in the Empire's official announcements, the

Philippines and Burma . . . should be allowed to become independent at an appropriate timing in the future. It should be specially noted that theirs will be independence under the firm grip of the Empire of Japan over their military, diplomatic, and economic affairs.[1]

As will be discussed in the following pages, in 1943 independence of the Philippines and Burma once again became an issue for the Japanese central government. But the above directive made it clear that, even in those regions that had been scheduled to become independent, the type of independence in which interference with internal affairs would be minimized and sovereignty would be thoroughly respected—as envisioned by Minami Kikan (a secret organization for the independence of Burma) and Foreign Minister Tōgō Shigenori—would never be realized. The "independence" envisioned in the directive was the Manchukuo-type of independence under which key functions of the state were under the firm control of locally stationed Japanese military. While reasons for independence differed between Burma and the Philippines, complete independence was unthinkable when the defense of Greater East Asia became a strategic mandate and cooperation by local residents for the war became much more necessary than before. In Japan's historical experience, the typical example of an attempt at establishing an independent state whose core functions were under Japan's firm control but which, nevertheless, must be internationally recognized, was Manchukuo. While there were a number of unique features in Japan's government of Manchukuo, by far the most important externally was the establishment of inter-state relations in which Japan recognized Manchukuo's independence but in reality kept all the key functions in its own hands. Internally, the most important feature in Japan's government of Manchukuo was the establishment of a regime-supporting political party, which was essentially

---

1 Bōei Kenkyūsho Senshibu, ed., *Shiryōshū Nanpō no gunsei* [Documents on Military Administration in Southern Territories], Asagumo Shimbunsha, 1985, p. 294.

tantamount to rejection of party politics.[2] This Manchukuo format was first adopted in the government of Burma.

Here the Manchukuo model does not refer to the form of government sustained by Japanese officials' monopolizing key positions of the state. While many of Japan's collaborators in the occupied territories (as well as unoccupied regions) in Asia were apprehensive that this form of government would be reenacted, it was decided at the beginning that this type of governance was to be avoided both in Burma and the Philippines.[3]

2. Conditions for Independence and Dilemma

(1) Conditions for Independence

At the Liaison Conference on January 4, 1943, Prime Minister Tōjō Hideki announced that a step forward should be made concerning the independence of Burma, the Philippines, and Indonesia and instructed concerned government sections to study the issue.[4] The backdrop to this was the increasing seriousness of the war situation in the Southeast Pacific (Guadalcanal Island) as in the case of the new China policy. As the greatest strategic issue shifted from military advances to the Central Pacific and the Asian continent to defense of Greater East Asia, the solidarity of Asian peoples and cooperation

---

2 Regarding this issue, the present author is deeply indebted to Mitani Taichirō, *Manshūkoku kokka taisei to Nippon no kokunai seiji* [Manchukuo's State System and Japan's Domestic Politics], Iwanami Shoten, 1992, pp. 179–213. Also see William H. Elsbree, *Japan's Role in Southeast Asian Nationalists Movements 1940 to 1945* (Cambridge: Harvard University Press, 1953), pp. 28–30.

3 Immediately after the signing of the military alliance treaty between Thailand and the Empire of Japan in December 1941, it is said that Prime Minister Plaek Phibunsongkhram of Thailand stated, "If our country joined the camp of the Empire of Japan, we would be like Manchukuo even if Japan had won the war." At this point, what the prime minister was envisioning was participation by Japanese officials in Thailand's administration. See E. Bruce Reynolds, "Aftermath of Alliance: The Wartime Legacy in Thai-Japanese Relations" in *Journal of Southeast Asian Studies*, vol. 11, no. 2 (March 1990), p. 85 (n87). For the argument against this type of government, see Takeuchi Tatsuji, "Manila Diary: Dec. 1942–Oct. 1943" in Rōyama Masamichi and Takeuchi Tatsuji, *Philippine Polity: A Japanese View* (Yale University Press, Southeast Asia Studies Monograph Series, no. 12, 1968), pp. 243–244.

4 Imperial Japanese Army General Staff Office, ed., *Sugiyama memo, ge* [Sugiyama Memorandum vol. 2], Hara Shobō, 1985, p. 343.

in the war effort by citizens of the occupied territories became the most important political issue. Thus, a review of the independence issue from that viewpoint was warranted.

The argument that it would be necessary to promptly promise independence to the Philippines and Burma in order to induce local peoples' "political understanding" and "voluntary cooperation" had already become increasingly strong within the Army General Staff Office and the Ministry of Greater East Asia by the latter half of 1942.[5] Therefore, no objection to independence for these two regions was heard during the deliberations over the issue organized by the War Guidance Office.[6] The only issue under debate was the timing. Even within the Army General Staff Office, which had been passive toward the independence issue, it was decided at its department chiefs' conference on January 11, 1943, that Burma's independence should be timed at the first anniversary of the Burmese Executive Administration (August 1, 1943), while the Philippines should be granted independence promptly, or "at least prior to the timing of independence that the United States had officially promised at the latest."[7] On the same day, deliberation on a provisional proposal on the reversion (of the occupied territories) was conducted among officials of the pertinent ministries. In these deliberations, the Ministry of Greater East Asia argued for Burma's independence in

---

5   For instance, Lieutenant Colonel Tsuji Masanobu of the operations section of the Army General Staff Office submitted a proposal to the War Guidance Office in September 1942, saying, "In order to nullify the war objective of the United States and make sure peoples of Greater East Asia politically understand [the Greater East Asia Co-Prosperity Sphere], it should be announced to the Philippines and Burma that they would be granted full independence after a specified period of time," with which the War Guidance Office also concurred (see *Kimitsu sensō nisshi*, September 13, 1942). The newly established Ministry of Greater East Asia also argued in December 1942 that it should be promptly announced that the Philippines would be granted independence "in order to induce voluntary cooperation of the peoples in Greater East Asia by clarifying the Empire's war purpose." ("Hitō dokuritsu sengen ni kansuru shian" [A Proposal on Declaration of Independence of the Philippines], Ministry of Foreign Affairs Document A7.0.0.9-46, "Daitōa Sensō kankei ikken" [Matters Related to the Greater East Asia War], "Hitō dokuritsu to Nippi dōmei jōyaku teiketsu kankei" [Matters Related to the Philippines' Independence and Conclusion of the Japan-Philippines Alliance Treaty].)

6   *Kimitsu sensō nisshi*, entry of January 10 and 11, 1943.

7   Ibid., entry of January 11, 1943.

February, while the military affairs section of the Army Ministry insisted on simultaneous independence for the Philippines and Burma.

The point of contention was Indonesia. *Kimitsu sensō nisshi* on January 13 writes, "Because the view on the belongings of the former Dutch East Indies differed between the Army General Staff Office and the Army Ministry, it was decided that the proposal to be submitted to the Liaison Conference should include only decisions on the reversions of the Philippines and Burma, dropping all other cases."[8] At a glance, it appeared that the Army Ministry insisted on granting independence to Indonesia against the wish of the Army General Staff Office, which found doing so premature. Judging from subsequent developments, however, it is conjectured that not only the Ministry of Navy and the Army General Staff Office but also the Ministry of Greater East Asia were reluctant to grant independence to Indonesia, while the Ministry of Foreign Affairs and the Ministry of Army was more favorable toward it.

The provisional proposal on the reversions of the occupied territories thus adopted by the January 14 Liaison Conference stipulated that Burma and the Philippines would be independent, while the treatment of other territories would be decided separately in the future, based on two criteria. Those criteria were that (1) territories which are essential for the defense of Greater East Asia, those with inadequate ability to become independent, and those which are sparsely populated should be, in principle, added to the Empire's territory, and (2) territories whose independence is judged to be beneficial to the waging of the Greater East Asia War and construction of the Greater East Asia Co-Prosperity Sphere should be allowed to become independent. Prime Minister Tōjō clarified the purport of this decision in his speech at the eighty-first session of the Imperial Diet on January 28.

The conditions for independence for Burma and the Philippines were set as (1) commitment to joint defense with Japan, (2) acceptance of the

---

8   Ibid., entry of January 13, 1943.

stationing of Japanese troops and their use of military bases ("solidification of military unity" in the case of Burma); and (3) "close alliance" in diplomacy and "close economic cooperation."[9] Indonesia's status as an "Imperial territory" along with Malaya was decided by the *Daitōa seiryaku shidō taikō* (Outlines for the Political Guidance of Greater East Asia), adopted by the May 31 Imperial Council (see chapter 6).

According to the proposal on the jurisdiction of the occupied territories, although Burma was a strategically important region in the west for the defense of Greater East Asia, it was judged that responding positively to the Burmese people's willingness to cooperate with Japan's war efforts would be "a testimony to the Empire of Japan's fairness" and would have a positive effect on winning the hearts of the Burmese people. The political effect of Burma's independence on the people of India, however, was given a low priority. Regarding the Philippines, the same provisional proposal referred to its ability to govern itself, the US promise of its independence in 1946, and the prospective increase of burden on the Empire if the Philippines was governed as a "territory of the Empire" as the three reasons the Philippines should be granted independence. Those reasons were almost identical to those enumerated at the beginning of the war, except its connection to the scheme to end the war, indicating that the only issue in the case of the Philippines was the timing of independence.

(2) The Dilemma of "Independence": Korea and Taiwan

Burma was the first occupied territory that Japan granted independence to after the start of the war. As such, the Japanese government paid due attention to and consideration of the impact of that decision. The briefing document on measures for the independence of Burma submitted to the January 14, 1943, Liaison Conference called participants' attention to "stimulations that this independence [of Burma] might give to independence movements of

---

9   Sugiyama Memorandum vol. 2, pp. 352–353.

other peoples under the Empire's control." About Korea, the document stipulated that the Empire of Japan should apply "the principle of making both the Japanese and Korean peoples the emperor's children equally," while the Empire should guide the locals in the Dutch East Indies with understanding for their welfare and advancement, helping them improve their position if they willingly collaborated with the Empire.[10] This document reveals that, while the Japanese expected that granting independence to occupied territories in Southeast Asia would promote their cultural assimilation to Japan and their Japanization, the Japanese could not eliminate their apprehension about its provocation of the Korean people's independence movement.

At the February 1942 Liaison Conference, which had deliberated the prime minister's announcement on the occasion of the fall of Singapore, the Imperial Japanese Navy had referred to the independence issue of the Philippines and proposed that, "reference to the word 'independence' should be restrained because it is feared it could be applied to Korea's independence issue." In response, Prime Minister Tōjō had replied that, because he had already used this term in his Imperial Diet speech in January, he could not take it back and stressed that, "Because Korean people are genuinely Japanese, this would not cause any problem at all."[11] Around the same time, at the first working group of the Daitōa Kensetsu Shingikai (Greater East Asia Establishment Council), a member of the group, Kuhara Fusanosuke, had argued for the independence of Korea, saying, if construction of Greater East Asia was to be conceived as a step toward "universal brotherhood" or "an incremental step toward world peace," it would be a benevolent policy to let Korea become independent at the earliest date because "territorial status would be of no interest to Korea." In response, Prime Minister Tōjō

---

10 "Daitōa Sensō kansui no tameno Biruma dokuritsu shisaku ni kansuru ken setsumei" [Explanation on Matters Related to Burma's Independence Measures toward Completion of the Greater East Asia War], Sugiyama Memorandum vol. 2, pp. 351–352.
11 Sugiyama Memorandum vol. 2, pp. 19–20.

had said, "My position does not permit me to touch on the Korean issue."[12]

Kuhara did not argue for independence of occupied territories on the basis of the principle of the self-determination of nations. When the Japanese government attempted to promote measures for the independence of Burma and the Philippines or measures to tolerate the future autonomy of and political participation in the occupied territories, however, it had to be prepared for the inevitable emergence of the dilemma of how to treat Korea and Taiwan. And in order to break out of this dilemma, it became necessary to prove that, as Tōjō had declared, the Korean people were genuinely Japanese. The abolition of the Ministry of Colonial Affairs in November 1942, on the occasion of the establishment of the Ministry of Greater East Asia, and the transfer of Korea and Taiwan to the jurisdiction of the Home Ministry as territories of Japan were, in a way, the proof to support Tōjō's argument. In other words, the completion of the institutionalization of "assimilation to Japan" was also a premise for measures to grant independence to occupied territories in Southeast Asia. As Mark R. Peattie, who studied the meaning of assimilation in Japan, points out, because assimilation was Japan's ideology adopted in the rule of Korea, Japan had to carry through a fiction—that is, the logic that there was no colonialism within "the formal empire."[13]

---

12 Kuhara Fusanosuke Ō Denki Hensankai, ed., *Kuhara Fusanosuke* [Biography of Kuhara Fusanosuke] (unreleased), 1970, pp. 534–535.

13 Mark R. Peattie, "Japanese Attitude toward Colonialism," in Ramon H. Myers and Mark R. Peattie, eds., *The Japanese Colonial Empire, 1895–1945* (Princeton University Press, 1984), pp. 119–120, and "Introduction," p. 14. An excellent recent study on the relations between the Koiso cabinet's reform of the treatment of Korea and Taiwan and the new Greater East Asia policy is Asano Toyomi, *Nippon Teikoku saigo no saihen: "Ajia shominzoku no kaihō" to Taiwan-Chōsen tōchi* [The Last Reorganization of the Empire of Japan: "Liberation of Asian peoples" and the Rule of Taiwan-Korea], Waseda University Press, 1996, pp. 249–298. Taking up the issue of the right of Koreans and Taiwanese to participate in the Imperial Diet, this work did not only explain this improvement of treatment of Koreans and Taiwanese from the Japanese domestic political factors as a part of measures to strengthen the National Mobilization system but also in the context of change in the international environment when decolonization began to become an important point of contention in Asian wars. The author analyzed that, while the Home Ministry perceived this issue in the framework of "inland territorial expansionism," the Ministry of Foreign Affairs perceived it as an incremental step toward independence, taking into consideration the "peoples' liberalization policy" of the Japanese government as a part of its peace maneuvering toward the Soviet Union (see chapter 9).

Incidentally, Foreign Minister Shigemitsu always kept in mind the issue of treatment of Korea and Taiwan because he could not be party to the fiction. For instance, when Koreans were enfranchised as compensation for compulsory military service (application of Japan's conscription to overseas territories), which gave them seats in the Imperial Diet, albeit in a limited manner, Shigemitsu expressed his utmost support for this decision as "a step forward toward autonomy." According to Shigemitsu, that was because he "believed this measure would make Japan's conduct in the Greater East Asia policy less contradictory, albeit to an unsatisfactory degree."[14]

3. Structure of Government of Burma: Treaty of Alliance between Japan and Burma

(1) Pressure from the "One Person with Two Roles" Argument

On January 14, 1943, the Liaison Conference decided *Daitōa sensō kansui no tameno Biruma dokuritsu shisaku ni kansuru ken* (Matters Related to Measures for the Independence of Burma in Order to Bring the Greater East Asia War to a Successful Conclusion) along with the provisional proposal on the possessing of the occupied territories already mentioned. The resolution clearly defined the purposes of Burma's independence as contribution to completion of the Greater East Asia War and cooperation in the war effort, while it defined the state configuration of independent Burma as "a state centered around the Burmese people but also cooperatively embracing Indians and other races." In order to strengthen and simplify state operations, it was decided that "special consideration should be given to the mechanism of the government." As for cooperation in the war effort, the decision stipulated that Burma should declare war against Britain and the US and pledge complete military, political, and economic cooperation with Japan. And the

---

14 Shigemitsu Mamoru, *Shōwa no dōran, ge* [Shōwa in Turmoil, vol. 2], Chūō Kōronsha, 1952, pp. 250–251.

foundation of Japan-Burma relations was defined as "a pact with Burma as an integral unit of the Greater East Asian solidarity with the Empire of Japan as its hegemon on the maintenance of close military, diplomatic, and economic relations with the Empire." Based on this resolution, Prime Minister Tōjō announced in his Imperial Diet speech that Burma would be granted independence, upon which the pertinent government ministries and agencies started studies on the *Biruma dokuritsu shidō yōkō* (Guidelines for Burmese Independence) in early February.

After his speech at the eighty-first session of the Imperial Diet, Prime Minister Tōjō remarked, "If we had followed only the reports and advice from locally stationed troops alone, Burma probably would have continued to be under military administration for two or three more years. There is a time for everything. And when that time is missed, things do not go well."[15] One can perceive here the continued passive attitude of the locally stationed Japanese military toward the granting of independence, which found its expression in the controversy over the diplomatic mechanism of the independent Burma. The Imperial Army's proposal on the diplomacy of Burma simply stipulated that Burmese "diplomacy shall be conducted by Burma itself under substantive control of the Empire of Japan." The Ministry of Foreign Affairs proposed the following:

> Even if [Burma's] diplomacy were under the Empire's substantive control, still, [such diplomatic routines as] the exchange of diplomatic missions deserves special consideration. While it concerns the fundamental issue of how to manage diplomatic relations among countries within the Co-Prosperity Sphere, it should suffice, for the time being, to exchange diplomatic missions.

---

15 Itō Takashi et al., eds., *Tōjō Naikaku Sōri Daijin kimitsu kiroku* [Confidential Records of Prime Minister Tōjō], University of Tokyo Press, 1990, p. 500.

In the end, the Foreign Ministry argued that the "diplomacy [of Burma] should be closely coordinated with the Empire of Japan."[16]

During the course of the deliberations, one important point of contention was whether to appoint a career diplomat ambassador to Burma after the independence or to have the military commander serve concurrently as the ambassador. The Imperial Army stationed in Burma insisted on the "two roles in one person" tact of having the commander-in-chief of the army stationed in Burma serve concurrently as the ambassador and requested that important decisions of the Army Ministry should be communicated directly to the commander-in-chief cum ambassador via central general command (particularly the supreme command staff) of the Imperial Army. While the Army Ministry persisted with the system that allowed the minister for the army to directly order and instruct the ambassador to Burma, the Army General Staff Office insisted that all the orders and instructions should go through the commander-in-chief of the locally stationed army.[17] But the Ministry of Foreign Affairs would not give up its insistence on the appointment of a career diplomat ambassador to Burma. The Foreign Ministry's slogan, "Burma should not be a second Manchukuo," called for, among other things, avoidance of the "two roles in one person" formula (i.e., the commander-in-chief of the Kanto Army serving concurrently as the Japanese ambassador to Manchukuo). In the end, against strong counter-demands from the locally stationed army and the Imperial Army leadership, it was decided that a career diplomat would be appointed as ambassador to Burma.[18]

Nevertheless, coordination of the ambassador to Burma's authority once again ran into rough waters. At the conference among bureau chiefs and department directors of the Army and Navy Ministries as well as the Ministries of Foreign Affairs and Greater East Asia on March 4, it was argued that it was a "top priority matter" to facilitate the military operations

---

16 Sugiyama Memorandum vol. 2, p. 390.
17 *Kimitsu sensō nisshi*, entry of February 10, 1943.
18 Ibid., entry of February 27, 1943.

of the locally stationed troops and, thus, decided that, "Military affairs as well as matters that are currently attended to by the military administration should be placed under the jurisdiction of the commander-in-chief of the Imperial Army stationed in Burma, while other matters should be handled by the ambassador to Burma." Oka Takazumi, director-general of the Naval Affairs Bureau of the Ministry of Navy, in particular, was so annoyed by what he regarded as "the Foreign Ministry's argument not based on realities" that he took the hardline stance of asking whether they could do without appointing an ambassador.[19] Thus, although the *Guidelines for Burmese Independence* stipulated appointment of an ambassador plenipotentiary to Burma, the document also stated that, "for the time being, in light of special conditions in Burma, the Empire's officials in the field should, when carrying out their tasks, act in accordance with the actual circumstances with special consideration given to the military requirements." This substantively limited the authority of an ambassador. The War Guidance Office appreciated this decision, saying, "Even when Burma becomes independent, it still remains the right-wing bastion of the Greater East Asia defense. Therefore, this decision is only a matter of course."[20] Even though the "two roles in one person" style was blocked, the ambassador to Burma's missions were limited in the March 10 agreement (among the Army and Navy Ministries, the Ministries of Foreign Affairs and Greater East Asia, as well as the cabinet) to protection of the Empire's commerce, services for subjects of the Japanese Empire, migration and settlement, overseas colonization, and "pure diplomacy." While the concrete range of pure diplomacy was not specified as at the occasion of the establishment of the Ministry of Greater East Asia, it seems needless to point out that "pure diplomacy" would be subservient to "military requirements."

---

19 Ibid., entry of March 4, 1943.
20 Ibid., entry of June 18, 1943.

(2) The Leader State and the Single-Party State

On the configuration of the state or the statehood of Burma, the *Guidelines for Burmese Independence* stipulated that an independent Burma would take the form of a "leader state" centered around Ba Maw. In a leader state, a national representative assumes the roles of the chief of legislation, administration, and judicature. This style of statehood was deemed necessary because (1) a government that could promptly respond to the needs of the military in executing operations should govern Burma, which was at the front line of the Greater East Asia defense, and (2) Ba Maw's position needed to be enhanced because Burma had a strong tendency toward rampant minor political parties. Additionally, there was Tōjō's view that it would be more effective to have the country's leader grasp people's hearts than to accommodate nationalistic demands in order to win the locals' hearts and induce them to cooperate in the war effort. In order to accomplish this, Tōjō believed it wise to give the leader, Ba Maw, appropriate treatment and guarantee his post. This notion was derived from the same logic as Tōjō's that representatives of the occupied territories would be invited to the Greater East Asia Conference half a year later.[21]

As for the range and form of the Burmese people's participation in the politics of Independent Burma, the Imperial Army's proposal clearly stated that "No parliament or political party which has the characteristics of a legislative organ is allowed."[22] In contrast, the Ministry of Foreign Affairs argued, "We should not overlook the history of Burma's political improvement, which has come about via development of people's political participation. In the future, its parliament should continue to function not only as a means for top-down communication but also as a mechanism for the top to hear the

---

21 Tōjō once commented on Ba Maw that "He takes great pride in representing the entirety of Burma. Thus, every once in a while, he may become overbearing. In order to embrace Burma magnanimously, it would be better to let him and other leaders have their own way under our broad control." This comment derived from the same conviction (see Itō et al., eds., 1952, p. 509).

22 *Biruma dokuritsu shidō yōkō* [Guidelines for Burmese Independence], February 20, 1943, Imperial Japanese Army Proposal (Ministry of Foreign Affairs Document A7.0.0.9-39-2).

views of the bottom" and insisted on tolerance for a unicameral parliament with legislative functions, albeit with limited actual authority.[23]

Furthermore, the Foreign Ministry also argued, "It may be problematic to abolish all political parties. Instead, efforts should be made to organize one powerful political party (a national organization that pursues the ideal of the newly born Burma) which can unite and integrate all the existing parties." As a compromise between the two sides, it was decided in the end that, even though the Burmese people's wishes should be respected, it should be noted that, when a parliament is to be established, it should not hamper the execution of state affairs by the state leader. As for political parties, it was simply noted that their division and strife should be restricted. It was also stipulated that a Sangifu (Office of Councillors) was to be established as an advisory organ on important state affairs.[24]

The proposal of the Imperial Japanese Army stationed in Burma based on the *Guidelines for Burmese Independence* defined the parliament to be established in Burma as "a mere advisory organization devoid of any legislative power" and insisted that, in terms of political parties, Burma should aim at being a single-party state. Apparently, the army's vision of a political regime in Burma was based on the experiences of the government of Manchukuo.[25]

The same could be said about the ethnic composition of Burma in relation to its administration after independence. Following the decision on the *Matters Related to Measures for the Independence of Burma*, it was decided that, in terms of the ethnic composition of Burma, while ethnic Burmese were the core of the country, they were to "harmoniously embrace" other groups,

---

23 *Biruma dokuritsu shidō yōkō ni kansuru jakkan no kōsatsu* [Some Observations on the Guidelines for Burmese Independence], February 24, 1943, Ministry of Foreign Affairs Political Affairs Bureau (Ministry of Foreign Affairs Document A7.0.0.9-39-2).
24 Ibid.
25 *Biruma dokuritsu shidō yōkō ni motozuku Biruma dokuritsu shidō yōryō (an)* [Proposed Outline of Independence Guidance for Burma Based on the Guidelines for Burmese Independence] (May 14, 1943, Mori Shūdan Shireibu) (Ministry of Foreign Affairs Document A7.0.0.9-39-2).

including ethnic Indians. The point of contention was the issue of nationality. Various ideas were studied, including (1) giving Japanese residents dual citizenship, (2) treating Indians as alien but semi-Burmese citizens, and (3) depriving Indian residents of Burmese nationality.[26] In the end, adopting the Manchukuo philosophy of "Five Races Under One Union," it was decided that the Japanese residents would not become Burmese citizens and that provision of Burmese citizenship to Indian minorities, the largest minority group in Burma, would be left to the Burmese government's discretion.[27]

Overall, it was envisioned in the *Guidelines for Burmese Independence* that central control of Burma's statehood would be in the hands of Japan. Militarily, Burma was obliged to offer provision of all kinds of convenience to the Japanese military. While Burma was allowed to possess its own army and navy, its strength, organization, and tactical operations were to be guided and instructed by the Japanese military. In the economic sphere, Burma was allowed to enjoy free activities in accordance with the Greater East Asia establishment plan, but it had to go along with Japan's policies for areas that were particularly important for the building of Greater East Asia. As far as transportation and communication were concerned, they would be placed under Burmese jurisdiction, but Burma had to recognize and cater to Japan's "special requests."[28] Needless to say, these decisions strongly reflected demands from the Imperial Army and Navy.

One of the Foreign Ministry's concrete concerns, particularly from its Bureau of Political Affairs, about the *Guidelines for Burmese Independence* was the absence of a difference in treatment between Burma during the war and after the war. In the ministry's conviction, "Substantive control

---

26 *Kimitsu sensō nisshi*, entry of February 10, 1943.

27 According to the Burmese Nationality and Naturalization Act (promulgated on February 19, 1943), any individual that resided in Burma and satisfied certain conditions was granted Burmese nationality. Nevertheless, the issuance of permission to acquire nationality was left to the discretion of the Burmese government, which did not owe an explanation to those whose applications were denied. (See Ōta Tsunezō, *Biruma ni okeru Nippon gunsei no kenkyū* [Study of Japanese Military Government in Burma], Yoshikawa Kōbunkan, 1967, pp. 568–569.)

28 Sugiyama Memorandum vol. 2, p. 390.

of Burma by the Empire of Japan should be a temporary measure called for in the waging of warfare." But this notion was not necessarily carried through.[29] Furthermore, the Bureau of Political Affairs argued that the military agreement attached to the *Guidelines for Burmese Independence* should not be applied indiscriminately. The bureau took the position that "in principle, articles included in the military agreement should be applied only to purely military matters (military operations and tactics)."[30] Nevertheless, as the Bureau of Political Affairs itself had admitted, "Which action should be judged to be united with and inseparable from military operations and tactics (e.g., local currency and physical distribution, etc.) is in the final analysis a matter of certification. As long as the certification is reasonably conducted, it should be accepted." The delineation of purely military affairs from other affairs was, in reality, difficult.

During the March 10, 1943, Liaison Conference that had adopted the *Guidelines for Burmese Independence*, Navy Minister Shimada Shigetarō and Greater East Asia Minister Aoki Kazuo insisted that, since Burma had been under its own control from the beginning except for military and diplomatic affairs, Japan should leave the management of the country to Burma's own initiative as much as possible. Aoki, in particular, criticized the attitude of the Army General Staff Office, which persisted with the argument that Burma should remain under Japan's full control. In response, the chief of the Army General Staff Office retorted that, should operational needs increase twice over or even more, there would be a limit to how much could be delegated to authorities of the Burmese side. This exchange invited Prime Minister Tōjō to attempt to mediate between the two sides. Tōjō interjected, "The arguments by both sides are reasonable. It should be noted that the *Guidelines for Burmese Independence* was drafted with due consideration

---

29 *Biruma dokuritsu shidō yōkō ni kansuru jakkan no kōsatsu*, February 24, 1943, Ministry of Foreign Affairs Political Affairs Bureau.
30 *Nichimen kan no kihonteki kankei ni tsuite* [On the Basic Relations between Japan and Burma], March 3, 1943 (Ministry of Foreign Affairs Document A7.0.0.9-39-2).

to the two sides." In fact, Tōjō added,

> The proposal submitted by the Imperial Army stationed in Burma had argued for tougher control of Burma. But thanks to special consideration of the Imperial Army headquarters, particularly the supreme general command, that stance has been much mitigated to the current position.

This mediation by Tōjō revealed that the inter-ministerial strife at the government center was relatively subdued compared to the conflict between army headquarters and the locally stationed army. Even after the adoption of the *Guidelines for Burmese Independence*, the confrontation over Japan's control of Burma continued between the two. The locally stationed army's proposal on the *Guidelines for Burmese Independence*[31] included such demands as (1) Burma should consult in advance with Japan about diplomacy during wartime; (2) after the termination of the war, Japanese troops should be permitted to remain in Burma temporarily from the viewpoint of the defense of the Greater East Asia Co-Prosperity Sphere and Burma; (3) Japanese troops should be allowed to use military bases as the need arise and construct related facilities; and (4) the commander-in-chief of the Imperial Japanese Army stationed in Burma should provide necessary guidance on the troop strength of the Burmese army and navy, their composition, as well as their training. These demands were so high-handed that concerned ministries and agencies had to remind the military that these stipulations should be for the military's ears only and should not be disclosed to the Burmese side.[32]

The basic policy for Burma's independence and the basic structure of independent Burma were communicated to Ba Maw when he visited Japan in March 1943. A preparatory committee for Burma's independence was set

---

31 *Biruma dokuritsu shidō yōkō ni motozuku Biruma dokuritsu shidō yōryō (an)*, previously cited.
32 Ibid., (attached memorandum).

up in May with Ba Maw as its chairman. On August 1, a state establishment conference was organized with the preparatory committee as its nucleus. This body immediately adopted the declaration of independence and the state organic law. Simultaneously, military administration by the Imperial Japanese Army was to be terminated.

(3) Foreign Minister Shigemitsu and the Japan-Burma Treaty

At the same time, deliberation on an alliance treaty between Japan and Burma was carried out, based on the *Guidelines for Burmese Independence*, as were preparations for independence. The proposal on the treaty submitted by the Ministry of Foreign Affairs under Foreign Minister Shigemitsu set out the following three principles: (1) the treaty should include an article on Burma's cooperation with Japan's efforts to bring the war to a successful conclusion; (2) the treaty should be a unitary treaty with no accompanying agreement with separate articles on postwar cooperative relations between the two countries; and (3) the treaty should be an alliance treaty between equals.[33] The proposal from the Army Ministry also stipulated that the treaty should include an article on Burma's cooperation with Japan. A second stipulation by the Army Ministry was that Burma's cooperation with Japanese troops and the commanding authority in wartime should abide by a military agreement to be signed by the commander-in-chief of the Imperial Japanese Army stationed in Burma. While details on the actual deliberations remain unknown, the Foreign Ministry's third principle became the preamble of the finalized alliance treaty, while the gist of the Army Ministry's second stipulation was also adopted. Although, as the Foreign Ministry had proposed, no accompanying military agreement was attached to the treaty, it was decided that a detailed secret military accord and agreements on details were to be concluded separately between the Burmese government and the

---

33 *Biruma dokuritsu ni kansuru jōyaku teiketsu yōryō (an)* [Proposed Outline on the Conclusion of the Treaty Related to Independence of Burma] (June 5, 1943), ibid.

commander-in-chief of the Imperial Japanese Army stationed in Burma.

Meanwhile, Foreign Minister Shigemitsu attempted to insert a clause in Article 2 of the treaty. Article 2 read: "Both parties should closely cooperate with one another in the joint construction [of the Co-Prosperity Sphere] for the prosperity of Greater East Asia." Shigemitsu wanted to add a clause saying, "For this reason, when necessary, representatives of the two governments should conduct necessary consultations with representatives of other Greater East Asia governments." Shigemitsu's proposition was turned down on the grounds that "it harbors the same philosophy as the League of Nations." Shigemitsu also attempted to insert the wording "mutual benefits among the Greater East Asian countries" in the preamble because, he said, "It fits well with the emotion of smaller and weaker peoples." This suggestion was also rejected.[34]

The final draft of the treaty set forth in its preamble "mutual respect of autonomy and independence" and "joint establishment of Greater East Asia." Article 3 stipulated that details should be left to consultations between relevant officials of the two countries. Other than that, the treaty was a simple affair with, essentially, just the following two articles.

Article 1

Burma and Japan "should render exhaustive military, political, and economic cooperation in order to successfully conclude the Greater East Asia War."

Article 2

Burma and Japan "should closely cooperate with one another in the joint establishment [of the Co-Prosperity Sphere] for the autonomous development and rise of Greater East Asia, aiming at the co-prosperity of countries in Greater East Asia."

---

34 Sugiyama Memorandum vol. 2, pp. 440–441.

Toward the end of July 1943, when the draft treaty was consolidated, Kuboi Yoshimichi, councilor of the Privy Council, called the attention of participants in the Council's Board of Review to Article 3 of the Japan-Burma Treaty. Article 3 stated that "details on the implementation of the treaty shall be decided by consultations between the two countries." Kuboi reminded participants, "If the mandate on consultations is broadly interpreted, any matter can be subject to consultation under the pretext of military, political, and economic cooperation." In response, Prime Minister Tōjō simply said, "You should trust your government in deciding which details are to be subject to consultation," without any reference to the military agreement.[35] Kuboi's apprehension was materialized in the secret military accord signed by the commander-in-chief of the Imperial Japanese Army in Burma and the Burmese government.

The secret military accord signed on August 1, 1943, was packed with a wide range of stipulations, including that (1) the Burmese military should be under the command of the Imperial Japanese Army "in order to complete a joint defense"; (2) in terms of agreements on details, the Burmese government should provide all the necessary facilities to the Japanese troops (including tax exemption or tax reduction on military supplies and gratuitous provision of lands and buildings); (3) Burmese police organizations should, as the need arises, come under Japanese military police command; (4) Burmese local officials should be placed under the Japanese troops' command when such defense need arises; and (5) telecommunications and mails should be censored by the Japanese military police.[36]

---

35 Fukai Eigo, *Sūmitsuin jūyō giji oboegaki* [Memorandum on Important Agenda of the Privy Council], Iwanami Shoten, 1953, p. 301.
36 Ōta, op cit., pp. 413–414.

4. Independence of the Philippines

(1) Manchukuo Model

Discussions among related officials on the basic policy for the guidelines on independence for the Philippines commenced in April 1943. Deliberations followed the *Guidelines for Burmese Independence* that had been consolidated in March 1943. The proposed outline compiled toward the end of April set out the basic policy as "consolidation of material and moral preparedness to cooperate in the successful completion of the Greater East Asia War." And it clearly stated that the price that the Philippines paid for permission for independence would be its full military cooperation with Japan's war effort, full provision of all necessary facilities, and immediate declaration of war against the United States and Britain.[37]

The Liaison Conference adopted the *Hitō dokuritsu shidō yōkō* (Guidelines for the Independence of the Philippines) on June 26, 1943. It turned out to be almost identical to the *Guidelines for Burmese Independence*, including the attached *Shin-Hitō oyobi Nippi-kan no kihon keitai* (Basic Form of the Philippines and Japan-Philippines Relations, revised). A few important differences, however, deserve mention.

The first difference is found in the portion of the *Outline of Independence Guidance for the Philippines* that stated that "[Japan should] renew and strengthen the incumbent Philippine administrative body and guide it toward becoming the core of the government after independence." This seems to indicate that Japan had to recognize the Philippines' political maturity as an independent nation. The corresponding portion in the *Guidelines for Burmese Independence* was in its attached document on "composition of the state," which stipulated that "While the national polity and the form of government are to be decided by the Burmese people's initiative as much as

---

37 *Hitō dokuritsu shidō yōkō (dai 2-an)* [Guidelines for the Independence of the Philippines (second proposal)] (April 26), Ministry of Foreign Affairs Document A7.0.0.9-46.

possible, the form of government shall be a leadership state." In the case of Burma, the leadership state was to be set up around Ba Maw, administrative and judiciary branches would be placed under a "state representative" (i.e., Ba Maw), and the state representative would temporarily serve concurrently as the chief of administration. It was also stipulated that legislative power would be exercised by the state representative. In the case of the *Outline of Independence Guidance for the Philippines*, a leadership state was not envisioned, out of respect for the country's political autonomy. Nevertheless, local leaders in the Philippines in those days pointed out that, at least in wartime, a presidential dictatorship was desirable. This coincided with the ulterior motive of the Japanese side.[38]

The *Outline of Independence Guidance for the Philippines* also declared that the wishes and intentions of the Philippine side regarding the national polity and management of state affairs should be respected. This meant that, at least officially, the traditional separation of the three branches of government would be tolerated. Still, when it came to legislative power, the *Outline of Independence Guidance for the Philippines* stipulated that, "when parliament is established, care should be taken so that its nature should not obstruct prompt operations of the administrative branch," thus betraying Japan's intention to suppress supremacy of the parliament over the administrative authority. The same can be said regarding Burma, because the *Guidelines for Burmese Independence* stipulated that "when parliament was to be instituted, caution should be paid so that it should not obstruct prompt execution of state affairs by the state representative"—and this was supplemented with the additional remark "that political parties' divisiveness and conflict should be restricted." This goes to show that, out of the fear of emergence of parliamentary governments in Burma and the Philippines, a Manchukuo-type government, which imposed strong restriction on the legislative authority, was envisioned in these two countries.

---

38 Takeuchi Tatsuji, op cit., "Manila Diary," p. 248, pp. 257–258.

In terms of political parties in these countries, a political party supportive of the state resembling the Manshūkoku Kyōwakai (Concordia Association) was considered most appropriate for Burma and the Philippines. A research committee on the Philippines had been studying a scenario for contributing to the government of the archipelago under the leadership of Murata Shōzō, supreme adviser to the Japanese Fourteenth Army (stationed in the Philippines). The committee stressed in its September 1943 report the importance of the existence of a national organization like the Shin-Hitō Hōshidan (Association for Service to the New Philippines, or Kalibapi in Tagalog) over a representative system or a political party system, both of which are based on local interests and/or personal interests. The committee pointed out that "the Kalibapi spirit and the significance of this national association for service must also permeate the parliament."[39] Kalibapi at one time boasted more than 800 branches, and it is believed that adult membership exceeded 1.5 million people. But according to Jose Laurel, president of the Second Philippine Republic (a Japanese puppet state from 1943 to 1945), the Kalibapi was "a copy of Japan's Taisei Yokusankai [Imperial Rule Assistance Association] and the Manshūkoku Kyōwakai whose purpose was to dissolve all the political parties and integrate the entire Philippine population into a single totalitarian party."[40] The Kalibapi was, thus, not a mere political organization. It was a national organization mandated to "implement measures to consolidate the Greater East Asia Co-Prosperity Sphere, following the policies of the Imperial Japanese military."[41]

The second difference between the *Outline of Independence Guidance for the Philippines* and the *Guidelines for Burmese Independence* was

---

39 *Hitō chōsa hōkoku dai 2-hen: Tōchi* [Survey Report on the Philippines Second Edition: Governance], September 1943, vol. 1, p. 138.

40 Jose P. Laurel, *War Memoirs of Dr. Jose P. Laurel* (Manila: Jose P. Laurel Memorial Foundation, 1962), p. 40.

41 Ōta Kōki, "Nippon gunseika no Firipin to Shin-Hitō Hōshidan (Kalibapi)" [The Philippines under the Japanese Military Administration and Shin-Hitō Hōshidan (Kalibapi)], *Seiji Keizai Shigaku*, no. 145, p. 37.

the timing of the declaration of war against Britain and the US. Burma was instructed to declare war when it became independent. The *Outline of Independence Guidance for the Philippines* only stipulated that the Philippines "should declare war against the US and Britain at a proper moment." As explained earlier, the original wording of the gist of the outline shared among pertinent officials required immediate participation in the war by the Philippines as a condition for independence. The Imperial Japanese Army was particularly adamant on this point. But when the Philippine side strongly resisted the condition for immediate participation in the war, which could turn the Filipino people's hearts away from Japan and worsen the state of security and public order, the Japanese government had to concur. Nevertheless, this did not mean that the Imperial Army gave up on the idea of immediate participation in the war by the Philippines, as reflected in the adoption of the expression "at a proper moment."[42]

With the *Outline of Independence Guidance for the Philippines* as its roadmap, the Hitō Dokuritsu Junbi Iinkai (Philippine Independence Preparatory Committee) was formed with Jose Laurel as its chairman under the command of the Imperial Japanese Army stationed in the Philippines. The first task the committee tackled was to draft a constitution. The locally stationed Imperial Japanese Army (particularly its Inspectorate Military Administration) insisted on the inclusion of two principles in the draft constitution. First, that the Philippines would be a member of the Greater East Asia Co-Prosperity Sphere should be clearly stated. And second, that supremacy of the administrative authority should be confirmed. The original draft of the constitution, in fact, had followed these principles. The subcommittee of the Philippine Independence Preparatory Committee working on a second draft of the constitution, however, was highly critical of the original

---

42 *Hitō dokuritsu shidō yōkō (dai 2-an)*. As Camilo Osias, a member of the Philippine Independence Preparatory Committee, once stated, because Filipinos were apprehensive of being forced to fight in the Solomon Islands campaign under the Japanese command immediately upon gaining independence, participation in the war upon establishment of independence was the most feared prospect for the Philippine side. (See Takeuchi Tatsuji, op cit., "Manila Diary," p. 277.)

draft and revised it. The subcommittee's draft excluded all the references to Japan and the Greater East Asia Co-Prosperity Sphere in order to maintain the integrity of the Philippines as an independent republic and included new references to the principle of the people's sovereignty. The Japanese side was informed that subcommittee members had voiced the opinion that "if the new Philippines government comes to be criticized as a puppet of Japan, it would fail to win people's hearts. Therefore, in order to win public support, the new constitution should be as close to the old one as possible." Thus, the drafting process took the form of revising the Commonwealth Constitution rather than constructing a new constitution along the lines of Japanese preferences.[43]

Some at the center of the Imperial Army were not happy about the new constitution of the Philippines being drafted with deference to the old Commonwealth Constitution. The War Guidance Office, for instance, took issue with Article 8 of the draft constitution on preservation and use of natural resources and criticized the effective banning of entry of foreigners in the endeavor. Also, Article 11 on postwar coordination of property rights and other privileges that Japan had obtained during the war was criticized as a tactic to win Japan over by taking advantage of the Philippines' position as a small and weak nation—which was totally against the scheme of the Greater East Asia Co-Prosperity Sphere.[44]

Rōyama Masamichi, prominent member of a seven-member research commission, organized under the chairmanship of Murata Shōzō, supreme

---

43 "Hitō shinkenpō ni kansuru iken" [Views on the New Constitution of the Philippines] verbally explained on August 24 by Colonel Utsunomiya, director of general affairs of the Philippines Inspectorate Military Administration, at the officers' meeting hall. (Ministry of Foreign Affairs Document A7.0.0.9-46). "Brief Summary of the Activities of Manuel Roxas during the Japanese Occupation," in Mauro Garcia, ed., *Documents on the Japanese Occupation of the Philippines*. (Manila: The Philippine Historical Association, 1965), pp. 247–248. A detailed account on the process of constitutional drafting as seen by an officer in charge of the Inspectorate Military Administration is given by The Yomiuri Shimbunsha, ed., *Shōwashi no Tennō: 11* [The Emperor in Shōwa History: 11], Yomiuri Shimbunsha, 1970, pp. 219–226, which seems to exaggerate the involvement of the Japanese side.
44 *Kimitsu sensō nisshi*, entry of August 31, 1943.

adviser to the Imperial Japanese Army stationed in the Philippines, observed in the Hitō Chōsa Iinkai (Report of the Research Commission on the Philippines) that leaders of the Philippines showed a strong inclination to prioritize establishment of the country's own defense capabilities throughout the drafting process, no matter what the outcome of the war might be. Rōyama further observed, "They tried to demonstrate, on the one hand, that they have been forced to collaborate with the Japanese invaders, while stressing, on the other hand, that they have at the same time maintained the minimum level of cooperation with Japan."[45] The determination of these Filipino leaders to maintain their independence also found expression in the Philippine-Japanese Treaty of Alliance.

The new constitution was adopted by the Kalibapi convention in early September 1943. Jose Laurel was elected the first president of the newly independent Philippines by the election held in accordance with the stipulations of the new constitution.

As preparations for independence advanced, the Japanese government invited leaders of the new Philippines, including Laurel, Jorge Vargas (chairman of the Japanese-sponsored Philippine Executive Commission), and Benigno Aquino Sr. (director-general of Kalibapi), to Japan in early October 1943 to once again give instructions on the spirit of the *Outline of Independence Guidance for the Philippines*.

(2) Drafting Process of the Philippine-Japanese Treaty of Alliance

Around the time a new Philippine constitution was being drafted, the drafting process for the Philippine-Japanese Treaty of Alliance was also underway. In mid-August 1943, at a meeting of officials in charge of related ministries,

---

45 *Hitō dokuritsu shidō yōkō ni motozuku genchi shidō no fukuan (dai 3-an)* [Proposal on Local Guidance Based on the Outline of Independence Guidance for the Philippines (third proposal)] (Ministry of Foreign Affairs Document A7.0.0.9-46), a memo attached to *Nippi dōmei jōyaku ni kansuru uchiawase no ken* [On the Consultation on the Philippine-Japanese Treaty of Alliance] (October 2, Treaty Division I).

the following points were agreed on regarding the treaty between Japan and the Philippines: (1) both countries should cooperate in every possible way to bring the Greater East Asia War to a successful conclusion, (2) the two countries should cooperate closely with one another for the joint construction of Greater East Asia, and (3) the treaty should contain no accompanying agreement. It was also agreed that such matters as the provision of facilities, offices and posts in charge of facilities, and the wartime command authority belonged in a secret military accord. Proposals submitted by various ministries were carefully studied before the final draft of the Philippine-Japanese Treaty of Alliance was decided on October 5. Without going into the details of the deliberations, suffice it to say that the final draft strongly reflected the proposal from the Imperial Army. As Matsudaira Kōto, director of the Foreign Ministry's treaty division I, pointed out, "With a subsequent strong push from the supreme general command, it was decided that the first proposal [submitted by the Imperial Army] was to be adopted."[46]

Article 1 of the Philippine-Japanese Treaty of Alliance draft stressed mutual respect of sovereignty and territories, which had been included in the preamble in the case of the Japan-Burma Treaty. It is conjectured that this stipulation was made into a separate article in consideration of the stronger anti-Japanese sentiment in the Philippines than in Burma.

Article 2 mirrored the content of the treaty with Burma, but in consideration of domestic politics in the Philippines, it was stipulated that "the signees of the treaty should render close political, economic, and military cooperation in order to bring the Greater East Asia War to a successful conclusion," inserting the passage on military cooperation after that on political and economic cooperation. This sequence—that is, military cooperation following political and economic cooperation—was also applied in the Treaty of Alliance between Thailand and Japan, betraying Japan's concern about people's attitudes toward Japan in these two countries, which

---

46 Takeuchi Tatsuji, op cit., p. 272.

were not necessarily conducive to military cooperation with Japan. Also, the wording "exhaustive . . . cooperation" used in the treaty with Burma was avoided, again, out of consideration of domestic politics in the Philippines. Article 3 stipulated that Japan and the Philippines "should closely cooperate with one another in a joint establishment of Greater East Asia," as in the treaty with Burma. Phrasing regarding "to secure stability" and "exhaustive cooperation" found in the Treaty of Alliance between Tokyo and Nanjing were also removed from this Article 3.[47]

The document on the understandings attached to the draft treaty defined the mode of cooperation in the military field "in order to bring the Greater East Asia War to a successful conclusion." It stipulated that the Philippines should provide all the necessary facilities and that the two countries should render mutual cooperation to the defense of the Philippines.

Meanwhile, Laurel's party visited Japan toward the end of September 1943 and was shocked to hear Prime Minister Tōjō request participation in the war against Britain and the United States. The delegation demanded the following revisions to the draft treaty.

First, the Philippine side requested that the wording "in order to bring the Greater East Asia War to a successful conclusion" in Article 2 and the attached understandings be changed to "for the establishment of Greater East Asia." This would make Article 3 redundant, and Article 3 could thus be eliminated. Their second request was to change "to the defense of the Philippines" in the attached understandings to "for the maintenance of the Philippines' territorial integrity and defense of its independence." The first request was intended to avoid the risk of the Philippines being forced to immediately participate in the war against Britain and the United States, while the second was intended to reduce the risk of the Philippine military being forced to join the Japanese military in overseas campaigns.

---

47 "Nipponkoku 'Firipin' koku kan dōmei jōyakuan setsumei" [Explanation on the Draft of an Alliance Treaty between Japan and the Philippines] (Liaison Conference on October 5, 1943) (Ministry of Foreign Affairs Document A7.0.0.9-46).

The Philippine side warned that both of these two stipulations would, if not amended, provoke the Philippine parliament and Filipino sentiment. Consequently, "Laurel's government would lose its public mandate and become a regime without popular support."[48]

The Imperial Japanese Army in the Philippines was supportive of these amendments because they would "strengthen Laurel's domestic leadership, which would work to the benefit of the Japanese side."[49] But the central command of the Imperial Army would not give in, retorting that cooperation with the war effort had already been included in the list of instructions conveyed to the Philippine side earlier. If the request from the Philippine side was granted, the Imperial Army was afraid that the Japanese military would be called upon to remain in the Philippines not only during wartime but even after the end of the war and provide facilities to the Philippines side. The Army General Staff Office, in particular, complained that the expeditionary force to the Philippines had been too accommodative of requests from the Philippine side and took the stance that "it would not be permissible for Japan to treat the Philippines alone as an exception from other countries in Greater East Asia."[50]

Still, the Philippine side showed uncompromising resistance, to which the Japan side had to respond by revising some portions of the accompanying understandings out of fear of weakening the domestic standing of the newly formed Laurel government, which might pose an obstacle to the Philippines' participation in the war against the United States and Britain. More concretely, "to the defense of the Philippines" in the accompanying understandings was changed to "to protect the Philippines' territory and independence," making it clearer that the purpose of military actions by the Japanese troops was to defend the territory and independence of the

---

48 *Kimitsu sensō nisshi*, entry of October 1, 1943.
49 October 9 telegram from the expeditionary force in the Philippines addressed to the Army Ministry (Ministry of Foreign Affairs Document A7.0.0.9-46).
50 *Kimitsu sensō nisshi*, entry of October 11, 1943.

Philippines. Even the Treaty Bureau of the Ministry of Foreign Affairs had to admit that the original stipulation had been "inadequate in terms of military responses compared to the traditional notion of an alliance."[51]

During deliberations at the Privy Council on the draft treaty, whether the accompanying understandings were really necessary or not was questioned. The Tōjō government admitted that it was not necessary from the Japanese viewpoint when Article 2 would be sufficient, but that it was included out of consideration for the position of Laurel, who had argued that immediate participation in the war would be impossible. The government explained that "the document of understandings settled the issue between the two sides because it would make it easier for Laurel to govern the country."[52] In fact, it was about one year later in September 1944, after US troops started attacking Manila, that the Laurel government declared war against the US.

Compared with the Treaty of Alliance between Japan and Burma, the Philippine-Japanese Treaty of Alliance had the following two distinctive features. One was that the portion of the treaty that corresponded to the preamble of the treaty with Burma became a separate article—that is, Article 1: Both countries should eternally maintain neighborly friendship based on the respect of mutual sovereignty and territories. A second feature was that in Article 2 of the treaty with the Philippines, which corresponded to Article 1 of the treaty with Burma (that both countries "should render exhaustive military, political, and economic cooperation"), "military" was placed after "political and economic" and "exhaustive" was struck out. These changes indicate that, as in the case of the drafting of the new constitution of the Philippines, the Japanese side had to show due consideration to the Philippine side's irreversible aspiration for independence and its refusal to cooperate militarily with Japan. And the Philippine side had to pay the price

---

51 Draft telegram by the Treaty Bureau dated October 5, 1943 (Ministry of Foreign Affairs Document A7.0.0.9-46).
52 *Sūmitsuin shinsa iinkai gijiroku* [Minutes of the Privy Council's Board of Review] (October 20, 1943).

for this consideration in the form of the secret military accord of October 14, 1943.

Taking into consideration the Philippine side's hesitation to declare war against Britain and the US, the Imperial Army's first proposal stipulated that "Whether the Philippines declares war against Britain and the US or not, the Philippines should render all kinds of cooperation for the successful conclusion of the Greater East Asia War." The Imperial Army also proposed that military operations and tactics, command of the police forces, as well as troop strength and composition of the Philippine military should be placed under control of the Japanese military and, even during peace time, the Philippine side would be obliged to offer lands and buildings to Japanese troops. Moreover, the draft accord included stipulations on such matters as management of facilities, use of transportation and telecommunication, contribution of military supplies, application of court martial, dispatch of advisers to military, security, and financial sectors, and regulations on industrial sectors (key mines, weaponry, military supplies manufacturing, and shipbuilding, etc.)—all of which ended up being adopted.[53] The War Guidance Office entered in its diary that, as a result of putting basic matters and detailed stipulations all together in one sentence, "it appears that the sentence is packed with too many stringent demands."[54]

5. Conclusion: Significance of Granting Independence

The Political Affairs Bureau of the Ministry of Foreign Affairs entered into a document the following concern about the *Guidelines for Burmese Independence*, which was being drafted at that time:

---

53 *Hitō dokuritsu shidō yōkō ni motozuku genchi shidō no fukuan* [Proposal on Local Guidance Based on Outline of Independence Guidance for the Philippines] (Imperial Japanese Army proposal on August 27, 1943) (Ministry of Foreign Affairs Document A7.0.0.9-46).
54 *Kimitsu sensō nisshi*, entry of October 3, 1943.

Although the most important thing is for the measures of the Empire of Japan to be starkly different from those under British colonial rule, it appears from the drafted *Guidelines for Burmese Independence* that our Empire would grab substantive authority over almost all of the important affairs, including military, economic, political, diplomatic, transportation, telecommunication, and currency affairs. This is against the expectation of the Burmese people, who have longed for independence, and it would not be entirely improbable that they would harbor apprehension and dissatisfaction toward Japan.[55]

In other words, the Foreign Ministry expressed apprehension that the spread of the plans for "Burma under Japan's full control" over all sectors of the country, as opposed to the official slogan of "establishment of Burma for the Burmese people" could leave the Burmese feeling both "apprehension and dissatisfaction." It was certainly ironical that when the "Burma under Japan's full control" persisted, approval of Burma's independence would lead to more anti-Japanese sentiment among the Burmese people.

As many studies have pointed out, these apprehensions of the Ministry of Foreign Affairs ended up becoming the reality. Yet despite these apprehensions, it appears that the independence of Burma had an effect of nurturing an awareness of self-determination among the Burmese people. For instance, Burma's New Order Plan that the Burmese government compiled in 1944, while arguing for persistence with the stance to eliminate Japan's interference as much as possible and reject the return of Britain as the colonial ruler, stated that, "The Burmese people primarily understand that independence means possession of tangible authority and power to carry out their own agenda with their own method and legitimacy." The final memorandum on this plan adopted the Japan-initiated

---

55 *Biruma dokuritsu shidō yokō ni kansuru jakkan no kōsatsu* (Political Affairs Bureau, Ministry of Foreign Affairs, February 24, 1943).

slogan of "Burma for Burmese people" as their own assertion of the self-determination that they had nurtured.[56]

In the case of the Philippines, too, as its strategic importance increased, the situation grew increasingly conspicuous. Murata Shōzō, Japanese ambassador to the Philippines, deplored, "The way we treat the independent Philippines is no different from the military administration days, and our military still regards the Philippines as an occupied territory to such an extent that there is no room for us to refute the accusation of the local government being a puppet government."[57] The high-handed and discriminatory attitude of Japanese military officials toward Filipino citizens, in particular, violated the Philippine-Japanese Treaty of Alliance as well as the Greater East Asia Joint Declaration, as Foreign Secretary Claro M. Recto complained in a personal letter to Wachi Yōji of the Inspectorate Military Administration.[58] In this way, these two documents became worthless in the eyes of the people of the Philippines.

Touching on Philippine-Japanese relations in a regular cabinet meeting in August 1944, President Laurel stated that it should be the stipulations in the Philippine-Japanese Treaty of Alliance as well as the Greater East Asia Joint Declaration that governed the bilateral relations. What was called for on the part of the republic's government was not unilateral "absorption" but collaboration.[59] This goes to show that collaborators with Japan, including Laurel, concluded that Japan's granting of independence for the Philippines, as well as the alliance treaty, along with the Greater East Asia

---

56 W.H. Elsbree, op cit., pp. 28–30. On Burma's New Order Plan, Ba Maw pointed out, "We must substantiate our independence. . . . That is the right way of looking at ourselves in the service of state which has not only won its independence out of a war but also fighting a war to save that independence from the fires of a world configuration. . . ." (Ba Maw, *Breakthrough in Burma*, New Haven: Yale University Press, 1968., pp. 280–281).

57 Murata Shōzō, *Hitō nikki* [Philippines Diary], Hara Shobō, 1970, p. 78.

58 Mauro Garcia, ed., op cit., pp. 109–124.

59 *Hitō dokuritsu jisshi no jiki oyobi taiyō ni kansuru ichi-kōsatsu* [An Observation on the Timing and the Form of Independence of the Philippines] (May 6, 1943) (Ministry of Foreign Affairs Document A7.0.0.9-46).

Joint Declaration, encouraged the Philippine people's self-initiated efforts to attain independence.

From the outset, though, the Ministry of Foreign Affairs did not necessarily have high hopes for the impact of approval regarding Philippine independence on the promotion of the Philippines' cooperation with the war effort. Instead, the ministry had been trying to find a symbolic meaning in Japan's conduct that could clarify Japan's position in the Greater East Asia Co-Prosperity Sphere.

According to a document compiled by the General Affairs Bureau of the Ministry of Greater East Asia in May 1943, the significance of Japan's granting independence for the Philippines was to clarify that there was no aggressive intention in Japan's war purpose, while the significance of the Philippine-Japanese Treaty of Alliance lay in "demonstrating the outline of the postwar world management envisioned by the Empire of Japan."[60] Kotaki Akira, Imperial Japanese Army military administrator (former director of Section IV, Trade Bureau of the Ministry of Foreign Affairs), who had taken part in the negotiations on the alliance treaty in Manila, sent his own view on the significance of granting independence for the Philippines to the home office. Kotaki wrote, "Its effect would be immense as a foundation of future maneuvering aimed at the United States to lead the Greater East Asia War to a splendid conclusion."[61]

This indicates that, even at that point, there still remained a view which positively evaluated Japan's approval of Philippine independence from the perspective of maneuvering vis-à-vis the United States—just as there had been an argument for it at the beginning of the war. And it was one of the objectives of Foreign Minister Shigemitsu's new Greater East Asia policy to spread this thinking beyond the Philippines to issues of independence for

60 Mauro Garcia, ed., op cit., p. 105.
61 "Hitō dokuritsu mondai no toriatsukai ni kansuru ken (shiken)" [Matters Related to Handling of the Independence of the Philippines (personal view)] (Ministry of Foreign Affairs Document A7.0.0.9-46).

other areas, which will be discussed in detail in ensuing chapters.

While Japan's approval of independence for the Philippines did indeed stimulate American concerns about the issue, the American reaction was the complete opposite of what Japan had hoped for. In response to Prime Minister Tōjō's speech at the eighty-first session of the Imperial Diet on January 28, 1943, which disclosed the Tōjō government's policy to tolerate Philippine independence, Manuel Quezon (President of the Commonwealth of the Philippines), in exile in the United States, issued a counter-announcement on February 20. Quezon said he was apprehensive of the "harmful influence" of the speech on the Philippine people. US President Franklin Roosevelt, in his August 12 radio speech intending to catalyze the Philippine people's resistance against Japan, gave the Quezon government in exile effectively the same position as other independent sovereigns and remarked that, "The Republic of the Philippines shall be confirmed the moment the enemy country Japan is destroyed." Against the background of the establishment of the Republic of the Philippines, or its independence being prepared under Laurel, Roosevelt referred to the possibility of approving the country's independence immediately upon Japan's surrender—without waiting for July 1946, as stipulated by the Tydings-McDuffie Act. On September 24, the US Congress passed a resolution to amend the said act and immediately recognize Philippine independence. Roosevelt was about to give his approval to this legislation.[62] Fearing the possibility that this act of Congress and the president might be misunderstood as US recognition of the puppet government supported by an invader nation, "[Secretary of War Henry] Stimson among others managed, however, to prevent so precipitous a move. . . . and in the event the legislation was amended so that it referred

---

62 US Department of State, *Foreign Relations of the United States, 1943*, vol. 3 (US GPO, 1963), pp. 1097–1098 (*FRUS*, henceforth); *The New York Times* (August 13, 1943); F4230/462/23/ F0371/35954 (British foreign service document).

only to independence being given 'as soon as feasible.'" [63]

Incidentally, the US Congress's resolution on the immediate independence of the Philippines also cast a shadow on the Japanese decision regarding the schedule for Philippine independence. In fact, the September 15, 1943, Liaison Conference decided to move forward the independence day, which had originally been set for October 15. The date was changed back to the original date after a reprimand from the chief of staff of the 14th Army and Murata Shōzō, who found the decision "a bit too frivolous."[64]

On the occasion of the establishment of the Republic of the Philippines on October 14, 1943, US Secretary of State Cordell Hull sent his statement to diplomats from neutral countries, stating that the establishment of an illegitimate republic would not harm relations between the US government and the Commonwealth of the Philippines. Hull also called the neutral countries' attention to his analysis that the main objective of Japan was to use the Philippines and its natural resources for its military purposes.[65] US President Roosevelt also issued a similar statement on October 22.[66]

Throughout these developments concerning approval of independence or autonomy, among the Allies it was the US that showed the most conspicuous reaction to the Philippine case. Because the US Congress's decision on immediate recognition of the Commonwealth of the Philippines was expected to have a certain impact on Britain's handling of India's independence issue, which had been deadlocked,[67] US interest in the decolonization issue became increasingly amplified as warfare intensified.

---

63 *FRUS*, 1943, vol. 3, pp. 1103–1104; Christopher Thorne, *Allies of a Kind: The United States, Britain, and the War against Japan, 1941–1945* (New York: Oxford University Press, 1978), p. 368; Christopher Thorne, *Issue of War: States, Societies, and the Far Eastern Conflict of 1941–1945* (New York: Oxford University Press, 1985), pp. 190–191.

64 *Kimitsu sensō nisshi*, entry of September 29 and 30, 1943.

65 *FRUS*, op cit., pp. 1105–1106.

66 US Department of State, *Bulletin*, Oct. 23, 1943, p. 274.

67 *FRUS*, op cit., pp. 1102–1103.

Chapter 6

*Outlines for
the Political Guidance of
Greater East Asia
and the Japan-China
Alliance Treaty*

1. Foreign Minister Shigemitsu and the *Outlines for the Political Guidance of Greater East Asia*

(1) New Sino-Japanese Treaty and the Greater East Asia International Organization Scheme

In a sudden and unexpected cabinet reshuffling on April 20, 1943, Prime Minister Tōjō Hideki appointed Ambassador to China Shigemitsu Mamoru as minister for foreign affairs and Foreign Minister Tani Masayuki as ambassador to China. To persuade Shigemitsu to accept the appointment, Tōjō told Shigemitsu:

> Honestly speaking, His Majesty is immensely worried about the implementation of the new China policy as well as Japan's foreign policy in general. I wish to put all of myself into the task this time and that is why I am requesting you to join the team. The cabinet reshuffle this time is mainly to welcome you to my cabinet.[1]

As Shigemitsu had praised Prime Minister Tōjō's handling of foreign policy, from the new China policy through the Greater East Asia Conference, saying, "He has been doing a truly excellent job,"[2] Tōjō would not hesitate to render his full support to the realization of Shigemitsu's ideas.

Immediately before joining the Tōjō cabinet, Shigemitsu submitted to Foreign Minister Tani a fully revised version of the *Nikka kihon jōyaku* (Japan-China Basic Relations Treaty) under the title of "On Promotion of the New China Policy." It argued that, if the new China policy were to be thoroughly pursued, "It would not be entirely impossible to settle the China Incident [Second Sino-Japanese War]," and proposed reexamination of "treatment of North China as a special region" in order to respect the independence

---

1 Itō Takashi et al., eds., *Shigemitsu Mamoru shuki* [Shigemitsu Mamoru Private Memoir], Chūō Kōronsha, 1986, p. 323.
2 Ibid., p. 423.

of the Nationalist government in Nanjing and promote unification of China's domestic politics.[3] From China's viewpoint, the Japan-China Basic Relations Treaty of 1940 was "mostly an unequal treaty which imposed burdens only on the Chinese side and treated China like Japan's colony."[4]

From Shigemitsu's viewpoint, the revised treaty should not only stipulate equal and mutually beneficial relations between Japan and China but also contain content that could provide a foundation for establishment of relations with other peoples in Greater East Asia. The prototype of this scheme for a new treaty was found in a document titled *Nikka dōmei jōyaku an: Daitōa Kenshō* (Proposed Sino-Japanese Alliance Treaty: Greater East Asia Charter),[5] which Shigemitsu submitted to Foreign Minister Tani Masayuki immediately before he himself became the foreign minister. This document consisted of sections on objectives of the treaty and notes of caution on the conclusion of the treaty. The gist of the two sections was summarized as follows:

Objectives of the Treaty

(1) This treaty aims at promoting voluntary cooperation and solidarity among countries of Greater East Asia by expressing our righteous war aims.

(2) This treaty aims at sealing off the enemy's maneuvers by proclaiming our vision of a postwar world and, at the same time, allowing our side to utilize weapons confiscated from the enemy.

---

3 "Taishi shinhōshin no suishin ni tsuite" [On Promotion of the New China Policy]. (A note was attached saying this was handed by Ambassador Shigemitsu to Foreign Minister Tani on April 16, 1943) (Ministry of Foreign Affairs Document A7.0.0.9-41-2). "Daitōa sensō kankei ikken" [Matters Related to the Greater East Asia War], "Chūka Minkoku Kokumin Seifu sansen kankei" [Matters Related to War Participation of the Nationalist Government in China], and "Nikka dōmei jōyaku kankei" [Matters Related to the Japan-China Alliance Treaty].

4 "Kihon jōyaku ni kansuru mondai" [Problems Related to the Basic Treaty], April 14, 1943 (Ministry of Foreign Affairs Document A7.0.0.9-41-2).

5 "Nikka dōmei jōyaku an/Daitōa Kenshō" [Proposed Sino-Japanese Alliance Treaty: Greater East Asia Charter], written on April 18, 1943 (Ministry of Foreign Affairs Document A7.0.0.9-41-2).

(3) (omitted)

(4) This treaty, which constitutes the substance of the proposed Charter on Greater East Asia Construction, aims to establish a joint organization among countries of Greater East Asia (Japan, Manchukuo, China, Thailand, Burma, and the Philippines) that gathers, either regularly or as needs arise, in Tokyo or other locations to discuss mutual collaboration in waging the war as well as cooperation in peacetime.

(5) Therefore, it is prudent for us to uphold the official stance of equality among members and thoroughly refrain from proclaiming that the Empire of Japan is the leader of the Greater East Asia Co-Prosperity Sphere, even though in actuality that is indeed the case.

Notes related to the Conclusion of the Treaty

(1) The inaugural meeting of leaders of Japan and China should be convened in Tokyo at the earliest possible date after the signing of the treaty.

(2) After conclusion of this treaty, a similar treaty should be concluded with Manchukuo and Thailand.

(3) A similar treaty should also be concluded with Burma and the Philippines, through which an international organization in the Greater East Asia region should be established.

In short, it was Shigemitsu's vision to, first, pronounce the Daitōa Kikō Kensetsu Kenshō (Charter on Greater East Asia Construction), based on a more appropriate philosophy of solidarity among countries in Greater East Asia, as Japan's war purpose. Subsequently, following this philosophy, a joint organization (or an international organization) for mutual consultation among member countries should be established, which would be the pillar of wartime and postwar cooperation. Shigemitsu further stressed that the substance of the Daitōa Kikō Kensetsu Kenshō (Charter on Greater East Asia Establishment) on Japan's war aims should allow Japan to utilize tools such as the Atlantic Charter of Britain and the United States or "seal off the enemy's maneuvers," as asserted in the second item of the list of objectives of the treaty. In other words, Shigemitsu appeared to be highly conscious of the Atlantic Charter (of August 1941) as the manifesto of the Allies' war aims.

According to Shigemitsu, although Britain and the United States in the Atlantic Charter posed as protectors of small ethnic groups and small nations, advocating the restoration of freedom for these people, in actuality, such small nations were victimized, as exemplified by the Baltic countries and Poland, which had been trampled on and broken up by the Soviet Union, one of the Allied countries. And the promise to restore freedom was nothing but an empty promise issued as a means for waging the war. In contrast, Shigemitsu argued,

> [Japan] has assumed the position of granting and protecting the freedom of small nations, at least those in Asia. It must be the Empire of Japan's state policy to grant independence and freedom to the Chinese people, help Thai people accomplish their national desire, grant independence for the Burmese and Philippine people, and satisfy the wishes of other peoples in East Asia.[6]

Shigemitsu had been convinced that, in terms of mutual relations among independent nations in Greater East Asia, Japan, Manchukuo, and China should not be given a superior position. Thus, Shigemitsu devised the idea of setting up a Daitōa Kokusai Kikō (Greater East Asia International Organization), as it was to be called, with the participation of countries in Greater East Asia as equal partners. And the first step toward this goal was a full revision of the Japan-China Basic Relations Treaty, which was the core of the new China policy, and conclusion of a new alliance treaty with China. The new treaty to be concluded should not only stipulate construction of mutually beneficiary relations but should also include the following three

---

6 *Shigemitsu Mamoru shuki*, p. 329.

items: (1) military cooperation during wartime; (2) withdrawal of Japanese troops after the end of the war; and (3) establishment of a consultative organization on the waging of war and postwar cooperation that included countries of Greater East Asia.

It was envisioned that conclusion of a Japan-China alliance treaty containing these three stipulations should be followed by similar treaties with Thailand, Manchukuo, the Philippines, and Burma.[7] The draft of the Japan-China Alliance Treaty prepared by the Foreign Ministry and circulated among relevant ministries in early June 1943 contained all the above elements plus the following two articles which presupposed the future establishment the Greater East Asia International Organization. Article 3 stipulated that "representatives of the two countries should meet regularly and as the need arises in a conference among representatives of the governments of the Greater East Asia region." Article 4 proposed that "At the conference stipulated by Article 3, consultations should be conducted on various matters related to autonomous development based on equality and mutual benefit among countries in Greater East Asia, the maintenance of peace and stability, joint defense, and joint construction of Greater East Asia."[8]

(2) Drafting of the *Outlines for the Political Guidance of Greater East Asia*

In his first report to the emperor on May 13, 1943, Shigemitsu stressed the significance of the new China policy. It is reported that the emperor gave his firm approval and repeatedly said, "Although I am aware there have been a variety of criticisms related to the China issue, you should not lend your ears to them and dauntlessly carry out the new policy thoroughly."[9] Encouraged by the emperor's words, Shigemitsu forged ahead with a full revision of

---

7　Ministry of Foreign Affairs document A7.0.0.9-3-3 (documents donated by Ambassador Miyake Kijirō).

8　"Nikka dōmei jōyaku-an" [Japan-China Alliance Treaty Draft], June 11, 1943 (Ministry of Foreign Affairs Document A7.0.0.9-41-2).

9　*Shigemitsu Mamoru shuki*, pp. 338–339.

the Japan-China Basic Relations Treaty. His immediate goals were to make sure that the *Daitōa seiryaku shidō taikō* (Outlines for the Political Guidance of Greater East Asia), which the prime minister had promoted explicitly, stipulated the conclusion of a new alliance treaty with China and to gain a foothold toward realizing his own Greater East Asia International Organization scheme.

On May 12, 1943, immediately after he returned from the Philippines, Prime Minister Tōjō presented his own outline of external measures that Japan should take by November of that year to directors-general of the Army Affairs and Naval Affairs Bureaus of the Imperial Army and Navy as well as to the chief cabinet secretary. Tōjō instructed everyone to study his outline. Although the content of Tōjō's proposal has not been disclosed, it is known that it became the genesis of the *Outlines for the Political Guidance of Greater East Asia*, which was adopted by the Imperial Council toward the end of May.[10]

In the background were the following two necessities. The first was the need to consolidate political solidarity among peoples of the occupied territories in Asia in preparation for (1) the full-scale counteroffensive from Britain and the US in the Asia Pacific region predicted to be launched in the fall of 1943 and (2) the anticipated conclusion of the war in Europe.[11] The second was the convening of a Greater East Asia Conference, to which leaders of the occupied territories would be invited. The conference was scheduled for the latter half of November, in anticipation of the launching of

---

10 Itō Takashi et al., eds., *Tōjō naikaku sōri daijin kimitsu kiroku* [Confidential Records of Prime Minister Tōjō], University of Tokyo Press, 1990, entry of May 12, 1943. (*Tōjō kimitsu kiroku*, henceforth)

11 According to Tōjō's explanation, it was judged that, "The global situation could change considerably, depending on the outcome of the German-Soviet war. It is predicted that the prospect of this war should be confirmed around November this year. It is also predicted that around the same time the counteroffensive by Britain and the United States would grow increasingly fiercer." (*Kinbara Setsuzō gyōmu nisshi tekiroku* [Excerpts from Kinbara Setsuzō's Diary], entry of the division directors' conference on June 17, 1943, a collection at the National Defense Medical College.) A similar assessment is found in *Sugiyama memo, ge*, p. 412 among others.

a full-scale counteroffensive by the Allies around that time.

As introduced in chapter 3, the Greater East Asia Conference was originally proposed by Privy Councilor Ishii Kikujirō as an alternative to the establishment of the Ministry of Greater East Asia. Although Prime Minister Tōjō did not withdraw his proposal on establishment of the new ministry, he recognized the concern about "establishment of the said ministry's having adverse effects on the minds of the peoples of partner countries" and promised that his cabinet would study the feasibility of the proposed conference.[12] Therefore, it seems appropriate to say that it was the fear that establishment of the Ministry of Greater East Asia could make peoples in the occupied Asian territories turn away from Japan, which, eventually, would pose an obstacle to Japan's war effort, that led to the convening of the Greater East Asia Conference. For Tōjō, this conference, which would bring together all the leaders from the occupied Asian territories, would be an opportunity to respond to the issue of how to secure cooperation in the war effort from peoples in the occupied territories. Behind this was the perception that, in order to induce peoples in Asian occupied territories to cooperate with the war effort, it would be effective to show their leaders appropriate consideration and guarantee their positions, because that would allow those leaders to grasp the hearts of their people.[13]

In any event, the *Outlines for the Political Guidance of Greater East Asia* was adopted by the Imperial Council less than half a month after it was

---

12 Fukai Eigo, *Sūmitsuin jūyō giji oboegaki* [Memorandum on Important Agenda of the Privy Council], Iwanami Shoten, 1953, pp. 264–265. According to Satō Kenryō, director-general of the Bureau of Military Affairs of the Army Ministry, Prime Minister Tōjō and himself learned from Wachi Takaji, chief of staff of the Imperial Japanese Army 14th Army in the Philippines cum Inspectorate Military Administration, that presidential candidate Jose Laurel had proposed a Greater East Asia Economic Conference, which inspired them to come up with the idea of a Greater East Asia Conference. (See Satō Kenryō, *Daitōa sensō kaikoroku* [Memoir on Greater East Asia War], Tokuma Shoten, 1966, pp. 313–314.) Even if that was indeed the case, it does not negate the connection with the Ministry of Greater East Asia issue.

13 It was stated on p. 500 of the previously cited *Tōjō kimitsu kiroku* that "We must think of ways to convince Thai people that Luang Pibulsonggram is indeed great so that he can win the Thai people's hearts."

first proposed. This speedy development owed a lot to Prime Minister Tōjō's strong drive. The details of deliberations on the Outlines are unknown, but it is known that the first point of contention during the deliberations was whether or not it was wise to expedite measures to allow independence for the occupied territories and regional people's political participation in order to secure the cooperation of Asian peoples in the war effort and against the British and American counteroffensive. The Ministry of Foreign Affairs took a positive position toward promoting these measures. On the other hand, the Imperial Japanese Navy, according to the *Kimitsu sensō nisshi*, argued most strongly that those measures were premature.[14] The Imperial Navy took the position that these measures would obstruct Japanese military operations and hamper the acquisition of national defense resources. But the Army Ministry as well as the Foreign Ministry insisted that these measures should be decoupled from military operations.[15] As discussed elsewhere in this book, the Imperial Navy had a tendency to perceive the Pacific War from the angle of survival and self-defense, which made it consistently critical not only of the *Outlines for the Political Guidance of Greater East Asia* but also of tolerance for autonomy and independence for the Asian occupied territories in general, which it saw as potential hindrances to resource procurement, self-subsistence of locally stationed Japanese troops, and obtainment of national defense resources. To the navy, these measures were a possible cause for the obstruction of military operations.

The confrontation between these two positions is believed to have been fierce. The Foreign Ministry, with the help of Prime Minister Tōjō, obtained a small victory by gaining confirmation of the promotion of independence for Burma and the Philippines (even though tolerance for the independence of these two territories had already been firmly established) and stipulation of the signing of the proposed alliance treaty with China. In terms of

---

14 *Kimitsu sensō nisshi*, entry of May 26, 1943.
15 Sanbō Honbu, ed., *Sugiyama memo, jō* [Sugiyama Memorandum, vol. 1], Hara Shobō, 1989, pp. 403–406.

realization of Shigemitsu's plan, however, no progress was made.

During the May 26 Liaison Conference, Shigemitsu made two proposals. The first was for the "conclusion of pro forma alliance treaties on an equal footing" with Manchukuo, China, the Philippines, and Burma. This proposal departed from the fixed notion of a unity among Japan, Manchukuo, and China. The second proposal was that Japan should refrain from inserting an article in the outlines that would allow Japanese troops to remain stationed locally after the war (or, in other words, permanently), while freedom of action should be guaranteed to Japanese troops so they could take necessary militarily actions during wartime.[16] Hata Hikosaburō, deputy chief of staff, pushed back on the first proposal, saying, "I am afraid it would be unacceptable to China and Manchukuo if Burma and the Philippines were treated equally with them. An alliance treaty should be concluded between Japan and each of these countries individually." All present agreed. Thus, Shigemitsu's first proposal was rejected.[17]

As for the second proposal, it was the position of the supreme command of the Imperial Japanese Army and Navy that the issue of troop withdrawal after the end of the war should not be referred to and that treaties with the countries in Greater East Asia should be concluded individually but not along a uniform format. The army and navy also found "a joint consultative mechanism among Greater East Asian countries similar to the League of Nations or the Pan-American Conference not appropriate." The Ministry of Greater East Asia took a similar position.[18] Thus, the scheme for conclusion of an alliance treaty on equal footing with independent countries in Greater East Asia, including Manchukuo and Thailand, which stipulated the withdrawal of Japanese troops after the end of the war suffered a setback.

But the more important point of contention was revision of the

---

16 *Shigemitsu Mamoru shuki*, pp. 356–366.
17 *Sugiyama memo, ge*, p. 404.
18 Ministry of Foreign Affairs document A7.0.0.9-3-3 (documents donated by Ambassador Miyake Kijirō).

Japan-China Basic Relations Treaty, the number one goal for Shigemitsu. The debate at the Liaison Conference concluded with Shigemitsu succeeding in making the *Outlines for the Political Guidance of Greater East Asia* stipulate revision of the said treaty, as he had hoped for. Because treaty revision was closely linked with the "full peace" issue, including that with the Chongqing government, however, it remained a constant irritant to the Japanese leaders. Eventually, the treaty revision issue developed into a major problem that almost toppled the decision on the *Outlines for the Political Guidance of Greater East Asia*. This issue will be discussed later in this volume.

(3) Setback of the Scheme for the Greater East Asia International Organization and the Greater East Asia Conference

The third and last point of contention was concerned with the positioning of the proposed Greater East Asia Conference. As introduced earlier, Prime Minister Tōjō envisioned this conference solely from the viewpoint of preventing a change of heart toward Japan by peoples of the occupied territories by bringing together leaders of the Greater East Asian countries. In Shigemitsu's perception, however, the Greater East Asia Conference was the first step toward establishment of the Greater East Asia International Organization. In his mind, the Greater East Asia International Organization would be a forum for Greater East Asian countries to discuss their common goal of "stability and prosperity of East Asia" from an equal and mutually beneficiary standpoint, "either regularly or as the need arises." And the first declaration from the conference (the Greater East Asia Joint Declaration) should "clarify the meaning of joint defense militarily, stress mainly an equal partnership politically, and stipulate open and mutually beneficial economic relations."[19] In other words, it was Shigemitsu's plan to institutionalize the

---

19 Itō Takashi et al., eds., *Zoku Shigemitsu Mamoru shuki* [Shigemitsu Mamoru Private Memoir, vol. 2], Chūō Kōronsha, 1988, pp. 156–166.

Greater East Asia Conference as a Greater East Asian international organization and promulgate a "Charter of Greater East Asia Establishment" (a "Greater East Asia Declaration") as the philosophy and operational principle of this joint consultative body.[20]

Thus, keeping in mind the scheme he had instructed the Foreign Ministry to study, Shigemitsu proposed at a subsequent Liaison Conference that "On the occasion of the Greater East Asia Conference, a Greater East Asia Alliance (i.e., Greater East Asia International Organization) should be launched instead of issuing a mere declaration."[21] Among the ideas being studied at the Foreign Ministry was a proposal compiled by the first division of its Political Affairs Bureau. Envisioning the Greater East Asia Conference as a permanent consultative body composed of Japan, China, Manchukuo, Thailand, Burma, the Philippines, and French Indochina, this division proposed establishment of such annex organizations as the Greater East Asia Court of Arbitration, the Greater East Asia Police Force, and the Greater East Asia Liquidation Bank (to stabilize currency and trade). As for diplomatic relations, the proposal stated, "Each Greater East Asia country should conclude no treaty with any outside country against the interest of Greater East Asia. When such a treaty is concluded, it could be invalidated by the Greater East Asia Conference." In economics, the proposal envisioned a powerful regional organization that could impose on member countries such partial transfer of sovereignties as reduction of tariffs on trade with non–Great East Asia countries, in compliance with the reciprocity principle, as well as the mandatory deposit of one-third of tariff incomes to the proposed Greater East Asia Liquidation Bank. The explanatory document

---

20 This scheme is also found in the "Nikka dōmei jōyaku an: Daitōa Kenshō." Also see *Shigemitsu Mamoru shuki*, pp. 328–330 and p. 407. In the former document, Greater East Asia International Organization was used, while other documents used Daitōa Kyōgi Kikō (Greater East Asia Consultative Organization) or Daitōa Renmei (Greater East Asia League). All of them being substantively the same, the present author has decided to use Greater East Asia International Organization to represent all of these terms.

21 *Sugiyama memo, ge*, p. 404.

attached to this proposal stated, "The Greater East Asia declaration would be aimed at creating a variety of federation of states. It would be necessary to organize this federation of states like the United States in North America. . . . It would be proper to make it a community of common destiny stronger than an alliance."[22]

Shigemitsu's scheme also found expression in proposals on alliance treaties with individual countries. The Japan-China Alliance Treaty aside, the proposal on the new alliance treaty with Thailand stipulated that (1) the existing alliance treaty between Japan and Thailand of December 1941 should be abolished; (2) both countries should respect mutual autonomy and independence and construct relations of equality and mutual benefit; and (3) the two countries should contribute to mutual development as members of the Greater East Asia International Organization.[23] In the preamble of the newly drafted treaty with Manchukuo, it also proclaimed that both governments would "respect autonomy and independence" of countries in Greater East Asia and proposed that representatives of the two governments should convene meetings with representatives of other Greater East Asian governments regularly or as the need arose in order to discuss the postwar withdrawal of Japanese troops and Japan-Manchukuo cooperation measures.[24] From Shigemitsu's standpoint, it was only natural to treat both Thailand and Manchukuo as equal members of the Greater East Asia International Organization.

As mentioned, however, the High Command of the Imperial Army

---

22 *Daitōa kyōdō sengen-an* [Proposal on the Greater East Asia Joint Declaration] (June 4, 1943, Division I, Political Affairs Bureau) and *Daitōa kaigi unyō gensoku-an* [Proposal on Operational Principles of the Greater East Asia Conference] (June 5, 1943) included in the microfilm *Japan Ministry of Foreign Affairs, 1868–1945* WT Series, Reel 52, a collection of the National Diet Library.

23 *Nichi-Tai shin dōmei jōyaku teiketsu ni tsuite* [On Conclusion of a New Japan-Thailand Alliance Treaty] (April 29, 1943), Ministry of Foreign Affairs Documents A7.0.0.9-41-2 and A7.0.0.9-3-3 (documents donated by Ambassador Miyake Kijirō).

24 *Nichi-Man kyōtei-an* [Proposed Japan-Manchukuo Treaty] (Jō-1, June 2, 1943) (Ministry of Foreign Affairs Documents A7.0.0.9-41-2).

and Navy as well as the Ministry of Greater East Asia had maintained the position that it would be improper to establish a League of Nations–like consultative body and, consequently, Shigemitsu's proposal was flatly dismissed. Although it appears that Shigemitsu did not subsequently withdraw his proposal, he failed to secure supporters. Ambassador to Thailand Tsubogami Teiji, when asked to review the newly proposed alliance treaty between Japan and Thailand, asserted, "Because this proposal is likely to unnecessarily provoke apprehension among the ever so suspicious Thai people, it would be difficult to convince them of its virtue." Also, the Japanese military stationed in Thailand was reluctant to withdraw after the war. In the end, it was decided that "this proposal should be put on hold as an ideal goal for the future."[25] The proposal on the Japan-Manchukuo treaty was also killed by opposition from the supreme general command of the Imperial Army and Navy, the Ministry of Greater East Asia, and many other related government bureaus, particularly because of its inclusion of articles on postwar withdrawal of Japanese troops and the establishment of a Greater East Asia organization.[26]

Shigemitsu's persistence with the establishment of the Greater East Asia International Organization also influenced deliberations on the proposal for an alliance treaty with Burma; those deliberations had become deadlocked. Shigemitsu attempted to submit his proposal directly to the Liaison Conference, bypassing the bureaucrats. On July 15, 1943, in order to realize "Shigemitsu's philosophy," the Foreign Ministry decided to resort to the radical measure of terminating deliberations on a draft treaty with Burma by appropriate government officials and immediately convening a Liaison

---

25 Ministry of Foreign Affairs Documents A7.0.0.9-3-3 (documents donated by Ambassador Miyake Kijirō). On Shigemitsu's scheme to conclude a new alliance treaty with Thailand, something similar to the Japan-China alliance treaty, which was opposed by the locally stationed Japanese military as well as Ambassador Tsubogami, see E. Bruce Reynolds, *Thailand and Japan's Southern Advance, 1940–1945* (London: Macmillan Press, 1994), p. 155.
26 *Kimitsu sensō nisshi*, entry of July 15, 1943.

Conference in which the foreign minister presented his view for approval.[27] Although officials in the relevant government bureaus resisted, Shigemitsu himself engaged in drafting the treaty and succeeded in submitting it to the July 19 Liaison Conference. Article 2 stipulated:

> Both countries [i.e., Japan and Burma] should cooperate with one another for the joint establishment to promote autonomous development and the rise of Greater East Asia to enhance mutual benefit of countries in Greater East Asia. And, when necessary, representatives of the two governments should conduct necessary consultations with representatives of other Greater East Asian governments.

Thus, the necessity for the Greater East Asia International Organization was implied. However, the Liaison conference rejected the stipulation following "And, when necessary" on the grounds that "it contained a philosophy somewhat reminiscent of the League of Nations."[28] And the term "mutual benefit," which Shigemitsu had used to represent the wishes of "smaller and weaker peoples" was replaced by the phrasing "coexistence and mutual co-prosperity."

At this point, the scheme for a Greater East Asia International Organization was substantively buried. Still, Shigemitsu never gave up on his idea to make the Greater East Asia Joint Declaration harbor the substance of a Charter of Greater East Asia Construction based on independence, equality, and mutual benefit.

---

27 Ibid.
28 *Sugiyama memo, ge*, pp. 440–441.

2. Bottleneck in the *Outlines for the Political Guidance of Greater East Asia*

(1) *Outlines for the Political Guidance of Greater East Asia* and Malaya and Indonesia

The *Outlines for the Political Guidance of Greater East Asia* defined Malaya, Java, Sumatra, Borneo, and Celebes as "territories of the Empire of Japan" and decided on the continuation of military administration in these territories for the time being, along with the incremental allowance of political participation in accordance with the local people's cultural standards. Inclusion of measures for political participation can be interpreted as the Japanese way of providing consideration of the petition from Mohammad Hatta, an independence activist who later became the first vice president of Indonesia. Hatta made his request to Greater East Asia Minister Aoki Kazuo when the latter visited Jakarta on May 2, 1943. Hatta told Aoki that Indonesia, which had been unified as a single nation, possessed a "strong will and determination to obtain a glorious position as a nation" and candidly pleaded for the future destiny of Indonesia to be "stipulated in the *Outlines for the Political Guidance of Greater East Asia*."[29] The form of political participation for Indonesians was disclosed by Prime Minister Tōjō immediately after adoption of the *Outlines for the Political Guidance of Greater East Asia*. Political participation for Indonesians was limited to local residents' participation in such advisory organs as the Chūō Sangiin (Central Advisory Council). By no means was this a presupposition of independence for Indonesia.[30]

It can be imagined that to make Indonesia and Malaya, which combined

---

29 Waseda Daigaku Ōkuma Kinen Shakai Kagaku Kenkyūsho, ed., *Indoneshia ni okeru Nippon gunsei no kenkyū* [Study of Japanese Military Administration in Indonesia], Kinokuniya Shoten, 1958, p. 353 and 399.

30 Prime Minister Tōjō's speech at the 82nd Extraordinary Imperial Diet Session on June 16, 1943. His statement was nothing but a reward to Indonesia, from which Japan requested the cooperation of people in Java, which was a key point of the southern defenses for Japan. See *Indoneshia ni okeru Nippon gunsei no kenkyū*, pp. 353–354, and Harry J. Benda, ed., *Japanese Military Administration in Indonesia: Selected Documents* (Yale University Press, 1965), pp. 49–52, 253–259.

included more than 60 percent of the entire population of Southeast Asia, "territories of the Empire of Japan" and to continue military administration there for the time being was unacceptable to Shigemitsu and the Ministry of Foreign Affairs. There is no undisputable evidence, however, that the Foreign Ministry or Shigemitsu himself explicitly insisted on independence or autonomy for Malaya and Indonesia during the deliberations on the *Outlines for the Political Guidance of Greater East Asia.*

As introduced in chapter 1, in his explanation on the compromise solution for the Ministry of Greater East Asia issue, Foreign Minister Tōgō Shigenori argued that, by making regions that were necessary for the war effort and the defense of Greater East Asia the territories under direct control of the Empire of Japan and expanding the principle of respect of sovereignty in other territories, Japan could avoid the pitfall of the British and American-style "colonialism." One may wonder whether Shigemitsu and the Foreign Ministry concluded that the territorializing of Indonesia and Malaya did not contradict the above logic. The document on the process surrounding the measures on Indonesia being decided for inclusion in the *Outlines for the Political Guidance of Greater East Asia* (compiled in 1944) disclosed that, "It had already been debated in some corners in those days whether such an inflexible notion as 'any region that was not independent was Japan's territory' was really valid."[31] This document, thus, implied that this sort of notion had been upheld in those days and, at the same time, some in the Japanese government actually opposed the decision to make those regions territories of the Empire. At the eighty-second Extraordinary Session of the Imperial Diet on June 17, Prime Minister Tōjō announced that his government "intended to take successive measures within this fiscal year to promote local residents' political participation in accordance with their respective cultural standards" in Malaya, Sumatra, Java, Borneo, and Celebes. Behind this announcement seemed to be the rebuttals against the

---

31 *Indoneshia ni okeru Nippon gunsei no kenkyū*, p. 561.

black-or-white policy toward the occupied territories—that is, either an area would be the Empire's territory or an independent country.

In accordance with Tōjō's announcement, measures to promote political participation of the locals were taken in Indonesia (particularly in Java), which presupposed the future granting of independence. An advisory council system modeled after the Executive Councils of the British colonial rule was also established on the provincial and city levels in Malaya from the summer of 1943 through the beginning of 1944. These bodies were merely nominal advisory councils and their existence did not presuppose the future granting of independence.[32]

In the process of the occupation of Malaya as well as during its military administration, Japan almost entirely relied on cooperation from the Malay population rather than the more economically predominant ethnic Chinese population. Consequently, such anti-Japanese struggle as the Malayan Communist Party had to be borne chiefly by the ethnic Chinese residents. It is well known that measures taken toward the ethnic Chinese residents were repressive and draconian in nature—unlike the relatively moderate policy line in the central government, particularly under the Watanabe Wataru military administration from March 1942 through March 1943. Toward the end of the Watanabe military administration, the economic ability and experience of the ethnic Chinese residents became an essential element of self-support indispensable to the Japanese forces stationed locally, resulting in some modifications of the governance. More full-fledged policy changes were witnessed under the succeeding Fujimura Masuzō administration.

The *Outlines for the Political Guidance of Greater East Asia* was adopted soon after the beginning of the Fujimura military administration. In accordance with the position taken in the *Outlines*, the central Japanese government started studying the possibility of ethnic Chinese people's

---

32 Itagaki Yoichi, "Some Aspects of the Japanese Policy for Malaya under the Occupation, with Special Reference to Nationalism," in K.G. Tregonning, ed., *Papers on Malayan History, Singapore* (University of Singapore, 1962), pp. 257–260.

participation in central and local politics in Malaya along with Indians and Malays. The hardliners in the Imperial Army, however, remained passive regarding the political participation of Chinese residents. As a result of mutual compromise between the hardliners and advocates of this measure, a policy was adopted stipulating that the political participation of Chinese residents should be decided in accordance with the progress of political participation by Malays and Indians. But following the last few months of 1943, the percentage of Chinese residents appointed to the central and local advisory councils had grown larger than those of other ethnic groups, partly because appointments were made in proportion to the total population. While some highly evaluated the advisory council system, which invited participation of such ethnic minorities as Indians as more than a mere appeasement measure toward the Chinese population and as something which aimed at the unification of ethnic groups in Malaya, the system was not perceived as a step toward expansion of various ethnic groups' political participation.

Meanwhile, Colonel Hamada Hiroshi, who had long been assigned to China previously, was appointed as director of general affairs of the 29th Army's Inspectorate Military Administration. Hamada carried out various measures sharing similar goals with the new China policy one after another. Hamada's measures to fully utilize the ability of Chinese residents in the economic realm included a revision of discriminatory treatment against Chinese residents, provision of the same degree of citizenship to Chinese residents as the Japanese had enjoyed, and the guarantee of free economic activities and no interference to Chinese residents. These measures, however, hardly had any impact on the economy of Malaya.[33]

It appears that it was after the Greater East Asian Conference that the Ministry of Foreign Affairs started engaging in Malaya's independence

---

33 The above explanation owes a lot to the study of Akashi Yōji. See Akashi Yōji, "Japanese Policy towards the Malayan Chinese 1941–1945," in *Journal of Southeast Asian Studies*, vol. 1 no. 2 (September 1970), pp. 61–89, and Cheah Boon Kheng, "The Social Impact of the Japanese Occupation in Malaya (1942–1945)," in Alfred W. McCoy, ed., *Southeast Asia under Japanese Occupation* (Yale University, Southeast Asia Studies Monograph Series no. 22, 1980), pp. 91–124.

issue. The working paper compiled by the ministry's Political Affairs Bureau toward the end of the Fujimura military administration pointed out that even the Inspectorate Military Administration had recognized the need to change its "Malay-centrism" and that the Chinese residents could not and should not be ignored when independence was granted to Malaya. Finding it difficult to grant independence for Malaya, because, the working paper said, "Malaya has not formed an independent nation in the modern sense of the term," the working paper presented three options for handling Malaya: (1) to annex Malaya into China except for the region that should belong to Thailand; (2) to let a collaborative government organization of the Chinese and the Malay, ethnic majorities in Malaya, govern Malaya; or (3) to make Malaya a part of the "Indonesian Federation." What was particularly noteworthy in this document was the fact that the idea of an Indonesian Federation, which would include Malaya, still remained a subject of study at this point. The Foreign Ministry documents related to this issue, however, concluded that it would be difficult to grant independence for the Indonesian Federation in light of the absence of a political entity that could be a central driving force of independence, to which subsequent political management could be entrusted. The dearth of a prominent independence activist, a decline in the sultan's influence, and the lukewarm reception by independence activists of the Indonesian Federation scheme were factors contributing to this situation.[34]

---

34 "'Marai' dokuritsu mondai" [Malay Independence Issue] (Political Affairs Bureau, Ministry of Foreign Affairs), and "'Marai' dokuritsu no kanōsei ni tsuite" [On the Possibility of Malaya Becoming Independent] (Ministry of Foreign Affairs, February 20, 1945) (part of The Wason Collection, Cornell University). The above two documents are also introduced in Okabe Makio and Otabe Yūji, "'Tōa kyōeiken' no shihai to mujun" [Rule of East Asia Co-Prosperity Sphere and Contradictions], Fujiwara Akira and Imai Seiichi, eds., *15-nen sensōshi 3* [History of the 15-Year War: Part 3], Aoki Shoten, 1989.

(2) Position of Thailand and French Indochina

After all was said and done, the *Outlines for the Political Guidance of Greater East Asia* stipulated the status quo for the two unoccupied territories in Greater East Asia—Thailand and French Indochina. While the *Outlines* confirmed Japan's endorsement of the revanchist policy over four northern states of the Sultanates (i.e., Kelantan, Trengganu, Perlis, and Kedah) in order to powerfully support the Pibul Songgram government, the proposal for a new alliance treaty with Thailand based on Shigemitsu's scheme never resurfaced. As for French Indochina, although there was some discussion about separation and independence of Annam, that was judged to be infeasible. In the end, the policy proposed by the Army Ministry—to refrain from granting independence and, instead, put Jean Decoux, governor-general of French-Indochina, under tight control and make him collaborate with Japan without cutting him off from the French home government—was adopted, thus allowing the status quo in French Indochina.[35]

As is well known, both Thailand and French Indochina had been in delicate positions in international relations, while strong nationalistic pressure for independence had accumulated inside both regions. Therefore, Japan had multiple reasons for worry when it came down to winning the hearts of the people. At an in-house lecture at the Society for Promotion of Japanese Diplomacy in 1943, Iwata Reitetsu, director of information at the Japanese embassy in Thailand, touched on the Thai people's nationalism and strong desire for remaining independent and pointed out,

> Japan guarantees Thailand's independence by Article 2 of the Japan-Thailand Alliance Treaty, which has allowed Thailand to promote nationalism with Japan's interference in domestic affairs completely shut off. At this point, it should be said that the alliance treaty has been

---

[35] Minutes of the June 17 division directors' conference and June 30 senior division officials' conference (*Kinbara Setsuzō gyōmu nisshi tekiroku*).

turned to Thailand's own advantage.[36]

On French Indochina, too, Mizuno Itarō, director of the southern territory office of the Ministry of Greater East Asia, around the same time explained the complicated conditions surrounding the region. Mizuno claimed that it would be almost impossible to turn French people pro-Japan and concluded that French residents in French Indochina "have cooperated with Japan only because they wish to protect French sovereignty in French Indochina and they wish to retain the region as their own colony, regardless of the outcome of the war." Still, Mizuno suggested, if Japan chose to positively respond to the Annam people's aspiration for independence and support their independence movement, it would rub the French residents' cooperative attitude toward Japan the wrong way.[37]

And yet, for Japan, the role of Thailand and French Indochina as bases for logistics and supplies was too important to be overlooked. Both territories had contributed greatly to the supply of food provisions (rice). In Thailand, the Japanese military relied almost entirely on the Thai government for its local military expenditures. Stressing these facts, Iwata remarked,

In my judgment, it is only Thailand and French Indochina in Greater East Asia that have maintained positive account balances vis-à-vis Japan. Of course, Manchukuo also maintains a positive account balance, but one way to look at it is that even its politics have been managed by the Japanese. It can be said that Japan has done everything for Manchukuo, not to mention all the factories there. Compared to Thailand, the form of cooperation with Manchukuo has been considerably different.

---

36 Iwata Reitetsu, "Saikin ni okeru Taikoku no naijō" [Recent Situations in Thailand], March 5, 1944 (a reference material prepared for a special committee of the Society for Promotion of Japanese Diplomacy).
37 Mizuno Itarō, *Saikin no nanpō jijō* [Recent Situations in the Southern Territories] November 28, 1943 (a reference material prepared for a special committee of the Society for Promotion of Japanese Diplomacy).

It can be said that the reality that only Thailand and French Indochina maintained positive account balances in the economy of Greater East Asia was an important reason for Japan to choose the status quo vis-à-vis these two territories.

3. Conclusion of the Japan-China Alliance Treaty

(1) "Same Bed, but Different Dreams" as the Reality of the New China Policy

In the *Outlines for the Political Guidance of Greater East Asia*, Japan set out two important policies vis-à-vis China.

One was conclusion of a new alliance treaty to replace the Japan-China Basic Relations Treaty. As mentioned in chapter 4, the Japanese government leaders, including Minister for Greater East Asia Aoki, were of the view that the new policy toward China should be carried out within the framework of the existing treaties and agreements such as the Basic Relations Treaty. And the *Taishi shori konpon hōshin* (Basic Policy toward China) of December 1942, too, stipulated modification of the existing treaties. It was due to the strong leadership of the Ministry of Foreign Affairs under its new minister, Shigemitsu Mamoru, that the policy was shifted toward conclusion of a new alliance treaty.

Around the time of the appointment of Foreign Minister Shigemitsu, the Foreign Ministry admitted,

When the Japan-China Basic Relations Treaty was concluded, we had been pressed by rivalry with Britain, the United States, and the Soviet Union as well as the pressure to hastily confirm Japan's vested interests in fear of a resurgence of anti-Japanese resistance in China . . . resulting in a treaty which was substandard in places, containing mutually contradictory stipulations.

The Foreign Ministry also argued that, when the existing treaty was to be revised,

> The form of treaty that would violate the sovereignty of the partner nation, like the existing Basic Relations Treaty, should be avoided (which would also apply to treaties with the Philippines and Burma in the southern territory.) Instead, it should be an alliance treaty between equal partners that includes articles of the Basic Relations Treaty that are militarily necessary.[38]

Judging from the position of the alliance treaty with China as a model for alliance treaties with other Greater East Asian countries, the Foreign Ministry could not back away from its policy to conclude a new alliance treaty. Nevertheless, as far as the content of the new treaty was concerned, the Foreign Ministry's argument was not necessarily accepted.

The second important policy vis-à-vis China was recognition of the Nanjing government's political maneuvering toward the Chongqing regime. While it is believed that this decision was adopted thanks to Prime Minister Tōjō's strong recommendation, Tōjō himself was not certain of its success. In response to a question from Hara Yoshimichi, president of the Privy Council, at the Imperial Council, Tōjō replied, "I cannot say that it is promising, but, given the current situation, it is absolutely necessary for successful war guidance."[39] In the judgment of the Imperial Army General Staff Office, although the center of the Chongqing regime had maintained alignment with Britain and the United States, its peripheral elements could be broken down with the use of proper political maneuvers. Therefore, a peace settlement with the Chongqing regime would not be entirely impossible if political

---

38 "Taishi shinhōshin no suishin ni tsuite" [On Promotion of the New China Policy] (April 5, 1943), "Kihon Jōyaku ni kansuru mondai" [Issued Related to the Japan-China Basic Relations Treaty] (April 14, 1943) (Ministry of Foreign Affairs Document A7.0.0.9-41-2).
39 *Sugiyama memo, ge*, p. 409.

engineering was applied at the proper timing in terms of the effects of the new China policy and the situation of the German-Soviet war.[40] However, the Ministry of Foreign Affairs did not share these views. To begin with, the use of the term "political engineering" instead of "peace engineering" signifies a failure to reach an agreement on whether the primary goal should be a peace settlement directly with the Chongqing government or strengthening of the Wang Jingwei government while undermining peripheral segments of the Chongqing government on the side.

It was not that a perfect agreement was reached on the above two new policies among government and military leaders. As for the first policy, partly because circumstances forced work on a new alliance treaty to take the form of revision of the Basic Relations Treaty, the argument for revision of the existing treaty instead of concluding a new treaty resurfaced. Subsequent pursuit of the second policy also continued to be turbulent. Resurrection of political engineering toward the Chongqing government as an option had the effect of bringing to the surface such issues as positioning of the alliance treaty with the Nanjing government and whether the goal of the proposed alliance treaty should be limited to strengthening of the Wang regime or eventual accomplishment of peace with the Chongqing government. And this contention was reflected in the content of the alliance treaty.

(2) Intra-Government Politics over Revision of the Basic Relations Treaty

Full-fledged working-level consultations on the revision of the Basic Relations Treaty commenced among officials in charge from the Ministries of Greater East Asia, Foreign Affairs, Army and Navy, and the Imperial Army General Staff Office in early August 1943. The first issue that was found controversial was the continued presence of Japanese troops in China. Immediately after the May 31, 1943, Imperial Council, the Imperial Army

---

40 Ibid., pp. 415–416.

General Staff Office announced that, "Because no agreement was reached among ministers on measures vis-à-vis China, the first thing to be accomplished is to unify their thinking." The Imperial Army General Staff Office promptly attempted to obtain a consensus within it as follows: "Since the main purpose of the proposed alliance treaty is training and strengthening of the Wang regime, in principle it should not touch on the withdrawal or stationing of Imperial troops."[41]

At the inter-ministerial joint study on August 6, however, the view became predominant that:

... the notions that Chinese people cannot be trusted for the maintenance of public order, given their nature, and that Japan's interests in China cannot be expected to grow without the right for the Japanese troops to remain in China go against the fundamental spirit of concluding a treaty with China with sincerity.

Consequently, it was confirmed that troop stationing for the purposes of anti-Communist defense measures and maintaining the public order as well as the stationing of Army vessel corps in North China and Mengjiang would be abolished, while "no request should be made at all" on the right to maintain troops for anti-Communist defense and the maintenance of public order or in accordance with precedent.[42]

The coordination of specific regions, including North China, Mengjiang, the lower Yangtze region, and islands off South China, was another point of major contention. In accordance with the aim of the new China policy, continuation of these special regions should be denied. In fact, such was confirmed at the August 6, 1943, joint conference. Still, this decision met

---

41 *Kimitsu sensō nisshi*, an entry of May 31, 1943.
42 "Nikka dōmei jōyaku no kaitei mondai ni kansuru kenkyū" [Study on the Issue of Revision of the Japan-China Alliance Treaty] (a joint study on August 6, 1943) (Ministry of Foreign Affairs Document A7.0.0.9-41-2).

fierce criticism from the Japanese military stationed in China. On August 16, the view of the Japanese North China Area Army on revision of the treaty was submitted to the central government in Tokyo with the approval of the China Expeditionary Army. This view argued for continuation of the special regions, citing, (1) "the Japanese military's guidance for anti-Communist defense measures is indispensable because both interest in and the capability for anti-Communist measures on the part of the North China Political Affairs Committee are low"; (2) "North China's rate of contribution to Japan's materials mobilization plan is 40 percent of Japan's total external dependence, occupying an extremely important position"; and (3) "it is, therefore, necessary to substantively maintain the special regions of North China, and it is premature for the Nanjing government to advance into North China."[43] The War Guidance Office criticized this view, saying, "It appears that the Japanese North China Area Army is so preoccupied with immediate realities that it loses sight of the ultimate goal of the settlement of the China Incident. . . . It also appears that its resistance to the new China policy may be at work to no small extent."[44] This view, thus, reveals the persistent criticism of the new China policy among the Japanese military stationed in China.

Encouraged by the reluctance of locally stationed Imperial Navy troops regarding abolishment of the special region designation for the coastal region in South China, the Imperial Japanese Navy also resisted abolition of the special regions. Thus, at the working-level consultation, the Imperial Navy had to insist on attaching a condition exceptionally to the development and use of national defense resources, which had important linkage with Japan's materials mobilization plan. The Imperial Navy suggested this wording: "It should be managed in a way that will contribute to the Empire of Japan into the future."[45] In the end, though, it was decided that this issue (i.e., the

---

43 *Kimitsu sensō nisshi*, an entry on August 16, 1943.
44 Ibid.
45 "Nikka dōmei jōyaku no kaitei mondai ni kansuru kenkyū" [Study on the Issue of Revision of the Japan-China Alliance Treaty], (a joint study on August 6, 1943) (Ministry of Foreign Affairs Document A7.0.0.9-41-2).

development and use of national defense resources) should be managed as a part of general economic cooperation and, as such, Japan would not request preferential treatment or interest after the end of the war in accordance with the principle of mutual cooperation.

Prior to this decision, Wang Jingwei conveyed to the Japanese government a request that, while his government was willing to supply national defense resources to Japan, "it would please us immensely if the Japanese government could amend the article of the treaty so that we, too, can use those resources for China and, also, give special consideration to our wish to develop resources with China's own capital."[46] It appears that the decision at the above joint conference was a response to this request.

Deliberations on revision of the existing treaty were started in late August with the proposal submitted by the Ministry of Greater East Asia (the details of which are unknown) as the central reference. These deliberations yielded a secretariat's proposal encompassing articles on troop withdrawals, cooperation with the construction of Greater East Asia, economic partnership, and neighborly friendship. But the more important issue was the relations between revision of the treaty and measures vis-à-vis the Chongqing government. At the third joint conference on August 24, the Imperial Army General Staff Office questioned whether the aim of the revision was a complete peace that included the Chongqing government.[47] The content of the revision would differ depending on whether it aimed at strengthening the political power of the National government in Nanjing or achieving a complete peace encompassing the Chongqing government. At the consultation based on the secretariat's proposal, it was more or less a general consensus that "the degree of expectation for a complete peace was

---

46 Yasuda Rie, "Daitōa Kaigi to Daitōa Kyōdō Sengen ni tsuite" [On the Greater East Asia Conference and the Greater East Asia Joint Declaration], *Hōgaku Kenkyū*, vol. 63 no. 2, 1990, pp. 386–387.
47 "Nikka Jōyaku kaitei mondai dai 3-kai kaigi yōroku" [Minutes of the Third Conference on the Revision of the Sino-Japanese Treaty], August 24, 1943 (Division II, Political Affairs Bureau, Ministry of Foreign Affairs) (Ministry of Foreign Affairs Document A7.0.0.9-41-2).

extremely low."[48] As the drafting work progressed, however, the expectation for such a peace grew increasingly higher.

For instance, in its written opinion submitted on September 1, 1943, the Research Division of the Ministry of Navy criticized the government's proposal to conclude the treaty exclusively with the Nanjing government and to so announce that. The Research Division commented, "As things stand today, it is hard to imagine that the Chongqing government would give in and join what the Nanjing government announces." The Research Division suggested two options from the viewpoint of "strategic utilization of revision of the treaty": (1) to confidentially negotiate revision of the treaty with the Chongqing government, using it as a tool for maneuvering toward it, and present the revised version co-drafted with the Nanjing government to the former as a souvenir; or (2) to informally present a revised treaty simultaneously to both the Nanjing and Chongqing governments . . . and announce it as a joint product of three governments.[49] This goes to show that there had emerged an excessive expectation on the strategic effect that revision of the treaty would have on the Chongqing government.

The Imperial Army General Staff Office had cautiously refrained from involving itself in the content of the said treaty since mid-August. On August 26, it presented the following views: (1) the principle purpose of the revision should be to have political impact on the Chongqing government; and (2) there is no actual problem in Japanese-Chinese relations that should be coordinated with the help of a new bilateral treaty, and settlement and coordination of various existing bilateral problems should be pursued within the framework of the Japan-China joint declaration.[50] The Japan-China joint declaration referred to here was the January 9, 1943, bilateral (Japan-Nanjing

---

48 Ibid.

49 "Nikka dōmei jōyaku kaitei ni kanshi iken" [An Opinion on Revision of the Japan-China Alliance Treaty] (September 1, 1943) in Doi Akira, ed., *Shōwa shakai keizai shiryō shūsei: Kaigunshō shiryō dai 21-kan* [Compilation of Documents on History of Shōwa Society and Economy: Documents on the Ministry of Navy, vol. 21], Gennandō Shoten, 1994.

50 *Kimitsu sensō nisshi*, entry of August 26 and 28, 1943.

government) joint declaration on war cooperation, which had announced that the two countries would "pursue complete military, political, and economic cooperation" in order to bring the joint war against Britain and the United States to a successful conclusion. It was the Army General Staff Office's position that all of the current problems between Japan and China could be handled within the framework of this declaration and, therefore, the main target of revision of the treaty should be political impact on the Chongqing government. This was a correctional intervention by the Army General Staff Office into the "excessively radical scheme" found in the government's proposal.

The final deliberations among concerned government ministries and bureaus on August 28 adopted the correctional view of the Imperial Army General Staff Office. The essence of the government proposal compiled on August 31 took the form of a preliminary revision of the Japan-China Basic Relations Treaty. The preliminary revision assumed that Sino-Japan relations during the Greater East Asia War were to be regulated by the Japan-China joint declaration, but it left some room for a new treaty, declaring, "a new treaty should be concluded between the Chiang Kai-shek government and the Empire of Japan immediately when the situation requires it."[51]

The main text of the revised treaty in the government proposal stipulated that (1) signees should mutually respect sovereignty and territories in order to perpetually maintain neighborly friendship; (2) signees should mutually cooperate closely for construction of Greater East Asia; and (3) signees should pursue economic partnership based on mutual benefit. Additionally, abolition of Japan's right to station troops in China after the war was stipulated in the attached protocol, while the "coordination of special regions" in North China and other regions was addressed by an exchange of notes (E/N) between the two. During the September 1 deliberation on the government's proposal, the Army General Staff Office expressed its wish that the dispatch

---

51 Ibid., entry of August 28 and September 7, 1943.

of the Japanese military should not be restricted in the event that the Greater East Asia War continued even after the settlement of the China Incident. This was not accepted by the participants.[52]

Characteristic of this government proposal was its assumption that it should be a revision of the existing bilateral Japan-China Basic Relations Treaty, as the Army General Staff Office had hoped for, instead of a new treaty. Also, the government proposal set the principal purpose at political engineering vis-à-vis the Chongqing government rather than the strengthening of the Nanjing government. Because the text of the proposed revision set out such principles as respect of sovereignty, equality and mutual benefit, and neighborly friendship, it was thought to be attractive also to the Chongqing government.

(3) "Shigemitsu Proposal" and Conversion into an Alliance Treaty

It was expected that the final draft of the treaty based on the government's proposal would be agreed on among officials in charge of related government ministries and bureaus by September 7, 1943. But the Ministry of Foreign Affairs announced that Foreign Minister Shigemitsu was adamantly against the government's proposal and submitted its own alliance treaty proposal. The main thrust of this Foreign Ministry proposal, called the Shigemitsu proposal, for the sake of convenience, was to insert the Japan-China joint declaration into the treaty in the form of an article, abolish Japan's right to station military troops in China as long as that would not interfere with military requirements, and abolish matters related to the special regions as long as doing so would not interfere with military needs. The Shigemitsu proposal called for the treaty to include the following: (1) reconfirmation of the Japan-China joint declaration; (2) abolition of the special regions designation and the right to station Japanese troops in China after the end of the war; (3) mutual respect of sovereignty and territories; (4) mutual

---

52 Ibid., entry of September 1 and 7, 1943.

cooperation in construction of Greater East Asia ("and joint defense," which was deleted later); and (5) economic partnership based on mutual benefit.[53]

The Ministry of Greater East Asia reacted sharply to the Shigemitsu proposal. It criticized the Foreign Ministry and Shigemitsu for neglecting to pay adequate attention to the deliberations at the working level up until then. Aside from that point, the argument of the Ministry of Greater East Asia could be summarized in two points: (1) the Shigemitsu proposal was not attractive at all as a condition for a peace settlement from the viewpoint of the Chongqing government, and (2) from the viewpoint of the Nationalist government in Nanjing, the Shigemitsu proposal would only impose the obligation to render war cooperation and worsen its domestic political standing because the treaty offered little, if any, constructive information with which the Wang Jingwei regime could explain postwar relations with Japan to its own people.

The Army General Staff Office (the War Guidance Office in particular) observed that the Shigemitsu proposal was "mainly to manage relations between Japan and China." The Army General Staff Office judged that the gravest problem of the proposal was that "it would give away the final and greatest gift that Japan could offer China under the current situation to the Wang regime, which would be extremely disadvantageous to Japan's engineering vis-à-vis Chiang Kai-shek."[54] In short, in the eyes of the Army General Staff Office, the Shigemitsu proposal paid major attention to current Japan-China relations and did not pay enough attention to the peace settlement with the Chongqing government.

Shigemitsu, however, took a totally opposite view and argued that conclusion of an alliance treaty with the Nationalist government in Nanjing, which Japan had officially recognized, would result in the strengthening of the said government, which would present the precondition for the

---

53 Ibid., entry of September 7, 1943.
54 Ibid.

Chongqing government to agree to a full peace settlement. Shigemitsu's vision can be summarized as follows.

To begin with, the Chongqing government was, in Shigemitsu's judgment, not in the state to join peace negotiations easily and "conventional conspiratorial negotiations would do no good; they would only reveal shortcomings on our side." Shigemitsu argued that "the China issue should be handled by an orthodox method from beginning to end." And this orthodox method entailed, first of all, conclusion of an alliance treaty between equal partners, completely abolishing the existing Basic Relations Treaty, with an explicit reference to the withdrawal of Japanese troops at the end of the war. The next step would be to announce this new treaty to the entire world, proclaiming Japan's "fair and selfless stance," after which the Nanjing government's peace proposal to the Chongqing government would follow. Through these steps, "because the treaty explicitly stipulates that Japan would withdraw its troops [from China], it is expected that the Chongqing government should accomplish peace with the Nanjing government and restore the sovereignty of China." And this peace proposal from the Nanjing government would not be a request for the Chongqing government to surrender but a peace proposal based on equal footing (uniting the central executive committees of the two governments). This way, "even if Chiang Kai-shek refuses to join, the proposed peace process could still obtain the Chinese people's understanding and, politically speaking, the China issue will advance almost to the point of settlement."[55]

At the Liaison Conference on September 18, 1943, the focus of discussions was whether to adopt Shigemitsu's proposal on an alliance treaty or the Ministry of Greater East Asia's argument for revision of the Basic Relations Treaty. Greater East Asia Minister Aoki and Suzuki Teiichi, director-general of the Cabinet Planning Board, insisted that the "mood for peace is intensifying in Chongqing, and President Wang [Jingwei] is willing to engage

---

55 *Shigemitsu Mamoru shuki*, p. 406, *Zoku Shigemitsu Mamoru shuki*, pp. 153–154.

in political engineering. Therefore, [revision of] the Basic Relations Treaty should be preferred over conclusion of an alliance treaty." Shigemitsu refused to back off, arguing, "Because we need the Nationalist government's war cooperation, we should follow the orthodox approach and conclude an alliance treaty." A similar debate continued in the Liaison Conference two days later. In the end, the Liaison Conference reached the conclusion that an alliance treaty should be concluded, based on its judgment that the Chongqing government was not in a position to work for a peace settlement.[56] During this process, Prime Minister Tōjō's stance remained obscure. While at first he had consistently supported the proposal for a new alliance treaty, in mid-September he announced that he would not pursue realization of an alliance treaty—highlighting a drastic change of his allegiance.[57]

Meanwhile, the "joint defense" that the Shigemitsu proposal had envisioned was struck from the final draft. The details of the background to this decision are unknown, but it can be conjectured that the following developments took place. From the viewpoint of burden sharing for mutual defense among Greater East Asian countries, the Army Ministry had assumed that, when stationing of Japanese troops was needed, it would take the form of "Japan stationing its troops based on a request from the partner country." This is "totally different from the coercive imposition of Japanese troops in the name of joint defense or anti-communist defense. It is different from the conventional notion of so-called cooperative defense (including the stationing of troops)." The Army Ministry assessed that in the Army General Staff Office, "there are a considerable number of officers who still hold to the conventional notion of joint defense."[58] It must have been this perception gap between the Army General Staff Office and the Army Ministry that was behind the dropping of the phrase "joint defense" from the draft treaty. The

---

56 *Kimitsu sensō nisshi*, entry of September 20, 1943.

57 Ibid., entry of September 17, 1943.

58 "Nikka dōmei jōyaku teiketsu ni kansuru ken" [Matters Related to the Signing of the Japan-China Alliance Treaty] (note of dialogue with the officer in charge of the Army Ministry on June 21, 1943) (Ministry of Foreign Affairs Document A7.0.0.9-41-2).

Imperial Navy, for its part, had refrained from expressing its opinion toward the non-inclusion of the words "joint defense" in the alliance treaty.[59] From this, it can be conjectured that the Imperial Navy, too, shared the same view on this issue as the Army General Staff Office.

The alliance treaty draft, which was approved by the Liaison Conference on September 20, 1943, can be summarized as follows. The Foreign Ministry's proposal (the Shigemitsu proposal) on inclusion of an article to confirm the Japan-China joint declaration was dropped. The articles on stationing and withdrawal of troops as well as abolition of special regions were moved to the attached protocol and by an exchange of notes (E/N), respectively. In other words, articles on war cooperation were moved to other agreements such as the Japan-China joint declaration, making the proposed treaty a document to stipulate the principles concerning construction of perpetual Japanese-Chinese relations. In that sense, it can be said that the draft presupposed a full peace between the two countries.

The preamble states that the two countries "should mutually cooperate closely as good neighbors, respecting the autonomy and independence of one another, and construct Greater East Asia based on moral principles and, thereby, contribute to peace of the entire world." Three articles followed:

Article 1

In order to perpetually maintain neighborly friendship relations, both signees should take friendly and cordial measures for mutual assistance, mutually respecting the partner's sovereignty and territory.

Article 2

Both signees should closely cooperate with one another and render all possible assistance in order to construct Greater East Asia and secure its stability.

---

59 "Nikka dōmei jōyaku chū ni kansuru kenkyū chūkan hōkoku" [Interim Report on Study on the Japan-China Alliance Treaty] (August 13, 1943) (Ministry of Foreign Affairs Document A7.0.0.9-41-2).

Article 3

Both signees should pursue close economic partnership with one another based on mutual benefit.

This Japan-China Alliance Treaty, signed on October 30, 1943, had several features not found in the alliance treaties with Burma or the Philippines. First, regarding mutual respect of the other partner's sovereignty and territories, the treaty with China combined features of the treaties with Burma and the Philippines. The wording "to cooperate closely with mutual respect of autonomy and independence" in the treaty with Burma was inserted in the preamble of the Japan-China Alliance Treaty, and the wording "mutual respect of sovereignty and territories" from the treaty with the Philippines was adopted in Article 1 of the treaty with China.

Second, the reference to "in order to bring the Greater East Asia War to a successful conclusion" was nowhere to be found. In contrast to the treaties with Burma and the Philippines in which cases of "close cooperation" were divided into wartime and peacetime, making the treaties as a whole applicable to both times, no such demarcation between peacetime and wartime was included in the treaty with China. As mentioned earlier, the Japan-China Alliance Treaty stipulated principles of long-lasting Japan-China relations that included the Chongqing government.

Third, the Japan-China Alliance Treaty turned out to be the only one that adopted "mutual economic benefit" (in its Article 3), the concept that Shigemitsu had stressed most. Because the Greater East Asia Joint Declaration (officially, Joint Declaration of the Greater East Asia Conference), which Burma and the Philippines had also signed, set out "close cooperation upon a basis of reciprocity," the said declaration obviously was not based on the actual alliance treaties. Moreover, it was only the Japan-China Alliance Treaty (its attached protocol, to be exact) that explicitly pledged withdrawal of Japanese troops after the end of war.

On a separate note, on September 18, 1943, the Ministry of Great

East Asia abruptly submitted a proposal to the Liaison Conference which argued that "on this occasion, we should induce the Nanjing government to commence political engineering toward the Chongqing government." This proposal was approved. But this proposal led to another debate over whether this engineering should be guided by the Great East Asia minister or the foreign minister. To appease the two sides, it was ultimately decided that the prime minister would directly guide the Nanjing government.

At the same time, political engineering toward the Chongqing government had also become a subject of discussions among pertinent government ministries and bureaus since August. While few historical documents are available from which to discern details of the debate, it is clear that it was the Ministry of Navy that was most enthusiastic about political maneuvering toward the Chongqing government. The view of Oka Takazumi, director-general of the Naval Affairs Bureau, was representative. Oka commented, "On this occasion, it is appropriate to dauntlessly conduct political activities toward the Chongqing government," without waiting for the revision of the treaty. In contrast to the positive attitude of the Navy Ministry and, to a somewhat lesser extent, the Ministries of Greater East Asia and Army, the Ministry of Foreign Affairs and the China Expeditionary Army were most reluctant regarding political engineering toward the Chongqing government. The China Expeditionary Army, in particular, argued against it, saying, "Given the lack of intention to pursue a peace settlement on the part of the Nationalist government in Nanjing and the Chongqing government's animosity toward the Nanjing government, it would be impossible to make the Nationalist government engage in the said political maneuvering." Besides, direct guidance by the prime minister had "no prospect for success."[60]

---

60 "Jiki no jūyō seiryaku ni kansuru ken" [Matters Related to Important Strategies in the Next Phase] (August 13, 1943) (Ministry of Foreign Affairs Document A7.0.0.9-61, "Daitōa Sensō 1-ken honpō no tai Jūkei kōsaku kankei" [A Matter Related to the Greater East Asia War: Matters Related to Japan's Political Engineering toward the Chongqing Government]).

Nevertheless, Prime Minister Tōjō strongly supported the proposal on the Nanjing government's political maneuvers regarding the Chongqing government, which helped in dismissing oppositions from the China Expeditionary Army and the Foreign Ministry to bring about the final decision to "make the Nationalist government start political maneuvering toward the Chongqing government" upon confirmation of President Wang Jingwei's true intention and plans.[61] This reveals that this measure was not an arbitrary action of the Ministry of Greater East Asia but a drive supported by the prime minister.

It seems safe to say that the conditions for peace presented by the Japanese side were made regarding the content of the revised treaty. A detailed and concise explanation of the contents of the Japan-China Alliance Treaty can be found in *Nikka Kihon Jōyaku kaitei jōyaku teiketsu yōkō* (Outline of the Signing of the Revision of the Japan-China Basic Relations Treaty), adopted by the September 18, 1943, Liaison Conference. On military-related matters, for instance, the *Outline* stipulated abolition of the entire right to station Japanese troops in China, including those troops whose presence was based on the need for anti-communist defense measures or the maintenance of public order or other precedents, as well as full withdrawal of troops after the end of war. As for the coordination of special regions, the *Outline* stipulated the abolishment of special regions, including North China, Mengjiang, and the lower Yangtze region. And development and use of important national defense resources were to be treated as "part of a general economic partnership." These stipulations essentially showed that, following the aims of Article 3 of the Japan-China Alliance Treaty, Japan would not demand preferential treatment or special benefits. These conditions presented by the Japanese side were truly unprecedented in the sense that they would not only restore bilateral relations to the pre–China Incident state but also explicitly announce abolition of the right to station Japanese troops in China based on

---

61 *Kimitsu sensō nisshi* entry of September 17, 1943.

the Boxer Protocol of 1901.[62]

As for the conditions to be imposed on the Chongqing government, such demands as disarmament of the British and American troops stationed in China or their withdrawal from China and the severance of communication with Britain and the United States were considered.[63] From the minutes of the Liaison Conference, one can detect that the Bureau of Naval Affairs of the Navy Ministry persisted with "methods to verify withdrawal of the American and British troops." In any event, these conditions, which were tantamount to requesting the neutralization of China, indicated that by this stage awareness of the importance of American influence on the Chongqing government had deepened.

(4) The Nanjing Government and the New Treaty

As an overview of trends on the Chinese side (the Nanjing government side), one could say that Prime Minister Tōjō's reference to a fundamental revision of the Japan-China Basic Relations Treaty at the eighty-second Extraordinary Session of the Imperial Diet on June 10, 1943, triggered active discussions on the treaty revision issue in the Nanjing government. The Wang regime argued that it would be futile to use revision of the treaty to bait the Chongqing government as long as the Allied side was on the whole taking the lead in the war. It took the position that Japan should not use the treaty as a tool to lure the Chongqing government to peace negotiations. Japan should, instead, announce to the world that respect for the independence and freedom of China (including the Chongqing government) was Japan's state policy whether the Chongqing side agreed to peace negotiations or not. More concretely, the Wang regime argued that it would be only a matter of course for Japan to abolish the right to station its troops in China. The

---

62 Tobe Ryōichi, "Shina Jihen to Daitōa Sensō" [The China Incident and Greater East Asia War], *Gaikō Jihō*, no. 1320, 1995, pp. 50–51.
63 "Tai Jūkei seiji kōsaku ni kansuru ken" [Matters Related to Political Maneuvering toward the Chongqing Government] in *Sugiyama memo, ge*, p. 463.

more important measure would be abolishment of the designation of North China and Mengjiang as special regions (or separation of these regions from others) and regulations contributing to the division of these regions. The Wang regime also stressed the need for simultaneous conclusion of an interim treaty to regulate the present conditions and a basic treaty of mutual benefit and equality.[64] The Shigemitsu proposal was meant to respond to these realistic arguments from the Nanjing side.

The attitude of the Imperial Army (particularly its General Staff Office) and the Ministry of Greater East Asia, which perceived the signing of a new treaty with the Nanjing government as a tool for political engineering toward the Chongqing government, displeased the Wang Jingwei regime. Zhou Fohai told Colonel Nagai Yatsuji, staff officer of the China Expeditionary Army, on June 23 that "Revision of the treaty should not be used as a strategic tool for luring the Chongqing side to peace negotiations." Zhou stressed that, regardless of whether the Chongqing government agreed to join peace negotiations, Japan should maintain respect for the independence and freedom of China (the Nanjing government) as an unshakable state policy. The most important determinant of the realization of full peace was the situation of war against Britain and the United States. When these two enemy powers were about to take the lead in war, it would be impossible to lure the Chongqing side to the peace negotiation table with the bait of revision of the treaty.[65] Shigemitsu clearly understood this logic and wrote in his journal, "The notion of using the alliance treaty as a bargaining chip with the Chongqing government is of no value. The other party would instantly recognize it as a deceptive ploy and our side would be left in an awkward

---

64 Sai Tokukin (Cai Dejin), ed., *Shū Futsukai nikki* [Zhou Fohai Diary], translated by Murata Tadayoshi et al. Misuzu Shobō, 1992 (entry of June 23, July 12 and 14, 1943), Itō Takashi et al., eds., *Zoku gendaishi shiryō 4 rikugun Hata Shunroku nisshi* [Documents on Modern History, Part II-4, Diary of Imperial Japanese Army's Hata Shunroku], Misuzu Shobō, 1984 (entry of July 12, 1943).
65 *Shū Futsukai nikki* (entry of June 23, 1943).

spot."[66]

One of the Nanjing government's important demands related to revision of the treaty concerned the content of "economic partnership." Nanjing requested that Japan allow China's ethnic capital to develop natural resources. Another important demand was to make the treaty comply with the policy of strengthening, both in name and in substance, the Nationalist government. In other words, the Nanjing side did not want a treaty that presupposed full peace with the Chongqing side.

On September 22, 1943, President Wang of the Nanjing government visited Japan to be briefed on the proposed Japan-China Alliance Treaty. Wang met with Prime Minister Tōjō and Foreign Minister Shigemitsu in Tokyo. After explaining the contents of the the treaty's draft, Tōjō told Wang, "The revised treaty will be concluded with the Nanjing government, regardless of whether peace is accomplished or not, by which the Chongqing side would be deprived of the pretext for resistance." In response, Wang proposed conclusion of two new treaties. One would permanently prescribe the basic relations between Japan and China, which had to explicitly stipulate China's unity and independence. The other would be a treaty that mainly focused on bilateral war cooperation, including the use of national defense resources during wartime.[67] Although the proposal from the Japanese side was not divided into two treaties, it substantively met the requests from the Chinese side. Upon being debriefed by Wang after his return from Japan, Zhou remarked that Japan's pledge to withdraw all of its troops, abolish the right of Japan to station troops in China, and dissolve the special regions was "one of the fruits of my tenacious efforts."[68]

In his meeting with Wang, Tōjō gave his word to (1) carry out political maneuvers toward the Chongqing government via the Nationalist government, (2) have the Japanese military immediately stand down and withdraw

66 *Shigemitsu Mamoru shuki*, p. 411.
67 *Tōjō kimitsu kiroku*, pp. 242–251.
68 *Shū Futsukai nikki* (entry of September 24, 1943).

if and when the Chongqing government severed its ties with Britain and the United States, and (3) enforce the Alliance Treaty whether a full peace was accomplished or not. Particularly, Tōjō's commitment that Japan would not engage in peace negotiations directly with the Chongqing government over the head of the Nanjing government meant that "the pace of the peace process is now entirely in the hands of President Wang." Wang, for his part, changed his attitude toward maneuvering vis-à-vis the Chongqing government and began to show a more positive posture toward peace mediation.[69] Other leaders of the Wang government, however, remained pessimistic about achieving full peace. Zhou Fohai, for instance, frequently exchanged views on full peace with the Japanese side after the signing of the Alliance Treaty, and he never forgot to remind his Japanese counterparts, "If Japan hopes to win the trust of the Chongqing government, it has to be trusted first by the citizens under the Nanjing government."[70] It is considered that one of Zhou's aims was to obtain economic assistance from Japan for financial reconstruction of the Nanjing government, which had been hard-pressed by hyperinflation. Nonetheless, it has to be said that the Nanjing government's enthusiasm for a peace settlement with the Chongqing government was minimal at best.

(5) Japan-China Relations, Ideal vs. Reality

At the September 30, 1943, Imperial Council, which had decided to designate a *Zettai kokubōken* (Absolute National Defense Zone), Foreign Minister Shigemitsu declared, "It is only the relations with China (the Chongqing government) that have the potential to lead the current war situation to a

---

69 On the motives behind Wang's change of attitude, Hata Shunroku, commander-in-chief of the China Expeditionary Army, observed that, "It might be because he detected the momentum toward peace settlement in Chongqing." (Itō et al., 1984, entry of September 12, 1943). During his meeting with Tōjō, Wang remarked that, due to the effect of the new China policy, the Chongqing side became more positive toward full peace. He even referred to concrete measures, but no progress was observed subsequently. (*Shū Futsukai nikki*, entry of September 21, 1943; *Tōjō kimitsu kiroku*, pp. 240–241).
70 *Shū Futsukai nikki*, entry of October 2, 1943.

settlement." He continued that to bring the "China issue" to a settlement, "it is imperative to strongly implement the new China policy." Although Shigemitsu did not specifically refer to the Japan-China Alliance Treaty, which had been in the final stage of negotiations, this new treaty obviously occupied the central position in his assertion. After the treaty was signed, Tani, Ambassador to the Nanjing government, debriefed staff officials of the embassy regarding the gist of Shigemitsu's remarks as follows:

> Although its full effect is expected only after the realization of a full peace agreement, the bilateral Alliance Treaty is none other than a portrayal of Japan-China relations as they naturally have to be in light of actual situations in East Asia. By no means was the treaty concluded as a tool to realize a full peace. . . . The gap between today's reality and the situations envisioned by the Alliance Treaty has become even wider, which calls for nothing less than engergetically and fearlessly pursuing the *Daitōa Sensō kansui no tameno taishi shori konpon hōshin* (Basic Policy toward China in Order to Accomplish the Goal of the Greater East Asia War).[71]

This debriefing idealized the Japan-China relations envisioned by the Alliance Treaty and strongly denied that conclusion of the treaty was a tool toward full peace, which very well represented Shigemitsu's wish to prioritize the position of the Nanjing government. And Shigemitsu had argued that the gap between the reality of Japan's being in a state of war with the Chongqing government, on the one hand, and the ideal shape of Japan-China relations envisioned by the Alliance Treaty, on the other hand, could be closed by thoroughly implementing the new China policy. However, as long as the new China policy took as its core the Alliance Treaty, the treaty would

---

71 "Nikka Dōmei Jōyaku narabini taishi shisaku yōryō ni kansuru kōjutsu (yōshi)" [Lecture on the Japan-China Alliance Treaty and the Outline of Future Policy toward China (summary)] (Ministry of Foreign Affairs Document A7.0.0.9-41-2).

have to be perceived as a tool for full peace, betraying the confusion, as well as the contradiction, between the goal and the means. Thus, it has to be said that, out of too much consideration for the position of the Nanjing government, which Japan had formally recognized, a means for a peace settlement with the Chongqing government was missing. The new China policy was not only about conclusion of a new treaty, but Shigemitsu's argument went round and round and got nowhere when all the other measures had been completely deadlocked.

It was not that the Japanese government and the military had placed high hopes from the beginning on a revised treaty's influence on the Chongqing government or its possibility to lure full peace. The document that the Foreign Ministry prepared for the prime minister's private report to the emperor on September 18, 1943, pointed out, "We submit that, under the current situation, an excessive expectation should not be placed on the proposed revision of the treaty for immediate realization of full peace or settlement of the China Incident."[72] It was wishful thinking that "to boldly carry out revision of the treaty today would undoubtedly become an extremely effective weapon, at least, when taking political offensive toward the Chongqing government."[73] And the role that Shigemitsu played helped tilt the balance from revision of the existing treaty to conclusion of a new treaty. For Shigemitsu, full peace between Japan and China did not mean the Chongqing government's surrender to the Nanjing government or Japan. It had to mean mutual acceptance, on an equal footing, of an alliance treaty that pledged full troop withdrawal and respect of sovereignty, upon which "China's sovereignty would be restored."[74]

---

72 "Nikka kihon jōyaku kaitei ni kansuru seifu naisō shiryō" [Material for Governmental Private Reporting to the Emperor on Revision of the Japan-China Basic Relations Treaty] (Division II, Bureau of Political Affairs, Ministry of Foreign Affairs, September 3, 1943) (Ministry of Foreign Affairs Document A7.0.0.9-41-2).
73 Ibid.
74 *Shigemitsu Mamoru shuki*, p. 406 and *Zoku Shigemitsu Mamoru shuki*, pp. 153–154. Also see Tobe Ryōichi (1995).

As of September 1943, it was obvious from the deliberation process of the new *Sensō shidō taikō* (New War Instruction Outline), which had been underway at the same time as the Alliance Treaty, that this understanding of Shigemitsu was not shared by Japan's war leaders. The *New War Instruction Outline* sketched "settlement of the China issue" and "winning the popular favor of peoples in Greater East Asia" as measures to be taken in Greater East Asia along with the setting of the Absolute National Defense Zone. The perception gap between Foreign Minister Shigemitsu and Greater East Asia Minister Aoki on these measures was obvious even in their explanations at an Imperial Council. While Aoki stressed the need for activation of political maneuvering toward the Chongqing government via the Nanjing government for the settlement of the China issue, Shigemitsu argued for settlement of the issue through pursuit of the new China policy. Concerning the significance of such ongoing measures as granting independence for Burma and the Philippines, while Aoki did not delve any deeper than the strengthening of cooperation with the war effort, Shigemitsu stressed that those measures were a part of the new Greater East Asia policy (an expanded version of the new China policy) and even referred to the possibility of these measures becoming a tools to be used in causing the United States to lose the will to fight.[75] This perception gap between the two camps was more of a reflection of the striving and confrontation over the series of ongoing new East Asia policy measures between the two rather than a reflection of differences in the policy areas the two sides were in charge of.

When the conclusion of the Japan-China Alliance Treaty was publicly announced, Kiyosawa Kiyoshi, Taishō-Shōwa era journalist and foreign policy critic, wrote in his journal as follows:

> [Because this treaty advocates mutual benefits and equality as well as neighborly friendship, its signing] should be perceived as a part of

---

75 *Sugiyama memo, ge*, pp. 481–482.

Japan's political actions toward the Chongqing government. But I am convinced that the Chongqing government will not be impressed. Had this treaty been concluded two years earlier, the China Incident would have already been settled and the Greater East Asia War would have been avoided.[76]

In contrast, Prime Minister Tōjō, speaking before the Review Committee of the Privy Council, said,

Earlier [when the Japan-China Basic Relations Treaty was concluded] it was necessary to put pressure on China. But today, it is more important to win the favor of the Chinese public. While doing so may be somewhat regrettable from the viewpoint of Japanese vested interests in China, we should abandon them to accomplish our grand goal.[77]

These two comments perceptively represent the two ends of a spectrum of views on the Japan-China Alliance Treaty.

---

76 Kiyosawa Kiyoshi, *Ankoku nikki* [The Diary of Darkness], Nippon Hyōronsha, 1979 (entry of October 30, 1943).
77 Fukai (1953), p. 329.

Chapter 7

Greater East Asia Conference and Joint Declaration

1. Drafting of the Greater East Asia Joint Declaration

(1) Sensō Mokuteki Kenkyūkai and the Greater East Asia Declaration

The Greater East Asia Conference, which was scheduled in November 1943, was, for Foreign Minister Shigemitsu Mamoru, one of the steps toward establishing the "Greater East Asia new policy." Particularly, the Joint Declaration of the Greater East Asia Conference (Greater East Asia Joint Declaration) would become a code of conduct for self-driven solidarity among Asian peoples and the establishment of Greater East Asia, which would also allow Japan to show how its "righteous war aims" contrasted with those of the Allies.[1] Originally, however, the purpose of the conference was to secure the cooperation of Asian peoples in the war effort in preparation for the predicted full-scale counteroffensive by US troops. The conference was not intended to serve as a stage for the realization of Shigemitsu's plan. As such, when drafting the joint declaration, Shigemitsu had to repeatedly cope with the military's demand to wage the war as well as the argument for the Empire of Japan to act as the guiding leader in Greater East Asia.

The Sensō Mokuteki Kenkyūkai (Study Group on War Aims), established on instructions from Shigemitsu within the Ministry of Foreign Affairs in early August 1943, drafted the Greater East Asia declaration. While the committee members consisted of its president, Yamakawa Tadao, adviser to the minister for foreign affairs, directors-general of major bureaus of the Foreign Ministry, and members of the Senji Chōsashitsu (Wartime Research Office, comprised of ex-ambassadors and ministers on the ambassador waiting list), actual deliberations were conducted by the executive

---

1 Among Shigemitsu's wartime writings, his intention to contrast Japan's redefined war purposes against those of the Allies is found in "Taiseiyō Kenshō to Taiheiyō (Daitōa) Kenshō" [The Atlantic Charter vs. the Pacific (Greater East Asia) Charter] in Itō Takashi et al., eds., *Shigemitsu Mamoru shuki* [Shigemitsu Mamoru Private Memoir], Chūō Kōronsha, 1986, pp. 328–330.

committee of the Research Committee on War Purposes under the chairman-
ship of Andō Yoshirō, director-general of the Treaty Bureau. The executive
committee was made up of division directors including Kadowaki Suemitsu
(Division I, Political Affairs Bureau), Sone Eki (Division II, Political Affairs
Bureau), Ogata Shōji (Research Division II), Matsudaira Kōtō (Division I,
Treaty Bureau), and Hara Kanjirō (Trade Division I).[2]

When the first executive committee met on August 20, Andō's draft
"Daitōa matawa Taiheiyō Kenshō Sō-an" (Greater East Asia or Pacific
Charter Draft), compiled by Andō at Shigemitsu's suggestion, was submitted
as a reference.[3] In a nutshell, the Andō draft included the following stipulations: (1) permanent liberation of Greater East Asia from external
interference, domination, monopoly, and exploitation; (2) establishment
of neighborly cooperative relations based on mutual respect of autonomy,
independence, and territory and on the principle of reciprocal benefit and
equality; (3) joint defense; (4) development and use of natural resources
under the principle of mutual benefit and cooperation; (5) nurturing indigenous culture and promoting further exchange, fusion, and development of
cultures; and (6) cooperating in the maintenance of world peace with armed
forces and peacefully settling all international disputes with the principle of
non-menace and non-aggression.

The minutes of the executive committee reveal that some participants
argued that the content of the joint declaration should be limited to propaganda aimed at luring the peoples of Greater East Asia into voluntarily cooperating with the war effort. Beyond mere wartime propaganda, however,
the Andō draft had a more proactive mission of stipulating the principles of

---

2   Useful studies referring to the Sensō Mokuteki Kenkyūkai include Kawahara Hiroshi, *Shōwa
seiji shisō kenkyū* [Study of Shōwa Political Thought], Waseda Daigaku Shuppanbu, 1979, pp.
285–302, and Yasuda Rie, "Daitōa Kaigi to Daitōa Kyōdō Sengen o megutte" [On the Greater East
Asia Conference and the Greater East Asia Joint Declaration], *Hōgaku Kenkyū*, vol. 63, no. 2, 1990,
pp. 403–406.
3   Andō draft on "Daitōa matawa Taiheiyō Kenshō Sō-an" [Greater East Asia or Pacific Charter
Draft] (included in the microfilm, *Japan Ministry of Foreign Affairs, 1868–1945*, WT Series, Reel
52, a collection of the historic documents on the Constitution in the National Diet Library).

construction for the postwar international order in Asia which could provide the foundation for the maintenance of world peace. Members of the executive committee exchanged views more or less with this mission in mind.

At this juncture, allow me to introduce views expressed by Sone Eki and Ogata Shōji, who took the lead in the discussions.

Sone:

While the Greater East Asia declaration must be useful to promote solidarity among Greater East Asian peoples, it must also be an appeal to countries within Greater East Asia as well as to the entire world. Therefore, the co-prosperity philosophy that places excessive stress on the conventional notion of the Empire of Japan as the guiding nation must be reviewed. At the same time, we must pay due consideration to domestic arguments on such issues as political structure and the extended economic zone of Greater East Asia. It would be the most difficult task to keep a proper balance between the two.

Ogata:

Although the official theme of the declaration will be liberation, liberation is only a step toward the ultimate goal—that is, world cooperation. Therefore, while the official aim is, of course, construction of Greater East Asia, it is imperative to steadfastly announce to the world that this Greater East Asia is not a closed entity that Japan monopolizes. Particularly since the proposed Greater East Asia Conference is likely to project the image of a conference to make Greater East Asia an exclusive region, issuing this kind of joint declaration will be all the more effective.

In the end, the key point is what fundamental structure of this Greater East Asia we should present as external propaganda. And when the joint declaration is issued, there is a risk that Greater East Asia will be seen as extremely exclusive—whose main purpose is to unite the peoples of Greater East Asia . . . The ultimate aim of the Greater East Asia declaration is to give an impression to the United States and Britain that what Japan is doing in Greater East Asia is a good thing. This may eventually make them approve of our conduct.

In short, a point of contention was whether to limit the goal of the declaration to extol, from militaristic and strategic requirements, solidity among Greater East Asian peoples or to make the goal a more universal one that also embraced the war purposes that the Allies held out, thus eliminating an image of an exclusive and monopolistic entity. As Ogata pointed out, "The ultimate aim of the Greater East Asia Declaration is to impress upon the United States and Britain that what Japan is doing in Greater East Asia is a good thing. This may eventually make them approve of our conduct." If to "make them approve of our conduct" was indeed one of the goals of the Greater East Asia Declaration, then the document had to refer to the Atlantic Charter, which was an explicit manifestation of the Allies' war purposes. And this is why Andō had aptly stated, "It is challenging to lead both countries within the Greater East Asia Co-Prosperity Sphere and those without to the right direction with only one declaration."

Matsudaira Kōtō, chairman of the executive committee, remained critical of these arguments from beginning to end.

Matsudaira

I have a fundamental doubt about the issue of the Greater East Asia Declaration. While the Atlantic Charter proclaimed by Britain and the United States stipulates objectives and procedures of the postwar plan, our Greater East Asia version must be something that is directly useful for reinforcing our war capabilities. The solidarity of Greater East Asia, too, is nothing less than solidarity for the sake of victory in the current war. In this sense, it is highly doubtful if Japan can truly adopt something akin to the Atlantic Charter in its Greater East Asia Declaration. . . .

The Greater East Asia Declaration . . . will be issued with the aim of uniting peoples residing in Greater East Asia. Should it be written along the lines of an Atlantic Charter–like philosophy, it is feared that we may find ourselves trapped in the future. Rather than speaking haphazardly about concrete issues, we might as well refrain from saying anything at all. It is also highly questionable whether there is anything creative that Japan can do for the world aside from construction of Greater East Asia.[4]

Matsudaira's remark contained two important points concerning the philosophy behind the drafting of the proposed declaration. One was the fact that the executive committee intended to adopt an "Atlantic Charter–like philosophy" in drafting the declaration. The Atlantic Charter had announced the principle of postwar management. The proposed Greater East Asia Declaration aimed to request the immediate cooperation of Asian peoples in the war effort. Given this difference, Matsudaira warned that if the Greater East Asia Declaration was also charged with the principles for postwar management, it could constrain Japan's external conduct in postwar days. This was Matsudaira's second point. In other words, Matsudaira argued that it would be senseless for Japan to issue a declaration that, following the argument of the Andō draft, went beyond Greater East Asia, both regionally and ideologically, and beyond war issues.

The majority of the executive committee was critical of the view expressed by Matsudaira. In the end, discussions converged on the argument that the Greater East Asia Declaration should not only serve as a means for waging the war but also as a guideline for postwar management. In any event, the commonly shared awareness by members of the executive committee was that to simply repeat the conventional Greater East Asia Co-Prosperity

---

4 "Sensō mokuteki kenkyūkai dai 1-kai kanjikai gijiroku" [Minutes of the First Executive Committee Meeting of the Study Group on War Aims] (convened at the office of the director-general of the Treaty Bureau on August 20, 1943). (Included in the microfilm, *Japan Ministry of Foreign Affairs, 1868–1945*, WT Series, Reel 52, a National Diet Library collection of historical documents on the Constitution.)

Sphere scheme would project an image of an exclusivity and would not be convincing to the outside world.

(2) Tangled Debate on the Opening of Resources to Outside Countries

A few important points of contention were observed during the deliberations at the executive committee.

First there was the contradiction between the political and economic principle of mutual respect for the independence of countries in Greater East Asia and the principle of mutual benefit and equality, on the one hand, and the concept of the Greater East Asia Co-Prosperity Sphere, on the other hand, which assumed Japan's hegemonic position vis-à-vis Asia. The denial of Japan's guiding authority vis-à-vis Greater East Asian countries, even after the end of the war, was predicted to meet strong opposition from within Japan. Eventually, the executive committee had to fend off opposition with the explanation that such terms as "joint," "cooperation," and "partnership" implicitly harbored a nuance of "guidance." For instance, when asked how Japan's guidance in the economic field was to be described, Andō explained that his draft had adopted the phrase "mutually beneficial cooperation" and that "the term 'cooperation' encompasses guidance."

Second, there was the problem of the operation of the Greater East Asia Conference. As mentioned in chapter 6, Foreign Minister Shigemitsu initially had envisioned institutionalizing the Greater East Asia Conference into a Greater East Asia international organization to be jointly organized by countries of Greater East Asia. And, as the philosophy of this consultative body, Shigemitsu wished to announce the Greater East Asia Charter (Greater East Asia Joint Declaration). While Shigemitsu's vision had met opposition from various government ministries and experienced setbacks one after another, the executive committee once again studied its feasibility. This was the final feasibility study on Shigemitsu's idea. It was predicted, though, that the scheme to expand the authority of the Greater East Asia international organization to allow it to settle fundamental political and economic problems within the region would be challenged by numerous objections from within Japan. Anticipated objections included the concern that Japan's authority as the "guiding state" would decline and that the Greater East Asian countries, which were currently collaborating with Japan, might collude with each other and secede from Japan. In the end, the executive committee judged that, in managing the Greater East Asia Conference, "such League of Nations–like structure and management as the decision by vote among equal member countries" should be avoided.[5]

The third point of contention was an argument in the economic field around the issue of "open access to natural resources." The Ministry of Foreign Affairs commissioned The Japanese Society of International Law to prepare a study, which included a section on the development and use of natural resources. Part of the report the society submitted included a passage stating that "Japan should open its doors to the world and establish mutually beneficial and cooperative trade relations with countries throughout the world—thereby contributing to the development and prosperity of the world economy." A note was attached to this proposal, revealing that this was the most controversial issue and that no consensus was reached.[6] Let me introduce the executive committee's discussions in the field of economics below.

During the first executive committee meeting, Andō Yoshirō argued that "the opening of natural resources should be announced widely to the world." Sone Eki followed with, "It is necessary to make it clearly understood among Japanese that it will be impossible to maintain perfect autarchy only

---

5　"Daitōa Kyōeiken no seiji taisei" [Political System of the Greater East Asia Co-Prosperity Sphere] (August 23, 1943, Division II, Political Affairs Bureau, Ministry of Foreign Affairs), (included in the microfilm, *Japan Ministry of Foreign Affairs, 1868–1945*, WT Series, Reel 52, National Diet Library collection of historical documents on the Constitution).

6　"Daitōa Sengen an" [Draft Greater East Asia Declaration] (July 23, 1943, Special Committee, the Japan Society of International Law) (included in the microfilm, *Japan Ministry of Foreign Affairs, 1868–1945*, WT Series, Reel 52, collection of the historic document on Constitution of the National Diet Library).

within Greater East Asia after the war. Unless Japan announces that surplus resources will be traded, countries in Greater East Asia, with the exception of Japan, will not follow and cooperate with Japan's lead." Additionally, another executive committee member also pointed out, concerning economic relations between the Co-Prosperity Sphere and external countries, that, "it is proper to refrain from predicting whether the world outside the Co-Prosperity Sphere will be divided into several so-called wide-area regional economic spheres." Overall, the executive committee became inclined to approve the "opening" of access to Greater East Asian natural resources.

But the problem was the assumption on which the argument for open access to natural resources was based. Views were divided not only within the Foreign Ministry on whether the postwar world economy would head in the direction of free trade or regional economic communities and bloc economies. This issue became one of the most fiercely contended issues. For instance, the *Daitōa sengen an (keizai bumon)*[7] (Greater East Asia Declaration in the Field of Economics Draft) compiled by the Trade Bureau of the Foreign Ministry was based on the notion that developing natural resources and liberalizing trade would require such conditions as the realization of a "world without exploitation" and the improvement of living standards, which would make it difficult, for the time being, to apply the principle of equality and reciprocal benefit.

The *Daitōa sengen keizai gensoku* (Economic Principles of the Greater East Asia Declaration) thus compiled on August 25, 1943,[8] by the executive committee of the Study Group on War Aims was based on the premise that "world peace will be hard to come by unless it is composed of states

---

7 *Daitōa sengen an (keizai bumon)* [Greater East Asia Declaration in the Field of Economics Draft] (August 23, 1943, Trade Bureau, Ministry of Foreign Affairs) (included in the microfilm, *Japan Ministry of Foreign Affairs, 1868–1945*, WT Series, Reel 52, National Diet Library collection of historical documents on the Constitution).

8 *Daitōa sengen keizai gensoku* [Economic Principles of the Greater East Asia Declaration] (August 25, 1943, proposal of the executive committee of the Research Committee on War Purposes) (included in the microfilm, *Japan Ministry of Foreign Affairs, 1868–1945*, WT Series, Reel 52, National Diet Library collection of historical documents on the Constitution).

or groups of states that are economically stable." On that assumption, the *Economic Principles of the Greater East Asia Declaration* stated:

> Countries of the Greater East Asia Co-Prosperity Sphere should come together to cooperate with unification of stable states based on the grand principles of independence, equality, and mutual assistance. States in the Co-Prosperity Sphere shall never intend to monopolize natural resources found in the Sphere as long as economic stability allows them.

The proposal created by the Trade Bureau of the Ministry of Foreign Affairs on August 31, 1943, on the basis of this executive committee draft[9] proposed, "a regulatory economy or cooperative regime based on a certain comprehensive plan within a necessary boundary with an aim to accomplish common purposes" basically under Japan's guidance, while, formally, stressing the necessity for the "formation of each country's consensus." In the meantime, the Trade Bureau organized a meeting of the Economic Committee of the Study Group on War Aims on August 28 at the official residence of the vice minister for foreign affairs. Using its own proposal as a basis for discussion, the Trade Bureau aimed to collect the views of members of the research committee on desirable postwar economic policies. One of the participating members, Ishii Itarō, wrote in his diary, "The economic self-sufficiency of the East Asia Co-Prosperity Sphere is a fantasy. So many things are inadequate there," displaying his skepticism of the Trade Bureau proposal.[10]

The second conference of the Study Group on War Aims, convened on

---

9 "Daitōa Kyōeiken no keizai taisei" [Economic Structure of the Greater East Asia Co-Prosperity Sphere] (August 31, 1943, Trade Bureau, Ministry of Foreign Affairs) (included in the microfilm, *Japan Ministry of Foreign Affairs, 1868–1945*, WT Series, Reel 52, National Diet Library collection of historical documents on the Constitution).

10 Itō Takashi and Ryū Ketsu (Liu Jie), eds., *Ishii Itarō nikki* [Ishii Itarō Diary], Chūō Kōronsha, 1993 (entry of August 28, 1943).

September 2,[11] discussed mainly the economic nature of Greater East Asia, based on the Trade Bureau proposal. Aside from the committee's executive members, the following also participated: Deputy Foreign Minister Matsumoto Shun'ichi; directors-general of bureaus of the Foreign Ministry; Hoketsu Kōta, councilor of the Foreign Ministry; directors of the Trade Bureau Division I, the Research Bureau Division II, and the Treaty Bureau Division II; Yamakawa Tadao, adviser to the Foreign Ministry; and Ishii Itarō, Matsuda Michikazu, and Kurusu Saburō from the Study Group on War Aims. First, Matsumoto pointed out that, even though the Trade Bureau proposal argued for tolerance of autonomy and independence for Greater East Asian countries in terms of the political regime, it presupposed a planned and controlled economy within the Sphere. This was, in Matsumoto's judgment, retrogression.

In response, Hoketsu, who had participated in the drafting of the proposal, refuted by saying, "Even though we shall formally respect [Greater East Asian countries'] autonomy and independence, in actuality we must control their political regimes as we do their economy." Upon hearing this, Matsumoto stressed that, if economic control would indeed be applied within the Co-Prosperity Sphere as need arose, as suggested by the Trade Bureau proposal, "Countries in the region would be panic-stricken." He continued to argue,

As a matter of fact, fundamental change and transformation are underway in the political realm, including, most notably, Japan-China relations. Given this situation, is it not time to reflect on our conduct in the economic realm in a fundamental way? Peoples of Greater East Asia, due to their temperament, do not desire the planned economy and, thus,

---

11 "Sensō Mokuteki Kenkyūkai dai 2-kai kaigō gijiroku" [Minutes of the Second Meeting of the Study Group on War Aims] (included in the microfilm, *Japan Ministry of Foreign Affairs, 1868–1945*, WT Series, Reel 52, National Diet Library collection of historical documents on the constitution).

a planned economy is not applicable to Greater East Asia. Therefore, we should revise the conventional notion of a planned economy. While it might be applicable to the South Sea territories, we must contemplate what to do in China.

Still Hoketsu argued, "It is obvious that the Co-Prosperity Sphere would not be realized unless we win the war," "application of the controlled economy in the Sphere would be a matter of course," and "[nothing less than a controlled economy] would secure the agreement of Japan's business circle." Ishizawa Yutaka, director of Division II of the Trade Bureau, seconded Hoketsu's remarks and stressed that the planned economy would be essential [for Greater East Asia]. The director-general of the Treaty Bureau, on his part, suggested that it would be "most important to secure understanding of the military." In the end, no agreement was reached among the participants.

Meanwhile, Yamakawa remarked, "I hope to see Greater East Asia take the route of an unregulated economy as much as possible," and if the Japanese economy could not withstand free economic competition, "we should judge that Japan is not capable of managing a co-prosperity sphere." Thus, this debate on whether a controlled economy or a free economy should be opted for as the economic regime of the Greater East Asia Co-Prosperity Sphere went on without reaching a conclusion. In the end, the final draft of the declaration argued for the "open access to natural resources" along the lines insisted on by Deputy Minister for Foreign Affairs Matsumoto. It should be noted that, the backdrop of the decision to persist with the development and use of natural resources was, albeit by a slim margin, a viewpoint which advocated that, regardless of the outcome of the war, Japan should boldly open East Asia, liberate its trade with other countries as much as possible, and promote the introduction of capital and technology. At least that was what was reported in an operational report produced by the Treaty Bureau.[12]

(3) Revised Declaration Draft Proposed by Shigemitsu

Based on these deliberations, the executive committee of the Study Group on War Aims compiled a proposed Greater East Asia declaration (executive committee proposal) on September 11, 1943. After a few modifications, this proposal was turned into the *Gaimushō kenkyū-an* (Proposal Based on the Foreign Ministry's Study) on October 4.[13] What follows is the full text of the *Proposal Based on the Foreign Ministry's Study*. (Incidentally, the executive committee's proposal was almost identical to this Foreign Ministry proposal.)

Proposal Based on the Foreign Ministry's Study

In order to permanently free Greater East Asia from aggression or colonial exploitation by external powers, construct Greater East Asia based on moral principles, and thereby contribute to the foundation of universal co-prosperity and peaceful development of mankind, representatives of Greater East Asian governments declare as follows:

(1) Each of the Greater East Asian countries wishes to collaborate in

---

12 Behind the arguments on "wide-area regional economic spheres" and "bloc economy" were strong demands from the Imperial Army and Navy, which took it for granted that Japan should receive preferential treatment on procurement of national defense resources and their development and use, as well as ministries or agencies engaged in materials mobilization. Free trade was not necessarily a natural course to take internationally, i.e., it was only one of many options in those days. See Judith Goldstein, "Ideas, Institutions, and American Trade Policy" in G. John Ikenberry et al., eds., *The State and American Foreign Economic Policy* (Ithaca, NY: Cornell University Press, 1988), pp. 187–210. Only a few raised an alarm regarding Japan's inclination toward the wide-area economic sphere; among them were Ishibashi Tanzan and an extremely small number of economists. See Matsuo Takayoshi, ed., *Ishibashi Tanzan hyōronshū* [Collection of Ishibashi Tanzan's Essays], Iwanami Shoten, 1991, pp. 232–238, Treaty Bureau, Ministry of Foreign Affairs, *Shōwa 18-nendo shitsumu hōkoku* [Operational Records of FY1943], p. 140.

13 "Daitōa sengen-an" [Proposed Greater East Asia Declaration] (September 11, 1943), "Daitōa sengen-an/Gaimushō kenkyū-an" [Proposed Greater East Asia Declaration/Proposal Based on the Foreign Ministry's Study] (October 4, 1943) (included in the microfilm, *Japan Ministry of Foreign Affairs, 1868–1945*, WT Series, Reel 52, a collection of the historic document on constitution of the National Diet Library).

construction of an order that eternally liberates Greater East Asia, promotes self-motivating improvement and development, and guarantees co-existence and co-prosperity as well as the stability of the entire Greater East Asia.

(2) Each of the Greater East Asian countries wishes to mutually respect its partners' autonomy, independence, and territories and firmly establish relations of neighborly fraternity and mutual assistance and cooperation.

(3) Each of the Greater East Asian countries wishes to jointly protect Greater East Asia from exogenous threats and aggressions.

(4) Each of the Greater East Asian countries wishes to closely collaborate and cooperate with each other in the economic realm in order to improve peoples' living standards and stabilize Greater East Asia and, at the same time, open its resources widely to the world under the principle of equality and reciprocal benefit and promote trade so as to contribute to the development and prosperity of the world economy.

(5) Each of the Greater East Asian countries wishes to mutually respect its partners' natural characteristics of ethnic cultures, promote "Asian" civilization, and, thereby, contribute to advancement of the peoples and civilizations of the entire world.

The principle of free religion must be respected by each country of Greater East Asia.

Particularly noteworthy in this proposal was retrogression to the argument of the Trade Bureau for a "planned economy" and a "controlled economy"—which had been a point of contention—in the form of an emphasis on the "principle of reciprocal benefit" and the "opening of resources." However, one could detect in the use of such terms as "reciprocal cooperation" and "joint," the Foreign Ministry's consideration of the military's wish to substantively secure Japan's political and economic leadership, as Andō had argued. Meanwhile, there is a reason to believe that the Trade Bureau convened the Economic Committee of the Study Group on War Aims several times in order to make the declaration adopt the Trade Bureau's economic policy argument, which, it appeared, the Research Committee could not ignore.[14]

Shigemitsu himself applied amendments to the *Proposal Based on the Foreign Ministry's Study* twice, and these are shown below.[15] But the most conspicuous change was the deletion of article three.

Shigemitsu Revision of the *Proposal Based on the Foreign Ministry's Study*

In order to eternally liberate Greater East Asia from aggression and exploitation by external powers, construct relations of fraternity in Greater East Asia based on moral principles, and thereby contribute to the construction of a world of universal co-prosperity and to the peaceful development of mankind, representatives of Greater East Asian governments declare as follows:

(1) Each of the Greater East Asian countries is firmly determined to eternally liberate Greater East Asia and consolidate stability and security as well as the co-existence and co-prosperity of the entire Greater East Asia on the basis of self-motivating improvement and development of the peoples of Greater East Asia.

(2) Each of the Greater East Asian countries wishes to mutually respect partners' autonomy, independence, and territories and firmly establish equal and mutually cooperative relations of neighborly fraternity.

(3) Each of the Greater East Asian countries wishes to improve peoples'

---

14 For instance, the Economic Committee was convened on September 29 and October 12, 1943, in which "economic policy of the Greater East Asia Co-Prosperity Sphere" was discussed. One of the participating members, Ishii Itarō, criticized these two meetings, saying, "The so-called co-prosperity sphere is utterly infeasible because Japan is not endowed with the power and virtue to carry it out," and "It can be likened to an attempt to introduce an armored state camouflaged with clothes to East Asia." *Ishii Itarō nikki*, entries of September 29 and October 12, 1943.

15 *Gaimushō Kenkyū-an* revised by Shigemitsu. (included in the microfilm, *Japan Ministry of Foreign Affairs, 1868–1945*, WT Series, Reel 52, National Diet Library collection of historical documents on the Constitution).

living standards and promote economic development of the entire Greater East Asia through close economic partnership under the principle of equality and reciprocal benefit. At the same time, every member country wishes to cooperate for economic development and prosperity of the Sphere by voluntarily opening its resources to the world, expanding trade with the external world, and eliminating obstacles to international traffic.

(4) Each of the Greater East Asian countries wishes to mutually respect indigenous traditions, religions, and culture, promote exaltation of indigenous spiritual civilization in Asia, promote broad cultural exchange, and thereby, contribute to development of the peoples and civilizations of the entire world.

Particularly noteworthy about this Shigemitsu revision was avoidance of the use of such terms as "cooperation" and "jointly" among countries in the Sphere in the core portion of the declaration. More specifically, article three on joint defense of the *Proposal Based on the Foreign Ministry's Study* was completely removed, the wording "relations of neighborly fraternity and mutual assistance and cooperation" in article two was replaced by "equal and mutually cooperative relations of neighborly fraternity," and the phrase "to closely collaborate and cooperate with each other in the economic realm" in article four was changed to "close economic partnership." If reference to "cooperation" and "jointly" indeed harbored, as Andō had pointed out, an intention to leave some space for Japan's leadership, Shigemitsu rejected that intention and, instead, tried to grant full independence and equality to each country in the sphere. In other words, Shigemitsu turned down, both in name and substance, all the references that could imply tolerance of Japan's political, economic, and military leadership in the sphere.

Aside from the above factors, the complete elimination of article three on joint defense was also attributable to the confirmation of a policy to avoid reference to joint defense in the drafts of alliance treaties with the Burmese,

Philippine, and Nanjing governments, leaving the matter subject to separate consultations after the end of the war. Behind this was the aforementioned schism of views within the Imperial Army over the shape of joint defense (see chapter 6).

(4) Intra-government Politics Regarding the Draft Declaration

But this Foreign Ministry proposal revised by Shigemitsu, which was supposed to be the final draft, had to once again face a setback in the course of coordination with the draft declaration proposed by the Ministry of Greater East Asia. The drafting of the latter had been almost exclusively commissioned to Ōkawa Shūmei and the Kokusaku Kenkyūkai (Research Institute of National Policy). Because the War Guidance Office of the Imperial Army General Staff Office had commented that the draft "contains no satisfactory ideas, including some which are too ideological to be realistic, and others which merely stress the Imperial Way beyond the comprehension of the peoples of Greater East Asia," the draft was conjectured to be significantly different from the Foreign Ministry proposal.[16]

The coordination of the Foreign Ministry's final draft with the Greater East Asia Ministry's proposal resulted in an October 20 draft. The main characteristics of this October 20 draft were its denouncement of the Allies' "insatiable lust for aggression, exploitation, and enslavement of Greater East Asia" and the addition of a lengthy preamble which declared that each

---

16 *Kimitsu sensō nisshi* (entry of October 14, 1943). Ōkawa Shūmei, founder of Tōa Keizai Chōsakyoku Fuzoku Kenkyūsho (Research Institute of the East Asiatic Economic Investigation Bureau, commonly known as "Ōkawajuku") was requested to draft the declaration by Uyama Atsushi and Sugihara Arata, director of General Affairs Division, Ministry of Greater East Asia. (See Ōkawa Shūmei Kenshōkai, ed., *Ōkawa Shūmei nikki* [Ōkawa Shūmei Diary], Iwasaki Gakujutsu Shuppan, 1986, entries of July 1, August 12 and 18, October 5 and 6, and November 27, 1943). According to *Yabe Teiji nikki: Ichō no maki* [Yabe Teiji Diary: Gingko Tree Volume] edited by Yabe Teiji Nikki Kankōkai (Yomiuri Shimbunsha, 1974), the Ministry of Greater East Asia commissioned Yabe to draft the declaration on October 6, 1943, and the ministry sent to Yabe what it had submitted to the Research Institute of National Policy as a draft declaration (see p. 653). But in the end, neither the Ōkawa proposal nor the Yabe proposal was adopted. (See Ōkawa Shūmei nikki's entry of February 25, 1944 and *Yabe Teiji nikki*, p. 683.)

country of Greater East Asia had "resolved to construct a new order based on moral principle in Greater East Asia." Still, the text of the October 20 draft essentially adopted the principles set out by the Foreign Ministry's draft. Let us explore here why the addition of the lengthy preamble was decided.

Upon hearing Shigemitsu's intention, the executive committee of the Research Committee on War Purposes argued for two separate declarations: a joint declaration stipulating the fundamental principles of "postwar management" and "establishing of Greater East Asia," and a separate declaration on the successful conclusion of the ongoing war. Thus, the first one—the joint declaration—had to manifest "principles of postwar management" that overshined the Atlantic Charter so as to "induce among peoples of Greater East Asia the desire to voluntarily cooperate with the war effort and, at the same time, eliminate their anxieties over the future," rather than contribute to the waging of the current war. The joint declaration also had to "make the United States and Britain realize that the war was caused by them, not us" and that we were upholding "principles that are objectively fair and appropriate in anyone's eyes."[17] However, the Ministry of Greater East Asia and the Army Ministry insisted on a unified declaration, arguing that the "successful conclusion of the war and construction of Greater East Asia are two sides of the same coin and, therefore, inseparable." Although the Foreign Ministry refuted with the argument that "it would be inconvenient to unify the two from the viewpoint of termination of the war and postwar settlements," its proposal to prepare two declarations was turned down in the end. Instead, a preamble that was incongruent with the text of the declaration was drafted by the Ministry of Greater East Asia and added to the declaration.[18]

The draft declaration, in which the argument of the Ministry of Greater East Asia had been adopted, was submitted to the Liaison Conference

---

17 Ministry of Foreign Affairs' "explanation" (on October 18) (included in the previously cited microfilm, *Japan Ministry of Foreign Affairs, 1868–1945*, WT Series, Reel 52, National Diet Library collection of historical documents on the Constitution). *Shōwa 18-nendo shitsumu hōkoku*, pp. 142–143.
18 Ibid. "Ippondate to suru riyū" [Reasons for Unification of the Declaration], October 19, 1943.

between the government and Imperial General Headquarters on October 21, 1943. While details of the deliberations there are unknown, it was recorded that the meeting became a clamorous session in which Minister for Greater East Asia Aoki's insistence on upholding the submitted draft was met by Shigemitsu's argument against the "blatant expression of exclusivist sentiment to view Greater East Asia as a bloc" and the need to make the declaration readily acceptable by participating countries.[19] In the end, the draft declaration was handed down to assistants of the executive members of the Liaison Conference for further coordination. Consequently, the following draft declaration was compiled. (Portions in brackets were inserted at the final stage. Underlined portions were deleted.)

Preamble

To begin with, it is the fundamental essence of the establishment of world peace for each country in the world to find its own place and share the pleasure of universal co-prosperity through mutual cooperation and assistance. However, Britain and the United States would not hesitate to suppress other states and other peoples for their own prosperity. In particular, Greater East Asia has been the target of their insatiable lust for aggression and exploitation, and they gave rein to their ambitions to enslave Greater East Asia. In the end, they attempted to undermine the stability of Greater East Asia from its foundation and this became the cause of the Greater East Asia War.

It is the hope of each and every member country of Greater East Asia to cooperate with one other to bring the Greater East Asia War to a successful conclusion and accomplish genuine self-sufficiency and self-defense by breaking away from the fetters of Britain and the United States. And it is our hope to build Greater East Asia on the basis of the following codes of conduct and, thereby, contribute to the establishment of world peace.

---

19 Imperial Japanese Army General Staff Office, ed., *Sugiyama memo, ge* [Sugiyama memorandum vol. 2], Hara Shobō, 1989, p. 503.

Text of the Declaration

(1) Each country of Greater East Asia wishes to cooperate with others to attain stability of Greater East Asia and construct a <u>new</u> order based on moral principles.

(2) Each country of Greater East Asia wishes to respect each other's autonomy and independence, bring about the result of reciprocal assistance and friendship, and establish harmony in Greater East Asia.

(3) Each country of Greater East Asia wishes to <u>mutually eliminate inter-ethnic biases</u>, respect each other's traditions, [encourage development of the creativity of each race], and boost Greater East Asian culture.

(4) Each country of Greater East Asia closely joins hands on equal footing to induce the sphere's economic development and promote prosperity of Greater East Asia.

(5) Each country of Greater East Asia wishes to promote friendship with all the countries in the world, [thoroughly eliminate racial discrimination,] carry out broad cultural exchange, willingly open its resources to the world, and, thereby, contribute to advancement of the world.

The following three points of contention were disputed among assistants of the Liaison Conference's executive members. First was the portion of "to mutually eliminate inter-ethnic biases," which was eventually deleted and replaced with "encourage development of the creativity of each race," which had been a part of article three of the October 20 draft. The reason given for this change was that "the item article three as a whole appeared wanting." The second source of contention was the strong insistence on the part of the Military Affairs Bureau of the Army Ministry to insert "thoroughly eliminate racial discrimination" in article five. Satō Kenryō, director-general of the Military Affairs Bureau, recalled how legitimate the Japanese proposal for elimination of racial discrimination at the Paris Peace Conference in 1919 was, and it dawned on him that it was this proposal of the Japanese delegation that had chiefly justified the insistence that Japan understood Asian peoples' hearts.[20] Ministries other than the Army Ministry were of the view that "it is best not to touch on the racial issue" and, if reference to the racial issue was unavoidable, that it should take the form of a noncommittal assertion "to persist with the cause of fraternity among humanity." In the end, though, the Military Affairs Bureau's proposal was adopted unmodified.[21]

The third contention was about "willingly open its resources to the world" in article five. The Imperial Japanese Navy strongly opposed this wording. The Imperial Navy feared that this statement might "lead to serious problems in the future." The Imperial Navy was also skeptical about other countries in Greater East Asia agreeing with this commitment. The Navy submitted a counterproposal that "[Each country of Greater East Asia intends] to mutually trade resources broadly," which the Ministry of Finance also supported. Nevertheless, this wording failed to be inserted in the face of united opposition from the Ministry of Greater East Asia, the Ministry of Foreign Affairs, the Army Ministry, and the Ministry of Navy. Of the three points of contention, the second and the third ones were carried over to the Liaison Conference on October 23.[22]

The October 23 Liaison Conference deliberated on the joint declaration draft for the final time. The proposed "new order" in article one was changed to "order." The Imperial Navy submitted a proposal to revise article five by adding, "to persist with the cause of fraternity among humanity" and "to mutually trade resources broadly." As the result of deliberations, "thoroughly eliminate racial discrimination" and "willingly open its resources to

20 "Sengen'an shingi dai-6 dokkai" [Sixth Deliberation on the Draft Declaration] (Division I, Political Affairs Bureau, Ministry of Foreign Affairs) (included in the microfilm, *Japan Ministry of Foreign Affairs, 1868–1945*, WT Series, Reel 52, National Diet Library collection of historical documents on the Constitution), Satō Kenryō, *Daitōa Sensō kaikoroku* [Memoir on the Greater East Asia War], Tokuma Shoten, 1966, p. 319.
21 Ibid., *Sugiyama memo, ge*, pp. 503–504.
22 Ibid.

the world" were both formally adopted as originally proposed.[23] The fact that the Imperial Navy was particularly critical about the Greater East Asia declaration itself from the viewpoint of securing necessary natural resources has also been discussed in preceding chapters of this book.

Readers should be reminded that, in the final draft declaration, such terms as "to cooperate with each other" and "closely join hands," which Shigemitsu had cautiously tried to avoid, were revived in the first and fourth articles, respectively. A far more important setback, however, was adoption of a preamble that was substantively incongruent with the text of the declaration. The preamble, which was adopted so as to address the viewpoint of contribution to the waging of the war, was an attempt to accommodate the argument of the Greater East Asia Ministry, albeit in a somewhat simplified manner. The addition of the preamble had the effect of weakening the character of the joint declaration as a postwar scenario. When Shigemitsu remained in the Koiso Kuniaki cabinet formed in July 1944 as its foreign minister, he accepted a concurrent appointment to minister for Greater East Asia. One of the reasons Shigemitsu agreed to serve as the Greater East Asia minister was that he found the ministry to be an obstacle to implementation of the Greater East Asia new policy.[24]

2. The Greater East Asia Conference

(1) Contexts of Speeches by Delegates of Participating Countries

The Greater East Asia Conference convened on November 15, 1943, at the Imperial Diet was attended by Zhang Jinghui, prime minister of Manchukuo; Wang Jingwei, president of the Reorganized National Government of the

---

23 Kajima Institute of International Peace, ed., *Nippon gaikōshi 30: Daitōa Sensō senji gaikō* [History of Japan's Foreign Relations 24: Wartime Diplomacy, 1941–1945], Kajima Institute Publishing, 1971, pp. 473–474.
24 For details on this development, see *Shigemitsu Mamoru shuki*, pp. 421–422.

Republic of China; Ba Maw, head of state of the State of Burma; Jose Laurel, president of the Second Philippine Republic; and Prince Wan Waithayakon, envoy from the Kingdom of Thailand. Additionally, Subhas Chandra Bose, head of state of the Provisional Government of Free India, participated as an observer. The attitudes of these participants toward the conference were by no means uniform. Their evaluations of the Greater East Asia Declaration as well as the contents of their speeches reflected the differences in their attitude toward cooperation with Japan and their respective domestic situations. Therefore, they deserve to be studied closely.

It should be pointed out that the draft of the Greater East Asia Declaration had been finalized on October 23, and it had been circulated among conference participants via their respective ambassadors to collect their feedback. Ba Maw and Wan Waithayakon submitted requests for revisions to the final draft. Ba Maw proposed that "Since this declaration also has an element of a counterargument against the Atlantic Charter, it should address beyond Greater East Asia to all the anti-British, anti-US peoples in the world (e.g., Arabians, Egyptians, and Palestinians) and include an appeal to these peoples to join us." Although Sawada Renzō, Japanese ambassador to Burma, found this argument "not entirely unreasonable" and included it in the agenda of pre-conference consultations, the Japanese government did not accept this suggestion.[25] While there is no knowing how Shigemitsu took this particular suggestion, we do know that Shigemitsu had no intention to make the Greater East Asia Conference a conference among ethnic representatives, and he perceived the declarants of the Greater East Asia Declaration vaguely as "independent states" within the Greater East Asia Sphere. Therefore, it is imagined that Shigemitsu had no space to

---

25 "Daitōa Kyōdō Sengen-an ni kansuru setsumei" [Explanation on the Greater East Asia Declaration Draft] (Ministry of Foreign Affairs Document A7.0.0.9-48 "Daitōa Sensō kankei ikken: Daitōa Kaigi kankei" [Matters Related to the Greater East Asia War: Matters Related to the Greater East Asia Conference]).

accommodate Ba Maw's suggestion.[26]

As a result of the above intercourses, Ba Maw's speech on November 5 merely stressed "Asian unity." His speech on the second day on the joint declaration, however, was more provocative, stating, "From an idealist viewpoint, some of its wordings appear to be too narrowly focused. . . . The spirit contained in the Greater East Asia Declaration should be applied more broadly in the future to embrace all the problems in 'Asia.'"[27] While it is unknown if this particular portion of Ba Maw's speech had been censored by the Japanese side or not, it can be conjectured from this that his speech must have included his suggestion that the declaration should also be addressed to all the "anti-Britain, anti-US peoples in the world," along with his above pre-conference suggestion.

Wan Waithayakon, in contrast, requested that the declaration should emphasize economic "reciprocal benefit" relations between the Greater East Asia region and external regions of the world. Upon consultation with Prime Minister Plaek Phibunsongkhram, Wan Waithayakon proposed revising article five along this line. Although the Japanese government did not concur with this suggestion either, Wan Waithayakon nevertheless argued in his first-day speech that relations between the Greater East Asian countries and the rest of the world should be administered with "the principle of mutual respect for independence and sovereignty" and "the principle of economic reciprocity." In his speech on the second day, while praising the

---

26 According to *Sugiyama memo, ge*, p. 404, Shigemitsu remarked in the Liaison Conference toward the end of May, which decided the organization of the Greater East Asia Conference, that "Participants of the Greater East Asia Conference should be representatives of independent states in the sphere. It would be inconvenient to invite representatives of all the races in the region in light of relations with independent states." He perceived that "each state of Greater East Asia" should be a declarant and, therefore, he had no intention of making the conference a forum of ethnic representatives. This was to avoid including Korea and Taiwan, which were in the process of reinvigorated "internalization" and "assimilation as the emperor's subjects" as well as Indonesia, which failed to go beyond autonomy, as declarants.

27 For the speeches of delegates at the Greater East Asia Conference, see "Daitōa Kaigi giji sokkiroku" [Stenographic Record of the Greater East Asia Conference], pp. 304–345 of Itō Takashi et al., eds., *Tōjō naikaku sōridaijin kimitsu kiroku* [Confidential Records of Prime Minister Tōjō], University of Tokyo Press, 1990. (*Tōjō kimitsu kiroku*)

declaration's emphasis on "the spirit of mutual benefit" in economic development of Greater East Asia, this envoy from Thailand confined himself to remarking, "In terms of relations between the Greater East Asian countries and the rest of the world, this declaration fits very well with the real state of affairs." Again, it is not known whether his speech manuscript was censored and edited by the Japanese side. His remark in the second-day speech could be interpreted as a euphemistic criticism of Japan's rejection of his pre-conference suggestions.

It should be noted also that Wang Jinwei's speech was charged with another mission of sending a signal to the Chongqing regime. This was because it had been decided by the Liaison Conference in September that maneuvering toward Chongqing would be carried out through the Nanjing government. When Prime Minister Tōjō met Wang in Tokyo, he requested the Nanjing government's cooperation toward achieving "a complete peace." Wang promised that he would "take all possible measures in order to appeal specifically to the Chongqing side on the occasion of the Greater East Asia Conference."

Thus, in his first-day speech, Wang commemorated a deed of Sun Yat-sen, quoting his Pan-Asianism speech delivered in Kobe in 1924, and repeatedly emphasized the significance of the "independence and autonomy" of Greater East Asian states. In his second-day speech, Wang again stressed, "It is the spirit of the Greater East Asia Declaration that we should strive to realize co-existence and co-prosperity through independence and autonomy." Moreover, Wang requested another chance to speak on the second day. That time, he reiterated the importance of the joint declaration and concluded his remarks by saying, "China has yet to be integrated. The earlier it is united, the sooner we can concentrate all of our spiritual and physical powers on the entirety of China and share the burden of management of Greater East Asia."

By far, the most noteworthy speech, however, was that of Jose Laurel. Particularly in his first-day speech, he explained, "Establishment of the co-prosperity sphere is not for the benefit of the Empire of Japan alone, nor is it for the benefit of other specific states in the sphere. The fundamental spirit of the East Asia Co-Prosperity Sphere is to recognize the freedom and independence of each member state and, on that basis, construct a sphere in which states prosper together." Laurel repeated that, "Even when Japan alone prospers and Japan alone survives, I do not think that Japan would be happy if peoples in the Orient are in decay or in distress." By emphasizing the universality of the spirit of the declaration, Laurel skillfully rejected Japan's hegemonic position in Greater East Asia.[28]

In the same speech, by stating, "Asian peoples wish to mutually assure ourselves that we will never become the prey of Western exploitation," Laurel appealed to participating states to consolidate the attitude to reject the comeback of Western colonial masters. In other words, Laurel's speech was a manifestation of not only his denial of the revival of Western colonialism but also his rejection of the establishment of Japan's hegemonic position beyond the hidden intention of the Japanese side. And this might indeed have been the significance of the Greater East Asia Conference that participating representatives commonly wished to find.

(2) Thailand and Indonesia

Among invited representatives of Greater East Asian states, Prime Minister Plaek Phibunsongkhram of Thailand adamantly refused to participate in the Greater East Asia Conference. The reasons for his decline, as communicated via Ambassador Tsubogami Teiji, included, aside from his health concern, (1) Thailand differed in its "motive of history and shape of state" from Burma, the Philippines, Manchukuo, and the Republic of China and (2) participation in the conference would be interpreted as submission to Japan, which could embroil domestic political situations. It was reported

---

28 A similar assessment of this speech is found in *Daitōa Kaigi to Daitōa Kyōdō Sengen o megutte*, p. 414.

by the Japanese legation in Thailand that, should Plaek Phibunsongkhram be further pressed to participate, he would convene the parliament to resign from the prime ministership so that a newly appointed prime minister would be dispatched to Tokyo.[29]

Around the time the invitation to the Greater East Asia Conference was sent out, Prime Minister Tōjō commented, "Thailand is most worrisome in terms of the solidarity of Greater East Asia." The Japanese government did not necessarily fully trust the Plaek Phibunsongkhram government's collaboration with Japan, and the prime minister's reasons for not participating in the conference revealed the instability of the political foundation of his regime.[30] Therefore, an extraordinary measure that was possible only under military occupation was taken regarding Thailand—that is, the devolution of territory, or, from Thailand's viewpoint, the recovery of lost territory.

In February 1943, Tōjō commented that, in order to strengthen the Plaek Phibunsongkhram government and win over Thai people's hearts, it would be necessary to provide the prime minister with a "gift" so that the Thai people would hold him in high esteem. And the gift for Plaek Phibunsongkhram was the transfer of the provinces of Kengtung and Mong Pan of Shan State (formerly British Burma) to Thai territory and the recovery of four Malay provinces (the states of Perlis, Kedah, Kelantan and Terengganu of British Malaya that had been surrendered by Siam after the Anglo-Siamese Treaty of 1909).[31] These measures were included at Tōjō's request in the *Daitōa Seiryaku shidō taikō* (Outlines for the Political Guidance of Greater East Asia) issued in May 1943 without any prior consultation with the Thai people. (It is reported that although Plaek Phibunsongkhram had preferred the Tenasserim Division of Burma and a portion of Indochina over the two Shan provinces, which were poor in natural resources and costly to govern,

---

29 *Kimitsu sensō nisshi*, entry of October 9, 1943.
30 *Tōjō kimitsu kiroku*, p. 208, Gotō Ken'ichi, *Kindai Nippon to Tōnan Ajia*, [Modern Japan and Southeast Asia], Iwanami Shoten, 1995, pp. 274–275.
31 *Tōjō kimitsu kiroku*, p. 208, p. 500.

the Japanese government did not accede to his request in consideration of relations with France and Burma.)[32] In early July in Singapore, Prime Minister Tōjō announced to Ba Maw that the provinces of Kengtung and Mong Pan would be transferred to Thailand. Ba Maw commented to Isomura Takesuke, vice chief of the Army General Staff, "While it might be possible to make the Independence Preparatory Committee and others understand Japan's intention, it will take considerable devising to make the Burmese people understand it." In the end, he decided to accept Japan's offer.[33]

The announcement of Plaek Phibunsongkhram's non-participation in the Greater East Asia Conference signified that the special considerations his government had received had born no fruit at all. The reaction of the Imperial Japanese Army General Staff Office was that "There is no one who is not infuriated by Plaek Phibunsongkhram's conduct." Prime Minister Tōjō himself was so annoyed that he proposed to the chief of the Army General Staff at the Liaison Conference on this particular issue that the Imperial Army should probably consider dispatching two or three army divisions to Thailand.[34] The Liaison Conference, in the end, decided that participation in the conference by proxy was permissible and successfully persuaded the Thai side to dispatch Prince Wan Waithayakon, allowing Japan to narrowly save face.

Plaek Phibunsongkhram would not listen when Minister for Greater East Asia Aoki visited Thailand in April 1943 to persuade him to participate in the conference for the sake of the solidarity of Greater East Asia.

---

32 E. Bruce Reynolds, *Thailand and Japan's Southern Advance, 1940–1945* (London: Macmillan Press, 1994), pp. 154–155.

33 Bōei Kenkyūsho Senshibu, ed., *Shiryōshū Nanpō no gunsei* [Documents on Military Administration in Southern Territories], Asagumo Shimbunsha, 1985, p. 486. While the British government rejected this measure outright, it refrained from making an announcement and simply ignored it. The British Colonial Office viewed this measure as part of a series of compromise policies toward the occupied territories and conjectured that it must have been devised by Shigemitsu. Although this "gift" from Japan would never solve Thailand's economic problems, the Colonial Office nonetheless apprehended that it could temporarily please the Thai people. ("Malay and Shan States: Japan and Siam," 16 July 1943, F13634/F0371/35949.)

34 *Kimitsu sensō nisshi*, entry of October 9, 1943, *Sugiyama memo, ge*, p. 501.

According to Aoki, the Thai prime minister had been determined not to accept the invitation from Japan as long as Thailand was treated on the same level as Manchukuo and the Nanjing government, both of which were puppet governments of the Empire of Japan.[35]

Iwata Reitetsu, who had been director of intelligence at the Japanese embassy to Thailand since before eruption of the war, attempted to persuade the Thai prime minister to accept the invitation. In his speech (restricted to members only) at the committee on southern territories of the Society for Promotion of Japanese Diplomacy in early 1944, Iwata introduced the following three points in relation to Plaek Phibunsongkhram's refusal to participate in the conference. First, while the Philippines and Burma could interpret their independence as a gain from the war, being involved in the war itself was a loss for Thailand, which had maintained its independence since long before the war. Hence, a point of pride on the part of Thailand was that its starting point was different from those newly independent states. And this pride coincided with the report of Tsubogami Teiji and the observation of Minister Aoki that Thailand's "motive of history and shape of state" was different from the Philippines or Burma.

Second, Iwata concluded that, to Thailand's prime minister, "Being a member of the Greater East Asia Co-Prosperity Sphere entails Thailand being a colony of Japan," making him wish to avoid any commitment. Third, from its own experience of having survived by putting itself in the middle between Britain and France, two major colonial powers in the region, "Thailand would hardly welcome the emergence of a unifying hegemon in East Asia. The Thai people cannot cast aside apprehension over what might happen in the future when Japan becomes the solitary hegemon in the region."[36]

---

35 Reynolds, op cit., pp. 162–163.
36 Iwata Reitetsu, "Saikin ni okeru Taikoku no naijō" [Recent Situations inside Thailand] (Document prepared for a special committee of the Society for Promotion of Japanese Diplomacy, March 5, 1944), pp. 23–25.

Iwata found the Thai government's unified wish to maintain its independence to be a more significant political background behind its nonparticipation in the Greater East Asia Conference than the fear of the government's political foundation. In Iwata's assessment, despite an alliance treaty between Thailand and Japan, the government and people of Thailand had not given up "the hope of restoring the country's neutrality." In other words:

> Japan guarantees Thailand's independence by Article 2 of the Japan-Thailand Alliance Treaty, which has allowed Thailand to promote nationalism with along with Japan's guarantee not to interfere in domestic affairs. At this point, it should be said that the alliance treaty has been turned to Thailand's own advantage."[37]

It was quite sharp of Iwata to recognize that Thailand had taken advantage of the bilateral alliance treaty to fend off interference from Japan and nurture its own nationalism. This analysis coincides with findings from recent studies on Thailand. According to the study of the nature of the Plaek Phibunsongkhram government's collaboration with Japan by E. Bruce Reynolds, for instance, realism was the essence of Thailand's stance. That is to say, in order to survive as an independent nation, Thailand would not hesitate to skillfully maneuver major powers such as Japan, Britain, and the United States based on shrewd calculations. Thailand's pose to uphold alliance relations with Japan only when its security appeared to depend on the Japanese military was, in Reynolds' assessment, a typical manifestation of this realism—and so was Plaek Phibunsongkhram's non-participation in the Greater East Asia Conference.[38]

In contrast with Thailand, Indonesia ached in vain to be invited to the Greater East Asia Conference. Perhaps in consideration of this intricacy of

---

37 Ibid., pp. 22–23.
38 Reynolds, op cit., pp. 167–168.

the Indonesian situation, Jose Laurel stressed in his two speeches that there was no difference in interest between peoples in Java, Borneo, and Sumatra and the countries participating in the conference, referring to the need for solidarity with Indonesia. Needless to say, this significant proposal from Laurel on the change of Indonesia's status never made it into the agenda of the conference, which was managed according to the scenario prepared by Japan.[39] While the true intention of Laurel remains unclear, it seems beyond doubt that it was at least in part a form of restraint on Japan's stubborn attitude toward Indonesia.

As introduced earlier in chapter 6, the *Outlines for the Political Guidance of Greater East Asia* (adopted by the Imperial Council in May 1943) gave Indonesia the position of an "Imperial territory." It was extremely difficult for Indonesia to graduate from that status to attain independence. At the 82nd extraordinary session of the Imperial Diet one month after the adoption of the *Outlines for the Political Guidance of Greater East Asia*, the Japanese government made an announcement on a measure regarding the political participation by the citizens of Java. This was followed by the Japanese military administration in Java's decision to set up a Chūō Sangiin (Central Advisory Council) as an advisory organization to military administration. However, the Imperial Japanese Army and Navy as well as Prime Minister Tōjō were reluctant to commit to any further move toward autonomy or independence for Indonesia.

The Indonesian wish to obtain a position similar to those of the Philippines and Burma had been communicated to the Japanese side repeatedly. When Greater East Asia Minister Aoki toured the southern territories in May 1943, Sukarno and Hatta pleaded with Aoki for Indonesia to obtain a "glorious position" as an integrated country by combining territories divided into several military administration districts. It is reported that Aoki replied to this request as follows:

---

39 Gotō (1995), pp. 195–196, p. 266.

While Japan has no objection to recognizing Indonesia's independence, I am afraid Indonesia has only a few people with administrative experience because the Netherlands failed to have local people participate in its administrative organ. Therefore, we prefer to grant independence to Indonesia after a certain period of experience in autonomous administration.

Sukarno and Hatta were not satisfied with Aoki's reply, and they were apparently unhappy about Indonesia's being treated differently from the Philippines and Burma.[40]

The Japanese business circle sent an observation mission to Java about two months prior to the Greater East Asian Conference. At the mission debriefing for Prime Minister Tōjō on September 26, the mission's leader, Kodama Kenji, conveyed requests from the Indonesians, including, "While residents of Indonesia have always trusted and supported Japan, they do not wish to be left behind other Asian peoples," and "Indonesia should not be divided into several regions." Kodama also reported to Tōjō that Indonesians had also asked concrete questions about the conditions to be cleared to realize Indonesian independence. Tōjō's response to these requests is not known.[41]

Even when Indonesian leaders including Sukarno and Hatta visited Japan in mid-November 1943, after the Greater East Asia Conference, no measure was taken by Japan to accommodate their requests. The only exception was the lifting of the ban on the use of the Indonesian anthem and flag that had been imposed since the start of military administration. However, due to strong protests in Indonesia, the ban was reinstated

---

40 Aoki Kazuo, *Waga 90-nen no shōgai o kaerimite* [Looking Back on my 90-Year Life], Kōdansha, 1981, pp. 176–177, Waseda Daigaku Ōkuma Kinen Shakai Kagaku Kenkyūsho, ed., *Indoneshia ni okeru Nippon gunsei no kenkyū* [Study of Japanese Military Administration in Indonesia], Kinokuniya Shoten, 1959, p. 399.

41 *Kimitsu sensō nisshi*, entry of September 26, 1943.

except in Java.[42] Shigemitsu also met with the delegation visiting Japan, but he confined himself to giving "encouragement" to their efforts toward independence.[43]

Because Indonesia had not been invited to the Greater East Asia Conference and due to the fact that the trip to Japan by Sukarno and other leaders had not borne fruit, Indonesians increased their distrust of Japan to the extent that they began to suspect that "Japan might draw a distinction between Java and Burma and the Philippines and eventually make it a territory under Japan's direct control along with the Malay Peninsula."[44] On the Japanese side, too, some like Hayashi Kyūjiro, diplomat and adviser to the Java Military Administration, submitted a view in 1944 that if Japan desired Indonesia's collaboration, it would be essential to promptly announce the policy to grant Indonesia independence.[45] While Shigemitsu highly valued this view submitted by Hayashi, it was not easy to change the status of Indonesia as a "territory of the Empire of Japan."[46]

3. Recognition of the Provisional Government of Free India and the Independence Issue

(1) Scenario for Recognition of the Provisional Government of Free India

Ba Maw, who took the podium last, immediately after the unanimous adoption of the Greater East Asia Joint Declaration, took up India's independence as "an issue that is inseparable from the objective of the Greater East Asia Conference," and, after declaring that there was "no freedom for

---

42 Gotō (1995), pp. 196–197.

43 Shigemitsu Mamoru, *Shōwa no dōran, ge* [Shōwa in Turmoil, vol. 2], Chūō Kōronsha, 1952, pp. 248–249.

44 "Jawa tō no dokuritsu kyoyo seimei ni kansuru kinkyū kōsatsu" [Urgent Examination of the Statement to Grant Independence to Java and Other Territories].

45 Gotō (1995), pp. 197–198. Hayashi's view is also included in *Indoneshia ni okeru Nippon gunsei no kenkyū* on pp. 591–593.

46 Shigemitsu (1952), p. 248.

Asia without freedom for India," he requested Chandra Bose to speak. Bose revealed his resolve to face the last decisive battle against British imperialism and concluded his speech by praising the Greater East Asia Joint Declaration as "not only a charter on the liberation of the peoples of Greater East Asia but also a charter on the liberation of all peoples in Asia." Hearing this speech, Prime Minister Tōjō announced that Japan was ready to transfer the Andaman and Nicobar Islands, which the Imperial Japanese Navy had been occupying, to the Provisional Government of Free India. This policy to provide the Provisional Government of Free India, which did not possess territory of its own, with these two sets of islands, was Tōjō's response to requests from Bose at the time of the meeting between the two on November 1, 1943. The decision to handle things this way was hastily made at the round-robin Liaison Conference on the morning of November 6.[47] And the scenario of Ba Maw's intervention after adoption of the Greater East Asia Declaration to be followed by Bose's speech, and, subsequently, Tōjō's speech on provision of the two sets of islands to India, had been proposed by Hata Hikosaburō, vice chief of the Army General Staff. This scenario had been negotiated with the provisional government for several days.[48]

Behind this scenario was the need to appease Chandra Bose, whose hope for Japanese troops to advance into India to assist India's independence movement was unlikely to be fulfilled with Japan's decision to abandon its strategy of "bringing Britain to its knees."

As mentioned earlier, Bose, during his stay in Germany, had been disappointed with Hitler's lack of intention to advance into India as well as with the increasingly remote possibility that Japan would do the same. And yet, Bose still remained motivated enough to return to Asia and contribute to India's independence. Bose departed the Kiel Naval Base onboard a submarine in January 1943 and arrived in Southeast Asia in mid-May that

---

47 *Tōjō kimitsu kiroku*, p. 287, *Kimitsu sensō nisshi*, entry of November 6, 1943.
48 *Kimitsu sensō nisshi*, entry of November 6, 1943.

year. Immediately after his arrival in Asia, he delivered a speech in which he argued that the "civil disobedience movement must evolve into an armed struggle. Unless Indian people are caught in a hail of gunfire, they will never be able to obtain independence." This statement demonstrates Bose's unbending eagerness for an armed struggle.[49]

Also in 1943, Bose visited Shigemitsu in early July and argued for, along with Japan's prompt implementation of military operations in India, the establishment of the Provisional Government of Free India so as to obtain recognition by the Axis countries. While the Imperial Japanese Army General Staff Office remained reluctant about advancing into India, it promised to extend its support for the establishment of a provisional government. The army's promise was partly in response to a request from Shigemitsu, who subsequently instructed the Treaty Bureau of the Ministry of Foreign Affairs to proceed with the recognition procedures. The Treaty Bureau, for its part, on June 11 compiled a memorandum on this issue from the viewpoint of international law. The memorandum pointed out the problems that might arise from recognizing the provisional government in India. According to the bureau, official recognition of a sovereign government presupposes the existence of a sovereign state with its own citizens and territory. If the Japanese government recognized a government without any property as a sovereign state, such as the Provisional Government of Free India, this could not be justified with legal theory, and doing so could "result in inadvertently giving such entities as governments in exile or the Korean Provisional Government in Chongqing theoretical grounds for demanding recognition as a state." Based on these reasons, the Treaty Bureau suggested that, instead of immediately recognizing the Provisional Government of Free India, "it would be more advisable to go a step further and make the Andaman Islands, which are currently the only free Indian area, its territory as a quick fix to

---

49 Milan Hauner, *India in Axis Strategy: Germany, Japan, and Indian Nationalists in the Second World War* (Stuttgart: Klett-Cotta, 1981), p. 562.

give it the appearance of a state and a government."[50]

There was opposition, however, within the Japanese government, including the Imperial Navy, to making the islands of Andaman and Nicobar, which had been occupied by the Imperial Navy as strategic key areas, territories of the Provisional Government of Free India on the grounds of international legal theory. Accordingly, this suggestion by the Treaty Bureau was left without concrete action being taken. In the meantime, Tsubogami Teiji, the Japanese ambassador to Thailand, had been closely watching the activities of Indians in Southeast Asia, including Chandra Bose. Tsubogami realized that, "It is feared that, if Japan's attitude remains obscure, it could make Indians outside India harden their suspicion of Japan, adversely influencing their independence movement." On the basis of this observation, Tsubogami conveyed Bose's strong desire for "Japan's unambiguous recognition of the Provisional Government of Free India from a broader perspective," and requested prompt recognition of the provisional government.[51]

At this point, the Japanese government decided at the October 9 Liaison Conference on recognition of the provisional Indian government without clarifying its position vis-à-vis the islands of Andaman and Nicobar. In Singapore, Bose for his part continued to work on organization of the Indian National Army and the plan to establish a provisional Indian government. The convention of representatives of the Indian Independence League East Asia on October 21 decided on the establishment of the Provisional Government of Free India, which was officially recognized by the Japanese government two days later.

Nevertheless, some argued that, because official recognition must be

---

50 "Jiyū Indo 'rinji seifu' shōnin ni kansuru hōritsujō no iken" [Legal Opinion on Recognition of the Provisional Government of Free India] (June 11, 1943, Division II, Treaty Bureau) (Ministry of Foreign Affairs Document A7.0.0.9-29-2, "Daitōa Sensō kankei ikken: Indo mondai" [Matters Related to Greater East Asia War: India Issue], "Subasu Chandora Bōsu no Indo kari seifu juritsu kankei" [Matters Related to Establishment of Subhas Chandra Bose's Provisional Indian Government]).
51 Telegram of Ambassador Tsubogami addressed to Foreign Minister Shigemitsu on September 25, 1943 (#1395), Ministry of Foreign Affairs Document A7.0.0.9-29-2.

preceded by establishment of the state of Free India according to inter-national law, what Japan did was merely to recognize an entity called the Provisional Government of Free India. And this is the significance of the Treaty Bureau's suggestion on a method to make it a fully recognized sover-eign state or government in the eyes of international law by making the Andaman and Nicobar Islands the territory of Free India.[52] Bose proposed this method during his meeting with Prime Minister Tōjō on November 1, 1943, but, as previously mentioned, this idea had already been studied on the Japanese side.

Bose was apprehensive about the compensation that might be demanded of India in return for the territory, but Prime Minister Tōjō repeatedly stressed that Japan had no territorial or economic ambition.[53] Ayyappan Pillai Madhavan Nair of the Indian Independence League, who had accompanied Bose on his trip to Japan, however, reminisced that the measure was merely "a symbolic gesture" on the part of the Japanese government to provide the provisional government with "a territory" as a tentative base for its activ-ities. As such, Nair maintained, Tōjō had no intention of actually parting with those islands. As Nair had correctly conjectured, it had been planned that Japanese troops would be stationed on the islands under the pretext of Japan-India joint defense after the islands were transferred to the Indian provisional government.[54]

Upon the recognition of the Provisional Government of Free India, Amō Eiji, director-general of the Cabinet Intelligence Bureau, issued a comment saying that, "Although the so-called Atlantic Charter sets out the war aims of Britain and the United States as the principle of self-determination, the

---

52 Gaimushō Kiroku Henshū Iinkai, ed. "Sensōchū ni okeru waga tai-Indo shisaku keii" [Details of Japan's Measures toward India during the War] (Ministry of Foreign Affairs Document A7.0.0.9-29-2, "Daitōa Sensō kankei ikken/Indo mondai" [Matters Related to Greater East Asia War: India Issue]).
53 *Tōjō kimitsu kiroku*, pp. 285–288, p. 303.
54 A.M. Nair, *An India Freedom Fighter in Japan: Memoirs* (Bombay: Oriental Longman, 1982), pp. 290–291, *Tōjō kimitsu kiroku*, pp. 355–360.

fact that India has been left out from this principle reveals the fallacious-ness of their policy."[55] Thus, the plan to give recognition to India's provisional government immediately prior to the Greater East Asia Conference had the hidden agenda of shedding light on the deceitfulness of the war aims of Britain and the United States which, despite the Atlantic Charter, denied independence to India. If Shigemitsu intended to place his hopes on "crushing" the British and American war aims with the Greater East Asia new policy, recognition of India's independence, albeit that of a provisional government, was found to be compatible with such an intention.[56]

(2) Post-Greater East Asia Conference Indian Independence Issue

As Amō aptly pointed out, India's independence issue had not advanced from the viewpoint of the principle of self-determination following the Quit India Movement in August 1942. The British government did not soften its attitude even to Gandhi's civil disobedience movement, nor did it explicitly promise future autonomy or independence. Across the Atlantic, President Franklin Roosevelt of the United States had abstained from being involved in the Indian issue since the 1942 anti-British movement, calling it "an internal problem within the British Empire," and this attitude continued into 1943. Even when his personal representative, William Phillips, reported to Roosevelt that India, like China and Burma, had wanted liberation from foreign control and said that concrete action was called for because the more time passed, the more distrustful of the United States India grew, Roosevelt would not listen.[57] Around the same time, the Chongqing

---

55 On the connection between the Greater East Asia Declaration and the Indian issue, see Francis C. Jones, *Japan's New Order in East Asia* (London: Oxford University Press, 1954), p. 368.

56 Amō Eiji Nikki/Shiryōshū Kankōkai, ed., *Amō Eiji nikki/shiryōshū dai 4-kan* [Amō Eiji Diary/Document Collection, vol. 4], 1982, entry of October 23, 1943.

57 US Department of State, *Papers Relating to the Foreign Relations of the United States, 1943,* vol. 3 (US Government Printing Office), p. 217, Gaddis Smith, *American Diplomacy during the Second World War* (New York: Alfred Knopf, 1985), pp. 84–86.

government in China prepared a draft proposal on the Cairo Conference of November 1943, in which it was proposed that, along with the return of Taiwan and the Pescadores Islands to China and international recognition of Korea's independence, "China, the United States, Britain, and the Soviet Union should jointly issue a declaration to guarantee that India will obtain the status of a self-governing territory immediately after the war and, subsequently, independence within a few years of the end of the war."[58] It appears that, because discussion on the Indian issue was inevitable both at the Cairo Conference and the Tehran Conference, this proposal from the Chongqing government failed to catch the attention of the leaders of Britain, the United States, and the Soviet Union. Nevertheless, it should be said that this proposal clarified the Chongqing government's position vis-à-vis the independence of Asian peoples.

The Chongqing government had been in a difficult international position regarding the independence movement in India since 1942. This was because it was feared that support and assistance for the anti-British movements by the Indian National Congress and others would worsen the Chongqing government's own relations with Britain.[59] Nevertheless, after Chiang Kai-shek's visit to India in February 1942, the Chongqing government maintained the position to basically support India's independence. Thus, the Chongqing government was able to compile the above concrete program for independence for the Cairo Conference.

In contrast, Japan's assistance for India's independence after the Greater East Asia Conference, even for movements outside India, was confined to the range of stratagem accompanying military operations—and this despite

---

58 "Kairo Kaidan no tameno Kokumin Seifu junbian" [Proposal for the Cairo Conference Prepared by the Nationalist Government] (November 14, 1943), Jingchun Liang, *Kailuo hui yi* [Cairo Conference], Commercial Press Taiwan, 1973, pp. 51–55, (translated by Usui Katsumi), Gaddis Smith, op cit., pp. 86–87.

59 Ona Yasuyuki, "'Quit India' to kokusai kankei" ["Quit India" Movement and International Relations], Tanaka Hiroshi, *Nippon gunsei to Tōnan Ajia no minzoku undō* [The Japanese Military Administration and Nationalist Movement in Southeast Asia], Institute of Developing Economies, 1983, pp. 199–219.

the harshness of Japan's criticism of Britain and the United States and its persistence in taking into account the liberation of Asian peoples. From the viewpoint of the Ministry of Foreign Affairs, the Imperial Army's India policy was "a measure with more significance as a stratagem to facilitate military operations than as a measure with political significance." The ministry based its opinion on the "view that it is essential [for Japan] to secure the authority for inner leadership over the provisional government as well as the Nationalist government forces." The Imperial Army's India policy was incompatible with the Foreign Ministry's position, which made much of Bose's "initiative" by "strongly arguing for promotion of measures for Indian independence based on the spirit of the Greater East Asia Declaration."[60] This conflict of positions between the Foreign Ministry and the Imperial Army found its expression in Japan's India policy after the Greater East Asia Conference.

After the conference, Bose met Prime Minister Tōjō, Chief of the General Staff Sugiyama Hajime, and Foreign Minister Shigemitsu and submitted the following requests: first, the prompt launching of a Japanese military advance into India; second, reorganization of the Hikari Kikan, the Japanese liaison office responsible for Japanese relations with the Provisional Government of Free India; and third, dispatch of a Japanese diplomatic legation to India. The Hikari Kikan had been set up by the Imperial Japanese Army General Staff Office under the command of the Southern Expeditionary Army in May 1943 on the occasion of Bose's return to East Asia.

Sugiyama refrained from giving a definitive reply to the first request. Tōjō, too, confined himself to saying, "It seems necessary to thoroughly compare viewpoints of military operation and politics."[61] In March 1944, amidst objections from many corners including the Southern Expeditionary Army, Bose's first request was realized in the form of the Battle of Imphal.

---

60 "Sensōchū ni okeru waga tai-Indo shisaku keii."
61 *Tōjō kimitsu kiroku*, p. 359.

While it was announced that the purpose of this military operation was the defense of Burma, it was hoped that it could yield some hope militarily, however slight, on improvement of the war situation in the Pacific and politically on advancement of maneuvering for the independence of India.[62] At first, the Battle of Imphal went well for the Japanese side. The Indian National Army also extended cooperation by dispatching two army divisions. In early April, when the war situation still appeared to be favorable to the Japanese, a proposal to dissolve the Provisional Government of Free India and upgrade it to the Government of Free India began to be studied and discussed in various government ministries and bureaus.[63] The war situation, however, took a rapid turn for the worse, and the operation was called off altogether in early July 1944.

Concerning the second request, the Indian side argued that interference by the Hikari Kikan in activities of the provisional government and the Indian National Army was so extensive that it had blocked development of a self-driven independence movement. Bose also complained that the desires of the Indian side had not been heard properly when they were conveyed through the channel of the Hikari Kikan–Southern Expeditionary Army–Imperial General Headquarters. To improve the situation, the Indian side requested that either the Hikari Kikan's tasks be limited to military missions or the Hikari Kikan be abolished altogether and a diplomatic legation be dispatched to India. After the failure at Imphal, Bose pointed out that the defeat of the Indian National Army during the battle was an unfavorable factor both for the provisional government's appeasement attempts aimed at Indian citizens and for its external propaganda. Therefore, Bose argued, strengthening government-to-government relations through an exchange of diplomatic legations would be essential in order to activate these measures—attempts at appeasement and propaganda—by the provisional government.

---

62 *Kimitsu sensō nisshi*, entry of December 23, 1943.
63 Ibid., entry of April 2, 1943.

While the Ministry of Foreign Affairs tried to respond positively to the requests from the Indian side, the Army General Staff Office and the Southern Expeditionary Army remained reluctant. Thus, these problems were not resolved before the end of the war.[64]

4. Conclusion

The primary objective of the Greater East Asia Conference was to solidify Asian peoples' unity and contribute to the mobilization of manpower and materials in preparation for the counteroffensives by the Allies that were predicted for the autumn of 1943. And this was where the aim of many Japanese leaders, including Prime Minister Tōjō, lay. For Shigemitsu, however, the conference was an integral part of the new Greater East Asia new policy, and it was meant to be a venue where a Greater East Asia Charter would be set out as a joint code of conduct based on the principles of mutual respect for sovereignty, equality, and reciprocity as the foundation of the self-driven solidarity among "independent states" of Greater East Asia. The conference was also a diplomatic offensive with the roundabout intention of "laying the groundwork for a peace settlement" by contrasting the Atlantic Charter, the ideal of international order that the Allies had pursued, against Japan' war aims, which, the thinking went, should deprive the Allies of reasons to continue waging the war. And this notion was also shared by the Foreign Ministry bureaucrats who had

---

64 "Sensōchū ni okeru waga tai-Indo shisaku keii" and "Jiyū Indo kariseifu ni taisuru gaikō shisetsu hakenkata ni kansuru ken" [Matters Related to the Dispatch of Diplomatic Legation to the Provisional Government of Free India] (no date given), Ministry of Foreign Affairs Document A7.0.0.9-29-2.

supported Shigemitsu.[65]

In short, it was necessary for the Greater East Asia Declaration to fulfill at least the following three requirements: that it contribute to the waging of the war; that it be a joint code of conduct to facilitate solidarity among peoples in Asia; and that it harbor a universal ideal about international order so as to function as a tool for the "diplomatic offensive." The declaration as it was finalized barely fulfilled these three requirements. Its entire text, including its preamble, became questionable in any of the three positions. The other way to look at it was that the declaration ended up being equivocal. And that was why the propaganda policy of the Greater East Asia Declaration ended up being inconsistent, as we will see in chapter 8, resulting in further confusion in Japan in debates on the war aims.

Seen from a different perspective, the Greater East Asia Declaration failed to evoke any response beyond an interpretation that it was an expression of Japan's anxiety concerning both procurement of cooperation for the war effort by peoples in the occupied territories in Asia and its impact on the Allies. It was utterly unthinkable for the Chongqing government to respond positively to the highly unusual call from Wang Jingwei, and its

---

65 For instance, Kamimura Shin'ichi, director-general of the General Affairs Bureau, testified that they "pursued the [New Greater East Asia] policy to prepare the groundwork for peace settlement and, at the same time, to make Japan's postwar position more favorable." (Kamimura Shin'ichi, *Gaikō 50-nen* [Fifty Years of Diplomacy], Kajima Institute Publishing, 1960, pp. 224–225). Yamada Hisanari, director of the General Affairs Division cum Inspection Division, General Affairs Bureau, Ministry of Greater East Asia, reminisced that the Greater East Asia Declaration harbored the policy consideration of incorporating the "ideal of liberation of Asia" because "the future prospect of the war was so bleak that it was found necessary to imbed some meaning in this war by stressing such an ideal and, at the same time, try to make the conclusion of the war as tolerable as possible with the cooperation of peoples in Asia." (Yamada Hisanari, *Beranmei gaikōkan* [Rough-Tongued Diplomat], Kongō Shuppansha, 1966, pp. 73–74). Sone Eki, director, Division II, Political Affairs Bureau, Ministry of Foreign Affairs, remarked that the aim of the Greater East Asia Conference was to stress to leaders of Greater East Asian countries that the objective of Japan's occupation policy was not to prolong the military administration but to liberate Asian peoples. It was, as Sone reminisced, "A highly roundabout way to induce a peace settlement . . . stressing that Japan does not necessarily persist with the territorial issue of the occupied territories." (Sone Eki, *Watashi no memoāru* [My Memoir], Nikkan Kōgyō Shimbunsha, 1975, pp. 95–96).

attitude toward the Greater East Asia Conference was also extremely cool.[66] Moreover, the fact that Chiang Kai-shek signed the Cairo Declaration issued three weeks after the Greater East Asia Conference revealed that, as Ishii Itarō had commented, "a complete peace had gone a thousand miles away."[67]

If the significance of the Greater East Asia Conference for representatives of participating Asian peoples had to be pointed out, it might be that it was confirmation of a common intention among them that they would reject Japan's hegemonic position but, at the same time, reject the return of Western colonialism, as exemplified by Jose Laurel's speech. As introduced in chapter 5, it was the United States that reacted most sensitively to the series of developments from the recognition of Burma, the Philippines, and the Provisional Government of India through to the Greater East Asia Conference. The United States had consistently persisted with anti-colonialism in Asia, which was reflected in its prompt reaction to Japan's recognition of the independence of the Philippines. Facing Japan's series of "Asian liberation" policies in 1943, the former European colonial masters that expected to return to Asia after the war, however, failed to provide citizens of the Asian region with any concrete promise on postwar management or their future treatment. And this was precisely what the United States had been apprehensive about. As Christopher Thorne has pointed out, a political situation had been emerging in Asia that would not allow former colonial

---

66 Ministry of Foreign Affairs' record (draft) on the Greater East Asia Conference revealed that one of the important aims of the conference was to call on the Chongqing government to reflect on its past conduct. (Ministry of Foreign Affairs Document A7.0.0.9-48-1, *Daitōa Sensō kankei ikken: Daitōa Kaigi kankei* [Matters Related to the Greater East Asia War: Matters Related to the Greater East Asia Conference]). It indicated that, along with Wang Jingwei's speech, the Greater East Asia Conference was a part of measure to lure the Chongqing government to peace negotiations. Major British and American newspapers, including *The New York Times*, *The Washington Post*, and *The Times*, did not report on the Greater East Asia Conference or Declaration at all. It was, instead, the resolution of the US Congress on the establishment of a postwar international organization based on respect of mutual sovereignty adopted on November 5, 1943, around the date of the Greater East Asia Conference, that was extensively reported by these papers. It was ironical that these reports reiterated the significance of the Atlantic Charter.

67 Itō Takashi and Ryū Ketsu (Liu Jie), eds., *Ishii Itarō nikki* [Ishii Itarō Diary], Chūō Kōronsha, 1993 (entry of December 3, 1943).

masters to easily return to the region (see chapter 8).[68]

Yet if one had to look for the concrete impact of the Greater East Asia Conference on Japan, it should be pointed out that a certain degree of policy restriction was imposed on Japan's independence-related actions, particularly those of the Ministry of Foreign Affairs. Materialization of the major thrust of the Greater East Asia new policy in the form of a joint declaration gave an incentive to Shigemitsu and the Foreign Ministry to persistent in pursuing the promotion of autonomy and independence for countries of Asia. Thus, as the war situation became increasingly critical, strife emerged between the military, which wanted to strengthen interference in local governments and augment authority through internal guidance, and the Ministry of Foreign Affairs, which hoped to promote autonomy and independence for countries in Greater East Asia. This strife became a pattern over such issues concerning India after the Greater East Asia Conference as well as Indonesia and French Indochina, as we will see in chapter 9.

---

68 See chapter 6 of Christopher Thorne, *The Issue of War: States, Societies, and the Far Eastern Conflict, 1941–1945* (New York: Oxford University Press, 1985).

Chapter 8

Repercussions of the Greater East Asia Declaration

1. Introduction: Significance of the Atlantic Charter

In 1943, when Burma and the Philippines attained independence and the Greater East Asia Conference was convened, the Atlantic Charter began to take on a much more important meaning than its drafters had intended. One British intellectual, for instance, argued in early 1944 that, because the current international situation—with Britain, the United States, the Soviet Union, and China in essence becoming allies and with Japan advancing into Southeast Asia, thus setting forth a "new order"—differed greatly from that of 1941, when British Prime Minister Winston Churchill proclaimed that the target of the Atlantic Charter was primarily Europe, the Charter needed to be redefined as a program for world peace and a means to bring about victory to the Allies.[1]

In the autumn of 1943, the US Department of State found French treatment of Arabs in Tunisia to be against the principle of the Atlantic Charter.[2] Around the same time, Republican leaders in Spain contributed a commentary to *The New York Times* arguing that Anglo-American nations should abandon their appeasement policy toward the Franco government, because it would only prolong the suffering of the Spanish citizens and Moroccans in Spanish Sahara. Instead, they wrote that those two nations should abide by the Atlantic Charter to guarantee peoples' liberation and free elections. As this episode reveals, the Atlantic Charter had become widely accepted by the Allied powers as a principle to guide even real politik.[3] In that sense, it can be said that the decision of the Study Group on War Aims of Japan's Ministry of Foreign

---

1 W. Arnold-Forster, *Charters of the Peace: A Commentary on the Atlantic Charter and the Declaration of Moscow, Cairo and Teheran* (London: The Camelot Press, 1944), pp. 39–40, 132–134.

2 "Memorandum for the President" (November 1, 1943), *F.D. Roosevelt Papers*, Office Files, 1939–1945, Part 3: Departmental Correspondence File (Microfilm, University Publications of America).

3 *The New York Times*, October 17, 1943, Christopher Thorne, *Allies of a Kind: The United States, Britain, and the War against Japan, 1941–1945* (New York: Oxford University Press, 1978), pp. 160–162.

Affairs to draft the Greater East Asia Declaration with the Atlantic Charter as a reference, had some meaning. Prime Minister Tōjō Hideki formally referred to the Atlantic Charter for the first time in his speech at the Greater East Asia Conference, saying, "No matter what logic Anglo-American nations resort to in their claim to abide by the Atlantic Charter and in what they are actually doing in India, it would be utterly impossible to reconcile the two." Of course, this remark did not mean that Tōjō was ready to accept the Atlantic Charter, but it at least indicated that the Charter had come to be recognized as a prominent principle of international order.

After the Greater East Asia Declaration was announced, Takagi Yasaka contributed an article to the English-language newspaper *Contemporary Japan* in which he prudently argued that, while the war aims of the United States as conveyed in the Atlantic Charter were connected to such idealism as the "four freedoms," the country had also pursued power balance politics and "economic imperialism," thus betraying its dual nature. But Takagi's emphasis was more on the defense of Japan's position. Takagi stressed the non-aggressive nature of Japan's war aims and justified independence for Burma and the Philippines as well as settlement of unequal relations with China as acts of the "war of liberation." To put it in other terms, Takagi found the gap between war aims officially set out by Japan and the United States and their actual war policies more problematic than the respective war aims themselves. And from this viewpoint, he rated Japan's Greater East Asia new policy highly as an effort to fill the gap. Takagi did not refer to the Greater East Asia Declaration at all in his article, which might betray his apprehension about the "universality" of the declaration working more toward the widening of the gap as the war situation became increasingly strained.[4]

In any event, the Greater East Asia Declaration had no small impact and repercussions on speech and writing in wartime Japan, stimulating debate on

4   Takagi Yasaka, "War Aims of America," *Contemporary Japan* (vol. 12, no. 12), pp. 1563–1581.

war purposes and postwar management plans. One example was Shigemitsu Mamoru's secret agenda to use the declaration as a basis for redefining Japan's war aims, a usage that he repeatedly promoted both publicly and privately.[5] This had the effect of confusing debates on war aims in Japan. A second example is evident in the writings of Ishibashi Tanzan and Kiyosawa Kiyoshi: the declaration provided those who criticized it with opportunities to present their own visions of postwar management. A third example is that the Greater East Asia Declaration necessitated the convening of a second Greater East Asia Conference, which, as a corollary, gave new Foreign Minister Tōgō Shigenori an opportunity to set out a new declaration. This chapter is almost entirely devoted to discussing these repercussions of the Greater East Asia Declaration.

2. Confusion over War Aims

(1) Propaganda Policy of the Greater East Asia Declaration

At the Imperial Council on September 30, 1943, Minister for Greater East Asia Aoki Kazuo characterized measures to grant independence to Burma and the Philippines and permit political participation by local citizens as a means to "promote voluntary cooperation with the Empire of Japan's war efforts." His remark must have been made from the viewpoint that the solidarity and collaboration of Greater East Asian peoples with Japan were indispensable for mobilizing human and material resources.[6] To many Japanese in positions of leadership at that time, including Amō Eiji, director-general of the Cabinet Intelligence Bureau, the Greater East Asia Declaration was an

---

5 For instance, at the press conference held when Shigemitsu decided to remain foreign minister, he declared, "To thoroughly realize the major thrusts of the Greater East Asia Declaration and the Japan-China Alliance Treaty, liberate Asia, and restore East Asia . . . is what makes the current war a holy war and they are indeed our war aims." (*Tairiku nenkan* [Continental Annual], 1945, pp. 62–63). Shigemitsu's advocacy of this type of argument became particularly conspicuous at the time of the Koiso cabinet.

6 Imperial Japanese Army General Staff Office, ed., *Sugiyama memo, jō* [Sugiyama memorandum vol. 1], Hara Shobō, 1989, pp. 484–485.

extension of this call to promote voluntary cooperation. In his briefing to the emperor in early 1944, Amō explained, "The Greater East Asia Declaration was the most effective propaganda tool for announcing the determination of Greater East Asian peoples to bring the war to a successful conclusion and for stressing the solidarity of these peoples."[7] From the viewpoint of Shigemitsu and the Ministry of Foreign Affairs, however, the declaration was more than just a means to contribute to Japan's current war effort. It was, to them, the manifesto of the ideal for postwar management of Greater East Asia. This gap over the understanding of the Greater East Asia Declaration was also to be reflected in the Japanese government's propaganda policy.

As we have seen in the drafting process of the Greater East Asia Declaration, the Ministry of Foreign Affairs had originally planned to separate a statement on a successful conclusion of the Greater East Asia War from a proclamation on construction of Greater East Asia and publish only the latter as a joint declaration. Through deliberations among relevant government ministries and bureaus, however, it was decided that the two should be integrated in a single declaration. Since that was how the declaration was drafted, subsequent conflict over it as a tool of government publicity policy was inevitable. Conflict surfaced, for example, during discussions on the *Kikugō senden jisshi yōkō* (Implementation of the Outline of *Kikugō* Publicity). Should the outline stress successful completion of the war or the establishment of Greater East Asia? As revealed during the discussions at the Study Group on War Aims, the Foreign Ministry put more emphasis on the establishment. The Cabinet Intelligence Bureau, which had been the center of Japan's propaganda policy, insisted,

At present, it should be more appropriate to concentrate everything on winning the war. Issues relevant to actions following the war should be

---

7   Amō Eiji Nikki/Shiryōshū Kankōkai, ed., *Amō Eiji nikki/shiryōshū* [Amō Eiji Diary and Documents], 1982, p. 890. (*Amō nikki*, henceforth)

deliberated as the second stage. Therefore, even though this conference [the Greater East Asia Conference] is also concerned about postwar issues, the emphasis should be placed on the successful completion of the war first.[8]

And this was also the position that the Ministry of Greater East Asia took. In the meantime, the "basic direction" section of the October 25 draft implementation outline compiled mainly by the Foreign Ministry claimed that, "Efforts should be made, on the occasion of the Greater East Asia Conference, to let the world know of the solidarity and cooperation among Greater East Asian peoples toward the construction of Greater East Asia, so as to cripple the war aims of the Allies and weaken their desire to continue the war." Here the apparent emphasis was on the "construction of Greater East Asia." But this particular portion was revised to "on the occasion of the Greater East Asia Conference, to promote and strengthen the determination to successfully conclude the Greater East Asia War as well as solidarity and cooperation toward construction of Greater East Asia, so as to cripple the war aims of the Allies . . . [identical wording thereafter]." Also added was a separate sentence that read, "Repeated publicity should be conducted regarding the Greater East Asia Declaration over the long term." It is almost beyond doubt that these revisions were added by the Cabinet Information Bureau.[9]

The Cabinet Intelligence Bureau was also dissatisfied with the draft of the Greater East Asia Declaration adopted on October 23—to the degree that its executive meeting that day was reported to have been filled with calls

---

8 "Kikugō kaigi ni tsuite" [On the Kikugō Conference] (October 20), *Japan Ministry of Foreign Affairs, 1868–1945*; WT Series, Reel 52 (microfilm collection of the Modern Japanese Political History Materials Room, National Diet Library), *Amō nikki*, entry of October 20.

9 "Kikugō Senden Yōkō" [Kikugō Propaganda Outline] (October 25) (same microfilm as above footnote 8). It is also written on p. 750 in *Amō nikki* that "Senior members of the Cabinet Intelligence Bureau are dissatisfied with the Ministry of Greater East Asia's handling of the propaganda policy."

for "more emphasis on the idea of the Co-Prosperity Sphere."[10] Through these interactions, the Greater East Asia Declaration became more of a publicity tool to let the world inside and outside of the region know about the determination on the part of each member country of Greater East Asia to successfully conclude the Greater East Asia War. And it can be said that the five principles of construction of Greater East Asia were now downgraded to the elements of long-term goals. To put it differently, attempts were made to wipe away any impression that the five principles of Greater East Asia construction, to which Shigemitsu had devoted his efforts, were meant to change the war aims.

Thus, the more Shigemitsu emphasized the content of the Greater East Asia Declaration as the articulation of Japan's war aims, the more confused the debate became. While the Ministry of Greater East Asia commissioned such leading intellectuals as Ōkawa Shūmei (founder of the Tōa Keizai Chōsakyoku Fuzoku Kenkyūsho [Research Institute of the East Asiatic Economic Investigation Bureau], commonly known as "Ōkawajuku")[11] and Yabe Teiji (a Tokyo Imperial University professor) to draft the text of the declaration, as we saw in chapter 7, it also occasionally asked for the advice of the Research Group on National Policy, via Yatsugi Kazuo, president of the institute (Ōkawa and Yabe had been affiliated with the group).[12] Toward the end of February 1944, after hearing Yatsugi's explanation regarding what had happened to the draft submitted by Ōkawa and his associates, Ōkawa wrote, "It appears that our draft on the new world order has been put on hold by Minister for Greater East Asia Aoki. He is apprehensive about China and Thailand denouncing our reference to 'the guiding nation.' This is absurd and spineless of Aoki." This remark represented Ōkawa's bewilderment over the government's injection of an argument for a new international

---

10 *Amō nikki*, entry of October 23, 1943.
11 Ōkawa Shūmei Kenshōkai, ed., *Ōkawa Shūmei nikki* [Ōkawa Shūmei Diary], Iwasaki Gakujutsu Shuppan, 1986, entry of October 5, 1943.
12 Yabe Teiji Nikki Kankōkai, ed., *Yabe Teiji nikki: Ichō no maki* [Yabe Teiji Diary: Gingko Tree Volume], Yomiuri Shimbunsha, 1974, entry of June 22, August 12 and 18, 1943.

order as if to deny the argument for a new order with Japan as the hegemon (i.e., the Greater East Asia Co-Prosperity Sphere), rather than his lack of understanding of the Greater East Asia Declaration. The remark indicates the confusion in the contemporary discussions of war aims in Japan. Even after the Greater East Asia Conference, Ōkawa continued to insist, "It is only natural and necessary for Japan to take the leadership position in the Greater East Asia Sphere," and he refused to give in to the government's "guidance" to suppress his position.[13]

It should be noted that within the Japanese government it was the Imperial Japanese Navy that was most hesitant about designating the liberation of Greater East Asia, or the Greater East Asia Declaration, as the aim of the war for Japan. The Imperial Navy argued that stating that the aim of the war was "to liberate Asian peoples," thus stressing Asian peoples' autonomy and independence, would block the "rapid mobilization of national defense resources to the war" and eventually consign the war to becoming a "war between races." Therefore, the Imperial Navy insisted, the Greater East Asia Declaration should concentrate on the argument for "survival and self-defense."[14] These were the reasons the Imperial Navy remained aloof regarding the Greater East Asia Declaration and the Greater East Asia Conference, both of which prompted various peoples to aspire for independence. Recent studies point out that, following occupation of the South Sea Islands, the fundamental objective of the Imperial Navy's

---

13 Ōkawa Shūmei Zenshū Kankōkai, ed., *Ōkawa Shūmei zenshū dai 2-kan* [Complete Works of Ōkawa Shūmei, vol. 2], 1962, p. 920.

14 For instance, according to *Nanpō kaigun senryō chiku shisatsu hōkokusho* [Report of the Mission to Inspect Southern Territories Occupied by the Imperial Navy] (April 1944, a collection of the National Institute for Defense Studies, Japan), "Because military administration has been carried out in the territories mainly under the Imperial Navy's charge with an aim of securing them as Japan's territory for a long time to come . . . unlike regions that are permitted independence . . . it is necessary to apply the same policy as in Japan to these territories at the Japanese people's expense." And it also argued, "The true meaning of the Greater East Asia War is that it is a battle for the survival of the Japanese race. Its true purpose is to rapidly mobilize national defense resources in the southern occupied territories in the war so as to complete the Empire's goal of 'survival and self-defense.' To make the current holy war into a war for the liberation of East Asia peoples not only consigns the war to a battle of races but also allows the Japanese people to remain bystanders."

occupation administration had always been "internalization," [equal treatment of overseas territories as homelands] which was closely connected with the need to secure necessary resources.[15] As discussed elsewhere in this book, this position of the Imperial Navy found expression on various occasions in the decision-making related to the independence of the occupied territories.

The Imperial Navy, however, was not alone in its criticism of the perception of the Greater East Asia Declaration and liberation of Asian peoples as Japan's war aims. The instruction on the priorities of military administration in 1944 issued by the Southern Expeditionary Army in January 1944, after the Greater East Asia Conference, reiterated the "three major objectives of military administration": maintenance of public order, procurement of important national defense resources, and self-sufficiency of locally stationed operational troops. The directive continued as follows:

Anticipating that the success or failure in reinforcing military strength in the next one or two years will determine the overall outcome of the Greater East Asia War, military administration should not be entrenched in the construction of ideals or the convenience of postwar management. Instead, military administration should aim at promptly incorporating the southern occupied territories into Japan's war capability. Particularly, measures to concentrate full efforts in making the occupied territories render immediate cooperation to ongoing military operations and those under preparation should be carried out.[16]

Obviously, the reference to "establishment of ideals or the convenience

15 Koike Seiichi, "Kaigun Nanpō 'minsei'" [Imperial Navy's Civil Administration in the Southern Territories], Hikita Yasuyuki, ed., "Nanpō Kyōeiken": Senji Nippon no Tōnan Ajia keizai shihai ["Southern Co-Prosperity Sphere": Economic Domination of Southeast Asia by Japan during the War], Taga Shuppan, 1995, pp. 135–172.

16 Bōei Kenkyūsho Senshibu, ed., Shiryōshū Nanpō no gunsei [Documents on Military Administration in the Southern Territories], Asagumo Shimbunsha, 1985, p. 312.

of postwar management" was driven by the awareness [on the part of the Southern Expeditionary Army] of the general acceptance of the Greater East Asia Declaration as the purpose of the war. The directive implicitly criticized the fact that at a time when prompt incorporation of the southern occupied territories into Japan's overall war capability was called for, emphasis on such idealized aims for the war as those in the Greater East Asia Declaration would obstruct accomplishment of the war aims.

(2) Buried in the Argument for the Greater East Asia Co-Prosperity Sphere

One of Shigemitsu's goals for the Greater East Asia Declaration as a diplomatic offensive was to "crush the enemy's war aims," and he once again stressed this at the Imperial Council on September 30, 1944. Yet how would it be possible to "crush" the Anglo-American "war aims?" Shigemitsu argued that the underlying tone of the Greater East Asia Declaration was "not to oppose capitalist democracy but rather to cooperate on the basis of rightful independence and survival. It has been most damaging to the Anglo-American nations that Greater East Asia is evidently pursuing this." To put it differently, it was Shigemitsu's logic that because Japan's war aims were based on justice or moral principles, they were equipped with a universality that could overwhelm capitalist democracy, which presupposed sacrifices by smaller and weaker peoples, and this universality could be effective in crushing the war aims of the Anglo-American nations.[17]

Another logical argument that Shigemitsu resorted to, which was not unrelated to the first, was that the principles contained in the Greater East Asia Declaration had "originated with the national policy of Japan since the founding of the nation." Of course, Shigemitsu was well aware that such notions of peoples' independence and equality and mutual benefit were

---

17 Itō Takashi et al., eds., *Zoku Shigemitsu Mamoru shuki* [Shigemitsu Mamoru Private Memoir, vol. 2], Chūō Kōronsha, 1988, pp. 149–150.

attributable to the Western spirit of democracy, not to Japan's traditional philosophy. And that may have been why he was able to secretly perceive that when the principles contained in the Greater East Asia Declaration "coincided with the war aims [of the Allies] called the Atlantic Charter, Japan might be able to get hold of a key to end the war."[18] As a matter of fact, as we have seen earlier, the Atlantic Charter—the manifesto of the war aims of the Anglo-American nations—was indeed referred to when the Greater East Asia Declaration was drafted. However, even if the proximity of the principles of the Greater East Asia Declaration to the Atlantic Charter had been recognized, it would have been impossible for the foreign minister to publicly acknowledge this under the domestic circumstances where "any thought that aspires for a peace settlement or any other sign of war weariness" had become subject to thorough crackdowns immediately after the Greater East Asia Conference.[19] Thus, taking a sympathetic position toward Shigemitsu, it could be interpreted that domestically he resorted to the totally opposite logic—out of necessity to "avoid being regarded as a peace feeler"—that the Greater East Asia Declaration and the war aims of the Anglo-American nations were totally different.

The Foreign Ministry's record on the Greater East Asia Conference (draft) pointed out, concerning the principle of independence and mutual benefit in the Greater East Asia Declaration, that "it is undeniable that the movement for peoples' liberation and peoples' independence has received some influence from European nationalism thought." It continued to say,

Nevertheless, the nationalism movement in East Asia is not confined to mere resistance to oppression. A spiritual awareness of returning to where East Asian peoples are meant to be has been an undercurrent of

18 Ibid., p. 443, Shigemitsu Mamoru, *Shōwa no dōran, ge* [Shōwa in Turmoil, vol. 2], Chūō Kōronsha, 1952, pp. 167–168, pp. 173–174.
19 "Senji kokumin shisō kakuritsu ni kansuru kihon hōsaku yōkō" [Outline of Basic Policy Concerning Establishment of Wartime National Thought] (December 1943) (Uchikawa Yoshimi, ed., *Gendaishi shiryō* [Contemporary History Documents], vol. 41, Misuzu Shobō, 1965), p. 511.

nationalism in East Asia. This signifies that a sense of Asian peoples' spiritual dignity versus spiritual enslavement is at the crux of the matter.[20]

That is to say, the Foreign Ministry's record argued that those principles contained in the Greater East Asia Declaration were indigenous principles that had been embedded in Japanese people's philosophy on external relations from the beginning.

But the above logic stimulated arguments in Japan that were substantively no different from the old argument for the Greater East Asia Co-Prosperity Sphere. Furuno Isuke, for instance, contributed an article to the monthly *Chūō Kōron* which, while admitting that "no matter how hard the Japanese government repeats dogmatic arguments that are appreciated only by the Japanese people, it will only end up placing Japan in an isolated position in the world," he elucidated an interpretation that the Greater East Asia Declaration was based on a "family-oriented world view" that had defeated the Anglo-American "individualistic world view," and reinterpreted "the principle of peoples' independence" and "the principle of mutual benefit" as "the principle of independence and harmony" and "the principle of economic prosperity," respectively.[21]

The commentary on the Greater East Asia Declaration that the Dai-Nippon Genron Hōkokukai (Japanese-Speech Patriot Association) compiled, with the input of such leading intellectuals as Saitō Tadashi, Ōgushi Toshio, Sakuta Sōichi, and Shiratori Toshio, also presented the same type of argument. Shiratori, for instance, argued as follows:

Everything must be explicated by going back to its basis. And to go

---

20 Manuscript of the Record on the Greater East Asia Conference (untitled) (Ministry of Foreign Affairs Document A7.0.0.9-48-1, "Daitōa Sensō kankei ikken" [Matters Related to the Greater East Asia War], "Daitōa Kaigi kankei" [Matters Related to Greater East Asia Conference]).
21 *Chūō Kōron*, January 1944.

back to the basis means to return to the fundamentals of the way of the gods of the Japanese people. That is where the true significance of the current war lies. In my judgment, the Greater East Asia Declaration's pledge to contribute to advancement of the world was none other than an extremely discreet expression of this.[22]

And it seems safe to say that Shiratori's logic was close to the rhetoric applied by Shigemitsu. The *Tai-teki senden hōsaku yōkō* (Outline of Anti-Enemy Propaganda Measures) agreed on at the Supreme Council for War Guidance in October 1944 also set out an interpretation that the Greater East Asia Declaration was precisely "the national policy of Japan since the founding of the nation" and a "concrete indication of Japan's war purposes."[23]

On the extensive coverage of the Greater East Asia Declaration by magazines and newspapers, Kiyosawa Kiyoshi, a Taishō-Shōwa era journalist and political commentator, deplored that the commentators were "eccentric right-wingers" or "imperialists" who were "alien to the Greater East Asia Declaration." Kiyosawa said that when these commentators "spoke of the Greater East Asia Declaration, no other country in the world would believe in it" and singled out Shiratori as one such commentator.[24] Kiyosawa's deploration portrayed exactly how the Greater East Asia Declaration became buried in the conventional argument for the Greater East Asia Co-Prosperity Sphere.

---

22 Kawahara Hiroshi, *Shōwa seiji shisō kenkyū* [Study of Shōwa Political Thought], Waseda Daigaku Shuppanbu, 1979, p. 323.
23 Honjō Shigeru, *Haisen no kiroku: Sanbō Honbu shozō* [Record of a War Defeat: A Collection of the Imperial Japanese Army General Staff Office], Hara Shobō, 1967, p. 196.
24 Kiyosawa Kiyoshi, *Ankoku nikki* [The Diary of Darkness], Hyōronsha, 1979, entry of January 12 and 15, 1944.

3. Criticisms of the Greater East Asia Declaration: Ishibashi Tanzan and Kiyosawa Kiyoshi

(1) Postwar Management Visions Proposed by Ishibashi and Kiyosawa

While in the world of journalism the Greater East Asia Declaration was about to be buried in the argument for a hegemonic co-prosperity sphere, journalists Ishibashi Tanzan and Kiyosawa Kiyoshi tried to evaluate the declaration from a different viewpoint. Ishibashi, in particular, had stressed the importance of study of postwar management policies of the Allies and Japan's postwar vision ever since 1942 through his own quarterly, *Tōyō Keizai Shinpō*. Fearing that "Japan would be in danger if free examination of any contingency were not allowed,"[25] Kiyosawa had begun to study postwar scenarios, paying close attention to the postwar world policy of the Allies, in such private gatherings as the Kokusai Kankei Kenkyūkai (Study Group on International Relations). This shows that it was possible for the two journalists to evaluate the Greater East Asia Declaration from the viewpoint of visions of postwar Japan. After "any thought that aspires for a peace settlement or any other sign of war weariness" became subject to thorough crackdowns in 1943, however, it became increasingly difficult for them to openly present their vision of the postwar world. It might be more accurate to say that they publicized their postwar scenarios by way of referring to and using the Greater East Asia Declaration.[26]

In any event, Ishibashi particularly praised Article 5 of the Greater East Asia Declaration as a "splendid philosophical offensive." He found it so because the ideas behind the Greater East Asia Co-Prosperity Sphere "are mainly about Greater East Asia and, although they do not touch on what to

---

25 Ibid., entry of September 6, 1943.
26 Matsuo Takayoshi, "15-nen Sensō ka no Ishibashi Tanzan" [Ishibashi Tanzan during the Asia-Pacific War], Japanese Political Science Association, ed., *Kindai Nippon no kokkazō* [National Vision of Modern Japan], Iwanami Shoten, 1982, p. 227.

do about the entire world, the relative weight of the latter bears no comparison to Greater East Asia, regarding which the Co-Prosperity Sphere argument is liable to be confined." If Japan wished to evict the Anglo-American nations from Asia, Ishibashi argued, "the responsibility to reconstruct the world order would fall on Japan's shoulders."[27] Kiyosawa, for his part, wrote in his diary for November 8, "It is Japan's tragedy to have had to draft a declaration that is similar to the Atlantic Charter, granting all peoples their independence and freedom. But, then again, here is the lesson that Japan should learn, too."[28]

While the cause of the eruption of war was, passively, "survival and self-defense," the more proactive motive for Japan was to "liberate the oppressed peoples of the world." If that was indeed the case, then Japan needed to produce some form of "concrete measures for postwar management." And that was one of the reasons Ishibashi and Kiyosawa decided to engage in the outlining of a vision of the postwar world.[29] In this sense, the Greater East Asia Declaration provided a valuable hint.

Soon after the Greater East Asia Conference, Kiyosawa invited Greater East Asia Minister Aoki to his study meeting, along with Takahashi Kamekichi, economist, and Ishibashi. At the meeting, Aoki stated simply, "We will uphold the Greater East Asia Declaration as it is now. No modification necessary. We will not create a permanent institution nor will Japan pretend to be the leader." Hearing this, Kiyosawa judged that Aoki was not too enthusiastic about a permanent institution and his hands were already filled with the war itself.[30] Although Kiyosawa and his associates wished to encourage the Japanese government to engage in planning for a

---

27 Ishibashi Tanzan, "Būgenbiru-tō oki kaisen" [Sea Battle off of Bougainville Island] (November 1943), Ishibashi Tanzan Zenshū Henshū Iinkai, ed., *Ishibashi Tanzan zenshū* [Complete Works of Ishibashi Tanzan], vol. 12, Tōyō Keizai Shinpōsha, 1972, pp. 527–529.

28 Kiyosawa (1979), entry of November 8, 1943.

29 Kiyosawa Kiyoshi, "Teki sengo shori-an o saiha subeshi" [Smash the Enemy's Postwar Handling Plans], Tōyō Keizai Shinpō, October 7, 1944, ibid., pp. 813–814.

30 Kiyosawa (1979), entry of November 25, 1943.

postwar institution on the basis of the Greater East Asia Declaration, Aoki's remark indicated that, at least as far as the Ministry of Greater East Asia was concerned, the declaration was nothing more than propaganda as a means to wage the war.

The Treaty Bureau of the Ministry of Foreign Affairs, in contrast, intermittently conducted a "study on a world peace organization centered around Greater East Asia" in cooperation with the Committee on Special Issues of the Japanese Society of International Law. This collaboration culminated in a *Draft Proposal on the World Peace Organization* compiled by Division II of the Treaty Bureau in early 1944. This draft proposal stated, "The proposed world union will not be like the League of Nations in Geneva, which is composed of equal nations; instead, it will be composed of each large-area regional organization as its direct members," and its "plenary assembly," to be attended by three representatives from each regional organization, would perform such functions as international peace keeping and conflict resolution.[31] But the study by the Foreign Ministry perhaps remained inside the ministry and did not reach Kiyosawa and his group. In any event, Kiyosawa became disappointed with the lack of ideas on the part of the government on materializing the Greater East Asia Declaration. Eventually he ceased to assertively approach the government on this matter.

During the latter half of 1944 Kiyosawa and Ishibashi had begun to engage in formulating a full-scale postwar vision, because, among other reasons, the Allies' vision on the postwar institution had begun to take concrete shape. In particular, the two men were stimulated by *Proposals for the Establishment of a General International Organization*, a vision of a new peace-keeping mechanism to replace the League of Nations released on October 9, 1944, as a conclusion of the Dumbarton Oaks Conference (August–October, 1944). Another reason was the appointment of Foreign

---

31 "Shōwa 18-nendo shitsumu hōkoku" [Report on Official Operations in FY1943] (Treaty Bureau), pp. 168–170.

Minister Shigemitsu to the concurrent post of minister for Greater East Asia of the Koiso Kuniaki cabinet; Shigemitsu now held the authority for wartime diplomacy in his own hands and began stressing the significance of the Greater East Asia Declaration. For instance, Kiyosawa highly praised Shigemitsu's reply to the House of Representatives' budget committee plenary meeting on September 10, 1944, that Japan's diplomacy would be based on the five principles (three major principles of the Greater East Asia Declaration plus the principles of non-interference in internal affairs and nationalism).[32] While the Five Principles of Japanese Diplomacy that Shigemitsu stressed was a truly epoch-making announcement, it was still void of concrete measures for carrying out those principles.

In mid-August 1944, Kiyosawa submitted, via Takayanagi Kenzō, adviser to the Ministry of Foreign Affairs, a "peace offensive" to Foreign Minister Shigemitsu. In the document, Kiyosawa suggested that, "Japan should announce, along the lines of the Greater East Asia Declaration, that it would withdraw all troops from China, Thailand, the Philippines, and other territories and 'feel' for a peace settlement on that basis."[33] While it is unknown how Shigemitsu received this suggestion, it must have been prompted by Kiyosawa's cynicism toward the Greater East Asia Declaration, which was devoid of any realistic basis.

Kiyosawa argued that, in order to "complement" the Greater East Asia Declaration, it would be necessary to deepen discussions on (1) concrete measures for cooperation among Greater East Asian countries and (2) the position that Greater East Asia should take in management of world peace.[34] In order to attain (1), some kind of a permanent institution was called for. As for (2), Kiyosawa argued that "construction of Greater East Asia would be possible only when world peace is firmly established," and:

---

32 Kiyosawa (1979), entry of September 14, 1944.
33 Kiyosawa (1979), entry of August 18, 1944.
34 Kiyosawa Kiyoshi, "Shigemitsu Gaishō ni kitaisu: Daitōa Kyōdō Sengen no gutaika" [Expectations on Foreign Minister Shigemitsu: Materialization of the Greater East Asia Joint Declaration], Kiyosawa (1979), entry of August 12, 1944, pp. 806–808.

The Japanese government would owe it to the world to answer what relations between the Greater East Asia Co-Prosperity Sphere and other co-prosperity spheres would be like and what the institution that presides over the various co-prosperity spheres that are expected to emerge in the world will look like.[35]

(2) Proposal on a Postwar World Economic Organization

After the proposal of a general international organization was publicized as an outcome of the Dumbarton Oaks Conference in October 1944, Kiyosawa and Ishibashi reinvigorated their arguments on behalf of visions of the postwar world, encouraged by the "freer atmosphere for speech under the Koiso cabinet."[36] While they actively contributed articles on the need for visions of the postwar world to media such as the quarterly *Tōyō Keizai Shinpō*, they also vigorously studied visions of the postwar world in Kiyosawa's Study Group on International Relations and other study groups.[37] The central issue in the discussions, which also included such intellectuals as Kamikawa Hikomatsu, Yokota Kisaburō, and Taira Teizō, was, in light of the Dumbarton Oaks proposal, whether the postwar international order would be regional-oriented or a centralized international system and whether "the postwar international organization should be placed above regionalism or above the general internationalism."[38]

Based on these discussions, Ishibashi completed his own "proposal for a postwar organization" toward the end of December 1944. Abstaining from political arguments, Ishibashi concentrated on painting a picture of postwar economic institutions and proposed in a nutshell that "the world should be divided into three spheres to be governed by three regional councils and a

---

35 Ibid.
36 Kiyosawa (1979), entry of October 20, 1944.
37 Ibid., entries of September 29, November 2, and November 25, 1944, and *Tōyō Keizai Shinpō*, November 4, 18, 25, 1944 and February 10, 1945.
38 Kiyosawa (1979), entry of November 25, 1944 and Kiyosawa Kiyoshi, "Teki sengo shori-an o saiha subeshi," p. 815.

world council."[39]

According to Kiyosawa, the institution envisioned in the Dumbarton Oaks proposal would be a ruling mechanism for the world major powers with international police power, and its executive council would be managed by the influence of major powers. If that was indeed the case, it was necessary for Japan, which had set out liberation of the oppressed in the world as its war aim, to prepare a new counter-theory based on the principles of Greater East Asia Declaration.[40] And it was Ishibashi's proposal that Kiyosawa found this "new counter-theory."

As mentioned, Ishibashi highly rated Article 5 of the Greater East Asia Declaration, but, like Kiyosawa, he criticized the declaration for its lack of concrete follow-up measures and a realistic foundation, as compared with the Dumbarton Oaks proposal. Regarding the Dumbarton Oaks proposal envisioning an institution for guaranteeing world peace, an attempt at concrete materializing of the Atlantic Charter, Kiyosawa expressed regret that "unfortunately, we have not produced a vision that can rival it." Finding the Dumbarton Oaks proposal more realistic because it was based on a five-country alliance (the United States, Britain, China, the Soviet Union, and France), unlike the League of Nations, Kiyosawa nevertheless found the proposal unacceptable because it entrusted the selection of members of the permanent council not to votes and elections but to the discretion of the United States, Britain, and the Soviet Union—which went against the principle of democracy. Therefore, Kiyosawa argued, a "new world organization" had to be conceived based on the principles of the Greater East Asia Declaration.[41]

Reflecting on these discussions, the Ishibashi proposal was an argument for "regionalism in the world economy," focusing, for the time being, on the economic organization to be established. Dismissing the vision of wide-area economic zones, each of which would aspire to be self-sustaining, as a notion

---

39 Ibid., entry of December 26, 1944.
40 Kiyosawa, "Teki sengo shori-an o saiha subeshi" p. 815.
41 Ibid.

that went against the international division of labor, which he considered a natural course of economy, Ishibashi first divided the world into three wide-area zones. Each of these zones would have its own permanent international committee and a regional committee. While the regional committee would be empowered to draw up economic plans for its own region and report to the permanent international committee regarding issues that called for interactions with other zones, the latter was entrusted with the mission to coordinate these plans from the viewpoint of the world as a whole.[42]

Kiyosawa also commented on the Dumbarton Oaks proposal in the quarterly *Tōyō Keizai Shinpō* that he too criticized the plan as being strongly centered around the major powers. In February 1945, Kiyosawa published *Sekai chitsujo ni kansuru shian* (A Personal Proposal on World Order), his revision of the Dumbarton Oaks proposal. Its major thrusts included (1) insertion of articles on the opening of natural resources to the outside world and elimination of the article on economic blockades; (2) elimination of the article stipulating that only "peace-loving nations" would be allowed to become members, because of the intention of excluding the Axis countries; (3) reduction of the power of the executive council; (4) founding of an international court of arbitration; (5) addition of a new article guaranteeing free trade and abolishment of racial discrimination; and (6) stipulation of the principle of across-the-board arms reduction. The contents of these articles were almost identical to those of the declaration to be issued at the Greater East Asia Ambassadors' Conference in April 1945. When publicizing this personal proposal, Kiyosawa explained why he had used the Dumbarton Oaks proposal as a basis, saying, "I wanted to show that I would not hesitate to take in anything that could contribute to world peace, no matter who envisioned it."[43] And this viewpoint was also shared by the Declaration of

---

42 "Sekai heiwa no yaburetaru konpon gen'in" [Fundamental Cause of the Destruction of World Peace] and "Sengo sekai keizai kikōan" [Proposal on Postwar World Economic Organization] (May 1945) in *Ishibashi Tanzan zenshū*, pp. 251–255 (Sekai heiwa . . .) and pp. 255–258 (Sengo sekai . . .).
43 *Tōyō Keizai Shinpō*, February 10, 1945.

the Greater East Asia Ambassadors' Conference, which will be discussed in the next section of this chapter.

In the fall of 1944, Ishibashi persuaded Minister of Finance Ishiwata Sōtarō to set up a Senji Keizai Chōsa Iinkai (Wartime Economic Research Committee) within the ministry in order to utilize outcomes of its research in actual policies.[44] While the committee was substantively a forum of discussions between businessmen and economists based on the Ishibashi proposal, it is conjectured that Ishibashi from the beginning envisioned a postwar world economic organization specializing in economic functions. The research committee continued its activities until late March 1945, and in June 1945 Ishibashi compiled the committee's final report centered around the vision of a postwar world economic organization. However, this report was never made public and it remains unknown how this report was used by the Ministry of Finance.

While it is not known how Foreign Minister Shigemitsu or Kiyosawa Kiyoshi evaluated the study by Ishibashi, the Japanese government's official view on the Allies' proposal of an international organization was revealed in Shigemitsu's reply to a question from Tsurumi Yūsuke, member of the House of Representatives, at the plenary assembly of the House's Budget Committee in March 1945. Tsurumi's question was on the Japanese government's response to the Allies' proposal on the international organization. Shigemitsu assessed that the international organization which the Anglo-American nations had wished to realize at the United Nations Conference on International Organization (San Francisco Conference) in April–June 1945 was "a mechanism for authoritarian autocracy by force based on cooperation among major powers" and denounced it as "an organization which neglects smaller and weaker nations and peoples, something far from democracy." As for the Japanese government's alternative proposal, Shigemitsu declared

---

44 Masuda Hiroshi, *Ishibashi Tanzan kenkyū* [Study on Ishibashi Tanzan], Tōyō Keizai Shinpōsha, 1990, pp. 292–298.

that it was explicitly presented in the Greater East Asia Declaration with the basic tone of peoples' liberation and cooperation.[45]

Shigemitsu's reply was nothing more than the Japanese government's stance. The government had flatly dismissed the Dumbarton Oaks proposal, saying that it proposed "an institution with the true aim of the Anglo-American nations to manage the world as they like and certainly not an institution to maintain world peace."[46] Thus, it has to be said that the vision of a concrete institution based on the Greater East Asia Declaration was out of Shigemitsu's consideration. It can be interpreted that by the time abandonment of the southern occupied territories had become self-evident, any effort toward a postwar institution was meaningless. Further, it should be said that the vision of a postwar world economic organization held by Ishibashi and Kiyosawa, on the basis of the criticism on the Greater East Asia Declaration, was an intellectual exercise that merits special mention.

4. Significance of the Declaration of the Greater East Asia Ambassadors' Conference

The Greater East Asia Ambassadors' Conference was convened on April 23, 1945, soon after the formation of the Suzuki Kantarō cabinet. While this conference has failed to attract much attention in historical studies, it shows the obvious originality of Tōgō Shigenori, diplomacy toward the end of the war—unlike his diplomacy vis-à-vis the Soviet Union which suffered seriously from domestic constraints. This conference had been conceived first as the second Greater East Asia Conference toward the end of Shigemitsu's tenure as foreign minister. The objective of the conference was to consolidate the unity of Greater East Asia during the decisive stage of the war and to "aggressively carry out political offensives toward the enemies against the

---

45 *The Asahi Shimbun*, March 24, 1945.
46 *Amō nikki*, p. 1050.

Anti-Axis San Francisco Conference."[47]

Invitations were to be sent out to the participants in the Greater East Asia Conference; three countries (the Empire of Vietnam, the Kingdom of Kampuchea, and the Kingdom of Laos) that had declared independence as a result of Meigō Sakusen (Operation Bright Moon), the Japanese coup d'état in French Indochina (March 9, 1945); and Indonesia, with the recommendation of Army Minister Sugiyama Hajime as well as Shigemitsu.[48] Subsequent preparations for the conference were handled chiefly by the Ministry of Foreign Affairs. But trips to Japan by representatives of East Asian countries became impossible due to the worsening war situation so the conference was postponed until the end of March. Under the leadership of newly appointed Foreign Minister Tōgō, it was decided to convert the plan for a second Greater East Asia Conference to a Greater East Asia Ambassadors' Conference, inviting ambassadors to Japan from Manchukuo, Thailand, the Philippines, the Republic of China, and Burma plus representatives of the Provisional Government of Free India.[49]

The resultant Greater East Asia Ambassadors' Conference was a single-day affair on April 23, 1945. Foreign Minister Tōgō reiterated that the Greater East Asia War was, for Japan, a war of "survival and self-defense," "a war of peoples' liberation" for Greater East Asia, and, globally, "a battle for a fair international order." Subsequently, Tōgō proposed the following seven principles as "guiding principles for construction of the world order."

Article 1

The fundamental cornerstone of the construction of international order should be the philosophy of co-existence and co-prosperity, devoid of

---

47 "Daitōa Taishi Kaigi kaisai no keii" [Circumstances surrounding the Greater East Asia Ambassadors' Conference] (Ministry of Foreign Affairs Document A7.0.0.9-53 "Daitōa Sensō kankei ikken" [Matters Related to Greater East Asia War] and "Daitōa Taishi Kaigi kankei" [Matters Related to Greater East Asia Ambassadors' Conference]).

48 Ibid., and *Haisen no kiroku*, p. 239.

49 *Haisen no kiroku*, p. 242, and "Daitōa Taishi Kaigi kaisai no keii."

any kind of discrimination based on race, under the principles of political equality, mutual economic benefit, and respect for indigenous cultures.

Article 2
In order to ensure equal status among states regardless of size and equal opportunities for their improvement and development, each nation should be able to choose its own form of government of without interference from others.

Article 3
We should liberate peoples currently under colonial status, allow them have their own proper place in the world, and together open the way for contributions to advancement of human civilization.

Article 4
We should strive to universalize economic prosperity, commensurate with each nation's ingenuity and labor, by eliminating monopolies of natural resources, trade, and international traffic to promote mutual economic interactions, and, thereby, eliminate economic inequality from the world.

Article 5
We should mutually respect each other's cultural heritage and, at the same time, promote international harmony and the advancement of humankind through cultural exchanges.

Article 6
Under the principles of non-threat and non-aggression, we should eliminate armaments that pose a threat to other countries as well as obstacles to international trade so that oppression or provocation of other countries not only by force but also by other economic measures shall be prevented.

Article 7

In terms of a security mechanism, we should eliminate arbitrary rule by major powers and a uniform measure covering an entire world and, instead, establish an international order underpinned by regional security regimes in line with each region's reality but concurrently supplemented by a world security institution as need arises. We should develop measures to transform international order peacefully in prompt accordance with situations around the world.

While the major points of the Greater East Asia Declaration were incorporated in Article 1 in summarized form, these seven principles had three characteristics that reflected the international situation in 1945.

First, much of the content of Article 2 stemmed from a consciousness of the Soviet Union, which had notified Japan that the treaty of neutrality would not be extended. Thus, it can be interpreted that such items as peoples' liberation in Article 3, emphasis on political equality among nations and the principle of non-interference in Article 2, and abolishment of armaments based on the "principles of non-threat and non-aggression" in Article 6 were expected to function as measures to dissuade the Soviet Union from participating in the war by stressing that what Greater East Asia stood for was no different from the Soviet vision of the postwar world and international politics.

Second, in the face of the San Francisco Conference, which had been predicted to further advance the argument for creation of a unitary security institution, the "guiding principles for construction of the world order" proposed a "regional security institution" (Article 7). It should be noted, however, that this regional institution was not meant to be an exclusive one. Described as being "concurrently supplemented by a world security institution as need arises," this concept seemed to resonate with the philosophy of the world economic organization—regionalism under globalism—that Ishibashi and Kiyosawa had envisioned.

Third, liberation of "people under colonial status" was reiterated in Article 3 as it was also stressed by Foreign Minister Tōgō's opening statement. In the background there seemed to be a need for a "diplomatic offensive" from Japan in the face of receding anti-colonialism on the Allies side. The trusteeship scheme, which had reflected the anti-colonialism stance of the United States, stipulated that it would be the task of colonial masters to assist independence for colonized peoples and that those colonies would be placed under the supervision of an international organization so that they would be given a chance for economic development and training in politics and administration before becoming independent. It was a scheme to incrementally expand the autonomy of colonized peoples.[50] US President Franklin Roosevelt's enthusiasm notwithstanding, the scheme had to experience a setback due not only to opposition from Britain and France but also to a conflict of views within the US government. By March 1945, the US government went so far as to essentially recognize France's return to Indochina.[51]

At the San Francisco Conference, a conflict over the objective of trusteeship to be stipulated by the United Nations Charter was seen between the United States, which insisted on limiting it to promotion of incremental autonomy, and the Soviet Union and China, which insisted on making the promotion of independence, rather than autonomy, a duty for colonial masters.[52] The record of the dialogue between former Prime Minister Hirota Kōki and Soviet Ambassador to Japan Yakov Malik showed that the Japanese

---

50 Cordell Hull, *The Memoir of Cordell Hull*, vol. 2 (New York: Macmillan, 1948), pp. 1234–1235.

51 For instance, see Christopher Thorne, op cit., chapter 27, Aruga Tadashi, "Amerika Gasshukoku no Tōnan Ajia seisaku: 1943–1952" [Southeast Asia Policy of the United States: 1943–1952], Hitotsubashi University *Hōgaku Kenkyū Nenpō*, no. 17, 1987, pp. 9–10, and Yamane Shin, "Rōzuveruto seiken no Indoshina seisaku" [The Roosevelt Administration Policy on the Indochina Question: Cooperation and Conflict among Wartime Allies, 1942–1945], *Dōshisha Hōgaku*, vol. 31, no. 4, 1979, pp. 58–60.

52 William R. Louis, *Imperialism at Bay: The United States and the Decolonization of the British Empire 1941–1945* (New York: Oxford University Press), pp. 532–547.

side was aware of this conflict of views at the San Francisco Conference.[53] In any event, learning that the principle of self-determination stipulated by the Atlantic Charter would not be immediately applied to the postwar world due to conflict of views within the Allies, marking the setback of anti-colonialism in the enemy camp inevitable, the Japanese side perceived it as a proof that Japan's argument for liberation of "people in colonial conditions" was rightful and just.

While the declaration that came out of the Greater East Asia Ambassadors' Conference might have been charged with all the above motives, it failed to stir any reaction domestically, not to mention any impact abroad. Nevertheless, its content was much more sophisticated than that of the Greater East Asia Joint Declaration. While the latter aspired to "regionalism" in international order, the declaration of the Ambassadors' Conference aspired to "universalism," which warranted the evaluation that the declaration "could have been drafted by the US State Department."[54] It can be said that presentation of such a philosophy that extended beyond contention over the war became possible due to changes in the environment, both overseas and domestic, involving the Ministries of Foreign Affairs and Greater East Asia.

In contrast to the Greater East Asia Declaration, which was drafted through rigorous negotiations with the military as well as the Greater East Asia Ministry, the declaration of the Greater East Asia Ambassadors' Conference was totally devoid of the resolve to meet the urgent need to

---

53 In his discussion with Yakov Malik on June 4, 1945, Hirota remarked, "I know that, at the San Francisco Conference, the Soviet Union insisted on India's independence and that Moscow promoted the policy of granting independence to occupied territories for the sake of future peace-keeping. I am also aware that the Soviet Union has a view of its own on the future peace-keeping mechanism. As for the international trusteeship for the occupied territories, I know Moscow hopes to grant independence to these territories. In this sense, the Soviet Union's policy coincides with Japan's policy toward the Eastern territories." (Ministry of Foreign Affairs record of the Hakone Talks supplemented with the record of the Russian side).

54 Akira Iriye, "Wartime Japanese Planning for Post-war Asia," in Ian Nish, ed., *Anglo-Japanese Alienation, 1919–1952* (Cambridge: Cambridge University Press, 1982), p. 195.

prepare for the homeland defense war or consideration for the need to respond to the realities of the occupied territories in Asia. Due to the defeat in the Battle of the Philippines, it became nearly impossible for Japan to maintain the occupied territories, particularly those in Southeast Asia, and the foundation for Japan's Greater East Asia diplomacy was quickly being eroded. Therefore, it can be said that it was a declaration which was liberated from the tension and pressure of domestic and international realities. In that sense, the Declaration of the Greater East Asia Ambassadors' Conference has to be clearly separated from the Joint Declaration of the Greater East Asia Conference (Greater East Asia Declaration) of the time of Shigemitsu's tenure as foreign minister. And this is the reason for judging that it was under Foreign Minister Tōgō, who had declared that the above seven principles were "the very war aims of Japan that I have long entertained,"[55] that the declaration of the Ambassadors' Conference was drafted.

At the conference among eight military governors in June 1945, Tōgō spoke of the recent international situation. In his speech, he touched on Japan's war purpose and argued that Japan's diplomatic policy must "show to the entire world, including Britain and America, the great principles for inducing permanent world peace." The Declaration of the Greater East Asia Ambassadors' Conference, Tōgō argued, was "a righteous war purpose" to not only liberate Greater East Asia but also "to establish a new international order for the entire world's co-prosperity," which had to be "a shared conviction for each and every one of the 100-million Japanese." It was as if Tōgō was trying to encourage participants to intellectually and psychologically prepare for the end of the war against the United States.[56]

---

55 Tōgō Shigenori, *Jidai no ichimen* [An Aspect of the Time], Hara Shobō, 1985, p. 323.

56 "Saikin no kokusai jōsei" [Recent International Situations] (Draft manuscript of foreign minister's briefing at conference among eight military governors on June 19, 1945), Akira Iriye, *Power and Culture: The Japanese-American War, 1941–1945* (Cambridge: Harvard University Press, 1979), pp. 240–241. Also see Iriye Akira, *Nichi-Bei sensō* [Japan-US War], Chūō Kōronsha. 1978, pp. 282–283.

5. Conclusion

The Greater East Asia Joint Declaration has been interpreted in numerous ways and has stirred controversies. Historian Iriye Akira, for instance, recognized "close parallels" or "an almost complete return to Wilsonian internationalism" in the Greater East Asia Joint Declaration and the April 1945 Declaration of the Greater East Asia Ambassadors' Conference that caused controversy.[57] Political scientist Miwa Kimitada, on his part, found in such principles of the declaration an "opening of natural resources," an early sign of values akin to the "endogenous development theory" of the present-day developmental theory or the notion of international common goods.[58] It was because the Greater East Asia Declaration contained highly universal philosophies above and beyond a mere hope for contributing to the waging of the war, that these and other interesting discussions developed regarding the declaration.

One of the government officials among the Allies who paid close attention to the above implications of the Greater East Asia Declaration was Robert Ward of the US State Department. Returning home after witnessing the Japanese troops' occupation of Hong Kong, Ward pointedly argued as follows in early 1945:

> The immediate purpose of the declaration is obvious: Japan hoped . . . to procure more widespread support in the decisive battles of the Pacific War that still lay ahead. . . . But the apparatus that was employed, and even some of the words that were used, suggested that the Japanese were more intent upon a subtler purpose. . . . That purpose is the projection of the political struggle in Asia beyond the issue of the present war. . . . This shift was followed by a series of maneuvers . . . a conciliatory policy toward

---

57 Iriye (1979), pp. 120–121, 240–241.
58 Miwa Kimitada, *Nippon: 1945-nen no shiten* [Japan: Viewpoint of 1945], University of Tokyo Press, 1986, pp. 100–101.

the puppet regimes in China . . . Burma was granted her independence, the Provisional Government of Free India was set up in Singapore, and the "government" of the Philippine Commonwealth was declared to be "free and independent." These acts cost Japan nothing; no actual change occurred in the condition of the subject peoples . . . rather they looked toward defeat and were calculated to make history plead the cause of Yamato before the bar of the East at some later judgment day.[59]

As it became increasingly clear that Japan would be defeated in the war, a calculation emerged in the minds of Shigemitsu and the Foreign Ministry bureaucrats who had supported Shigemitsu regarding promotion of a series of new policies on how "to make history plead the cause of Yamato before the bar of the East at some later judgment day," as we will see in more detail in chapter 9.

59 Robert S. Ward, *Asia for the Asiatics? The Techniques of the Japanese Occupation* (Chicago: University of Chicago Press, 1945), pp. 189–190.

Chapter 9

Foreign Minister Shigemitsu and Greater East Asia Diplomacy: Indonesia and French Indochina

1. Introduction: Resurrection of Greater East Asia Diplomacy

The new China policy was, according to Shigemitsu Mamoru, minister for foreign affairs, a series of Greater East Asia policy measures that included the granting of independence to Burma and the Philippines, Thailand's recovery of lost territories, and the promotion of people's political participation in Java. As part of the new China policy, the Greater East Asia Declaration was a culmination of these policy measures. According to Shigemitsu, the declaration represented a "grand diplomatic offensive by Japan" and, at the same time, the momentum for Japan to shift "from the initial stage of military offensive to that of political diplomacy." While Prime Minister Tōjō Hideki showed commendable political skill in supporting and carrying out the Greater East Asia policy, he failed to utilize the policy in domestic politics. It was a grave deficiency on the part of Tōjō to forge ahead with collectivism and militarism, believing "political diplomacy [would be only] an obstacle to the pursuance of militarism."[1]

It was the loss of diplomacy and politics in Japan's measures toward Greater East Asia throughout the Tōjō government's tenure that brought about economic and political hardship to Greater East Asia. The situation also brought about the weakening of the foundation of Japan's diplomatic offensive vis-à-vis the world. In February 1944, Shigemitsu stressed to Tōjō as follows:

> Since the issuing of the Greater East Asia Declaration, there have been no diplomacy or politics in Greater East Asia. Economically it has been seriously deadlocked and, if not attended to properly, Japan may even lose

---

1 Itō Takashi et al., eds., *Zoku Shigemitsu Mamoru shuki* [Shigemitsu Mamoru Private Memoir vol. 2], Chūō Kōronsha, 1988 (*Zoku Shigemitsu shuki* henceforth), p. 203 and Itō Takashi et al., eds., *Shigemitsu Mamoru shuki* [Shigemitsu Mamoru Private Memoir], Chūō Kōronsha, 1986 (*Shigemitsu shuki* henceforth), pp. 419–423.

Greater East Asia altogether . . . Because diplomacy toward Greater East Asia is the foundation of Japan's global diplomacy, a lack of Greater East Asia diplomacy will lead to ineffectual diplomacy all around.[2]

Several factors made Shigemitsu acutely aware of the importance of the unification of Japan's Greater East Asia diplomacy. These included the conspicuous interference from the Ministry of Greater East Asia in the drafting of the Greater East Asia Declaration and management of the Greater East Asia Conference, delays in the liberation and independence of Indonesia and French Indochina, and bankruptcy of the new China policy. In order to break those deadlocks in the new Greater East Asia policy, it was necessary to return the authority for measures toward Greater East Asia to the Ministry of Foreign Affairs. To realize this through organizational reform, however, would have been extremely difficult. The only option available to Foreign Minister Shigemitsu was to concurrently serve as minister for Greater East Asia. Thus, on the occasion of the formation of the Koiso Kuniaki cabinet, Foreign Minister Shigemitsu succeeded in being appointed concurrently as minister for Greater East Asia thanks to support from Kido Kōichi, Lord Keeper of the Privy Seal.

In the midst of the worsened war situation caused by collapse of the Absolute National Defense Zone in the Pacific and the defeat in Burma, however, it was not at all easy to resuscitate Greater East Asia diplomacy and pursue a Greater East Asia policy anew. Consequently, the argument for tightened control of the peoples of Greater East Asia, rather than for their autonomy and independence, became increasingly dominant in Japan as it sought to secure cooperation from the occupied territories on behalf of the war effort.

This chapter reviews the process through which Shigemitsu and the Ministry of Foreign Affairs, which had succeeded in realizing substantive

---

2 *Zoku Shigemitsu shuki*, p. 203.

unification of Greater East Asia measures, persisted with the second phase of the Greater East Asia policy—the promotion of people's political participation in Indonesia, the liberalization and independence of French Indochina, and so on—in the face of the above-mentioned militaristic arguments.

2. Attempts at Unification of Greater East Asia Diplomacy

When Shigemitsu succeeded in monopolizing authority for measures toward Greater East Asia by being appointed as both minister for foreign affairs and minister for Greater East Asia in the Koiso cabinet, marking the completion of preparations for the new Greater East Asia policy, attempts to counter Shigemitsu's efforts emerged from among those around Prime Minister Koiso. These attempts were based on the *Taigai seiryaku shidō yōryō* (Outline of Guidance on External Political Maneuvers), which had been compiled by the Army Ministry immediately after formation of the Koiso cabinet. The major thrust of this outline was twofold: establishment of the "one person, two roles" system for the representative of the Empire of Japan in China, Thailand, French Indochina, the Philippines, and Burma; and dissolution of the Nationalist government in Nanjing to create a better governing body, depending on the result of political maneuvers vis-à-vis the Chongqing government. The objective of these measures was the strengthening of cooperation of Greater East Asian peoples with Japan in the Greater East Asia War.[3] Although the Ministries of Foreign Affairs and Greater East Asia did not agree with these measures—which in their judgment, went against the traditional Greater East Asia policy—Prime Minister Koiso, nevertheless, was determined to carry them out. This indicated that the Greater East Asia policy that the Imperial Army wished to entrust to

---

3 Honjo Shigeru, *Haisen no kiroku: Sanbō Honbu shozō* [Record of a War Defeat: A Collection of the Imperial Japanese Army General Staff Office], Hara Shobō, 1967, pp. 35–36.

the Koiso government was beginning to differ significantly from the policy Shigemitsu promoted.

With the consent of Umezu Yoshijirō, chief of the Imperial Japanese Army General Staff Office, Koiso first set out to seize diplomatic authority in the southern occupied territories currently in the hands of the military and appoint particularly competent ambassadors to French Indochina, Thailand, and Burma to control these regions. Koiso wanted these ambassadors to function concurrently as military commanders when the need arose. More concretely, Koiso schemed to reinstate retired Army General Minami Jirō to active duty and appoint him as ambassador to Thailand with the title of "combined ambassador to the southern territories" and place all the Japanese ambassadors and ministers in the region under his command. To realize this scheme, Koiso intended to appoint Minami as the Japanese ambassador to Thailand as a beginning. But Shigemitsu and the Foreign Ministry found the scheme intolerable, saying, it is "total rubbish to say that because it not only brushes aside the spirit of the Greater East Asia Declaration but also ignores true conditions in the southern territories."[4]

Koiso's scheme must have reminded Shigemitsu and the Foreign Ministry officials of the "army formula"—the permission that Army Lieutenant General Ōshima Hiroshi, ambassador to Germany, had obtained from Foreign Minister Matsuoka Yōsuke before the outbreak of the war to supervise all the Japanese envoys extraordinary and ministers plenipotentiary assigned to other European countries. To forestall Koiso's scheme, Shigemitsu appointed Deputy Minister for Greater East Asia Yamamoto Kumaichi, Ambassador Ishii Itarō, and Ambassador Matsumoto Shun'ichi as ambassadors to Thailand, Burma, and French Indochina, respectively.[5]

---

4 Yamamoto Kumaichi's personal note, "Shūsen ni shosu" [Coping with Defeat in War], (Ministry of Foreign Affairs Document A7.0.0.9-69), Yasuda Toshie, "Daitōa Kyōdō Sengen to Daitōa Kaigi o megutte" [On the Greater East Asia Declaration and the Greater East Asia Conference], *Hōgaku Kenkyū*, vol. 63, no. 2, 1990, p. 420.

5 Yamamoto arrived at his post in Thailand on September 9, 1944, Ishii on October 7, 1944, and Matsumoto on December 24, 1944.

Shigemitsu also appointed Foreign Ministry officials who "appreciate the new policy" as ministers to Beijing, Shanghai, and Guangdong. He replaced Lieutenant General and Minister to Beijing Shiozawa Kiyonobu, who had been regarded as a "cancer against the thorough implementation of the new China policy" with Kitazawa Naokichi.[6] While the scheme for "one person, two roles" that would have blocked the rehabilitation of the Greater East Asia policy was thus stopped, yet another obstructive factor emerged. Prime Minister Koiso, with the help of Ogata Taketora, minister of state, turned positive toward peace maneuvering vis-à-vis the Chongqing government.

Koiso, in cooperation with Ogata, proceeded to make political maneuvering with the Chongqing government an Imperial Council decision. At the same time, he requested General Ugaki Kazushige, former army minister and foreign minister, to sound out the possibility of a peace settlement during his impending trip to China. Furthermore, Koiso aggressively pursued peace maneuvering vis-à-vis Miao Bin of the Nanjing government. Koiso's enthusiasm notwithstanding, Shigemitsu persisted with the position that, "Regardless of the success or failure of peace maneuvering activities, it is absolutely necessary for Japan to simultaneously pursue the so-called new policy vigorously in all areas, including politics and economy, and thereby induce the Chongqing government to come in line with us."[7] When Koiso proposed a review of the new China policy at the Supreme Council for the Direction of the War in mid-December 1944, citing the death of Wang Jingwei and the poorer-than-expected results of the peace maneuvering with the Chongqing government, Shigemitsu simply killed it.[8]

Ogata and Ugaki and his group had been supportive of Koiso's policies

---

6 *Shigemitsu shuki*, p. 485. Shiozawa was replaced by Kitazawa Naokichi (chargé d'affaires) in August 1944.

7 "Tai Jūkei seiji kōsaku no jisshi ni kansuru ken" [Matters Related to Implementation of Political Engineering toward Chongqing] (September 1) (Ministry of Foreign Affairs Document A7.0.0.9-61, "Daitōa Sensō ikken" [Matters Related to Greater East Asia War] and "Honpō no tai-Jūkei kōsaku kankei" [Matters Related to Japan's Engineering toward Chongqing]).

8 Ogata Taketora Denki Kankōkai ed., *Ogata Taketora* [Ogata Taketora], 1963, pp. 131–132.

toward China. Shigemitsu, from beginning to end, remained critical of their deep involvement in the political maneuvering with the Chongqing government as an attempt to topple the Wang Jingwei government, which had argued for the "demise of the Nanjing government." Shigemitsu was of the conviction that, "Once the Japanese government has recognized the Nanjing government, it has to follow the royal road of moral principle and international fidelity by thoroughly pursuing the new China policy."[9] Shigemitsu was convinced that the likes of Koiso and Ugaki could not possibly "understand the new China policy nor the Greater East Asia Declaration," and they "wrongly equate conspiracy and maneuver with diplomacy," just as the time when Koiso had been director-general of the Bureau of Military Affairs of the Army Ministry.

And it was at the reshuffling of the Koiso cabinet in December 1944 that the tangle between Shigemitsu and Koiso over the Greater East Asia policy reached its peak. When Fujiwara Ginjirō, minister for munitions, tendered his resignation, Koiso intended to appoint Education Minister Ninomiya Harushige as minister for Greater East Asia and replace Ninomiya with Tanaka Takeo, chief cabinet secretary. Koiso also planned to replace Maeda Yonezō, minister for transport and communications, with Murata Shōzō, Japanese ambassador to the Philippines.[10] Koiso conveyed his plan for the personnel shuffle to Shigemitsu.

It is rumored that the ulterior motive for Murata's appointment as a member of the Koiso cabinet was Murata's dismissal from the Philippines. The chief focus of this cabinet reshuffle was to appoint Ninomiya to minister for Greater East Asia instead of allowing Foreign Minister Shigemitsu to serve concurrently as the Greater East Asia minister.

Finding Prime Minister Koiso's proposal unacceptable from the viewpoint of unification of diplomatic channels, Shigemitsu replied in writing as

---

9   *Shigemitsu shuki*, p. 474, pp. 486–487.

10 Amō Eiji Nikki/Shiryōshū Kankōkai, ed., *Amō Eiji nikki/shiryōshū, dai 4-kan* [Amō Eiji's Diary and Documents, vol. 4], 1982. According to the entry of December 19, 1944, Koiso also planned to appoint Ugaki Kazushige as ambassador to the Soviet Union.

follows in consultation with Kido Kōichi[11]:

(1) Appointment of a separate minister for Greater East Asia would go against unification of diplomatic channels and obstruct pursuit of the Greater East Asia policy;

(2) If a separate minister for Greater East Asia has to be appointed, the system of unification of diplomatic channels would need to be established first. In that case, the Ministry of Greater East Asia would need to be renamed the Ministry of Greater East Asian Economy before a new, separate minister is appointed.[12]

The general outline of Shigemitsu's reply had been envisioned toward the end of the Tōjō cabinet. Item (2) above meant that when a separate minister for Greater East Asia was to be appointed, the ministry's authority over measures toward occupied territories would be transferred to the Foreign Ministry. A proposal on the reform of regulations for governmental organizations had already been determined by an in-house conference of the Foreign Ministry.[13] Shigemitsu was determined to resign as foreign minister if his replies were not accepted. He conveyed his determination to Navy Minister Yonai Mitsumasa via Arita Hachirō, adviser to the foreign minister. As a result of Yonai's persuasion, Koiso at last gave up the idea of appointing a separate minister for Great East Asia.[14]

Thus, Shigemitsu succeeded in defending the unification of diplomatic channels. At the same time, he intended to put forth the second Greater East Asia new policy targeted at Indonesia and French Indochina.

---

11 Kido Nikki Kenkyūkai, ed., *Kido Kōichi nikki* [Kido Kōichi Diary], University of Tokyo Press, 1966, entry of December 17, 1944 (pp. 1158–1159), *Shigemitsu shuki*, pp. 487–488.
12 *Shigemitsu shuki*, pp. 488–489.
13 *Ogata Taketora*, p. 131.
14 *Shigemitsu shuki*, pp. 490–491. According to *Amō nikki* (December 18), he met Shigemitsu, who said, "Depending on what will happen to the unification of diplomatic channels, I may have to make a personal decision."

3. Gyration of the Issue of Indonesia's Independence

(1) Koiso Statement and the Foreign Ministry

Toward the end of March 1944, top leaders of the Army Ministry and the Imperial Japanese Army General Staff Office were prompted by Shigemitsu and Prime Minister Tōjō to study the issue of independence for the Dutch East Indies. The backdrop to this was the fall of Truk Island, which was located on the outer rim of Japan's Absolute National Defense Zone, in February 1944. The study concluded that, although it would be appropriate to make a governmental announcement promising future independence in response to the "long-cherished aspiration" of the Dutch East Indies people, such an announcement had to wait until there was a turn for the better in the war situation. In other words, the study concluded that it would be premature to make the announcement at that time.[15] This was believed to be the origin of the Koiso Statement. Because the war situation further worsened, however, the chance to make the announcement never materialized.

Due to the distress caused by the fall of Saipan Island, which was a strategic point in the Absolute National Defense Zone, Japan was cornered into doing something for the solidarity of Greater East Asia, including political maneuvering, to counter the US forces' offensive deep into the central Pacific region. Thus, the issue of Indonesian independence abruptly resurfaced as soon as the Koiso government was formed. And it was perceived that "It would be difficult to secure the local people's cooperation if the issue of their independence was left in limbo."[16]

---

15 *Daihon'ei kimitsu sensō nisshi* [Imperial General Headquarters Secret War Diary], Imperial Japanese Army General Staff Office Section 20 (March 18 and 22, 1944). (*Kimitsu sensō nisshi*, henceforth)
16 *Dai 2-ji Sekai Taisen chū ni okeru Higashi Indo no tōchi oyobi kizoku kettei ni kansuru keii* [Details on the Decision on East India's Administration and Belonging during the Second World War] (Ministry of Foreign Affairs Document A7.0.0.9-56, "Daitōa Sensō ikken Ranryō Higashi Indo mondai ikken" [Matters Related to Greater East Asia War: Matters Related to the Dutch East Indies]).

On August 17, 1944, about a month after the formation of the Koiso cabinet, the Ministry of Foreign Affairs convened a meeting of the Nanpō Iinkai (Southern Territory Committee, Arita Hachirō, chairman) on the issue of Indonesia's administration at the official residence of the deputy minister for foreign affairs. The ministry invited Hayashi Kyūjirō, adviser to the Java Army's Inspectorate Military Administration and former Japanese ambassador to Brazil, to attend. The meeting was attended by the directors-general of almost all of the bureaus, as well as divisions directors, starting with Deputy Foreign Minister Matsumoto Shun'ichi. While the details are unknown, the meeting centered around Hayashi's argument for Indonesia's independence. According to Ishii Itarō, one of the participants, Hayashi argued that, in a nutshell, if Japan did not promise independence to the Javanese people, who had been collaborating with Japan, they would be disappointed and Japan could no longer expect their cooperation if the war situation grew even worse. And to offer his opinion on this issue to the Japanese government was why he had returned to Japan, Hayashi said.[17]

According to Hayashi's written opinion, although the Javanese people's cooperation with the war effort had been gradually reinforced thanks to guidance provided by the Jawa Hōkōkai (People Service Organization, organized in March 1944), it was "highly questionable whether the Javanese people would willingly collaborate with the war effort due to the hardships they would have to endure in their daily lives." Based on this analysis, in his paper, Hayashi argued for the prompt issuance of permission for independence for Indonesia. He continued to say, "It is because Javanese leaders, intellectuals, and youths believe that the current war is not only Japan's war but a war that can liberate Indonesian people, if they win it, that they have collaborated with our military. Nonetheless, their hope has not been formally endorsed by Japan yet."

---

17 Itō Takashi et al., eds., *Ishii Itarō nikki* [Ishii Itarō Diary], Chūō Kōronsha, 1993, entry of August 17, 1944.

Furthermore, Hayashi pointed to the conspicuous gap between the Javanese people's expectation for expansion of their political participation and the reality of the situation. He contended, "there is a tendency among people to suspect, as time goes on, that Japan treats Java differently from Burma and the Philippines and will, eventually, make it a directly ruled territory together with the Malay Peninsula."[18]

While Hayashi urged prompt issuance of approval of independence, regarding the timing of such, he was of the view that it would take time to train the locals to prepare for independence. He contended that Japan should utilize this preparatory period to familiarize the local people throughout the island with the Japanese language, and, "at the same time, mold their youths into a second Japanese nation imbued with the Japanese spirit, which would allow the Empire of Japan to gain an essentially reliable ally under our guidance." In other words, the form of independence envisioned for Indonesia was, like that of the Philippines and Burma, not a full independence but a guided independence under de facto Japanese leadership. And, moreover, this independence was premised on assimilation.

Although Hayashi's argument on Indonesia's independence was not fully in line with the Foreign Ministry's policy, it nevertheless appeared to have a certain impact both within and outside of the ministry, at least regarding the need for a prompt announcement on granting permission for independence to Java.

In anticipation of the opening of the 85th session of the Imperial Diet, in early August, pertinent government offices began drafting concrete measures in preparation for Indonesia's independence. The Ministry of Greater East Asia, for instance, proposed that, after making a declaration on granting approval for the independence for Indonesia, Japan should allow "Java and

---

18 Hayashi Kyūjirō, "Jawa tōchi ni kansuru ichi kōsatsu" [An Observation on Rule of Java] in Waseda Daigaku Ōkuma Kinen Shakai Kagaku Kenkyūsho, ed., *Indoneshia ni okeru Nippon gunsei no kenkyū* [A Study on Japanese Military Administration in Indonesia], Kinokuniya Shoten, 1959, pp. 591–594. Although the date of writing is unknown, it is conjectured that it was written in the fall of 1944.

other eligible regions to become independent one by one," starting with Java. The ministry's proposal also predicted that "Indonesia in the end can be made into an independent member of the federation in the future."

At the same time, the Imperial Japanese Army proposed that it should be "promptly announced that the Dutch East Indies will be made independent in the future." Unlike the Greater East Asia Ministry's proposal to permit regions of Indonesia, starting with Java, to become independent one by one, the Imperial Army's proposal regarding the regions of the Dutch Indies to be independent included Java, Sumatra, Southern Borneo, and Celebes—that is, almost the entire territory of Indonesia. Still, the army proposed that the timing of each region's independence should be decided separately, in consideration of the war situation and other factors, and stressed that, "premature independence must be avoided." As for the form of independence, the army argued, "It should be in a form that allows easy control by the Empire of Japan. Also, the degree of independence should vary from region to region, depending on a region's attributes."[19]

From the viewpoint of the Foreign Ministry, even though the army's proposal clearly stated its policy to grant independence for all the regions in the future, it gave priority to the continuation of military administration and, therefore, lacked concrete steps toward realizing independence. Despite this, the Foreign Ministry found the Greater East Asia Ministry's proposal to be close to its own. It commented, however, "The kind of independence that effectively requires protection arrangements should not be granted in haste. This kind of 'independence' would actually go against Greater East Asia policy."[20] While it remains unclear which portion of the Greater East Asia Ministry's proposal presupposed post-independence protection arrangements, for the Foreign Ministry, independence literally meant independence,

---

19 Proposals by ministries are quoted from Ministry of Foreign Affairs Document A7.0.0.9-56 and *Indoneshia ni okeru Nippon gunsei no kenkyū*, pp. 594–597.
20 "Higashi Indo dokuritsu shisaku ni kansuru ken (chūkan hōkoku)" [Matters Related to Independence Measures for the Dutch East Indies (an interim report)], (Ministry of Foreign Affairs Document A7.0.0.9-56).

and its criticism of the Greater East Asia Ministry's proposal showed that a form of independence that would allow Japan to maintain its leadership position was unacceptable.

It was, however, the Imperial Japanese Navy—not the Imperial Army or the Ministry of Greater East Asia—that obstructed the materialization of inter-bureau concrete measures toward Indonesia's independence. Critical of the proposal for a prompt announcement of the policy for independence from the beginning, the Navy Ministry also expressed its objection to the geographical range of regions to be allowed to become independent. The Foreign Ministry official in charge wrote about a brainstorming session on August 26 to study the proposals by Hayashi, the Ministry of Greater East Asia, and the Imperial Japanese Army, saying, "the Navy Ministry has no proposal and it opposes any change to the current status in areas under its own control."[21] As it turned out, the Imperial Navy continued to oppose independence for Indonesia right up to the time of the 85th session of the Imperial Diet.

Thus, related officials of the Ministries of Army, Navy, and Foreign Affairs failed to reach a conclusion concerning the timing and geographical range of Indonesia's independence before Prime Minister Koiso's speech at the Imperial Diet. Thus, Koiso's speech on September 7, 1944, became a simple affair, with Koiso stating, "The Empire of Japan hereto declares that it intends to grant independence in the future to the peoples of the Dutch East Indies in order to secure their lasting welfare." This remark is known as the Koiso Statement. At the Supreme Council for the Direction of the War on September 6, it was pointed out that this statement alone was "liable to become an obstacle in carrying out actual measures because it leaves unde-cided what should be done in Java or whether preparation for independence

---

21 "Higashi Indo dokuritsu shisaku ni kansuru ikken (chūkan hōkoku)" [Matters Related to Independence Measures for the Dutch East Indies (an interim report)], August 28, 1944, (Ministry of Foreign Affairs Document A7.0.0.9-56).

in Sumatra causes any problem."[22] Thus, the Koiso Statement fell short of becoming an effective guideline for measures to be taken for Indonesia.

At the same time, in Indonesia, too, a conflict between the 16th Army, which insisted on limiting independence to Java alone, and the Office of Naval Attaché in Jakarta, which envisioned independence for the entirety of Indonesia, was entangled in the strife between the Office of Naval Attaché, the Southwest District Fleet Civil Government, and the 25th Army, which had been consistently negative toward independence. This made materialization of the Koiso Statement all the more challenging.

(2) Turning toward Permission for Independence

Five concrete directives accompanying the Koiso Statement included (1) no specific date for independence should be given; (2) unofficial preparatory study by the Indonesian side should be permitted; (3) local people's political participation should be expanded; (4) enthusiasm for independence should be publicized; and (5) use of the Indonesian people's national anthem and flag should be permitted. While it can be interpreted that these five directives were extracted from the agreements reached through the inter-ministerial entanglements since early August, item (2) alone was an important one that had not undergone inter-ministerial coordination. While the Ministries of Foreign Affairs and Greater East Asia envisioned a formal independence preparatory committee that would include representatives of local residents as in the case of Burma and the Philippines, the Imperial Army supported the policy of allowing only unofficial studies on requirements for independence by local citizens. And the Imperial Navy was critical of the establishment of such institutions altogether.[23]

Of these five directives, only the third, on expansion of local people's political participation, made any headway. With such measures as the

---

22 *Kimitsu sensō nisshi*, entry of September 6, 1944.
23 Proposals by ministries are quoted from Ministry of Foreign Affairs Document A7.0.0.9-56.

promotion of Indonesian officials to executive positions, the adoption of the system of councilor and establishment of a councilor's conference, and the expansion of the number of seats of the Central Advisory Council, it almost appeared that permission for independence was substituted with an expansion of local people's political participation. The most problematic of the five instructions was instruction (2) on establishment of an organization to study issues with direct bearing on independence.[24]

An Independence Preparatory Study Committee was set up in March 1945, but it took half a year for this committee to be established. Its assigned task of "studying all the issues necessary to preparing for independence" was constrained by the insurmountable conflict of views over the mandate of the research organization, the scope of its work, and the nature and geographical range of the envisioned independent nation, among other factors. Suspecting this research organization to be a ploy for postponing independence, the Indonesian side nevertheless took on the attitude of aggressively utilizing it as, for instance, a venue through which the constitution of the new nation was to be drafted.[25]

The Imperial Navy and the Southwest District Fleet Civil Government confirmed that the Koiso Statement essentially said, "Unless otherwise instructed, current measures and systems should not be altered," and, accordingly, they continued to suppress nationalist movements by local populations and forbid use of people's anthems and flags. The Imperial Navy had no intention of following the government's policy of expanding local people's political participation or carrying it out in such areas under their control such as Sumatra and Celebes. Behind this attitude was a lack of awareness on the part of the Japanese Navy of the rising aspiration for independence among the locals stimulated by the Koiso Statement. Unlike Java, in the areas under the Navy's military administration, including Celebes, the

---

24 *Indoneshia ni okeru Nippon gunsei no kenkyū*, pp. 408–410.
25 Ibid., pp. 411–418.

Navy saw itself as dealing with "feudalistic chieftain systems" and a "lack of a modern-day intellectual class." Particularly, the Southwest District Fleet Civil Government did not recognize the need to change existing policies and systems; rather, it basically continued to view nationalistic movements as potentially undermining war capability.[26]

Because preparations for independence progressed in Java, the Southwest District Fleet Civil Government felt pressure to show some progress in Celebes, Borneo, and the Lesser Sunda Islands, too. This led to the founding of the Kenkoku Dōshikai (National Construction Comrades Society) and establishment of branches of the society in those three regions. But the society proved inadequate for the task of providing a basis for the subsequent nationalist independence movement because its founders over-estimated the governing capability of the traditional chieftain system. The National Construction Comrades Society was dissolved shortly afterward.[27]

It was the worsening war situation that created a change of attitude in the Imperial Navy. In particular, the defeat in the Battle of the Philippines left the Southwest District Fleet Civil Government with the following "war lesson": "The strains in the war situation and the failure of military operations in the Philippines have taught us that it is extremely important to strengthen our hold on the hearts of local people. For this purpose, it is considered to be a good policy to firmly grasp the hearts of nationalist leaders, no matter how small their numbers might be, and, subsequently, to appeal to the entire population, in order to stimulate the local people to participate in the war."[28]

---

26 Nansei hōmen Kaigun minseifu (Mitsuhashi Kōichirō), ed., *Genjō shinkokusho* [Declaration on Status], June 1945 (a collection of the National Institute for Defense Studies, Japan), George Kanahele, "The Japanese Occupation of Indonesia, Prelude to Independence" (Ph.D. dissertation, Cornell University, 1967). For the details of the reality of administration of the occupied territories by the Southwest District Fleet Civil Government, see Koike Seiichi, "Kaigun nanpō 'minsei'" [Naval Civil Government in Southern Territories], Hikita Yasuyuki, ed., *Senji Nippon no Tōnan Ajia keizai shihai*, [Wartime Japan's Economic Domination of Southeast Asia], Taga Shuppan, 1995, pp. 135–172.

27 *Indoneshia ni okeru Nippon gunsei no kenkyū*, pp. 422–423.

28 *Genjō shinkokusho.*

This shows the change in the Imperial Navy's attitude toward tolerance of independence by recognizing that emphasis on a few nationalist leaders was more effective than relying on traditional feudal chieftains in attempting to grasp public sentiment.

Toward the end of May 1945, related officials from the Ministries of the Army, Greater East Asia, Foreign Affairs, and the Navy gathered once again in order to study measures for the independence of Indonesia. This group decided on the policy that, "in order to stimulate the nationalistic sentiment of the Dutch East Indies people, in accordance with the established policy of the liberation of East Asia, and induce them to contribute to the Empire of Japan's war effort, the Empire shall grant independence to the Dutch East Indies as expeditiously as practicable." Furthermore, on June 1, related officials of the four ministries adopted a draft proposal saying, "the [Empire of Japan] should prompt immediate preparations for independence throughout the entire territory and let the entire region declare the independence of a new nation as soon as preparations are completed in key regions."[29] On July 17, the major thrust of this draft proposal was adopted almost in its entirety by the Supreme Council for the Direction of the War. Accordingly, all preparations for independence were left to the military stationed in Indonesia. Thus, the process toward independence greatly accelerated.

After the announcement of the Koiso Statement, within the Japanese government there expanded an expectation that it would take at least several years to prepare for independence. During that period, policy coordination and consensus with the Imperial Navy could be achieved, taking into consideration internal Japanese conditions and external factors. This was one of the reasons why the Koiso Statement had evolved into such a simple affair. At the time, in Japan it was believed that, even if the Indonesian side was permitted to make preparations for independence, it would take at least a

---

29 *Kanji hosa shian* [Assistant Executive Members' Draft Proposal], June 1, 1945 (Ministry of Foreign Affairs Document A7.0.0.9-56).

few years to complete them, because preparations included deciding on the form of the state (for instance, whether it would be a federation, a union, a republic, or a monarchy), establishing the constitution, overcoming issues related to multiple ethnicities and languages, and various religious problems, as well as the existence of multiple sultanates, large and small.[30]

However, as numerous witnesses and studies point out, the preparation for independence on the Indonesian side progressed much faster than the Japanese side had expected after the announcement of the Koiso Statement. To cope with the worsened war situation in the Pacific, Japan was pressed harder than before to utilize the physical and human resources of the occupied territories. Taking advantage of the euphoria and heightened morale over future independence among the Indonesian people, Japan moved forward on a variety of wartime measures. The most stressed of these measures were expansion and improvement of the military organization, strengthening of motivation for homeland defense, and, above all, expansion and reinforcement of the Jawa Bōei Giyūgun (Volunteer Army for Defense of Java, or PETA for short) group.[31] On October 8, 1944, the commander of the 16th Army announced a policy regarding PETA. The group was to "shoulder the important mission of being the forerunner and the core of the independent Dutch East Indies national army to be built in the future." The same commander outlined PETA's duty as including the following: (1) members of PETA should hasten toward defeating the archenemies the United States, Britain, and the Netherlands, for the sake of the independence and defense of their homeland, people, and religion; and (2) PETA should follow the instructions of the Japanese military.[32] This indicates that PETA was expected to participate in Japan's war against the American, British, and Dutch forces as the East Indies (Indonesian) independence army. Even

---

30 Miyoshi Shunkichirō, "Jawa senryōgunsei kaikoroku (dai 14-kai)" [Memoir of Military Government in Java, no. 14], *Kokusai Mondai*, no. 80, November 1966, p. 65.

31 "Jawa senryōgunsei kaikoroku (dai 13-kai)," *Kokusai Mondai*, no. 78, September 1966, pp. 65–66.

32 Local newspaper in the Japanese language, *Djawa Baroe*, October 15, 1944.

though these expectations were never realized, PETA continued to evolve as the core of the national military after Indonesia became independent.

Immediately following the announcement of the Koiso Statement, the local newspaper published by the Java Army's Inspectorate Military Administration carried an editorial welcoming the statement in which it reported for the first time on the Greater East Asia Declaration in detail, calling it "an epoch-making declaration which could be likened to a charter of Greater East Asia establishment." While highly praising the article in the declaration on elimination of racial discrimination, the editorial was unique in its abstention from referring to the principle of independence and autonomy as well as the principle of equality and reciprocity. Also unique was the following vision of international relations in which "the nation state of Indonesia to be recognized in the future" was to participate:

Relations among Greater East Asian countries are fundamentally different from the international relations of alignment and realignment based only on self-interest, something that is clearly visible among the anti-Axis countries. Members of Greater East Asia are connected with each other with amiable, almost familial ties, which is a traditional feature of Oriental ethics. . . . The Empire of Japan in the patriarchal position is pursuing implementation of the Greater East Asia Declaration, carrying high the banner of justice.[33]

This was not the direction that Shigemitsu had envisioned for Greater East Asia, nor was it a vision of international relations that Sukarno and Hatta had assumed. This was no different at all from the vision of the Greater East Asia Co-Prosperity Sphere with Japan as its guiding nation. Thus, the spirit of the Greater East Asia Declaration had suffered setbacks.

---

33 *Djawa Baroe*, October 1, 1944.

4. Liberation of Indochina

(1) Policy of Keeping the Peace and the Status Quo in French Indochina

Toward French Indochina, which had been under the control of Vichy France following France's surrender to Germany in June 1940, Japan maintained a policy of "keeping the peace and the status quo" (respect of French sovereignty). As the Southern Operations of the Japanese military progressed, however, this policy was shaken from two directions. One was the rise of voices demanding military government in the region. These voices were particularly loud among the Japanese military stationed in French Indochina. To go through diplomatic negotiations with the French Indochina authority or even the French government in order to carry out measures necessary for the war effort was found to be too time consuming compared with other occupied territories.[34] The second was criticism of the policy from the viewpoint of liberation of the East Asians. The Ministry of Foreign Affairs was particularly sensitive to this criticism. At the same time, it believed that it did not necessarily have to destroy French rule of Indochina to liberate its people. The Foreign Ministry was of a view that it would be possible to take such measures as improvement of the status of the Annam people through negotiations with the mainland French or the French Indochina authorities.

Nevertheless, whatever Japan attempted would end up threatening France's sovereignty in French Indochina and, for this reason, the Japanese government would not alter its policy of keeping the peace and the status quo in the region for fear of worsening relations with France. The grounds for the argument supporting this policy were provided, among other factors, by an inability to deploy massive forces to the region due to intensification of the Burma Campaign and the increased importance of French Indochina

---

34 Gaimushō Gaikō Shiryō Henshū Iinkai, ed., *Gaikō shiryō: Nichi-Futsuin kankei no bu* [Diplomatic Documents Japan-French Indochina Relations Section] (February 1946), p. 199.

as a base for supplies and logistics, which could be damaged by hasty application of the principle of people's liberation. French Indochina had played an important role as an operational and logistical base for the Southern Operations and it was "well known that it . . . made a great contribution to Japan's food supply." Thus, the view was widespread that, for the sake of obtaining a secure food supply, "it is wiser to keep the French Indochina government intact and use it at Japan's beck and call to collect necessary goods."[35]

During the deliberations on *Daitōa seiryaku shidō taikō* (Outlines for the Political Guidance of Greater East Asia) (adopted by the Imperial Council) in May 1943, although some argued for separation and independence of Annam, such was found to be infeasible under current circumstances. In the end, the status quo was chosen on the basis of the Imperial Army's policy "to refrain from granting independence and, instead, put Jean Decoux, governor-general of French-Indochina, under tight control and made him collaborate with Japan without cutting him off from the French home government."[36]

It was after the announcement of the Greater East Asia Joint Declaration (November 6, 1943) that this highly robust policy of keeping the peace and the status quo in French Indochina was shaken. While French Indochina was not invited to the Greater East Asia Conference, it was only natural, given the spirit of the Greater East Asia Declaration, for the issue of French Indochina, the last European colony remaining in Asia, to surface during the conference as an issue that called for "changes of existing conditions."[37]

After visiting French Indochina and Thailand, Mizuno Itarō,

---

35 Yamane Michiichi (Adviser, Indo-Shina Sangyō Kaisha or Compagnie Indochinose de Commerce et d'Industrie), "Futsuin o kataru" [Talking about French Indochina] (Nippon Gaikō Kyōkai, October, 1943).

36 Minutes of the June 17 division directors' conference and June 30 senior division officials' conference (*Kinbara Setsuzō gyōmu nisshi tekiroku*).

37 Akagi Kanji, "Futsuin buryoku shori o meguru gunji to gaikō: 'Jison jiei' to 'Daitōa kaihō' no aida" [Japanese Wartime Policy toward French Indochina Reexamined: The Designs and Realities], *Hōgaku Kenkyū*, vol. 57, no. 9, September 1984, pp. 42–43.

secretary-general of the Southern Territories, Ministry of Greater East Asia, gave a lecture at the Society for Promotion of Japanese Diplomacy in September 1943, in which he commented as follows:

Thinking about the Greater East Asia Co-Prosperity Sphere, it is not pleasant for us to see a European colony remaining in the middle of the Co-Prosperity Sphere. Many have insisted that we must grant independence to Annam promptly. The Annam people, too, might be frustrated by Japan. Although Japan has painstakingly helped the Philippines and Java obtain independence or autonomy, making all kinds of efforts and sacrifices, we do not pay enough attention to the Annam people. Many in Annam must find this attitude hard to understand and feel discontented, while many in Japan who are sympathetic with the Annam people may feel the same way.[38]

Nonetheless, Mizuno stressed, "Japan's involvement in French Indochina's independence must be avoided by all means." Mizuno concluded that French residents in French Indochina "have cooperated with Japan only because they wish to protect French sovereignty in French Indochina and they wish to retain the region as their own colony, regardless of the outcome of the war." Still, if Japan chose to positively respond to the Annam people's desire for independence and support their independence movement, Mizuno predicted, "The attitude of French people would little by little become less cooperative." As he aptly pointed out, the central government of Japan, particularly the Imperial Japanese Army General Staff Office, was extremely cautious about Japan's involvement in the independence movements in French Indochina out of fear of a deterioration of relations with the French Indochina government. Thus, the central government prohibited Japanese

---

38 Mizuno Itarō, *Saikin no nanpō jijō* [Recent Situations in the Southern Territories] November 28, 1943 (reference material prepared for a special committee of the Society for Promotion of Japanese Diplomacy).

troops in the region from contacting such pro-Japan independence advocates as the Vietnam Restoration League. At the same time, the French Indochina regime had also become increasingly oppressive toward these independence movements.[39]

Mizuno's analysis accurately pointed to the dilemma facing French Indochina, sandwiched as it was between France's colonialism, even under the Vichy regime, and Japan's policy for liberating Asia. Under these circumstances, it can be said that the Greater East Asia Conference had an impact on resolving this dilemma.

Subsequently, the Ministries of Foreign Affairs and Greater East Asia commenced deliberations on measures toward French Indochina in mid-November, after the Greater East Asia Conference. The Ministries of Army and Navy later joined the deliberations. The outcome was the adoption of the *Jōsei no henka ni ōzuru tai-Futsuin sochian* (Proposed Measures toward French Indochina in Response to Changes in Circumstances) in January 1944 by the Liaison Conference. While it is not possible to know what kind of deliberations took place during the two months, the Liaison Conference endorsed the ongoing policy by deciding that "Given the current situation, the Empire of Japan should persist with the policy of keeping the peace and the status quo in French Indochina. Thus, activities that could stimulate nationalist movements by the locals must be avoided." Yet it was also decided that, "When the homeland France ceases to be a pro-Axis independent nation in substance, French Indochina should be substantively seceded from the homeland France," and the four ministries began to study methods of achieving this aim, including the use of force. In any event, it was stipulated that the "utmost effort should be made to utilize the existing French Indochina administrative mechanisms."[40] In other words, even though Japan intended to go as far as separating French Indochina from

---

39 Akagi (1984), pp. 38–41.
40 Imperial Japanese Army General Staff Office, ed., *Sugiyama memo, ge* [Sugiyama Memorandum, vol. 2], Hara Shobō, 1989, p. 530.

France in case of the collapse of the Vichy regime or its self-exile, the option of granting independence to French Indochina was not given.

When Ambassador to French Indochina Yoshizawa Kenkichi returned home temporarily, he spoke with officials of the Army Ministry. During the meeting, Yoshizawa remarked that, when the Vichy government was dissolved, it would be useless to rely on the existing governing organization and, therefore, it would be more advisable, instead, to give the Annam people explicit hope for independence to make them hopeful for the future.[41] As this remark revealed, the notion of immediate independence of French Indochina upon the collapse of the Vichy government was already being considered within the Foreign Ministry.

Immediately after the decision at the Liaison Conference, Foreign Minister Shigemitsu Mamoru stressed to Prime Minister Tōjō the need to respond to "nationalism in French Indochina" by broadening the interpretation of the Greater East Asia Declaration as a part of the "second [Greater East Asia] new policy." Although Tōjō responded, "I am in full agreement with you. We should carry on along that line,"[42] he nevertheless failed to overturn the traditional policy of keeping the peace and the status quo and saving any steps toward tolerance for French Indochina's independence until after the liberation of Paris in August 1944. This was because the importance of French Indochina as a logistical base had increased due to the worsening of the war situation in Burma.[43]

(2) Liberation of Paris and Relations with the Soviet Union

The liberation of Paris in August 1944 pressured the Japanese government to revise its policy of keeping the peace and the maintaining the status quo. Upon his triumphant return to Paris, General Charles de Gaulle appointed Eugene Mordant, military commander of French forces in Indochina, to

---

41 *Kimitsu sensō nisshi*, entry of January 29, 1944.
42 *Zoku Shigemitsu shuki*, pp. 203–204.
43 Ibid., pp. 240–241.

delegate general of the French government for Indochina in an attempt to strengthen the organization toward liberation of French Indochina from the Japanese military. Although Mordant became the effective head of the French government in Indochina, replacing Jean Decoux, de Gaulle kept Decoux in the position of governor of Indochina lest Japan should be provoked.[44]

For his part, after de Gaulle returned to Paris, he devoted energy to securing international recognition for his government. This resulted in recognition as a provisional government by the United States, Britain, the Soviet Union, Canada and Australia toward the end of October. Through these processes, de Gaulle's government gradually consolidated its political foundation, both domestically and internationally. Although the French Indochina government continued to remain cooperative with Japan, political forces within the region eliminated Joseph Pétain's influence, showed signs of aligning with the de Gaulle government, and activated Annam independence movements. The information that the French Indochina government was trying to maintain an alliance with the de Gaulle government was also conveyed to the Japanese.[45]

In light of these circumstances, Foreign Minister Shigemitsu submitted a memorandum to the Supreme War Leadership Council on November 4, 1944. In this memorandum, Shigemitsu called the Council's attention to the de Gaulle regime's estrangement from Japan and the behind-the-scenes operations of the Annam independence advocates within French Indochina. He argued that, based on the Greater East Asia Declaration, which was the fundamental policy toward Greater East Asia for Japan, "It is of the utmost importance to make political and military preparations for the independence of Annam and make sure that when an appropriate time has arrived to

---

44 Tachikawa Kyōichi, "Furansu ga kaettekuru" [France is Coming Back] *Dai 2-ji Sekai Taisen: Shūsen* [World War II: End of the War], Kinseisha, 1995, pp. 232–233.
45 Foreign Minister Shigemitsu's telegram to Hanoi and Saigon (no. 211), *Gaikō Shiryō: Nichi-Futsuin kankei no bu* [Diplomatic Document: Japan-French Indochina Relations Section], pp. 255–256.

recognize independence, we have no regrets."[46] Although the Imperial Army agreed with Shigemitsu's basic argument, it opposed any hasty handling of the issue, citing a lack of military preparations caused by imminent operations in the Philippines that would not allow troops to be deployed to French Indochina. The Army's War Guidance Section, in particular, strongly criticized Foreign Minister Shigemitsu's insistence on hasty assistance for the independence of Annam.[47]

In mid-December, when the failure of the Philippine campaign became obvious to anyone, however, the issue of the use of force to handle French Indochina rapidly surfaced. Militarily speaking, the abortive Philippine campaign increased the possibility of the Allied forces landing in French Indochina, making French Indochina liable to become an advance base of operations for the Allies. Toward the end of the year, a US mobile force deployed in the South China Sea, and on January 12, 1945, the first strike by the mobile force was launched against Saigon. It was feared that a landing in South China and French Indochina was imminent. Under these circumstances, the Supreme Council for the Direction of the War on the last day of December 1944 approved Foreign Minister Shigemitsu's proposal that a decision should be made on handling French Indochina with armed forces by mid-January, after careful study of the international situation. Thus, the Imperial Japanese Army began preparations for military intervention in French Indochina. By late January 1945, an operational plan was being constructed between the Imperial Japanese Army General Staff Office and the Imperial Navy General Staff Office. Concentration of troops also commenced, starting with the incorporation of three divisions stationed in China and Burma into the 38th Army, which had been reorganized on December 20 from the occupation forces in French Indochina. Lieutenant

---

46 "Futsuin mondai" [French Indochina Problem] (November 2, 1944, Ministry of Foreign Affairs) *Gaikō shiryō: Nichi-Futsuin kankei no bu* [Diplomatic Document: Japan-French Indochina Relations Section], pp. 262–263.
47 *Kimitsu sensō nisshi* (November 4, 1944) and the above *Gaikō shiryō: Nichi-Futsuin kankei no bu.*

General Tsuchihashi Yūitsu replaced Lieutenant General Machijiri Kazumoto as commander.[48] Although the French Indochina authority did not agree with this transfer of Japanese troops at first, it eventually accepted it, based on the principle of joint defense. While hostility on the part of the French Indochina government became more pronounced, there was no sign yet of an anti-Japan resistance movement.

In its international relations, Japan had to pay closest attention to its relations with the Soviet Union. After obtaining international recognition by major Allied nations, the de Gaulle government was invited to the London conference of the European Advisory Commission in November 1944, which was followed by de Gaulle's visit to Moscow in early December. This diplomacy resulted in the signing of the Franco-Soviet Treaty of Mutual Assistance on December 10. The official announcement of this treaty was meant to regulate relations between the French provisional government and the Soviet Union in Europe. In other words, this treaty was solely intended to support the war against Germany and to prevent future German aggression. Nevertheless, the Japanese side perceived that if this treaty was also applied to Asia, Japan's handling of French Indochina with armed forces could give the Soviet Union an excuse for joining in the war against Japan.[49]

At this point, Shigemitsu sounded out the Soviet Union's intention via Ambassador to the Soviet Union Satō Naotake. Meeting Solomon Abramovitch Lozovsky, deputy people's commissar for foreign affairs, and Foreign Minister Vyacheslav Mikhailovich Molotov on December 21, 1944, and January 4, 1945, respectively, Ambassador Satō received confirmation from the Soviet side that the said treaty was targeted solely at Germany and the issue of the Far East had not even been discussed during the deliberations on the treaty. Thus, Japan's apprehension was resolved, at least

---

48 Shiraishi Masaya and Furuta Motoo, "Taiheiyō Sensō-ki no Nippon no tai Indoshina seisaku" [Japan's Indochina Policy during the Pacific War], *Ajia Kenkyū*, vol. 23, no. 3, 1976, pp. 18–19; Akagi (1984), pp. 47–48.

49 Murakami Sachiko, "Japan's Thrust into Indo-china, 1940–1945", Ph.D. dissertation, New York University, 1981, pp. 516–517; and Akagi (1984), pp. 49–50.

to some extent, and its policy toward armed intervention was unaffected. Nevertheless, the very fact that the Soviet Union and France entered into an alliance indicated that, when dealing with the nominal reason for military intervention and Indochina's independence issue, considering relations with the Soviet Union had become much more important for Japan than before.[50]

(3) The "Greater East Asia New Policy" and the French-Indochina Issue

A. Armed Liberation and the Independence Issue

In Indochina, a scheme for post-intervention government was compiled by the Japanese embassy under the leadership of Ambassador Matsumoto Shun'ichi (former deputy minister for foreign affairs), who was directly appointed by the emperor to replace Ambassador Yoshizawa. This Japanese embassy scheme set out the following as its fundamental policy: (1) military intervention is to be aimed at the independence of Annam in accord with the "spirit of the Greater East Asia Declaration," (2) while the independence of Annam is to be the initial goal, it should be followed by promotion of the independence of Cambodia and Laos and formation of the Federation of Vietnam, and (3) intervention in French Indochina "should primarily aim at the restoration of independence and autonomy for the local people, and the Empire of Japan should assist and extend cooperation in the attainment of this goal hand in hand with its partner nations in Greater East Asia." As regards measures for the independence of Annam, the scheme argued for "establishment of a government among independence advocates through a 'political coup d'état' to be conducted under the current monarch, which is to announce restoration of Annam's autonomy and independence." It was also suggested that no change should be applied to the existing government institutions in Annam and, instead, an advisory office should be set up within the Japanese embassy to conduct "internal guidance" of an

---

50 Akagi (1984), p. 49.

independent Annam.[51] Japanese troops stationed in French Indochina had taken an accommodative attitude toward this embassy proposal. But when the landing of US forces in French Indochina became an imminent danger after the attack on Saigon by the US mobile forces on January 12, 1945, circumstances forced the proposal to be reviewed.

Lieutenant General Tsuchihashi Yūitsu, who had been appointed commander of the 38th Army on December 4, 1944, was determined to expedite military intervention and submitted an outline of governance for French Indochina to the army leadership toward the end of January 1945. The outline's main points were: (1) the major aims of government in French Indochina should be prevention of confusion and turmoil and prompt restoration of public order; (2) for this purpose, existing administrative organs as well as officials should be used without modification, but the key posts of the administration should be filled by Japanese nationals (staff members of the Japanese embassy); (3) no change should be applied to administrative organizations; and (4) Annam, Cambodia, and Luang Prabang should be allowed to attain self-initiated independence and Annam should be governed by the incumbent emperor, who should not be dethroned.[52] While Tsuchihashi's proposal was tolerant toward self-initiated independence for the three French Indochina countries, it fell short of envisioning the establishment of the Federation of Vietnam. It argued for Japan, at least for the time being, to replace the French-Indochina government without destroying the existing government organizations.[53] Before long, however, the Tsuchihashi proposal was transformed into one that prioritized military operations—and this was utterly unacceptable to the embassy.

The Army Ministry's proposal for coordination (titled *On the Handling of French Indochina in order to Cope with Changes of Circumstances*)

---

51 *Gaikō shiryō: Nichi-Futsuin kankei no bu*, pp. 270–273, and Shiraishi & Furuta (1976), p. 21.
52 Tsuchihashi Yūitsu, *Gunpuku seikatsu 40-net no omoide* [Reminiscence of my 40 Years in Uniform] (privately printed book, 1985), pp. 533–534.
53 Based on interviews included in Shiraishi & Furuta (1976), p. 22.

compiled on January 28, 1945, proposed that, after the armed intervention, "While France's sovereignty and territorial claim to French Indochina should be respected, the Empire of Japan should administer French Indochina only for the duration required for armed intervention." Positing that Japan would recognize France's nominal sovereignty over French Indochina, in consideration of Japan's relations with the Soviet Union, the proposal argued for a de facto military government in the region.[54]

Before submitting its proposal, the Army Ministry asked for Foreign Minister Shigemitsu's view on the Franco-Soviet Treaty of Mutual Assistance. Shigemitsu assured the Army Ministry that the treaty had nothing to do with Far Eastern issues. Nonetheless, relations with the Soviet Union became an element that required the greatest of attention in the subsequent negotiations between the Ministries of Army and Foreign Affairs. Some even argued that, from the viewpoint of Japan-Soviet relations, the best option would not be to launch an armed intervention, but if it had to be done, it should be done after April 5, when the notice period for abolishment of the Soviet-Japanese Neutrality Pact expired and only after careful observation of Soviet actions. The Imperial Army was of the position that, in light of the war situation in East Asia, armed intervention in French Indochina was essential for the "survival and self-defense" of the Japanese troops and that postponement of armed intervention would be unacceptable. Thus, it was decided that, in order to avoid the appearance of a direct Japan-France war, Japan should appeal to the world that it had to singlehandedly defend French Indochina on the basis of a joint defense agreement because the French Indochinese side would not comply with the agreement.

At issue was the form of government after the proposed armed intervention. The Ministries of Foreign Affairs and Greater East Asia were in agreement with the proposal submitted by the Japanese embassy to French Indochina. They emphatically stressed that "in compliance with the spirit of

---

54 *Gaikō shiryō: Nichi-Futsuin kankei no bu*, p. 268.

the Greater East Asia Declaration, the Empire of Japan should take up the ethnic issue and take measures to realize the immediate independence of Annam, Cambodia, and Luang Prabang" and demanded avoidance of military government. The Imperial Japanese Army, in contrast, based its argument on the aforementioned army proposal, and stressed that the "Empire of Japan should put French Indochina under military government in order to secure its grip on the region, and from a purely militaristic viewpoint, the ethnic issue is only secondary." Thus, "the focus of discussions boiled down to how to handle the ethnic issue."[55] On the basis of the common understanding that a form of government that denied France's sovereignty had to be avoided in consideration of relations with the Soviet Union, the Imperial Army insisted that French Indochina should be temporarily put under military control after the armed intervention.

The Ministry of Foreign Affairs and Foreign Minister Shigemitsu argued that as long as military intervention was to be conducted, pro forma recognition of France's sovereignty would be meaningless. If the Japanese side persisted with the policy of peoples' liberation, allowed Annam and other French Indochina countries to become independent immediately, and defended their independence as it launched the armed intervention, Japan would show the world that it had no aggressive intention, which would also comply with the spirit of the Greater East Asia Declaration. Because even the Soviet Union could not oppose the official goal of people's liberation, the Foreign Ministry and Shigemitsu argued that the "immediate independence" of French Indochina countries should be the basic stance that Japan should take.[56]

Thus, the two sides failed to reach an agreement. The situation was tentatively settled with the policy of "putting French Indochina under military control without conducting military government and simultaneously

---

55 Ibid., pp. 68–69.
56 Akagi (1984), pp. 49–50, and Shiraishi & Furuta (1976), pp. 23–24.

carrying out measures to realize the independence of Annam and other French Indochina countries" when the armed intervention was conducted. In other words, a final proposal was made through adoption of both the Imperial Army's arguments and the Foreign Ministry's insistence.[57]

The decision at the February 1, 1945, Supreme Council for the Direction of the War to adopt the *On the Handling of French Indochina in order to Cope with Changes of Circumstances* proposal first defined the nominal reason for armed intervention as the fulfillment of the "absolute need for survival and self-defense." This meant, in other words, that the primary objective of the intervention was defense of French Indochina—which showed that the Imperial Japanese Army's argument was upheld on this point. In the section of the proposal stipulating the outline of the ultimatum on the launching of joint defense, however, the proposal argued that (1) if French Indochina does not comply with Japan's request, the Empire of Japan would resort to armed force to intervene and put French Indochina under military control for the time being; (2) the Japanese troops stationed in French Indochina would take necessary and timely measures to improve and assist the independent status of Annam and other French Indochina countries and allow them to actively cooperate with the Empire of Japan; and (3) Japan would, as need arose, explain the Empire's true intention, particularly the absence of any aggressive intention, to the Soviet Union. These specific measures also fulfilled the request from the Ministry of Foreign Affairs.[58]

During this conference of the Supreme Council for the Direction of the War, Shigemitsu requested a chance to speak and stressed two points concerning the importance of taking up the independence issue. One was the liability that, if Japan took the policy of resorting to arms and conducting military government in the occupied territories, stressing the official goal of survival and self-defense, the enemy could contend that this conduct

---

57 *Gaikō shiryō: Nichi-Futsuin kankei no bu*, p. 280.
58 *Haisen no kiroku* (1967), pp. 227–228.

betrayed the Empire's intention of occupying French Indochina in the place of France, and the Soviet Union and other neutral countries could take advantage of this. The second was that, if Annam and other French Indochina territories abolished the protection treaty and announced their intention to become independent and if Japan took the policy to assist and defend them, "it would appeal to the world that Japan has no aggressive intention, complying with the spirit of the Greater East Asia Declaration, and preventing the risk of being taken advantage of by third countries."[59]

In his telegram to convey the decision at the Supreme Council for the Direction of the War to Japanese Ambassador Matsumoto Shun'ichi (February 5), Shigemitsu called Matsumoto's attention to something he had said during the conference: "Only when measures taken by the Supreme General Headquarters, on the one hand, and the government's policy, on the other, align perfectly will this decision be carried out successfully." Shigemitsu's apprehension came true in the form of the obvious incongruence between the Japanese military stationed in the region and the Japanese embassy during the preparations for concrete action. In particular, the Japanese military stationed in the region interpreted the February 1 decision to mean that it left everything, including measures to be taken after the armed intervention, to its discretion. The military began taking the initiative, not only in preparation for the military operations but also regarding the planning for the management of French Indochina after armed intervention.[60]

After meeting with Commander Tsuchihashi and Chief of Staff Kawamura Saburō on February 13, Ambassador Matsumoto reported to Shigemitsu that they could not reach agreement on several important points. The first point of contention was the heavily military operation–oriented plan of the Imperial Army stationed in the region. The army intended to retain the existing office of governor-general, in preparation for the possibility

---

59 *Gaikō shiryō: Nichi-Futsuin kankei no bu*, pp. 277–229.
60 Ibid., p. 269.

that Indochina would become a battlefield, and planned to transfer embassy officials to the office of governor-general to explicitly use them in military operations. In other words, it was the policy of the locally stationed Imperial Army that the post-intervention measure would be, de facto, a military government, even though it would be referred to as "military control." This being the case, embassy officials were afraid of being transferred to the office of governor-general as military administration officials, including provisional administrators. The embassy side had resisted this idea, citing lack of administrative experience. Commander Tsuchihashi interpreted this attitude as resistance by the Foreign Ministry to having its personnel deprived of their status as diplomats.[61] But for the Foreign Ministry, which had intended to recognize the three Indochinese countries immediately when they gained independence, retention of the embassy's function was an important part of its measures toward independence of these countries.[62]

The second point of contention was closely related to the first. It was the perception gap concerning the independence issue. Matsumoto observed that, while the Imperial Army stationed in the region did not intend to upset the current status of Annam, Cambodia, and others, neither did it intend to nurture them into full-fledged independent countries in the future. According to Commander Tsuchihashi's perception, the aim of the armed intervention in French Indochina was to "protect and strengthen Japan's military readiness, in light of the overall war situation and the importance of French Indochina." In short, it was a perception that prioritized military operations most of all. The locally stationed army's arguments for abstention from post-independence intervention and continuation of personnel assignments in the office of governor-general were proposed from the viewpoint of preventing confusion after any armed intervention. These were not argued

---

61 *Gunpuku seikatsu 40-net no omoide* (1985), pp. 524–525.
62 Akagi (1984), pp. 50–51, Ambassador Matsumoto's telegram on February 14, 1945 addressed to Foreign Minister Shigemitsu (no. 5), Ministry of Foreign Affairs Document A7.0.0.9-54 "Daitōa Sensō ikken jōseihenka ni ōzuru Futsuin shori mondai" [Matters Related to Greater East Asia War: The Issue of Handling of French Indochina in Accordance with Changes of Circumstances], vol. 1.

out of appreciation for the significance of Asian peoples' independence.[63] The Southern Expeditionary Army, to which the 38th Army belonged, was of the same perception; it had planned to deal with the independence issue "in a few months," after public order was restored and the base of the military was established.

In response to the appeal from the Japanese embassy, Shigemitsu replied that, given the current war situation,

It is inevitable for the military to supervise everything. In this critical transitional period, it is of utmost importance to make efforts toward implementation of the policy within the military organization. What is called for is, in a nutshell, proceeding with maneuvering for the independence of these territories without delay when the military operations are conducted.

While it was not unimportant for the Foreign Ministry to save face, Shigemitsu requested the embassy side to devote its efforts to accomplishing the more important goal of realization of independence for these territories. To Shigemitsu, the utmost priority in armed intervention of French Indochina was to promptly realize the independence of Annam and other territories. From that position, "It is essential to request the military to take full responsibility in carrying out fundamental measures for prompt independence of Annam and other territories." In any event, Shigemitsu found it worrisome that the intention of central command had not been fully shared by the locally stationed Imperial Army troops. Thus, he had to raise this issue to the army minister at the February 22 Supreme Council for the Direction of the War.[64]

The Imperial Army worked out the details of post-intervention

---

63 *Gunpuku seikatsu 40-net no omoide* (1985), p. 523 and p. 528.
64 *Gaikō shiryō: Nichi-Futsuin kankei no bu*, pp. 280–281.

governance and shared them with the Ministries of Foreign Affairs, Greater East Asia, Army, and Navy for their review. After that, the Army submitted *Indoshina seimu shori yōkō an* (Outline of Political Treatment of Indochina Draft) to the Supreme Council for the Direction of the War on February 26. During the Council meeting, Shigemitsu reiterated the necessity to let Annam and others abolish protection treaties, without delay, and restore their independence along with military operations. This was accepted and, accordingly, adopted in the revision of the original proposal by the Army.[65] Consequently, it was explicitly stipulated in the adopted *Outline of Political Treatment of Indochina* that the "Empire of Japan should induce Annam and other territories to, without delay, voluntarily abolish protection treaties with France and make an announcement on restoration of their independence."

It was not because the Imperial Army recognized the significance of peoples' independence that it accepted the independence of Annam and other territories immediately following the armed intervention. It was to begin with, the setback in the Philippine campaign and the air raid of French Indochina by US Navy forces on January 12, 1945, that brought home to the Japanese military the imminency of US troops landing in Indochina. This understanding spread from the central command all the way through to the locally stationed troops. It was this that made the Japanese side choose the military option of armed intervention.[66]

And it was because the Imperial Army understood that stressing the non-aggressiveness of the armed intervention in French Indochina to the Soviet Union could prevent deterioration of Japan's relations with the Soviet Union that it stood closer to the Foreign Ministry's position of immediate independence. The telegram "Meigō sakusen ni tomonau seimu shori no ken" (Matters Related to Political Handlings Accompanying the Meigō Operation) that the deputy minister for the Imperial Army and vice chief of

---

65 Ibid., p. 281.
66 Akagi (1984), p. 48., Bōei Kenshūsho Senshishitsu, ed., *Shittan/Meigō sakusen* [The Battle of Sittang Bend and Operation Bright Moon], Asagumo Shimbunsha, 1969, pp. 598–599.

the Imperial Army General Staff Office sent to the locally stationed armies on February 23 explained that the Army's central command interpreted the February 1 decision of the Supreme Council for the Direction of War on "assistance to improvement of independence status," not as an instruction on "particularly urgent implementation of concrete measures for independence," but as "a tool to demonstrate to the Soviet Union that the armed intervention had no aggressive intention." The locally stationed armies were instructed to pay close attention to this interpretation.[67]

From another perspective, it can be said that Foreign Minister Shigemitsu and the Foreign Ministry, which had hoped for thorough realization of the spirit of the Greater East Asia Declaration, succeeded in luring the Imperial Army and the locally stationed troops to the unprecedented position of "immediately granting independence," taking advantage of the fear of worsening relations with the Soviet Union.

B. Liberation of French Indochina

In the meantime, the issue of the status of the embassy officials was discussed, at the insistence of Ambassador Matsumoto, among the Ministries of Army, Navy, Foreign Affairs, and Greater East Asia. As a result, it was decided that, in case the French Indochina government rejected the ultimatum from Japan and armed intervention became inevitable, officials of the embassy (including consul-generals and consuls) would retain their status but would be transferred to embedded civilians or civilian employees of the Army. It was also decided that the ambassador would be appointed as adviser to the commander in chief in charge of political affairs.[68] Thus, Ambassador Matsumoto would be appointed as supreme adviser to the locally stationed

---

67 "Meigō sakusen ni tomonau seimu shori ni kansuru ken" [Matters Related to Political Handlings Accompanying the Meigō Operation] (sent by the deputy minister for army and vice chief of the Imperial Japanese Army General Staff Office to the Southern Expeditionary Army, and to Chief of Staff for reference), Ministry of Foreign Affairs Document A7.0.0.9-54, Shiraishi & Furuta (1976).
68 *Gaikō shiryō: Nichi-Futsuin kankei no bu*, pp. 296–297.

army, Minister-Counselor Tsukamoto Takeshi as director-general of the office of governor-general, Consul-General Minoda Fujio as governor-general of Cochin China, Consul-General Nishimura Kumao as provincial governor of Tonkin, Minister-Counselor Yokoyama Masayuki as supreme adviser to the government of Annam, and Consul-General Kubota Kan'ichirō as supreme adviser to the government of Cambodia.

As for the handling of the Kwangchow Wan Bay leased territory, it was decided that it should not take the form of Japan transferring the administrative authority to the Nationalist government. Instead, "in light of the fact that France's administrative authority had been eliminated," it was decided to adopt a pro forma procedure in which the Nationalist government voluntarily confiscating administrative authority in the future in order to retrieve the leased territory.[69] This decision was taken partly as a measure to "demonstrate that Japan has no territorial ambitions in Indochina." But it was also out of respect for Foreign Minister Shigemitsu's argument, from the viewpoint of maintaining the spirit of the new China policy, that the Kwangchow Wan Bay leased territory should belong to the Chinese.[70]

Upon the completion of these preparations, the armed intervention in French Indochina (Operation Bright Moon) was launched on March 9, 1945. The key organs of the office of governor-general of French Indochina were occupied by Japanese troops, the French Indochina troops were disarmed, and both Admiral Jean Decoux and General Eugène Mordant were arrested. Thus ended some sixty years of French sovereignty in Indochina.

On March 11, the king of Annam announced the abolition of its treaty of protection with France and the restoration of the kingdom's independence. The king of Cambodia announced the invalidity of the treaty of protection as well as the independence of his kingdom on March 13. The Kingdom of Luang Prabang (Laos) also declared independence on April 8. Needless

---

69 Greater East Asia Minister Shigemitsu's telegram addressed to Ambassador Tani to China on March 4 (no. 13), *Gaikō shiryō: Nichi-Futsuin kankei no bu*, pp. 300–301.
70 *Gaikō shiryō: Nichi-Futsuin kankei no bu*, pp. 299–301.

to say, these three were not cases of full-fledged independence because the Japanese military commander essentially acted as governor-general supervising government affairs, using the administrative organizations of the office of the French Indochina governor-general. Although the Japanese side took the basic policy of transferring as much authority of the office of governor-general as possible to each kingdom to carry out administrative improvement in an attempt to allow each kingdom to strengthen its respective political foundation—except for such matters as transportation and communications, which required nation-wide measures—it was proven to be difficult for these kingdoms to carry out effective policies that befitted independent governments.[71]

Incidentally, it was Thailand that had been expected to be affected directly by Japan's armed intervention in French Indochina. Aside from the danger of French Indochina troops fleeing into the kingdom's territory, more importantly, it was worried that the intervention would adversely affect the issue of retrieval of lost territories from French Indochina, which had been an issue since the days of the Franco-Thai War. While the Imperial Army argued that it would be unnecessary to pay attention to Thailand's demand for retrieval of lost territories, which could provoke unnecessary conflict, the Ministries of Foreign Affairs and Greater East Asia insisted that some leeway should be left to accommodate Thailand's request, in light of the policy to coordinate nationalistic demands rationally. During the drafting of *Futsuin shori ni tomonau tai-Tai shisaku no ken* [Matters Related to Measures toward Thailand Accompanying the Armed Intervention in French Indochina] of March 1, 1945, which reconfirmed the policy of assisting Thailand's "self-initiated independence," the Imperial Army's proposal included an article which said, "It is so determined that Thailand's request

---

71 Shiraishi Masaya, "Chan Chon Kim naikaku no seiritsu no haikei" [Background of Formation of the Trần Trọng Kim Cabinet], Tsuchiya Kenji & Shiraishi Takashi, eds., *Kokusai kankeiron no furontia/Tōnan Ajia no seiji to bunka* [Frontier of International Relations/Politics and Culture in Southeast Asia], University of Tokyo Press, 1984.

for retrieval of lost territory will not be taken into consideration." This was revised by the Foreign Ministry to ". . . will not be taken into consideration for the time being." The Foreign Ministry wished to imply, by adding "for the time being," that the door was still open to accepting Thailand's request sometime in the future. This contention was carried over to the Supreme Council for the Direction of the War, at which this article as a whole was eliminated. Not touching on the issue of retrieval of the lost territory was an implicit message to the Thai side that Japan was prepared to respond to its request.[72]

5. Conclusion: Half of the Victory Is Mine

Although Shigemitsu, as a member of the Koiso cabinet, succeeded in defending unification of the channels of Greater East Asia diplomacy and tried his best to protect the position of the Foreign Ministry, it was difficult for even Shigemitsu to persist with advocating Greater East Asian peoples' independence, or anti-colonialism. If he wanted to realize his hopes of promoting Greater East Asian peoples' independence, it would inevitably lead to a compromise with the military's demand for operations. This was well-represented by the French Indochina issue.

As mentioned earlier, Ambassador Matsumoto Shun'ichi consulted with the locally stationed Imperial Army on liberation of French Indochina in mid-February 1945 and debriefed Shigemitsu on the "failure to reach an agreement with the military on several important points."

Matsumoto found that the Imperial Army stationed in the region intended to "preserve the existing government organization of the office of governor-general, in anticipation of Indochina becoming a battlefield" and that it had no intention of nurturing Annam, Cambodia, and others to help

---

72 *Gaikō shiryō: Nichi-Futsuin kankei no bu*, pp. 304–305.

them become full-fledged independent nations in the future.[73] Matsumoto resisted the Imperial Army's stance, arguing that de facto continuation of the existing governor-general government would be totally devoid of consideration of the issue of independence, leaving Japan without a leg to stand on in the face of allegations that it was an aggressor.[74] According to Matsumoto, the Imperial Army side showed no sign of changing its attitude.

After this interaction, Matsumoto recommended to Shigemitsu that Japan's unequivocal position vis-à-vis independence issues should be discussed and decided by the Supreme Council for the Direction of the War. While finding Matsumoto's suggestion highly reasonable, Shigemitsu replied that the primary concern was prompt realization of independence for Annam and other French Indochina territories under the Imperial Army's purview.[75]

In the end, it was decided that, after the armed intervention, French Indochina would not enjoy full-fledged independence; Japan would take over France's governor-general government. Shigemitsu fully recognized the validity of Matsumoto's argument that continuation of the governor-general government would only cause Japan to be accused of being an aggressor when, officially, Japan was claiming to uphold the slogan of Asian peoples' independence. But Shigemitsu was more apprehensive that refusing the military's request in order to pursue full-fledged independence would nullify the policy of prompt independence itself.

Sone Eki, who had participated in the drafting of the Greater East Asia Declaration, once referred to Shigemitsu's "aversion to openly antagonizing the military" as characteristic.[76] Given that Shigemitsu was well aware that

---

73 Ambassador Matsumoto's telegram on February 15 addressed to Foreign Minister Shigemitsu. (*Gaikō shiryō: Nichi-Futsuin kankei no bu*, pp. 304–305).
74 Ibid.
75 Foreign Minister Shigemitsu' telegrams on February 18 (no. 7) and February 19 (no. 8) addressed to Ambassador Matsumoto.
76 Sone Eki, "Shigemitsu Mamoru no jinbutsu" [Shigemitsu Mamoru as a Person], *Asahi Shimbun*, May 13, 1952.

independence attained through compromise with the military was only a superficial independence without substance, one wonders why he persisted in pursuing such perfunctory independence measures.

One document, which appears to have been produced by the Foreign Ministry in the last days of the Pacific War, addressed the issue of independence for Indonesia as follows. This war [the Greater East Asia War] "is in essence a war against the Anglo-American world order and it is, fundamentally, a war of world views." Whatever the outcome of the war might be, "a complete return to the old order" is no longer permissible. In particular, "even the enemy cannot deny . . . the philosophical principle that the Empire of Japan is waging war to liberate Greater East Asia," regardless of the outcome of the war. Therefore, if Japan can clarify its position by promptly expediting Indonesia's independence, instead of leaving it unattended, it should be recognized that "half of the victory is mine," even if Japan is defeated.[77]

In other words, the above document argued that Japan should clarify its stance toward the independence issue, regardless of the outcome of the war, paying attention to the universality of the philosophical principle of peoples' independence, which was predicted to be the founding principle of the postwar international order. A similar train of thought can be found regarding the liberation of French Indochina in other Foreign Ministry documents. For instance, a document produced in February 1946 included the following review on the armed intervention in French Indochina in March of the previous year:

At that time, while the Imperial Army strongly insisted that it should seize French Indochina with its own armed forces and conduct military administration in the occupied territories, the Japanese government, particularly the Ministries of Foreign Affairs and Greater East Asia,

---

77 *Indoneshia ni okeru Nippon gunsei no kenkyū*, pp. 561–562.

predicted that it would be impossible to maintain the Empire's position in southern territories in the future, given the prediction of an imminent end of the Greater East Asia War. Under these circumstances, these two ministries argued that to support nationalistic aspirations of French Indochina locals, it would not only be necessary but also facilitative toward realization of the peoples' desire for self-determination set out by the Greater East Asia Declaration. Also, the Foreign and Greater East Asia Ministries pointed to a common ground shared by prompt granting of independence to French Indochina peoples and the spirit of international democracy of the Allies, particularly the United States, manifested in the Atlantic Charter and the proposal on United Nations Trust Territories. In light of these considerations, the two ministries insisted that primacy should be given to peoples' independence in French Indochina. In the end, it was decided that, after the armed intervention on March 9, the Empire of Japan should support the declaration of independence for the Kingdoms of Annam, Cambodia, and Luang Prabang and assist facilitation and completion of their independence.[78]

This document is highly interesting for two reasons. First, one can detect the Foreign Ministry's determination to appeal to the world the righteousness of Japan's Greater East Asia policy by fulfilling "nationalistic aspirations of French Indochina locals," judging it obviously "impossible to maintain the Empire's position in the southern territories." Put differently, this document shifts the responsibility for "liberation and independence" on the victors of the war. Second, the document stresses the commonality between "the spirit of peoples' self-determination set out by the Greater East Asia Declaration" and "the spirit of international democracy of . . . the United States, manifested in the Atlantic Charter." In other words, Britain, which still persisted in colonialism, was no longer the issue; instead, it was the United States that was

---

78 *Gaikō shiryō: Nichi-Futsuin kankei no bu*, pp. 200–201.

perceived by the Foreign Ministry as the builder of the postwar world order. One may wonder, given the timing of the writing of this document, whether this assessment by the Ministry of Foreign Affairs was made in anticipation of Japan being occupied by the United States alone. The present author is of the view that it was not necessarily so. It is conjectured that this document was written either by Shigemitsu himself or one of the supporting Foreign Ministry officials, given the way it is phrased. In any event, it should be said that the hopes that Shigemitsu and the Foreign Ministry had conveyed in the Greater East Asia Declaration were represented in this document.

Chapter 10

Shigemitsu Mamoru and Wartime Diplomacy

1. Japan-China Partnership and Decolonization

In May 1952, by the time it became almost certain that Shigemitsu Mamoru would be elected president of the Kaishintō Party, his former subordinate, Sone Eki (Executive Committee member, Study Group on War Aims (1943) of the Rightist Socialist Party of Japan, at that time) contributed the following personal criticism of Shigemitsu to the daily *Asahi Shimbun*:

> Shigemitsu, who was a successor to Shidehara diplomacy, succeeded in advancing his professional career smoothly through the 1930s—unlike contemporaries such as Yoshida Shigeru and Ashida Hitoshi—from deputy foreign minister to ambassador to the Soviet Union, ambassador to Britain, and, eventually, foreign minister. And it was not so much by sheer luck but more due to Shidehara's personality traits, including his highly precise legal juristic mind, his resolute ambition and tenacious fighting spirit, his prudence and self-restraint regarding exposing his true feelings, and his avoidance of open antagonism toward the military. To put it differently, it must be Shigemitsu's nature that enabled to switch from mainstream Shidehara diplomacy until the Manchurian Incident to the argument for abolishment of the Nine-Power Treaty.[1]

Shigemitsu had started his full-fledged professional engagement in diplomacy in the 1920s in China. As a faithful follower of Shidehara diplomacy, he devoted himself to international recognition of China's tariff autonomy and abolition of extraterritoriality. During that time, Shidehara was already exploring Sino-Japanese relations based on such notions as respect for sovereignty and reciprocal benefit. This was the genesis of the later-day new China policy that he pursued when he became the Japanese ambassador to

---

1 Sone Eki, "Shigemitsu Mamoru no jinbutsu" [Shigemitsu Mamoru as a Person], *Asahi Shimbun*, May 13, 1952.

China and, subsequently, the minister for foreign affairs.[2] But his being an advocate of Shidehara diplomacy did not lead Shigemitsu directly to the later China policy. After all, as Sone pointed out, in the 1930s, Shigemitsu often presented an argument that could be taken as an argument for the abolition of the invalid Nine-Power Treaty—which contradicted Shidehara diplomacy. It appears that, in those days, Shigemitsu took an accommodating position toward the military.

In particular, during his tenure as deputy foreign minister (1933–1936), Shigemitsu was the de facto promoter of the so-called Amō Seimei (Amau Doctrine). Shigemitsu argued at the time that the Nine-Power Treaty and the Charter of the League of Nations were the Western norms that disciplined modern international relations. In contrast, "China in those days was in an extremely unique situation which defied easy application of the ordinary norms of international law." When "it is realized that improvement of this country would not be as easy a task as ordinary Westerners believe," the Amau Doctrine, which stipulated that Japan should be responsible for the maintenance of stability and public order in East Asia, became convincing.[3] It was not Shigemitsu's intention to deny the legal and universal rule of international norms. His logic was that those norms could not be applied for the time being to the "Far East, which is the arena of backward international relations."[4]

---

2 Shigemitsu, for instance, wrote in the tribute to the late Saburi Sadao, minister to China, that, while China prior to the Northern Expedition in 1926 had been a theater of "China-style struggle among warlords," the rise of the Kuomintang made the world aware of the Chinese people's nationalistic aspirations. And whether to recognize and approve this aspiration or to "perceive China to be eternally a land of warlord conflicts" was the dividing point for Japan's policy toward China. The former of the two positions was represented by "the spirit of the Washington Naval Conference." And the speech by Hioki Eki, plenipotentiary of Japan, at the Special Tariff Conference in Beijing in October 1925, which declared that Japan was prepared to recognize China's tariff autonomy, was the first step toward the new China policy based on "the spirit of the Washington Naval Conference." See Shigemitsu Mamoru, "Saburi kōshi no shi" [Death of Minister Saburi], *Chūgoku Kenkyū Geppō*, no. 489, November 1988.

3 "Teikoku no taishi gaikō seisaku" [Empire of Japan's Foreign Policy toward China] (September 1933) (Ministry of Foreign Affairs Document A1.1.0.10).

4 Ibid.

A half year after the announcement of the Amau Doctrine, Shigemitsu disclosed a plan to return various systems that the Western powers had constructed in China (e.g., customs inspection, foreign concessions, and Western troops stationed in North China) to the Chinese side in order to lure China toward reconciliation and partnership with Japan.[5] The plan was an expression of Japan's intention to eliminate the Western powers, which "had treated various regions in the Orient as their colonies," and construct new relations with China.[6] The North China Buffer State Strategy, which had been adopted by the Imperial Japanese Army, posed a major obstacle to Shigemitsu's attempt to promote cooperation with Britain through these diplomatic initiatives. Shigemitsu concluded that the strategy gave the world the impression that the Japanese government was incapable of controlling the military and that "militarism in Japan will eventually wipe out all interests of the Western powers and, in the end, disturb the order of the Orient, which will pose a threat to world peace."[7] Shigemitsu's criticism of the military became stronger after the army's announcement of the North China Buffer State Strategy.

Shigemitsu's memoir tells us that while he was Japanese ambassador to Britain (1938–1941), the China issue was constantly on his mind. Although he made various attempts to improve Japan's relations with Britain, hoping to "by all means prevent the China issue from leading to a war with Britain,"[8] the signing of the Tripartite Pact shifted Japan's policy in the opposite direction. According to Shigemitsu, "I cannot say

---

5 "Taishi seisaku ni kansuru Shigemitsu jikan kōjusu" [Verbal Explanation of Deputy Minister Shigemitsu on China Policy] (October 20, 1934) (Ministry of Foreign Affairs Document A1.1.0.10-3).

6 Sakai Tetsuya, "'Ei-Bei kyōchō' to 'Nicchū teikei'" ["Cooperation with Britain and the United States" vs. "Japan-China Partnership"], Kindai Nippon Kenkyūkai, ed., Nenpō kindai Nippon kenkyū 11: Kyōchō seisaku no genkai [Annual of Modern Japan Studies 11: Limits of Cooperative Policy], Yamakawa Shuppansha, 1989, pp. 61–92.

7 Sakai Tetsuya, Taishō demokurashī taisei no hōkai [Collapse of the Taishō Democracy Regime] University of Tokyo Press, 1992, pp. 58–61 and the Foreign Ministry document quoted on p. 128.

8 Itō Takashi et al., eds., Shigemitsu Mamoru shuki [Shigemitsu Mamoru Private Memoir], Chūō Kōronsha, 1986, p. 126.

that the plan to accomplish peace with China via Germany through the Tripartite Pact is based on any kind of firm conviction." This ruled out the option of entrusting settlement of the China issue to Britain and the United States. Once the Tripartite Pact was signed, the only option left to Japan for resolving the China issue was "for Japan to match its words with action and accommodate the desires of the Chinese side." Shigemitsu felt that "settlement of the China issue has become an urgent task of the day that has to be accomplished at any cost."[9] How, then, could the China issue be settled? Shigemitsu argued that it would take "thorough rectification of the 'conquest of China' psychology, which has been the source of chaos," and that such would be possible only when "Japan matches its words with action and becomes benevolent enough to accommodate the desires of the Chinese side."[10] This goes to show that the outline of the scheme for the new China policy—that is, the determination to rectify Japan's own attitude toward China—had already been envisioned by Shigemitsu during his tenure as ambassador to Britain.

Also noteworthy in Shigemitsu's wartime diplomacy was the attention he paid to the trend toward nationalism in post–World War I Asia and the international trend toward decolonization, one of the factors that had affected his psychology. That Shigemitsu was becoming increasingly convinced that one of the factors which would rule post–World War I international politics would be peoples' demands for decolonization and self-determination can be detected in the report on his observation tour to the South Pacific Mandate immediately following his return from the Paris Peace Conference as well as his talks with Sun Yat-sen.[11] Realizing

9   Ibid., pp. 221–222.
10 Ibid., p. 170, p. 221.
11 Immediately after Shigemitsu returned from the Paris Peace Conference (1921), he was instructed to observe situations in the South Pacific Mandate. Shigemitsu compiled a lengthy report on this. The purpose of Shigemitsu's visit was to judge whether these island territories should be placed under the Imperial Navy's military government or under the jurisdiction of the Ministry of Foreign Affairs. In his report, Shigemitsu attributed the unpopularity of the Imperial Navy's military government among locals as well as alien residents in comparison with the former German rule

from his discussions with Sun how intensely the Chinese people's nationalist sentiment burned, Shigemitsu became aware of its irreversibility and predicted that it would become an important factor to determining the political situation in postwar East Asia.[12]

Shigemitsu's realization was also reflected in his favorable response toward the sovereignty restoration movement in China. After the end of World War I, the principle of peoples' self-determination came to be formally recognized, and the "first step toward international democracy" was made by adopting such principles of domestic politics as freedom and equality for international relations as well. Nevertheless, the "perception of Asia as a colony" was not remedied because the "international status of humanity was not yet recognized [for Asian peoples]." That was why Shigemitsu was particularly mindful of the growth of nationalism in China. In his assessment, the "honest account of European people is that 'international democracy is for Europe and Europe alone . . . [and] justice is confined to

---

to the navy's determination to continue military government even after the war and to "sacrifice everything for the military cause."

Based on his analysis, Shigemitsu argued that it was "urgent to conduct civilian government, separating military elements" and proposed abolishment of military government, simplification of administrative organs, withdrawal of the Japanese garrison, and "incrementalism" regarding Japanese-language education. (See "Nan'yō inin tōchi-ku ni kansuru hōkoku (ko-go)" [A Report on the South Pacific Mandate (no. 1)] March 27, 1921, Ministry of Foreign Affairs Document "Teikoku no nan'yō tōchi ikken" [Matter Related to the Empire of Japan's Governance of the South Pacific Mandate].) Shigemitsu wrote in his memoir that he had devoted himself to writing this report (see *Gaikō kaisōroku* [Foreign Policy Memoir], Mainichi Shimbunsha, 1953, pp. 49–50), and it is believed that it was this visit to the South Pacific Mandate that gave him a chance to pay closer attention to the problems of militarism in the rule of occupied territories.

Immediately following the observation tour to the South Pacific Mandate, Shigemitsu headed for Guangdong to meet with Sun Yat-sen. Shigemitsu was strongly impressed by Sun, who passionately shared his "determination to accomplish revolution," saying, ". . . extraordinarily resolute, Sun was determined to, domestically, renovate Chinese society which is thousands of years old and, externally, settle all the inequal treaties and remove all the foreign influences in order to rehabilitate the Chinese state and nation." When Sun repeatedly stressed that "unless Japan's military clique changes its mind about invading China, it is utterly useless to talk about China-Japan friendship," it left a strong impression on Shigemitsu that stayed with him for a long time to come. (See Watanabe Yukio, "Sonbun o shinobu: Shigemitsu Mamoru" [Reminiscence of Sun Yat-sen: Shigemitsu Mamoru], *Chūgoku Kenkyū Geppō*, no. 487, September 1988, pp. 47–50.)

12 Sakai (1989), p. 64.

Europe.'"[13] Therefore, it was compatible with the "international justice of decolonization" for Japan to assist the nationalism of the Chinese people and respond to it with a policy to promote independence and equality.

Former Foreign Minister Shidehara Kijūrō shared his thoughts with Prince Higashikuni Naruhiko, who later formed his own cabinet, in August 1943, as follows:

The Treaty of Versailles concluded at the time of the previous world war [World War I] allowed smaller nations to become separate and independent. The treaty's principle of peoples' self-determination became one of the causes of the current world war [World War II]. The Empire of Japan has chosen to put the so-called pro-Japan leaders at the front to let Burma and the Philippines become independent. I am apprehensive about these smaller nations becoming a source of future trouble for Japan. . . .[14]

The perception that the principle of peoples' self-determination had brought about the fragmentation of numerous small nations, which in turn became one of the causes of World War II, was widely shared by leaders of wartime Japan. From Shigemitsu's viewpoint, however, it was not the principle of peoples' self-determination that served as a remote cause of the war. The problem was that the principle was used only for the benefit of major powers and, consequently, "justice was confined only to Europe."

---

13 Itō Takashi et al., eds., *Zoku Shigemitsu Mamoru shuki* [Shigemitsu Mamoru Private Memoir, vol. 2], Chūō Kōronsha, 1988, pp. 417–418.
14 "Higashikuninomiya nisshi" [Prince Higashikuni's Diary] (entry of August 4, 1943). It should be noted that the content of this journal is slightly different from the description on page 117 of the published *Ichi kōzoku no sensō nisshi* [War Diary of an Imperial Family Member].

2. Greater East Asia New Policy and Greater East Asia International Organization Scheme

As shown, it can be said that by the time Shigemitsu was stationed in Nanjing as Japanese ambassador immediately after the outbreak of the Pacific War, the basic direction of his new China policy had already been determined. First, his was a scheme to substantiate the principles of respect for sovereignty and independence and equality in relations with China, using those principles as a foundation for construction of bilateral relations to solve the China problem. The China problem was seen as the root cause of "today's fundamental disease" and, therefore, a major priority for Japan to deal with Second, in light of the universality and irreversibility of such principles as decolonization and peoples' self-determination after World War I, Shigemitsu perceived that the liberation of Asian peoples was a mission given to Japan. For this reason, the new policy should not be confined to China; rather, it should be universally applied to the entirety of Greater East Asia as the Greater East Asia new policy.

Shigemitsu as Japanese ambassador to China became a promoter of the new China policy, convinced that building relations with the Nanjing Nationalist government based on respect for sovereignty and reciprocal benefit would eliminate the reason for the Chongqing government to resist Japan—which would provide the basis for a full peace between China and Japan. The emperor became an avid supporter of this new China policy, as well. It was taken into consideration in the decision by the Imperial Council in December 1942 to adopt a new policy centered around respect for the Nanjing government's sovereignty and tolerance of its self-initiative.

In April 1943, Shigemitsu decided to join the Tōjō Hideki cabinet, encouraged by Tōjō himself, in the hope of realizing his new policy. The first thing Shigemitsu devoted his energy to as foreign minister was revision of the Japan-China Basic Relations Treaty and the signing of a new alliance treaty, which was the ultimate goal of the new policy. Shigemitsu succeeded in including a stipulation on this revision of the existing treaty and the signing of a new treaty in *Daitōa seiryaku shidō taikō* (Outlines for the Political Guidance of Greater East Asia) in May 1943. For Shigemitsu, nevertheless, this new alliance treaty with China not only had to clean the slate of Japan-China relations but also provide a foundation for relations with other Greater East Asian countries.

Shigemitsu's plan was to conclude alliance treaties based on respect for sovereignty, equality, and reciprocal benefit with other Asian "independent countries" (e.g., Manchukuo, Thailand, the Philippines, and Burma) around the nucleus of the Japan-China Alliance Treaty. This scheme for a Greater East Asia international organization was positioned as the core of a new Greater East Asia policy aimed at expanding the philosophy of the new China policy to cover the entire Greater East Asia region. The international organization for common consultation among the Greater East Asian countries was envisioned as a permanent pillar for wartime and postwar cooperation where "autonomous and independent states consult with each other as equal partners, either as the need arises or on a regular basis." And the scheduled first Greater East Asia Conference was to be a starting point toward this international organization, where a Greater East Asia Charter politically based on independence and equality and economically based on mutual benefit and an open-door policy was to be issued.

Therefore, Shigemitsu perceived the Greater East Asia Conference as the first step toward a Greater East Asia international organization in which the "independent" states of Greater East Asia participated on equal footing. This was a significant departure from Prime Minister Tōjō's initial idea. The premise of Shigemitsu's scheme was the conclusion of an "alliance treaty on equal footing," at least on the surface, among "independent states" in Greater East Asia, leaving behind Japan's traditional obsession with a Japan-Manchukuo-China union. Accordingly, individual alliance treaties with Thailand and Manchukuo were studied by the Foreign Ministry. The two treaty proposals shared several commonalities. First, both proposals presupposed the foundation of an international organization among equal member states, without giving Japan, Manchukuo, or China superior positions. Second, neither proposal included an article that would allow the continued stationing of Japanese troops after the end of the war. Thus, the international organization was to be founded on the basis of a network of treaties, each of which fulfilled the above common conditions. As introduced in chapter 6, it was with these proposals being studied within the Foreign Ministry in mind that Shigemitsu proposed at the Imperial General Headquarters–Government Liaison Conference that "On the occasion of the Greater East Asia Conference, instead of a mere declaration, a Greater East Asia Alliance [Greater East Asia international organization] should be launched."

These proposals by Shigemitsu, however, met opposition from participants of the Liaison Conference. His first proposal was turned down with the counter-argument that "China and Manchukuo would not be happy to be treated equally with Burma and the Philippines. Individual alliances should be concluded between the Empire of Japan and each of the Greater East Asian countries." His second proposal also met rebuttal from the Imperial Japanese Army and Navy General Staff Offices, which opposed reference to withdrawal of Japanese troops after the end of the war. Thus, both of Shigemitsu's proposals failed to overcome opposition from within Japan, and the scheme for the international organization itself was killed on the grounds that "It is not appropriate to establish an organization that is similar to the League of Nations." But this in no way affected the intention of Shigemitsu and the Foreign Ministry to attach to the envisioned Greater East Asia Charter (Greater East Asia Joint Declaration) the significance of a code of conduct for construction of Greater East Asia based on autonomy, independence, equality, and reciprocal benefit.

The proposed scheme for a Greater East Asia international organization to be composed of states within the Co-Prosperity Sphere joining as equal and mutually beneficial members harbored an aim to institutionally restrict

Japan from assuming a hegemonic position. As such, it can be said that this international organization aspired for significantly strong regional solidarity among members. One possible interpretation is that, while the declaration of the Greater East Asia Ambassadors' Conference that had convened when Tōgō Shigenori was foreign minister had aspired for universalism, the Greater East Asia Joint Declaration, which embraced the scheme to establish an international organization, was geared more toward regionalism.[15]

3. Greater East Asia Joint Declaration and Shigemitsu

(1) Impact of the Greater East Asia Declaration

One important factor that has to be kept in mind when evaluating the Greater East Asia Declaration is that the Greater East Asia Conference itself was an integral part of an attempt to promote solidarity among Asian peoples and consolidate a system of manpower and physical mobilization in anticipation of the Allies' counteroffensive predicted to take place in the fall of 1943. While many Japanese government leaders, including Prime Minister Tōjō,

---

15 For instance, a treatise contributed by "Japonicus" (whose true identity is unrevealed) under the title of "The Pacific Charter" (*Contemporary Japan*, vol. 13, no. 3, March 1944, pp. i–xvi) characterized the Greater East Asia Declaration as a Pacific Charter in juxtaposition with the Atlantic Charter. Taking into consideration the Moscow Declaration, this treatise explained that the Atlantic Charter explored a unitary world system under Pax Anglo-American or British-American-Soviet hegemony. In this sense, it should be said that the Atlantic Charter aspired for universalism. In contrast, the Greater East Asia Declaration primarily aspired for regionalism when organizing peace. And it did not aspire for a closed regionalism, but rather an open regionalism that negated imperialism both inside and outside of the region, promoted cultural exchange, and guaranteed free access to natural resources and markets. This treatise also pointed to the effectiveness of a regional framework as a means for localizing and resolving regional conflicts. This corresponds to Walter Lippman's criticism of Wilsonianism when he asked if Americans really wished the universalistic organization to solve the conflict when it erupted between the United States and Panama. (See Walter Lippman, *US War Aims*, Boston: Little Brown & Co., 1944, pp. 188–190.) The Foreign Ministry's draft record of investigation on the Greater East Asia Conference characterized the Greater East Asia Declaration as manifestation of a "regionalistic principle" that had been lacking in modern Europe ("Daitōa Kaigi ni kansuru chōsho no sōkō (untitled)" [Untitled Draft Record of Investigation on the Greater East Asia Conference], Ministry of Foreign Affairs Document A7.0.0.9-48-1).

SHIGEMITSU MAMORU AND WARTIME DIPLOMACY | 377

aimed at this goal, for Shigemitsu the conference was a part of the new Greater East Asia policy. In Shigemitsu's eyes, the conference was a first step toward prompt independence of the southern occupied territories and establishment of a Greater East Asia international organization for reciprocal benefit among these mutually equal independent states. And the Greater East Asia Declaration was to be the code of conduct for this international organization. This goes to show that the aim that Shigemitsu and other leaders charged the declaration with was different from the very beginning.

Moreover, the declaration was, for Shigemitsu, a roundabout means for attaining a peace settlement—an attempt at eliminating the Allies' reasons to wage a war by contrasting Japan's war purposes against those of the Allies. In that sense, the declaration was an instrument of Japan's diplomatic offensive. This understanding about the role of the Greater East Asia Declaration was also shared by officials of the Foreign Ministry who supported Shigemitsu.

In short, the Greater East Asia Declaration had to fulfill at least the following three requirements. First, it had to contribute to the waging of the ongoing war. Second, it had to serve as a common code of conduct for promoting solidarity among Asian countries. And third, it had to harbor a universal philosophy about the international order as a tool of diplomatic offensive.

As discussed in detail earlier in this book, Andō Yoshirō, director-general of the Treaty Bureau, Ministry of Foreign Affairs, declared at the executive committee of the Study Group on War Aims, which was entrusted with the task of drafting the Greater East Asia Declaration, that the declaration had to "induce peoples of Greater East Asia to voluntarily render cooperation [with Japan]" and, at the same time, "demonstrate that Greater East Asia is founded on objectively fair and appropriate principles in anyone's eyes and that it can be a major foundation for the maintenance of world peace." That was why the Atlantic Charter, which was an Allied scheme for the postwar international order, was referred to and why at the same time, "the traditional

Co-Prosperity Sphere philosophy, which excessively stressed the notion of a guiding nation, had to be eliminated." Nevertheless, it was also important for "some domestic consideration to be paid to the issues of the political structure and the regional economic zone of Greater East Asia."

More concretely, the first challenge was, on the one hand, how to overcome the gap between the spirit of the Greater East Asia Declaration and, on the other, how to overcome such schemes as the Greater East Asia Co-Prosperity Sphere and a regional economic zone, both of which presupposed Japan's position as the guiding nation. The executive committee had no choice other than to fend off criticism by arguing that "guidance" or "leadership" was implicitly included in such notions as "cooperation" and "jointly" among countries in the Sphere. During the inter-ministerial consultation based on the Foreign Ministry's proposal, the Imperial Navy, in particular, opposed to the end certain articles in the proposal from the viewpoint of securing natural resources in the occupied territories. The Imperial Navy judged that these statements "might lead to serious problems in the future." The Ministry of Greater East Asia, which was eager to stress the contribution to the successful conclusion of the ongoing war, submitted its own draft and applied revisions to the Foreign Ministry's proposal.

Thus, the Greater East Asia Declaration, its entire text and the preamble, as it was finalized barely fulfilled the three requirements—and yet it became defendable from any of the three positions. The other way to look at it is that the declaration ended up being equivocal. And that was why the propaganda policy of the Greater East Asia Declaration turned out to be inconsistent. The inconsistency resulted in further confusion in debates on the purpose of the war—to the extent that Shigemitsu even declared strongly that the five principles of the declaration were the precise war aims of Japan. As discussed earlier, while the Greater East Asia Declaration contained a scheme for regionalism, it was reflected only in a halfway manner in the declaration's text. The declaration also fulfilled the "universalism" requirement, which was inconsistent with the solidarity of Asia, the original meaning of the war, making discussions on the declaration all the more confusing.

In any event, the declaration was ineffectual in terms of securing cooperation with the war effort from peoples in the occupied territories in Asia—the end result of which can be described as, "we have played the pipes for you and yet you have not danced," to paraphrase Matthew 11:17. And in terms of having an impact on the Allies, the declaration failed to provoke any reaction from them other than the realization of frustration on the part of Japan. If one has to look for a concrete impact of the declaration, it would be that fruition of the spirit of the Greater East Asia policy in the form of a joint declaration accelerated Shigemitsu's and the Foreign Ministry's pursuit of independence and autonomy for Asian peoples.[16] For Shigemitsu and the Foreign Ministry, it was the "independent states" of Greater East Asia that were the main actors of the Greater East Asia Conference and its joint declaration, at least momentarily. It was not a conference of representatives of various ethnic groups in Greater East Asia.[17] Because the declaration was an integral part of the Greater East Asia new policy, however, tolerance for independence or autonomy should not be limited to Burma and the Philippines. It was a goal that should be promoted for other territories in the region. In this sense, the Greater East Asia Declaration worked to limit options available to the Foreign Ministry, which came to be dominated by a kind of sense of mission. Thus, as discussed in previous chapters, in the midst of the worsening war situation, a pattern of conflict emerged between the military, which wanted to expand intervention in local governments and

---

16 An almost identical evaluation is found in Yasuda Toshie, "Daitōa Kaigi to Daitōa Kyōdō Sengen o megutte" [On the Assembly of Greater East-Asiatic Nations and the Joint Declaration in 1943], *Hōgaku Kenkyū*, vol. 63, no. 2, 1990, pp. 410–415.

17 At the late-May Liaison Conference that decided the convening of the Greater East Asia Conference, Shigemitsu remarked, "It is better to limit participants in the Greater East Asia Conference to independent states. It would be highly awkward to invite leaders of every ethnic group in the region in the place of participating independent states" (*Sugiyama memo, ge*, p. 404). As this remark suggested, Shigemitsu envisioned it would be a conference among independent states of Greater East Asia, and he had no intention to make it a conference among representatives of each ethnic group.

become the guiding power, and the Foreign Ministry, which intended to promote autonomy and independence in the region. And this pattern was repeated in India, Indonesia, and French Indochina after the Greater East Asia Conference.

(2) Overcoming Militarism

Among criticisms of the Greater East Asia Declaration by its contemporaries, those of Ishibashi Tanzan and Kiyosawa Kiyoshi merit special attention. Part of what motivated Ishibashi and Kiyosawa following the latter half of 1943 to grapple with a vision of the postwar world was the need for some concrete measures for postwar management that took into account Japan's proactive war aim of liberating oppressed peoples in the world and its passive aim of survival and self-defense. In the exploration of measures for postwar management, the Greater East Asia Declaration presented promising hints. Both Kiyosawa and Ishibashi invited Greater East Asia Minister Aoki to their respective study meetings after the Greater East Asia Conference in hopes of prompting creation of concrete measures toward postwar organization. Aoki, nevertheless, showed no interest in the issue of the postwar organization, saying, "The Greater East Asia Declaration shall be unmodified. No postwar organization will be established and Japan will no longer pose as a leader."[18] This goes to show that, at least as far as the Ministry of Greater East Asia was concerned, the Greater East Asia Declaration was no more than wartime propaganda.

According to Kiyosawa, at least some kind of permanent organization was necessary to complement the Greater East Asia Declaration. And it is clear that both Shigemitsu and the Foreign Ministry shared this awareness in their plan for a Greater East Asia international organization and the *Draft Proposal on the World Peace Organization* compiled by the Treaty

---

18 Kiyosawa Kiyoshi, *Ankoku nikki* [The Diary of Darkness], Hyōronsha, 1979, entry of November 25, 1943.

Bureau. The setback that the scheme had met prior to the Greater East Asia Conference due to criticism from the government and the military, however, caused Shigemitsu and the Foreign Ministry to lose their grip in working out concrete measures. Nor did they believe it was possible for them to tackle the task.

Moreover, on the day before the Greater East Asia Conference, Shigemitsu confided to Kido Kōichi, Lord Keeper of the Privy Seal, that in contrast to the flashiness of the conference, the reality was that the new Greater East Asia policy was in a state of deadlock, symbolized by the economic crisis under the Nanjing government. Therefore, the priority for Japan at that time was to revitalize the policy.[19] In other words, even though Shigemitsu was fully aware of the gap between the reality of Greater East Asia and the ideal set out by the Greater East Asia Declaration, he still persisted with the strategy of upgrading the Greater East Asia Declaration and the series of new policy measures to the position of Japan's purpose for war. One of the reasons behind Shigemitsu's actions was his hopes of putting the war aims, which had been defined by the military, back in the hands of politicians.[20] Because it would be difficult to terminate the war as long as the declared aims were in the hands of the military, Shigemitsu must have decided that it was necessary to redefine Japan's war aims and manage them through civilian government. When Shigemitsu's scheme is seen in this context, it should become obvious that the Greater East Asia Declaration was aimed more toward the domestic audience than the international community.

In May 1943, Shigemitsu reported on remarks by German ambassador to Japan Heinrich Georg Stahmer and briefed the emperor on the situation in Germany as follows:

---

19 *Zoku Shigemitsu Mamoru shuki*, pp. 201–202.
20 For instance, to Colonel Matsutani Makoto, chief of Office of War Direction of the Imperial Japanese Army General Staff Office, who claimed that the war aim was "self-existence and self-defense," Shigemitsu replied in September 1943 that, "As far as the war aim of Japan is concerned, it has already been confirmed. The new China policy is a part of it, and so is the Greater East Asia new policy." (*Zoku Shigemitsu Mamoru shuki*, p. 168).

Similar to what occurred toward the end of the previous world war, the military's intervention in politics became overly apparent and, consequently, the conflict between the military and the government (the political parties) also became increasingly more adamant. Thus, this German tendency to rely on military might and pay little heed to politics also became blatant in foreign policy. . . . If this tendency for the military to intervene in politics continues to grow, it will eventually become impossible to get the war under control.

While there is no knowing how the emperor interpreted this report, it can be said that Shigemitsu, by way of explaining the situation in Germany, warned the emperor about the crisis facing Japan, which was entering a situation similar to Germany's.[21] According to Shigemitsu, the first opportunity to shift "from the initial military stage to the next political and diplomatic stage" was the implementation of the new China policy; the second opportunity was the Greater East Asia Conference. In other words, the series of Greater East Asia new policy measures had a hidden meaning as a means to restrict the military's involvement in politics. In particular, the Greater East Asia Declaration was not merely "an impressive diplomatic offensive" from Japan. It was also expected to have the effect of checking Japan's deeper inclination toward militarism. In that sense, it can be said that the Greater East Asia Declaration was the war aim that should have been shared by Germany, which had a "tendency to rely on military might and pay little heed to politics." When serving as the Japanese ambassador to Britain, Shigemitsu had already scrutinized the situation after the opening of the war between Germany and the Soviet Union and pointed out that, "Without a doubt, it is a liability for Germany that it has expanded its occupied territories, inviting the resentment of the

---

21 *Shigemitsu Mamoru shuki*, p. 339.

occupied peoples along with the expansion of the fronts."[22] This shows that German treatment of the occupied territories in Europe was a matter of great concern for Japan—as was its own treatment of occupied territories in Asia.

Furthermore, in late September 1943, Shigemitsu argued that, "At this point, Japan and Germany should jointly announce their war aims in a manner that is acceptable to the rest of the world. To do this, it will be necessary to make use of political measures, not to mention military means." Regarding specifically economic issues, Shigemitsu proposed to Ambassador Stahmer that a "reciprocal open-door policy" to eliminate monopolies "could be announced not only to our wartime allies but also to the entire world." A few days later, on the issue of the handling of such territories under German occupation as Serbia and Albania, Shigemitsu suggested, "If it is assured that these territories will become amicable instead of hostile, granting them independence or autonomy should not pose any problem." Needless to say, these suggestions from Shigemitsu were not accepted by the Germans. Shigemitsu was of the view that it would be on the issue of the treatment of occupied territories that military intervention in politics and diplomacy would be most conspicuous. In that sense, it appears that both Germany and Japan shared a similar problem.[23]

The issue of Japan and Germany sharing war aims was a subject of consideration by the Study Group on War Aims of the Ministry of Foreign Affairs (renamed Research Committee on War Aims) before and after the Greater East Asia Conference. Because the defeat of Bolshevism was the

---

22 Ibid., pp. 149–150, 155–156, p. 280, and pp. 398–399.

23 *Zoku Shigemitsu Mamoru shuki*, pp. 174–175. Joseph Goebbels' diary reveals that Japan's treatment of its occupied territories was a matter of concern for the German side. When hearing a report on this issue in the spring of 1943, Goebbels recorded in his diary, "It is enviable that Japan has succeeded in realizing it quite skillfully. While Japan manages occupied territory government under the Japanese military in all the occupied territories, paying attention to the peculiarity of each territory, it still manages to maintain the appearance of freedom of each state. . . . The way Japan treats its occupied territories can present a model to us." (Louis P. Lochner, ed., *The Goebbels Diaries, 1942–1943*, New York: Doubleday Co. Inc., 1948, p. 348).

only war objective for Germany, and because it was judged to be "inappropriate to openly present such principles as the self-initiated development of nation states,"[24] this consideration was terminated shortly.[25] The scheme to make a joint German-Japan declaration on common war aims concerning treatment of occupied territories was also a means to overcome the problem of "political intervention by the military," a flaw common to both countries. But, most of all, this proposed scheme revealed that Shigemitsu was aware that treatment of the occupied territories—that is, the issue of colonialism—had become an important point of contention as the war advanced.

4. Deadlocked Greater East Asia New Policy and the Second New Policy

(1) Unification of Greater East Asia Diplomacy

In contrast with the ostentatious Greater East Asia Conference, the Greater East Asia new policy was deadlocked. In particular, in China under the Nanjing government, which was supposed to be the central stage of the policy, inflation steepened and the economy seemed a catastrophe. The Liaison Conference of mid-July 1943 urged the Japanese government to decide on an emergency economic measure for China so that credibility of the currency issued by the central bank of the Nanjing government could be maintained. Toward the end of the Tōjō government, the situation became so serious that Shigemitsu deploringly remarked, "There has been neither politics nor diplomacy in Greater East Asia since the Greater East Asia Conference. . . . Economic conditions have become so deadlocked that, if left unattended, Greater East Asia might fall out of Japan's hands." This situation was chiefly due to the absence of any Greater East Asia diplomacy,

---

24 "Shōwa 18-nendo shitsumu hōkoku" [Operational Report for FY 1943] (Treaty Bureau, Ministry of Foreign Affairs), pp. 165–168.
25 Hosokawa Morisada, *Hosokawa nikki, jō* [Hosokawa Diary, vol 1], Chūō Kōronsha, 1979, pp. 69–70.

and it was a grave problem that called for "an innovation of organization and policy," not only for China but for the entirety of Greater East Asia. It was not something that could be remedied with a mere "expanded interpretation" of "pure diplomacy," the only realm that had been left to the jurisdiction of the Foreign Ministry in the Greater East Asia Sphere, as suggested by Lord Keeper of Privy Seal Kido.[26]

To break the deadlock, Shigemitsu, with the support of Kido, succeeded in serving in the Koiso cabinet concurrently as its foreign minister and minister for Greater East Asia, thus consolidating a new setup for Greater East Asia diplomacy. This provoked counter-movements within the Imperial Army. One was the scheme to promote the "one person, two roles" system for the Empire of Japan's representatives (a "guidance mechanism") in China, Thailand, French Indochina, the Philippines, and Burma. Another was the scheme to "constructively" dissolve the Nanjing Nationalist government depending on the outcome of the political engineering toward the Chongqing government. And the goal of these measures was the strengthening of cooperation in the war effort from Greater East Asia territories in anticipation of a decisive battle with the United States in the fall of 1944.[27] This goes to show that the collapse of the Absolute Zone of National Defense made the Imperial Army's measures toward Greater East Asia shift from the advancement of autonomy and liberation to military intervention, altering the Greater East Asia policy that the Imperial Army had entrusted to the Koiso cabinet divert widely from what Shigemitsu had envisioned.

Prime Minister Koiso endorsed the "one person, two roles" proposal of the Imperial Army. With the support of Umezu Yoshijirō, chief of the Imperial Japanese Army General Staff Office, Koiso tried to promote the scheme of having regional military commanders in the southern territories serve concurrently as ambassadors. Finding this attempt unacceptable as "a

---

26 *Zoku Shigemitsu Mamoru shuki*, p. 203.
27 Honjo Shigeru, *Haisen no kiroku: Sanbō Honbu shozō* [Record of a War Defeat: A Collection of the Imperial Japanese Army General Staff Office], Hara Shobō, 1967, pp. 35–36.

nonsensical measure that not only brushes aside the spirit of the Greater East Asia Declaration but also ignores the true situation in the southern territories," Shigemitsu pre-empted the scheme. Then another disruption emerged: Prime Minister Koiso's active promotion of a peace settlement with the Chongqing government. Koiso managed to make launching of maneuvers toward the Chongqing government an Imperial Council decision with the help of Ogata Taketora, Minister of State. General Ugaki Kazushige, former army minister and foreign minister, who was about to embark on a trip to China, was requested to sound out the possibility of a peace settlement. Koiso also aggressively pursued strategies vis-à-vis Miao Ping of the Nanjing government.

Koiso's enthusiasm notwithstanding, Shigemitsu persisted with the position that, if manipulations toward Chongqing were to be carried out, "it is absolutely necessary for Japan to simultaneously pursue the so-called new policy vigorously in all areas—including politics and the economy—and, thereby, induce the Chongqing government to align with us." Shigemitsu remained critical of the deep involvement of Koiso and the Ugaki group in the political activities toward the Chongqing government as an attempt to bring about the demise of the Nanjing government. From Shigemitsu's standpoint, it was the Nanjing government, Japan's alliance partner, which had to be the other party of Japan's peace settlement with China. Accordingly, Shigemitsu would pay attention to measures to strengthen the Nanjing government. He could hardly be party to actions leading to the demise of the Nanjing government. Shigemitsu maintained this posture throughout his tenure as foreign minister.

At the reshuffling of the Koiso cabinet in December 1944 the disagreement between Shigemitsu and Koiso over the Greater East Asia policy came to a denouement. The most controversial move in this reshuffle was the appointment of Lieutenant General Ninomiya Harushige of the Imperial Army as minister for Greater East Asia. The appointment went against the previous pattern of the foreign minister serving concurrently as minister for

Greater East Asia. Shigemitsu adamantly opposed this move, arguing that (1) appointment of a separate minister for Greater East Asia would go against unification of diplomatic channels; (2) the appointment would obstruct pursuit of the new China policy; and (3) if a separate minister for Greater East Asia had to be appointed, the system of unification of diplomatic channels should be established first. The third point further called for reorganization of the Ministry of Greater East Asia to a Ministry of Greater East Asian Economy in charge of economic affairs in the occupied territories before appointing a new, separate minister. Shigemitsu was determined to resign as foreign minister should his suggestions be rejected and he conveyed as much to Navy Minister Yonai Mitsumasa via Arita Hachirō, adviser to the foreign minister. As a result of Yonai's persuasion, Koiso ultimately gave up on the idea of appointing a separate minister for Great East Asia (see chapter 9).

Thus, Shigemitsu succeeded in defending the unification of diplomatic channels and, at the same time, he started working on the second Greater East Asia new policy.

(2) The Second Greater East Asia New Policy

One of the things that Shigemitsu tackled was to carry out the new policy vis-à-vis Indonesia. Indonesia had basically been given the status of a territory of the Empire of Japan under the *Outlines for the Political Guidance of Greater East Asia* that had been adopted by the Imperial Council in May 1943. As such, it was extremely difficult to liberate Indonesia from that status and make it independent. In spite of Shigemitsu's proposals, Prime Minister Tōjō was highly reluctant to take any measures other than expanding political participation by the locals. In 1944, however, with the intensification of Indonesian frustration over the situation, a simple, brief Koiso Statement was issued on September 7 recognizing the future independence of "East India [the Dutch East Indies]." The statement did not include concrete details such as the timing of independence, the geographical range of the territory to become independent, or the form of independence. This was basically and largely attributable to the Imperial Navy's resistance to a change of the status quo in the territories under its control. The Imperial Navy was critical of the perception of the Greater East Asia War as a "war of peoples' liberation" and insisted that the emphasis on the autonomy and independence of occupied territories would be detrimental to the "rapid mobilization of national defense resources for the war." It strongly argued for maintaining the principle of self-existence and self-defense.[28]

Much more important than the Indonesian issue, however, was the liberation of French Indochina. In particular, it was thought that the improvement of French-Soviet relations following the launching of General Charles de Gaulle's provisional government in August 1944, including the signing of the Franco-Soviet Treaty of Mutual Assistance on December 10 that same year, would have a great impact on the French Indochina issue. After the Greater East Asia Conference Shigemitsu began to argue strongly at the Liaison Conference for a shift in Japan's policy toward French Indochina. Since the commencement of the war, Japan's consistent policy had been geared toward keeping peace and maintaining the status quo. After the Great East Asia Conference, however, Shigemitsu began to advocate liberation and independence through force. Nevertheless, it was not until the de facto collapse of the Vichy government and establishment of de Gaulle's provisional government in August 1944 that Shigemitsu's argument became a realistic policy issue. This was because the demise of the Vichy government harbored the danger of French Indochina detaching itself from Japan.

The core of the French Indochina issue was governance after an armed intervention. At the Supreme War Leadership Council on February 1, 1945, Shigemitsu stressed the following two points regarding the importance of taking up the issue of independence. First was the liability that, if Japan took the policy of resorting to arms and conducting military government in the

---

28 For the Imperial Navy's opposition to "open access to natural resources," see *Kimitsu sensō nisshi*, entry of October 23, 1943.

occupied territories, stressing the official goal of autonomy and self-defense, "the enemy side could publicly claim that this conduct betrayed the Empire's intention to occupy French Indochina, in place of France, and this could be taken advantage of by the Soviet Union and other neutral countries." Second, if Annam and other French Indochina territories abolished the protection treaty and announced their intention to become independent and if Japan adopted a policy to assist and defend them, "It would appeal to the world that Japan has no aggressive intention, complying with the spirit of the Greater East Asia Declaration and avoiding the risk of being taken advantage of by third countries." In other words, Shigemitsu shared his conviction that in order to avoid provoking the Soviet Union through an armed intervention, it would be most important to maintain the principles contained in the Greater East Asia Declaration.

The Imperial Japanese Army and the locally stationed Japanese troops perceived the Asian peoples' independence issue as being of secondary importance. They insisted on putting these territories under "military management," or military government after the armed intervention. This made for a fierce confrontation between Shigemitsu and the Foreign Ministry. Still, in the end, the Imperial Army accepted Shigemitsu's argument for "immediate independence," and the locally stationed Japanese troops shifted their policy toward "prompt and voluntary declaration of independence." The army did not compromise because it recognized the significance of peoples' independence. It realized that a worsening of relations with the Soviet Union might be avoided by demonstrating to the Soviet Union the "non-aggressive nature" of its armed intervention in French Indochina.[29] At the same time, it can be

---

29 "Meigō sakusen ni tomonau seimu shori ni kansuru ken" [Matters Related to Political Handlings Accompanying Meigō Operation] (sent by the deputy minister for army and vice chief of the Imperial Japanese Army General Staff Office to the Southern Expeditionary Army, and to Chief of Staff for reference), Ministry of Foreign Affairs Document A7.0.0.9-54; Shiraishi Masaya and Furuta Motoo, "Taiheiyō Sensō-ki no Nippon no tai Indoshina seisaku" [Japan's Indochina Policy during the Pacific War], *Ajia Kenkyū*, vol. 23, no. 3, 1976, pp. 25–26; Akagi Kanji, "Futsuin buryoku shori o meguru gunji to gaikō" [Japanese Wartime Policy toward French Indochina Reexamined: The Designs and Realities], *Hōgaku Kenkyū*, vol. 57, no. 9, September 1984, pp. 44–49.

said that Shigemitsu and the Foreign Ministry, which had maintained the spirit of the Greater East Asia Declaration, succeeded in luring the Imperial Army and the locally stationed Japanese troops into the unprecedented position of supporting the immediate granting of independence.

5. Setbacks of Policies toward China and the Soviet Union and Decolonization

(1) Aberration of Policy toward the Soviet Union

It should be pointed out that the greatest diplomatic concern for the Tōjō and Koiso cabinets was stability of relations with the Soviet Union. The position of the Foreign Ministry was to rely on the goodwill accumulated through solutions to individual bilateral problems. Particularly noteworthy was the issue of oil and coal concessions in north Sakhalin. The Foreign Ministry succeeded in obtaining an agreement with the Soviets after some seventy tenacious negotiations between June 1943 and March 1944. The Japanese took this agreement as providing a new foundation to its plan to mediate peace between Germany and the Soviet Union. But the Soviet side's reaction was cold. The Soviet Union had turned down the Japanese proposal to dispatch a special envoy to Moscow—a proposal that had been accepted the previous year—and Japan's attempt to mediate a peace settlement between the Soviet Union and Germany was deadlocked as symbolized by this refusal. Under these circumstances Shigemitsu remarked at the Supreme War Leadership Council in mid-September 1944, "I hope to suspend all studies on the negotiations with the Soviet Union that we have pursued so far. From now on, I intend to study the more philosophical aspects of the common issues between our two countries." The philosophical aspects referred to the Greater East Asia Declaration as well as Shigemitsu's speech at the 85th session of the Imperial Diet. In short, Shigemitsu declared that he would shift the mode of negotiations with the Soviet Union from exchanges on compensations and interests to an approach centered on the philosophical aspects of common issues.

The first philosophical aspect refers to the Greater East Asia Declaration as "the righteous war aim of the Empire of Japan." It was Shigemitsu's scheme to lure the Soviet Union into cooperation with Japan by demonstrating that Japan's policy to liberate Asian peoples coincided with Soviet policies. As a second philosophical point, Shigemitsu argued that, in light of the Soviet Union's effort to expand the influence of communism in Europe and China, it was necessary "for Japan to show that it tolerates democracy by bringing down the banner of anticommunism in China." Shigemitsu's emphasis on the policy to promote Asian people's independence, the first point, was conveyed to the Soviet side during the dialogue between former Prime Minister Hirota Kōki and Soviet Ambassador to Japan Yakov Malik. Japan had actually started retreating from its anticommunist policy in China in the summer of 1944, from the viewpoint of blocking the Yan'an (Mao Zedong)-Chongqing collaboration, and Shigemitsu intended to use that in Japan's policy toward the Soviet Union.

Shigemitsu's Soviet diplomacy was characterized by a multifaceted approach based on a rigorous assessment of Soviet conduct from the viewpoint of both balance of power and ideology. In Shigemitsu's analysis, while the Soviet Union claimed it wanted to liberate the European continent from totalitarianism and "deliver it into the hands of democracy," it plotted restoration of the balance of power in the European continent. The scheme that Shigemitsu had consistently promoted to mediate peace between Germany and the Soviet Union was based on this analysis. In 1944, in particular, when the schism between the Soviet Union and the Anglo-American alliance deepened over the issue of postwar management of Europe, Shigemitsu predicted that it would be possible to lure Soviet troops to eastern Europe if Germany agreed to a compromise. In spite of repeated appeals from Japan, however, neither Germany nor the Soviet Union agreed to a peace settlement. The unexpected result was a hardening of Soviet policy toward Japan.

It appears that these experiences taught Shigemitsu that it would no longer be possible to move the Soviet Union with a balance-of-power argument or diplomacy over compensation and interests. Thus, in mid-1943, Shigemitsu wrote, "We must counter force with force and diplomacy with diplomacy. And we must meet philosophical offensives with our own philosophy." The shift in the fall of 1944 toward an approach centered more on philosophical aspects must have been made based on the realization that the opportunity for luring the Soviet Union into collaboration with Japan with force or diplomacy had already been lost. At that stage, it appears that Shigemitsu decided that to deal with the Soviet Union using a philosophy-to-philosophy approach—that is, more emphasis on the Greater East Asia Declaration and maneuvering of anticommunist ideology—was the only possible measure left vis-à-vis the Soviet Union.[30]

When a decisive battle on the Japanese homeland became imminent, however, it was not promotion of the Greater East Asia Declaration or a Greater East Asia new policy that was called for in wartime diplomacy. In order to terminate the war on more favorable terms by avoiding direct negotiations with Britain and the United States, which were expected to demand severe conditions, figuring out how to get the Soviet Union and China (Chongqing government) involved in the process was an urgent issue. For instance, Sugihara Arata, secretary-general of the China office of the Ministry of Greater East Asia who was essentially in charge of China policy under Minister Shigemitsu, proposed a scheme for a Japan-Soviet Union "agreement on peace and security in the Far East" that presupposed the participation of China. Shigemitsu adopted this proposal in his

---

30 *Zoku Shigemitsu Mamoru shuki*, p. 332. Ogata Shōji, director of Division II of the Research Bureau, Ministry of Foreign Affairs, who took part in the drafting of the Greater East Asia Declaration, made the following remark on the operation of the Soviet-Japanese Neutrality Pact in March 1945: "At this point, if the Japanese government intends to have talks with the Soviet government, it should explain the true intention of the Greater East Asia Declaration and the fact that Japan has been waging the Greater East Asia War as a means to accomplish world peace without touching on the issue of the treaty." This remark appears to have taken Shigemitsu's approach toward the Soviet Union into consideration. ("Honma hōkokusho" [Army General Honma Masaharu Report], Yahata University, *Hōritsu Kenkyūsho Hō*, no. 2, 1968, p. 278.)

foreign policy scheme—that is, his Japan–China–Soviet Union partnership scheme.[31] Various sources reveal that this scheme had significant support. One such source is the article added to the agreements of the conference of the Supreme War Leadership Council in mid-May 1945, which decided on termination of the war through mediation by the Soviet Union. The newly added article stipulated that, "It is most desirable to establish a joint Japan-Soviet-China cooperation system in China."[32]

One piece of information regarding the background of the emergence of the Japan-China-Soviet partnership as a diplomatic scheme in the last days of the war was the maneuvering vis-à-vis the Chongqing government, including that to Miao Ping, in the hope that peace establishment with the Chongqing government would lead to peace negotiations with Britain and the United States. And underlying these attempts was a judgment that settlement of the war with China could no longer be separated from settlement of the war with Britain and the United States, in which the Nanjing government posed a stumbling block. For instance, Prime Minister Koiso himself drafted a proposal stating that Japan and China should jointly construct a Pacific Charter if and when the maneuvering with the Chongqing government showed some progress; this Pacific Charter should then be submitted to Britain and the United States in order to start the peace negotiations among the three countries. It was a scheme to link the peace maneuvering toward the Chongqing government with a peace settlement with Britain and the United States. This was the background to the activities vis-à-vis Miao Ping that Koiso had pursued.[33]

The second part of the background was the assumption that the Soviet

---

31 "Taigai shisaku kanken" [My Humble View on Foreign Policy] (written by Sugihara Arata on September 29) compiled in *Takagi Sōkichi shiryō* [Takagi Sōkichi Documents]. Also see Sugihara Arata, "Tai-Jūkei mondai ni kansuru iken" [A View on the Issue of Relations with the Chongqing Government] (written on April 30) included in the above *Takagi Sōkichi shiryō*.

32 Ministry of Foreign Affairs, ed., *Shūsen shiroku* [End of the Pacific War Record], Shimbun Gekkansha, 1952, p. 323.

33 Tobe Ryōichi, "Taichū wahei kōsaku 1941–1945" [Peace Maneuvering toward China, 1941–1945], *Kokusai Seiji*, no. 109, 1995, p. 10.

Union did not necessarily hope for the collapse or even the weakening of Japan. Rather, what the Soviet Union hoped to see in the postwar Asia-Pacific region was construction of an international setup to block US advances into East Asia. The argument that stressed the "autonomy" of Soviet conduct in East Asia was also widely shared by the Imperial Army.

The third element hidden behind the scheme for Japan-China-Soviet collaboration was, perhaps, Japan's desire to prepare a framework for the maintenance of the postwar East Asian order in case it lost all of the colonies in Southeast Asia. Sugihara had envisioned the end of war with Manchukuo and the Korean Peninsula still under Japan's control. Although the proposal on conditions for a peace settlement with the Chongqing government, which the Ministry of Foreign Affairs drafted toward the end of August 1944, argued that Manchukuo would be a territory of China in the end, the Supreme War Leadership Council decided that the status quo should be applied to Manchukuo. Behind this decision was the council's resolve to maintain control of Manchukuo in exchange for relinquishing concessions in the southern territories. Coupled with conditions for compromise with the Soviet Union that the Japanese side had been studying separately, it seems safe to say that Japan's leaders had envisioned an end of the war in which Japan could keep at least the Korean Peninsula (and preferably Manchukuo, too) through compromising with the Soviet Union by abandoning the southern territories as a compensation.[34] Also, the scheme for a Japan–China–Soviet Union partnership, which the Imperial Army had pursued since the last days of 1944, was also constructed on the premise of Japan's withdrawal from the occupied territories in Southeast Asia.[35] To put it differently, it can be said that a kind of power system

---

34 "Jūkei kōsaku jisshi ni kansuru ken" [Matters Related to Implementation of Maneuvering toward Chongqing] (August 31) and "Jūkei kōsaku ni kansuru jyakkan no mondai" [A Few Problems Associated with Implementation of Engineering toward Chongqing] (September 1) (Ministry of Foreign Affairs Document A7.0.0.9-61). These documents stipulated that "Japan must decide to imply that it is prepared to consider abandoning the southern territories as a quid pro quo for Manchukuo."

35 "Tōa antei ni kansuru Nichi-So kyōdō sengen (an)" [Proposal on Japan-Soviet Joint Declaration

in which Japan would withdraw entirely from Southeast Asia, tolerating its becoming an Anglo-American sphere of influence, in return for which Japan could retain not only Korea but also Manchukuo as a joint sphere of influence between Japan, China, and the Soviet Union, was judged to be the most preferable form of the war's end.[36]

The foreign policy scheme of the Konoe group, centered around Konoe Fumimaro, the emperor's chief vassal, and Yoshida Shigeru, was at the opposite spectrum of the Supreme War Leadership Council's scheme. If, as Satō Naotake, Japanese ambassador to the Soviet Union, had protested, the Japan-China-Soviet partnership harbored the risk of Japan allowing itself to lean in the direction of tolerating communism, it was this Konoe group that embodied this sense of crisis most acutely.

At the time, the predominant view among Japanese leaders was that direct peace negotiations with Britain and the United States should be avoided because these two countries would demand Japan's unconditional surrender. Against this background, the Konoe group remained anxious to end the war as promptly as possible because its members shared a sense of crisis that the defeat could bring about communist revolution and convert postwar Japan to a communist country. The stance taken by Japanese leaders to seek benevolent mediation by the Soviet Union was so entrenched that the demand to let Nosaka Sanzō, a founder of the Japanese Communist Party, and his associates, who had aimed to form a democratic front in Yan'an, join the cabinet as compensation might not remain an imaginary threat.[37]

---

on Stability of East Asia] (September 18, 1944), "Tōa antei ni kansuru Nichi-So-Shi kyōdō sengen (dai 2-an)" [Japan-Soviet-China Joint Declaration on Stability of East Asia (second draft)] (December 15), "Nisso mondai o chūshin tosuru teikoku kongo no taigai shisaku ni kansuru kansatsu" [An Observation on the Empire's External Measures in the Future Centered around the Japan-Soviet Issues] (March 17, 1945). These three documents are bound in "Shōwa 19–20-nen Daitōa sensō shidō taikō kankei tsuzuri: Ippan no bu" [File of FY1944-45 Documents Related to the Greater East Asia War Instruction Outline in General Affairs] compiled by Section XX, Imperial Army General Staff Office.

36 Akira Iriye, "Wartime Japanese Planning for Postwar Asia," in Ian Nish, ed., *Anglo-Japanese Alienation, 1919–1952* (Cambridge: Cambridge University Press, 1982), pp. 185–187.

37 For the analysis of the Konoe group, see chapter 4 of Itō Takashi, *Shōwa-ki no seiji* [Politics in

The Konoe group was not simply motivated by a sense of crisis. Equally important was that they also saw some chance of success in direct peace negotiations with Britain and the United States. For instance, Konoe wrote as follows in his report to the emperor in February 1945:

To further continue the war with no prospect for winning would only enhance conditions for communist revolution. From the standpoint of "protecting the national polity," efforts should be made to promptly end the war. A stumbling block to an early end of the war is, however, "that particular group" in the military. If these elements are eliminated, peace settlements with Britain and the United States as well as the Chongqing government would become feasible.

Konoe based the above argument on a prediction as well as a conviction concerning the international environment that "the goal of Britain, the United States, and Chongqing is the downfall of Japan's military clique" and that such actions would not extend to "reforming of the national polity."[38]

Shōwa Period], Yamakawa Shuppansha, 1989, and Shōji Jun'ichirō, "Konoe jōsōbun no saikentō" [Reexamination of Konoe's Report to the Emperor], *Kokusai Seiji*, no. 109, 1995, pp. 54–69.

38 When asked by the emperor on February 14, 1945, if the Japanese military's observation that the United States even considered "reform of the national polity" was warranted, Konoe replied that he believed that at least former US Ambassador to Japan Joseph Grew, "holds the imperial family in high esteem and reverence" (Kido Nikki Kenkyūkai, ed., Kido Kōichi kankei bunsho [Documents Related to Kido Kōichi], University of Tokyo Press, 1967, pp. 497–498). Konoe referred to Joseph Grew, US Ambassador to Japan until the outbreak of the war, because he had been promoted from assistant secretary of state for Far Eastern affairs to undersecretary of state, thus increasing his influence within the State Department, and because his words and deeds were closely watched in Japan. Since the summer of 1943, Grew watched closely the "moderates" or "sound elements" in Japanese society and stated on various occasions that a sound government should be established around these elements by defeating the military clique. Grew's remarks were closely analyzed by Japan's Ministry of Foreign Affairs. The record of investigations compiled by the Ministry's Treaty Bureau in February 1945 wrote as follows, while describing the US attitude toward Japan's national polity issue as "noncommittal and cautious." Incidentally, this record of investigations summed up all the records of the Political Affairs Bureau on the Allies' proposals on treatment of Japan after the war since 1944 (Division II, Treaty Bureau, "Kenkyū shūroku" [Compilation of Studies] February 1945, "Takagi Sōkichi shiryō").

"It appears that, as far as the future political system of Japan is concerned . . . it intends to take thorough measures to defeat the military clique and eliminate militarism, and prompt democratic

(2) Contradictions in China Policy and Decolonization

Sandwiched between the two positions just described, Shigemitsu's position was ambiguous. To begin with, Shigemitsu was not necessarily enthusiastic about a peace settlement through mediation by the Soviet Union. Toward the end of January 1945, when Shigemitsu was invited to the senior councillors' conference to give a lecture on the international situation, Okada Keisuke proposed, by way of introducing Nakajima Chikuhei's argument, that now that the defeat seemed to be imminent, "we should plead to the Soviet Union for mediation in peace negotiations, rather than directly surrendering to the United States." Refuting this, Shigemitsu responded, "There is no knowing what the Soviet Union would demand as quid pro quo. Seeing that the Soviet Union is likely to demand cabinet posts for members of the troops or organizations in Yan'an with the mission to liberate Manchuria, it would be utterly impossible to ask for the Soviet mediation."[39] This shows that by that time Shigemitsu had become extremely reluctant regarding seeking a peace settlement with Britain and the United States via mediation by the Soviet Union. It appeared that he was anticipating that the Soviets would demand heavy compensation, including formation of a communist cabinet in Japan—a scenario that would face insurmountable opposition from within Japan.

During his speech at the 85th session of the Imperial Diet in September 1944, Shigemitsu had to add respect of nationalistic policy and the principle of non-interference in domestic politics to the five principles of the Greater

---

elements in Japan to naturally gain power. . . . The occupation forces and supervising organization shall assist the rise of these elements in Japan, and when it witnesses establishment of government by these elements, it will treat Japan as a member of international society."

Reading these Foreign Ministry's analyses, which coincided with the major thrusts of Grew's speeches, Konoe was convinced that it would be possible to protect the national polity. Thus, he wrote, "The war aim of the United States is not annihilation of the Japanese nor reform of the national polity (which would involve doing something about the imperial family) . . . Its war aim is in the change of the substance of the Imperial Army." ("Konoe kō iken" [View of Prince Konoe], January 22, 1945, Takagi Sōkichi shiryō).

39 *Hosokawa nikki, ge,* p. 67.

East Asia Declaration, stressing that the "form of government and the guiding principle are the domestic affairs of each country." His having had to do this betrayed the agonizing position in which Shigemitsu found himself. He had to pursue improvement of relations with the Soviet Union while, at the same time, preventing Soviet interference in Japan's politics. His position was similar to that of the Konoe group in the sense that he had to reject Soviet mediation of a peace settlement with Britain and the United States because of the communist threat. Still, Shigemitsu had no means of initiating direct peace negotiations with Britain and the United States, nor did he give any heed to its promotion. This was because, unlike Konoe, he could not envision Britain and the United States being tolerant during direct peace negotiations. From Shigemitsu's viewpoint, the only form of surrender that a loser in the age of all-out war deserved was unconditional surrender.[40]

Yet Shigemitsu could not be an advocate of the Japan-China-Soviet partnership on the premise of a peace settlement with the Chongqing government. Domestically, the position of Shigemitsu, who had been persistently critical of peace maneuvering toward Chongqing, became increasingly unpersuasive. His determination to persevere with the new China policy, keeping faith with the Nanjing government, obviously lost validity when at the same time the Chongqing government was deepening relations with the United States.

For Shigemitsu, China remained a presence whose sovereignty had to be restored—that is, become subject to decolonization. To him, a peace settlement, which had to be accomplished as a premise for the restoration of China's sovereignty, had to be lead both Nanjing and Chongqing to peace on equal footing.[41] But Shigemitsu's persistence with defense of the Nanjing government, which was no longer the main actor of Chinese politics, and his dismissal of the maneuvering toward the Chongqing government as "a

---

40 *Zoku Shigemitsu Mamoru shuki*, p. 237 and p. 388.
41 Tobe Ryōichi, "Daitōa Sensō to Shina Jihen" [Greater East Asia War and the Second Sino-Japanese War], *Gaikō Jihō*, no. 1320, July/August 1995, pp. 51–52.

plot to dissolve the Nanjing government" contradicted his own hopes of restoring China's sovereignty, putting him in an awkward position. Even when we review Shigemitsu's China policy from a long-term perspective, the contradictions in his actions were ill-concealed. While his awareness and understanding of nationalism in China was incomparable among other political leaders in Japan, he nevertheless continued to evade settlement of the Manchurian issue, which was by far the central point of contention.[42] After Manchukuo was actually founded, Shigemitsu tolerated it as a fait accompli, and after the opening of the Greater East Asia War, he treated Manchukuo as a member state of the Greater East Asia Conference—on par with the Nanjing government.

Thus, Shigemitsu ended up facing one deadlock after another in his diplomacy toward the Soviet Union, his foreign policy toward China, and his measures addressed to Britain and the United States before resigning as foreign minister, with liberation and independence for French Indochina as his parting present.

When, after Shigemitsu's resignation, Japan became geared toward a decisive battle on the homeland itself, Japan chose peace mediation by the Soviet Union as its foreign policy instead of direct peace negotiations with Britain and the United States—which Konoe advocated. It was hoped that the conditions for peace could to a certain extent be mitigated if peace was mediated by the Soviet Union rather than achieved through direct peace

---

42 Shigemitsu held the following principle in conducting foreign policy while he was Japanese minister to China in the 1920s. "Shigemitsu has been of a strong view that Japan-China relations should be permeated with the new policy. . . . But [Mr. Shigemitsu said that] diplomacy must be most practical. If, in particular, the Chinese side takes up the Manchurian issue and makes demands, there will be no smooth talks. While Japan must accommodate China's request in China proper, ahead of other major powers, China should compromise on Manchuria." To put it differently, Shigemitsu's diplomatic tactic was "to discourage the Chinese side from touching on the Manchurian issue, improve China-Japan relations for solutions of general problems, and, thereby, talk the Chinese side into settlement of the Manchurian issue" (Watanabe Yukio, "Saburi kōshi no shi: Shigemitsu Mamoru" [Death of Minister Saburi: Shigemitsu Mamoru], *Chūgoku Kenkyū Geppō*, vol. 42, no. 11, November 1988). If Shigemitsu applied this diplomatic tactic in the 1930s, the settlement of the Manchurian issue in the 1930s was de facto hopeless.

negotiations with Britain and the United States. In the case of direct negotiations, unconditional surrender would surely be demanded. As it turned out, at the last minute the Soviet Union turned down Japan's request to mediate peace negotiations. Therefore, Japan was not pressed to adopt a pro-Soviet political regime as quid pro quo. Nevertheless, this did not make the future prospects of political and economic regimes in postwar Japan any clearer. The Soviet Union's signing of the Potsdam Declaration and participation in the war was perceived in Japan to mean that the Soviet Union had obtained grounds to exercise its influence over Japan and advance to East Asia. This conduct of the Soviet Union was considered to have created "a situation for the United States and the Soviet Union to compete and contain one another in East Asia."[43]

A document produced by the Foreign Ministry about a month after the end of the war also contended that Japan was divided into two groups—those who relied chiefly on Britain and the United States for construction of a new Japan and those who hoped for the Soviet-China alliance to keep US influence in check.[44] Against the background of this rivalry between the pro-Soviet group and the pro-US group, Shigemitsu, now the foreign minister in the Prince Higashikuni cabinet, did not immediately steer Japan toward the pro-US camp. At the time, the most important thing for Japan to do was to willingly accept the reality of defeat through unconditional surrender, comply with the articles of the Potsdam Declaration—a document based on US-Soviet agreement—and prepare conditions to contribute to the peace and stability of East Asia by voluntarily carrying out domestic reform, regardless of which powers—meaning the US and Britain or the Soviet Union—ended up taking the initiative in the region.[45]

---

43 Remark by Councilor Yoshizawa Kenkichi at the Privy Council on September 3, 1945 (Fukai Eigo, *Sūmitsuin jūyō giji oboegaki* [Memorandum on Important Agenda at the Privy Council], Iwanami Shoten, 1953, pp. 435–436).

44 "Shūsen ni tomonau gaikō seisaku yōkō-an" [Draft Outline of Foreign Policy Accompanying the End of the War] (September 25, 1945) and Amō Eiji Nikki, Shiryō Kankōkai, ed., *Amō Eiji nikki, shiryō-shū* [Amō Eiji Diary and Documents] vol. 4, 1982, p. 1209.

45 *Zoku Shigemitsu Mamoru shuki*, p. 233, pp. 240–241, and p. 282.

In February 1945, toward the end of the war, Shigemitsu wrote, "A new era will not emerge until the 'myth of the omnipotence of the military' is demolished in Japan. One raison d'être of the current war was indeed reform of Japan. Today, the issue is what to do with Japan instead of how to wage the war. And this should be the main concern regardless of one's position in the hierarchy."[46] Recalling that Shigemitsu had once pinned his hopes on reform of Japan and the elimination of militarism in the Greater East Asia new policy, it can be said that the Potsdam Declaration finally provided the opportunity for realizing this goal. Complete elimination of militarism was perceived to be a necessary condition for what may be called the "de-imperialization" of the Empire of Japan itself.

6. Conclusion

Finally, let us review the nature of the Greater East Asia new policy, to which Shigemitsu had devoted himself throughout the war. As has been repeatedly pointed out, the nature of this policy was most explicitly reflected in its last application—that is, the issue of independence for Indonesia and French Indochina.

Needless to say, the independence of French Indochina after liberation was not a full independence. The Japanese government decided to rely on the existing government system of the former office of the French governor-general. Ambassador to French Indochina Matsumoto Shun'ichi urged Shigemitsu to reconsider, stressing that continuation of the existing government system totally lacked consideration of the "peoples' desire for independence" and that Japan could not find no excuse for itself if it was accused of being an aggressor state. While admitting the legitimacy of Matsumoto's argument, Shigemitsu nevertheless rejected Matsumoto's suggestion. Taking the stance that the "top priority is to promptly realize the independence

---

46 *Shigemitsu Mamoru shuki*, p. 438.

of Annam and others," Shigemitsu maintained that it was imperative to respond to the operational needs of the Japanese military first and to grant independence for French Indochina within that framework.[47] That is to say, Shigemitsu feared that, if the Japanese government rejected requests from the military and persisted with full independence for French Indochina, it might jeopardize the measures for prompt independence as a whole.

Shigemitsu was well aware that independence for French Indochina thus obtained through compromise with the military was only a superficial measure without substance. Why, then, did Shigemitsu persist with the promotion of such independence measures, even though they were almost entirely pro forma? A document believed to have been produced by the Foreign Ministry toward the end of the war comments on independence for Indonesia. In summary, it reads as follows:

> While the current war is, in essence, a war against the Anglo-American world order, it is, at the core, also a war of world views. No matter what the outcome of the war is, there will be no complete return to the old order. In particular, the philosophical principle of a war of liberation of Greater East Asia that the Empire of Japan has pursued is something even the enemy nations cannot deny, regardless of the outcome of the war. Even if the Empire is defeated, it should be permissible to acknowledge that "half of the victory is mine."[48]

A Foreign Ministry document that was produced half a year after the end of the war explains the positions of the Ministries of Foreign Affairs and Greater

---

47 February 15, 1945, telegram from Ambassador Matsumoto addressed to Foreign Minister Shigemitsu. February 18, 1945, and February 19, 1945, telegrams from Foreign Minister Shigemitsu addressed to Ambassador Matsumoto (#7 & #8). Gaimushō Gaikō Shiryō Henshū Iinkai, *Gaikō shiryō: Nichi-Futsuin kankei no bu* [Diplomatic Document: Japan-French Indochina Relations Section] February 1946, pp. 293–296.

48 Waseda Daigaku Ōkuma Kinen Shakai Kagaku Kenkyūsho, ed., *Indoneshia ni okeru Nippon gunsei no kenkyū* [Study of Japanese Military Administration in Indonesia], Kinokuniya Shoten, 1959, pp. 561–562.

East Asia when they had insisted on independence for French Indochina:

> As for the prospect for the termination of the Greater East Asia War, it
> appears that it would be challenging for the Empire of Japan to maintain
> its status in the southern territories. This being so, it is all the more neces-
> sary to support and promote the nationalist desires of the local peoples in
> French Indochina. Doing so would not only represent a realization of the
> spirit of peoples' self-determination advocated by the Greater East Asia
> Declaration but also would share something in common with the spirit
> of international democracy of the Allies, particularly the United States,
> as manifested in the Atlantic Charter and the notion of trusteeship.[49]

Common to these two Foreign Ministry documents was the argument that
Japan should clarify its position vis-à-vis the independence issue regardless
of the outcome of the war by focusing on the universality of the philosophical
principle of peoples' independence, because this was expected to become a
founding principle in the postwar international order. If Japan chose to promote
the prompt independence of Indonesia and French Indochina and, thereby,
clarify its stance, instead of leaving the issue unaddressed, Japan would be
able to claim that "half of the victory is ours" even if Japan were defeated.

In other words, as long as Japan wished to infuse the Greater East Asia
War with the meaning of "a war for the liberation of peoples," it was its
priority to give the appearance that its conduct in Asia promoted peoples'
independence, even if that conduct lacked substance. And this position,
which could be termed "a loser's assertion," was carried over into postwar
days. For instance, an early preparatory study on the peace treaty between
Japan and the Allies conducted by the Foreign Ministry included "a principle of recognizing independence for the peoples of colonized territories
in East Asia equipped with the ability to become independent" in the list

---

49 *Gaikō shiryō: Nichi-Futsuin kankei no bu*, pp. 200–201.

of principles to be stipulated in the peace treaty, along with principles such as elimination of racial discrimination, freedom of the seas, and freedom of trade.[50] However, as Robert Ward pointedly criticized in the last days of the war, it should be said that the Allied side had detected in Japan's loser's assertion "a calculation to have history defend Japan in the imminent war tribunal."[51]

Soon after the end of the war, Shigemitsu wrote in his diary that, his career in Japan "has been a history of conflict with the military and its supporters." He also wrote that his wartime diplomacy had been guided by his "conviction" that it was "undisputed justice" to help Asian peoples "become liberated from colonial status and obtain equal positions as free and independent nations."[52] To be sure, it was commendable that Shigemitsu stressed the need for unification of diplomatic channels to block military intervention in Greater East Asia policies and, at the same time, that he tried his best to carry through the policy of tolerating independence and autonomy for the occupied territories in the face of demands to the contrary from the military. Shigemitsu was conscious of decolonization as the point of contention in the war.

In light of the reality of the new Greater East Asia policy as symbolized by the so-called independence of French Indochina, however, it may be called quite paradoxical that, in his quest for the meaning of the war in the liberation and independence of Asian peoples, Shigemitsu ultimately left a legacy of independence for Asian countries that was without substance. Thus, Shigemitsu contributed to the perception in postwar Japan that the Pacific War was a war of liberation.

---

50 "Tainichi heiwa jōyaku ni okeru seiji jōkō no sōtei oyobi taisho hōshin (an)" [Envisioned Political Conditions in the Peace Treaty between Japan and the Allies and Countermeasures (proposal)] ("Heiseiken no ichi" Heiwa Jōyaku Mondai Kenkyūkai) Ministry of Foreign Affairs Document B'4.0.0.1 ("Tai-Nichi heiwa jōyaku kankei: Junbi kenkyū kankei" [Matters Related to the Peace Treaty with Japan: Preparatory Studies Related]).

51 Robert S. Ward, *Asia for the Asiatics? The Techniques of Japanese Occupation*, (Chicago: University of Chicago Press, 1945), pp. 189–190.

52 *Shigemitsu Mamoru shuki*, pp. 610–611.

Afterword

I became inspired to write this book through my work at and subsequent long association with two organizations: the Diplomatic Archives of the Ministry of Foreign Affairs and the Center for Military History at the National Institute for Defense Studies of the Ministry of Defense. In particular, it was an honor as well as an inspiration for me to have assisted Dr. Kurihara Ken, senior archivist at the Diplomatic Archives, who has trained his successors and supported researchers in various ways, to publish *Shūsen shiroku* [Record of the End of the Pacific War] (republication of the 1952 original), *Senryō shiroku* [History of the Occupation of Japan] (four volumes), and *Shūsen kōsaku no kiroku* [Record of Maneuvering to End the War] (two volumes), among other books. Having the opportunity to cultivate my awareness of the issues of Japan's diplomacy during the Greater East Asia War through these activities was an even greater fortune for me than exposure to the massive amounts of historical documents collected by these institutions. When I subsequently and quite unexpectedly took a position at a university, my academic interest expanded to prewar and postwar times, and I did not necessarily pursue my interest in Japan's diplomacy during the Greater East Asia War. Nevertheless, I continued to wonder about subjects such as what meaning the Ministry of Foreign Affairs and the Imperial Army and Navy found in the expansive war, how wartime leaders imagined the shape of postwar Japan and the world, and what legacy they wished to leave to future generations.

Takeuchi Yoshimi, a Shōwa Japan sinologist, once wrote, "[What Japan lost through the defeat was] our posture to think proactively about Asia, which we have nurtured since the Meiji era. It was an attitude of assuming responsibility toward Asia as a member of Asia." While the aggressive aspect of Japan's war was undeniable, Takeuchi deplored the fact that Japan was so ashamed of its own aggression that it even abandoned even a constructive posture toward Asia.[1] It is noteworthy that, even during wartime, there were a number of people in Japan, both in the government and the military, who sincerely tackled the issue of what kind of proactive relations Japan should have with other Asian nations. Otherwise, there would not have been such heated conflicts and confrontations over the issue of independence and autonomy for the occupied territories as discussed in the present volume. This book is, therefore, a record of these struggles.

As enumerated below, I have authored a number of treatises and books on subjects related to the topic of the present volume:

(1) *Shūsen kōsaku no kiroku* [Record of Maneuvering to End the War] in two volumes, co-authored and co-edited with Kurihara Ken, Kōdansha, 1986

(2) "Senji gaikō to sengo kōsō" [Wartime Diplomacy and the Vision of Postwar Japan] (a paper presented at the International Academic Conference to Commemorate the 50th Anniversary of the End of Pacific War—The End of War and the Asia-Pacific (August 23–26, 1999, Shimoda, Shizuoka) organized by the International House of Japan)

(3) "Shigemitsu Mamoru to Ajia gaikō" [Shigemitsu Mamoru and Asia Diplomacy], Institute of International Relations, Sophia University, *Kokusaigaku ronshū* [Treatises on International Relations], no. 10, January 1983

(4) "Shigemitsu Mamoru to Daitōa Kyōdō Sengen: Senji gaikō to sengo kōsō" [Shigemitsu Mamoru and the Greater East Asia Joint Declaration: Wartime Diplomacy and a Vision of Postwar Japan], *Kokusai Seiji*, no. 109, May 1995

(5) "'Wilsonianism' in Wartime Japan and Its Legacy," presented at the Second Workshop on Global Uniformity, Special Project on the New

---

1 Takeuchi Yoshimi, "Nipponjin no Ajia kan" [Japanese Views on Asia]) in volume 5 of *Takeuchi Yoshimi zenshū* [Complete Works of Takeuchi Yoshimi], Chikuma Shobō, 1981.

International System, University of Tsukuba (February 1994, the International House of Japan)

While many of these publications provided the basis for the present volume and helped me substantiate my arguments, no specific treatise or book constitutes a chapter or a section of this book. To briefly explain the relations between those earlier publications and the present volume, the *Shūsen kōsaku no kiroku* [Record of Maneuvering to End the War] is a collection of historical documents related to the ending of the Greater East Asia War and a product of the collection of historical documents of the Ministry of Foreign Affairs as well as the Imperial Japanese Army and Navy. Although these documents provided the basis for this book, I was able to incorporate only one-third of them, many of which I had to abridge. "Senji gaikō to sengo kōsō" [Wartime Diplomacy and a Vision of Postwar Japan] presents the outline of the analytical framework for wartime diplomacy that is discussed in the present volume. The other three publications listed are studies on Shigemitsu's diplomacy during the war. All were substantially revised before being used in the present volume.

As mentioned earlier, the basic model for this volume comes from my work at the Diplomatic Archives of the Ministry of Foreign Affairs and the Center for Military History, National Institute for Defense Studies of the Ministry of Defense. It would be my great pleasure if the present volume served to repay to even a minor degree the warm and unchanging support I received from these institutions. And, last but not least, I wish to express my deepest gratitude to Dr. Kurihara Ken, who has served as a bridge between me and these two institutions and who constantly encouraged me in the completion of this book.

I began working on this book in earnest several years ago. While I was working on this book, I was fortunate to be able to participate in the planning and organization of two international conferences under the chairmanship of Professor Hosoya Chihiro. These conferences enabled me to learn the trends of research both in Japan and overseas as well as the points of contention that needed to be addressed. These conferences were the International Academic Conference to Commemorate the 50th Anniversary of the Opening of the Pacific War in 1991 and the International Academic Conference to Commemorate the 50th Anniversary of the End of the Pacific War—The End of War and the Asia-Pacific in 1995. The second conference, in particular, allowed me to deepen my understanding of the framework of the wartime diplomacy that this book deals with.

I also had the good fortune of presenting some portions of the present volume to such groups as the Study Group on Perceptions of Asia at Waseda University (led by Professors Ōhata Tokushirō and Gotō Ken'ichi); the Study Group on Japan-US Diplomatic History at Doshisha University's International Institute of American Studies (led by Professors Asada Sadao and Hosoya Masahiro); the Research Project on the New International System of the University of Tsukuba (directed by Professors Satō Hideo and Imaoka Hideki); the History Study Group, University of Tsukuba (led by Professor Harald Kleinschmidt); the Study Group on Yoshida Shigeru, University of Tsukuba (led by Professors Yoshimura Michio and Tobe Ryōichi); and the Professor Hanabusa Nagamichi Memorial Lecture of Keio University (led by Professor Ikei Masaru). On each occasion, I benefitted from invaluable criticism and comments by participants on the framework as well as the substance of the present book and I am greatly indebted to them.

The same can be said regarding the two Grants-in-Aid for Scientific Research on Priority Areas from the Ministry of Education, Science and Culture (present-day Ministry of Education, Culture, Sports, Science and Technology). The grants were awarded to the Basic Study on Formation of Postwar Japan and the Comprehensive Area Study, two study groups in which I participated. I wish to express my gratitude to Professors Kitaoka Shin'ichi of Rikkyo University and Kojima Masaru of Ryukoku University, who organized these two study groups. I would also like to take this opportunity to express my heartfelt thanks to Shimizu Hajime (Professor, Nagasaki Prefectural

University, and formerly with the Institute of Developing Economies), Akagi Kanji (Associate Professor, Keio University), Henry Frei (Professor, University of Tsukuba), Kurosawa Fumitaka (Professor, Tokyo Woman's Christian University), Miwa Kimitada (Professor, Sophia University), Shiozaki Hiroaki (Professor, Nagasaki Junshin Catholic University), and Fujimura Kin'ichirō (formerly with the Ministry of Finance), who inspired me, directly or indirectly, in dealing with the subject matter of the present volume.

When completing the manuscript for this book, I took advantage of the facilities at the Reischauer Institute of Japanese Studies, Harvard University, where I stayed for two years as a visiting fellow in 1995–1996. I wish to convey my deepest gratitude to the institute's staff members for generously providing me with an ideal research environment. Last but not least, I must extend my deepest appreciation to Professor Iriye Akira, former director of the Reischauer Institute, whose studies gave me numerous useful hints for my research. Moreover, since I became acquainted with Professor Iriye at the aforementioned two Pacific War–related international academic conferences in 1991 and 1995, he has been most helpful, offering a number of suggestions on my manuscript and, above all, inviting me to the Reischauer Institute as a visiting fellow. I would be more than happy if the present volume reciprocates his kindness even slightly.

My appreciation also goes to Takenaka Hidetoshi and Shiba Hiroshi of the editorial department of the University of Tokyo Press who have encouraged me and helped me publish this book, which was nothing more than a preliminary essay when they had their first glimpse of the content.

I would also like to add that publication of the present volume benefitted from a publishing subsidy (fiscal year 1996) from Keio Hōgakukai. I am deeply grateful.

August 1996
Arlington, Massachusetts
Hatano Sumio

INDEX

Note: The abbreviation 'n' refers to footnotes.